AN OMELETTE AND A GLASS OF WINE

Elizabeth David in her kitchen, by John Ward, R.A., in the possession of the author

·ELIZABETH DAVID·

❖

An Omelette and a Glass of Wine

❖

Elisabeth Sifton Books

VIKING

ELISABETH SIFTON BOOKS · VIKING
Viking Penguin Inc.,
40 West 23rd Street,
New York, New York 10010, U.S.A.

First American edition
Published in 1985

ISBN 0-670-80769-9
Library of Congress Catalog Card Number:
85-3282 (CIP data available)
Second printing March 1986

Drawings by Marie Alix for *107 Recettes on Curiosités
Culinaires*, edited by Paul Poiret, published by Henri
Jouquières et Cie, Paris, 1928.

Printed in Great Britain by St Edmundsbury Press
Bury St Edmunds, Suffolk
Set in Linotron Sabon

For Anthony and Celia Denney
with love

CONTENTS

Introduction	9
John Wesley's Eye	19
Fast and Fresh	22
The True Emulsion	25
Lucky Dip	27
Summer Holidays	30
Big Bad Bramleys	34
Crackling	37
Your Perfected Hostess	39
Secrets	41
Ladies' Halves	46
Letting Well Alone	46
An Omelette and a Glass of Wine	49
Chez Barattero	53
Dishes for Collectors	63
Eating out in Provincial France 1965–1977	66
Confort anglais, French fare	75
Roustidou	82
Golden Delicious	83
A la marinière	85
Fruits de mer	87
Waiting for Lunch	91
Para Navidad	94
Pizza	98
Sweet Vegetables, Soft Wines	101
Bruscandoli	106
Mafalda, Giovanna, Giulia	113
Have It Your Way	120
South Wind through the Kitchen	124
The Englishman's Food	134
Home Baked Bread	135
West Points	137
If You Care to Eat Shark	139

Moorish Recipes   143
Fine Bouche   143
How Bare is Your Cupboard?   145
Chez Gee-Gee   148
Franglais   153
Exigez le véritable Cheddar français   156
Having Crossed the Channel   162
Pomiane, Master of the Unsacrosanct   175
Table Talk   185
Whisky in the Kitchen   187
A Gourmet in Edwardian London   192
I'll Be with You in the Squeezing of a Lemon   198
Pleasing Cheeses   203
Sweet Aristo   208
English Potted Meats and Fish Pastes   216
Syllabubs and Fruit Fools   229
Operation Mulberry   247
Foods of Legend   249
The Markets of France: Cavaillon   255
                     Yvetot   261
                     Montpellier   263
                     Martigues   267
                     Valence   271
Oules of Sardines   275
Trufflesville Regis   280
The Magpie System   284
Traditional Christmas Dishes   287
Welsh Doubles   293
Too Many Cooks   300
Isabella Beeton and her Book   303
Index   310

Introduction

In thirty five years of writing about food and cookery I have contributed articles to a very various collection of publications. From the *Sunday Times* to *Nova*, from *Vogue* to the *Spectator*, from the long defunct travel magazine *Go* to Cyril Ray's *Compleat Imbiber*, Peter Dominic's *Wine Mine* and quite a few others, I have put together the present volume. The bulk of the articles included were written during the decade between 1955 when I joined the *Sunday Times* as cookery contributor and 1965 when I launched my kitchen shop. For several of those years I was contributing a monthly article apiece to *Vogue* and *House and Garden* as well as a fortnightly one to the *Sunday Times*, and in 1960 had published *French Provincial Cooking*. In 1961, freed from the *Sunday Times* and the monthly stints for the Condé Nast magazines, I worked for a time for the moribund *Sunday Dispatch* and wrote my first contribution for the *Spectator* and, unexpectedly perhaps, thoroughly enjoyed writing for both publications. What matters is sympathetic editors who know how to get the best out of their contributors, and in that respect I have been, albeit with one or two notable exceptions, very fortunate.

It was the *Spectator's* editors who liberated me from the straitjacket of the conventional cookery article as decreed by custom. The old routine had been to open with a short introductory piece relevant to the products of the season, or to one particular type of dish, let us say soufflés, omelettes, rice dishes – the very first cookery article I ever wrote was for *Harper's Bazaar* and was called *Rice Again* – or it might deal with the cookery of a specific region of France, or of Italy, or perhaps it would be a little moan about the poor quality of our potatoes, or about not being able to buy courgettes. Whatever it was, once the opening piece was dutifully concluded, you filled the rest of your space with appropriate recipes and that was that. Sometimes the formula reminded me of English musical comedy. The recipes were the turns, the songs and dances, the introductory pieces the spoken dialogue which kept the flimsy plot moving. It was all very stilted. When in 1956 I was recruited by Audrey Withers, editor of *Vogue*, to write for the Condé Nast magazines, I made a bid to break away from the idiotic convention by planning, for *House and Garden*, a series on English cookery writers of the past. Kicking off with Eliza Acton – in those days not many people knew about her wonderful book, first published in 1845,[1] and even Longmans, her own publishers, had never heard of her – I followed up with Colonel Kenney Herbert, the Victorian officer who in his retirement opened a cookery school in Sloane Street, and copies of whose books on what in his opinion were the proper food and cooking for the British in India are today much sought after. In 1984 the subject is popular enough, but in 1956 the editors of *House and Garden* didn't take to the Colonel or the parade-ground tones in which he denounced the kitchens and cooks of the Raj. *House and Garden* readers, they said, wanted recipes, not history. It was back to the outdated formula.

For the temporary setback I made up during my years at the *Spectator*. They were stimulating years for me. Well, look at the company I found myself in. Katharine Whitehorn, Cyril Ray, Bernard Levin calling himself Taper, Alan Brien, Jean Robertson contributing a weekly piece under the pseudonym of Leslie Adrian. Brian Inglis was my first editor, succeeded by Iain Hamilton, in whose time most of my *Spectator* pieces were written, and at the end, briefly, the lamented Ian McLeod. If life as a contributor to the *Sunday Times* had been bumpy, and it had been made so by the late Ernestine Carter, editor of the fashion pages, always appropriately ready with her cutting-out shears when it came to my cookery pieces, at the *Spectator*, the co-operation, encouragement, support and on occasions most beneficial editing by Katharine Whitehorn, were compensation for the years of Mrs Carter's busy scissors. As can be seen from the selection of articles I have chosen to reprint (others have already been incorporated into books, some simply weren't good enough to reproduce, some, including the historical ones, will eventually appear in another volume) my subjects were in the main topical, and ranged all over the place, from reviews of eccentric books such as Sir Harry Luke's *The Tenth Muse* and Alan Davidson's very singular first version of *Mediterranean Seafood*, then entitled *Seafish of Tunisia and the Central Mediterranean*, a stencilled production sold for the benefit of the Tunisian Red Crescent – no doubt copies are now collectors' items – to harmless fun at the expense of restaurant guides and the baiting of public relations persons who made imbecile suggestions to the effect that

---

1. *Modern Cookery for Private Families*, a landmark in English cookery writing, and a work heavily borrowed from by Isabella Beeton.

two tins of tomato juice packed in a basket tied with red ribbons would make a nice neighbourly Christmas gift. Sometimes my fortnightly column would deal with an event such as a delicatessen exhibition, an encounter with some delicious and hitherto unknown wine or with a particularly awful restaurant, or even just with a glut of apples. Topics such as the well-known British disregard for the authenticity of other peoples' and indeed our own culinary specialities preoccupied me a good deal, as how should they not? It has to be remembered that it was only in 1954 that we had been freed from food rationing. The national fling with abundance didn't occur overnight, and it didn't by any means coincide with an instant disappearance of all the ghastly synthetic foodstuffs and ignoble substitutes to which as a nation we had become acclimatised during the war years and after. On the contrary, once entrenched, those boil-in-the-bag sauces I wrote about in a little article for *Punch*, included in the present collection, and other such expedients of scarcity, whether of ingredients, time, technical accomplishment, or simply of knowledge, are still with us today, and given the microwave's magic button, likely to remain so. I think that blithe acceptance of travesty in the matter of imported specialities, whether it be the *pizza*, the *quiche*, or the newest invention of M. Michel Guérard, is deep within our national temperament. This characteristic I examined in an article about mayonnaise entitled *The True Emulsion*. It reappears here without comment. It needs none.

Every now and again, during my joyous *Spectator* years, there would be a threat of trouble. Once Messrs Walls cut up a bit rough when I reported that, proffered a slice of their packaged chicken and veal pie, my cat had waved a disdainful tail and walked off. When I pointed out that cats were habitually more fastidious than humans, but like humans variable in their tastes, everyone calmed down. On another occasion I quoted a wartime recipe for a corned beef pudding contributed by a famous Mayfair restaurant to a Kitchen Front-type collection published in 1942. The enraged wife of the owner of the restaurant wrote defying me to prove that the recipe had ever existed. That was unwise of her. Chapter and verse were there, in print. If the recipe had been libel in the first place why had she and her husband not done something about it sooner? Then there was the time I criticised a terrible restaurant owned by Lyons. The trouble was that the owners weren't owning up to owning it, and I had rumbled them, hardly a great feat of detection. My punishment was to return to the same restaurant for dinner with one of the directors, or was it their public relations officer? A genial host, but he couldn't make the food any better. However, the evening was nothing like the ordeal I had suffered after publishing a derogatory article about British sausages in the *Sunday Times*. A guided tour of the Walls factory had been followed, first by lunch with the directors – we ate sausages, of course, but at least I wasn't eating my words – and during the ensuing weeks by a bombardment of sample after sample of their products. No doubt the public relations people at Walls were just doing their jobs. They can't really have thought that a few free sausages were going to convert me into a Walls sausage enthusiast.

It must have been at about this time that a fellow guest at a small private dinner party given by a wine merchant friend at Prunier's restaurant leant across the table and said to me, 'It must be awful to be you. Always criticising everything, enjoying nothing.' Well, if a food writer does not exercise his or her critical faculties to a high degree and with a backing of informed experience, he or she is not doing his or her job. He or she is a sham or, as would be said nowadays, a pseud. What, I wonder, would the person who made that remark to me have had to say if our host had not troubled to choose his wines with as much critical care as indeed Madame Prunier had exercised in the choice of her menu? Does a theatre critic offer his readers indiscriminate praise of every play or of the performances of every actor he has seen during the week, a music critic of every concert or opera he has attended? To be attacked for declining to say, whether in private or in public, that in the world of gastronomy, French, English, or any other, all was always for the best, and that that world was the best of all possible ones, seemed to me illogical, ignorant and thoroughly philistine. But lest it be assumed by anyone taking a superficial look at the essays assembled in *An Omelette and a Glass of Wine* that these consist wholly of carping criticism and unconstructive send-ups, I should point out here that, on the contrary, the majority of them are about benefits and pleasures, about good food, good wine, good cookery books. Those pleasures I did my best to express to my readers in lively terms. A delightful meal in a modest restaurant deep in Provence was the subject of one of my very early articles for the *Spectator*. True enough, I finished the piece with a plea to British restaurateurs of similar scope to refrain from the addition of redundant elements to every one of their dishes, to leave well alone if and when well was what they could do. Governessy, if you like, but at the time it was something which really did need saying. It still does, although quite frequently in a reverse sense. Today's young restaurant chefs, amateurs usually, tend to imagine that they can with impunity take some recently evolved *style moderne* recipe, omit one of only two key components, and with a flourish present a customer with nothing more than one and a half mushrooms and one small croûton in the centre of a vast expanse of otherwise empty plate. The descriptions of the mushroom as 'wild', and of the croûton as 'le brioche de notre pâtissier' do nothing to mitigate the ludicrous effect of the presentation, particularly when you know perfectly well that the 'wild' mushrooms have been brought by lorry from Rungis market, to where they had been conveyed in the first place from a French mushroom farm, and that 'notre pâtissier' is a Camden Town bakery. It is the kind of place where if you read *salade de foie de volaille* on the menu, it isn't due to a fault of written French but is the literal truth, salad of one chicken liver. The London *style moderne* restaurants become ever more reminiscent of that old music hall song in which the chorus line was something about one meat ball.

To return to the France of the old style 1960s, about four years after that Provence excursion of *Letting Well Alone*, a primitive but strikingly enjoyable lunch in an indescribably scruffy café somewhere close to the Loire was the starting point for a *Nova* story called *Pleasing Cheeses*. In those days so agreeable a surprise meal had already become a very exceptional happening in the French provinces. Could it ever happen again?

In February 1962, for the tenth anniversary of the death of Norman Douglas, I wrote about the times I had first met him in 1939, in Antibes, and again twelve years later in Capri. It was then 1951, the last year of his life. The piece had been very difficult to write, but appreciative letters from some of Norman's old friends were gratifying. Later, I expanded the original article, and that second version, taken from another publication,[1] reappears here. In the autumn of 1962, with assistance from a delightful lady at the French Embassy called Mademoiselle Bologna, I arranged a visit to Nantes to meet some of the people involved in the sardine industry and to find out how the sardine got into the tin. I had always wanted to know, and now I do. *Spectator* readers were pleased and in-

---

[1] The American magazine *Gourmet*.

terested, even the one who took the trouble to write from Canada saying that I wrote like a hairdresser – I had used that furiously disputed word *firstly* instead of *first*[1] – and he remained dear modom mine sincerely. A by-product of my Nantes visit was the discovery of the beauty of the fish in the market there and of the towering heaps of tiny, sweet, briefly cooked mussels to be found in the humbler restaurants of the city. So *Fruits de Mer* came out of Nantes as well as *Oules of Sardines*. The following autumn, 1963, after a disruptive illness, I went on a short trip to Turin and Alba, to see an exhausting exhibition of Piedmontese baroque at Stupinigi, the former palace of the royal house of Savoy, and more enjoyably, to eat white truffles and *fonduta*, white truffles with risotto, white truffles and scrambled eggs, white truffles spread on bread and butter. My article, *Trufflesville Regis*, was written rather hurriedly for the *Spectator*, and contained any number of Italian spelling mistakes. Nobody complained except the Italian friend I had been with on the trip. In due course she corrected them for me, and a second version of the article was published by Cyril Ray in his *Compleat Imbiber*. That is the one which appears here. Another happy autumnal article, *Para Navidad*, emerged from South East Spain in November 1964.

I suspect that there will be a few readers who will think what a lovely time I had going on all those trips with everything paid for by the paper. So I did have a lovely time, but nothing was paid for by anyone other than myself. It was only in one or two of my *Vogue* years that I had been allowed the princely sum of £100 by Condé Nast to cover expenses, hotels, restaurant meals, petrol, when I went on the occasional ten to fourteen day trip to France. During my *Spectator* period I didn't ask for expenses and didn't expect them. The pay was nothing to sing about either but because I retained all my copyrights, as indeed I have done ever since I started in journalism,[2] I was able to republish my articles in other forms and publications and thus earn the extra money which would eventually

---

1. Readers may be amused to learn what Bill Bryson, author of *The Penguin Dictionary of Troublesome Words*, 1984, has to say on the subject: 'The question of whether to write *firstly* . . . *secondly* or *first* . . . *second* constitutes one of the more bizarre and inane but most hotly disputed issues in the history of English usage.' The admirable Mr Bryson sends us back to Fowler, 'ever the cool head' and thinks he should have the last word in the matter. 'The preference for *first* over *firstly* in formal enumerations is one of the harmless pedantries in which those who like oddities because they are odd are free to indulge, provided that they abstain from censuring those who do not share the liking.'

2. That was thanks to Anne Scott-James, my first editor at *Harper's Bazaar*.

cover my expenses on trips such as the *Trufflesville* one. Many of my *Vogue* contributions published between 1956 and 1959, as also some of my *Sunday Times* articles, were eventually incorporated into *French Provincial Cooking* and earned their pay that way.

With the launching of my shop in November 1965 my cookery writing came to an end, although as things turned out only temporarily, so a few of the pieces in *Omelette* are of relatively recent date. Three are from Alan Davidson's *Petits Propos Culinaires* (although I am sometimes referred to in the press as sharing editorial responsibility for that publication, I do not in fact have any whatsoever. I am entirely lacking in the gifts requisite for such a task) and two of them were written before 1979 when *Petits Propos* was launched. At the time I had already embarked on research for an entirely new book, so no longer had much opportunity to engage in journalism, or indeed the taste to do so. From 1949 to 1979 was quite long enough. No more deadlines for me. But there is one minor aspect of my journalism which I have not mentioned here and feel that I should, particularly as it concerns the late Leonard Russell, for thirty years Literary Editor of the *Sunday Times*, who initially offered me the job as cookery columnist on the paper. It was Leonard who also first sent me books to review, appalling me with a task I had never before tackled. I don't think he found me very good at reviewing, and given that among his regular reviewers were Cyril Connolly and Raymond Mortimer, it took some courage to accept even the few books he entrusted to me. As far as I remember all the reviews I wrote for him are included in this volume. With one exception, all the books involved were interesting and unusual, in one case a highly important one, and although I never had quite enough space to fill, Leonard was a considerate editor to work for and he taught me a lot about a journalist's job. I have much cause to be grateful to him. On more than one occasion his intervention in the matter of Mrs Carter's shears saved my cookery contribution from reduction to meaningless shreds. The piece called *Pizza* in the present collection was just such a case. I never did discover what Leonard had said to the lady, but the article appeared word for word as I had written it. All the same, in the end, the job became impossible. After several more such episodes, and after five years, I resigned from the *Sunday Times* sometime in 1960.

There were other newspapers and many more periodicals to which I contributed during those decades. There were wine and food journals, and various publications put out by wine merchants who most agreeably paid for contributions in kind. At one time a few bottles of glorious white Burgundy from the cellars of Avery's of Bristol would occasionally find their way into mine. They were the ones which came at the bidding of André Simon. Their arrivals were rare occurrences. 'Interesting', said André on the first occasion he had invited me to choose my wine, 'women don't often care for white Burgundy.' I don't know how on earth he had worked that one out, but doubtless he had his own reasons for holding such a very odd belief. What I do know is that today I'd have to write a couple of books before I'd earn a case of wine equivalent to the Montrachet André used to choose for me. There were also, in those years, house journals such as that of the B.P. Company, which paid generously and were straightforward to work for, and there was *Housewife*, a long-vanished monthly, whose editor, Joanna Chase, gave me a good deal of well-paid work, welcome because it provided valuable experience as well as a big audience and big cheques. At the time, the early 1960s, cookery writers were a little better paid than they were when I started. In 1949, I earned eight and a half guineas for a thousand word monthly article. By 1955 it was twenty guineas, and there were still editors who tried to tie you exclusively to one publication *and* to hang on to your copyrights, so unless you worked for one of the mass circulation weeklies, 'better' was a very relative term, and it was necessary to accept nearly everything you were offered. But not quite everything. On one occasion I was summoned to see the editor of a popular Sunday paper. Asked what I had been paid on the one I had previously written for and which had lately folded, I replied 'forty guineas'. *Forty guineas* for a cookery article? The great man was apparently on the verge of explosion. 'No wonder the paper's gone broke.' I made for the door. 'Oh well, if that's what you've been getting I suppose you'll have to have it.' 'Thank you. I'm not going to work for your paper.' I fled from the building as fast as I could go. I'd had enough of bullies.

Although I was sacked by only one editor among the many I worked for, it was not my intention when I embarked on the writing of this Introduction to compose an essay on the theme of Some of my best friends are Editors, but journalism is after all inseparable from editors. When mine were good they were very very good. I, on the contrary, am not one of nature's journalists. I am incapable of writing to order. Editors of the experience of Leonard Russell and of Audrey Withers of *Vogue* could and did sometimes persuade or cajole me into writing what I had thought I couldn't, although never what *I* knew I wouldn't. They were too intelligent to try, and too busy. From the very beginning, the travel writer Elizabeth Nicholas, editor of *Go*, gave me as much encouragement and support as I received later from the youthful Hugh Johnson who edited the Wine and Food Society's *Quarterly* when André Simon retired, from Pamela Vandyke Price who eventually took over the editorship when the publication was bought by Condé Nast, and from *Nova*'s first editor, Harry Fieldhouse. Without these editors, and not a few others, I simply would not have had the impetus to produce enough journalism to fill a school exercise book, let alone a proper one between covers. I thank all those friends for their help and guidance.

I do not forget to thank also my readers, especially the many who over the years have troubled to write to me, even when occasionally their letters were furious, rude or sarcastic. Grumpy letters often reveal more about current attitudes to food and cooking than appreciative ones. Useful things are to be learned from those who tell you what you've done wrong. That is not to say that I harboured particularly charitable thoughts about the retired French professional chef who wrote regularly, not to me, but to trade publications, denouncing in almost paranoiac terms, me, my contemporary colleague on the *Observer*, and indeed all cookery writers since Escoffier, as frauds. Today's friendly cooperation, free exchange of ideas, and cordial relations generally between top-flight professional chefs and cookery journalists would scandalise that angry old man. It would never have occurred to him that mutual respect between the two categories of professional might be of benefit to the public, as well as to each other. In those days professional chefs were often very limited and narrow in outlook and education. There were of course many shining exceptions, but some knew only what they had been taught during their apprenticeships and were unbelievably bigoted. I well remember one French chef at a respected West End restaurant who, when asked to include a certain mushroom soup, for which the recipe appears in *French Provincial Cooking*, in a dinner to be organised by André Simon in honour of the book, refused point blank. The poor man emerged from his kitchens fairly fuming. 'A soup thickened with bread? No Frenchman has ever heard of such a thing. Ah non'. That couldn't or at any rate wouldn't happen today. The professionals all collect cookery books. Some actually read them and adapt ancient recipes. Others talk a good deal about using *trucs de bonne femme*, by which they mean their great aunts' or their great grandmothers' cousins' cooking methods, which of course would have to include thickening their soups with bread. These men would be ashamed to reveal ignorance and intolerance such as were demonstrated by the older chefs mentioned above. I've forgotten both their names, so I suppose neither of them was really a top flier, and not comparable with the stars of today's gastronomic firmament. I'm glad to think that in that particular cooking world there are many things which have changed very much for the better.

June 1984

John Wesley's Eye

In a brief and neatly-worded letter to the *Guardian* some three weeks ago Mr George Mikes expressed the view that we shall need no independent deterrent so long as we have English provincial cooking. I am not arguing with Mr Mikes. I simply wonder if he, as an old inhabitant of these islands and, I take it, a man of resource, was really making his way about our provinces unprovided with the wherewithal to sustain life without resort to hotel meals. Myself, it wouldn't occur to me to do such a thing. Once, I was involved in such a venture, and very odd consequences it had.

It was the winter of 1946–47. In the late summer of 1946 I had returned to England after some years spent in the Middle East and a brief period in the Farther one.

After years of enjoying comparative plenty, rationing was a challenge. Everyone else had hoards of things like powdered soups and packets of dehydrated egg to which they were conditioned. I started off untrammelled; an empty cupboard was an advantage. With whatever I could get I cooked like one possessed. The frustrations were great. All the same one managed some entertainment. Nobody ever came to a meal without bringing contributions. Unexpected ones sometimes. A wild goose. Snails from Paris. Mock liver pâté from Fortnums. British Government-bought Algerian wine. One of my sisters turned up from Vienna with a hare which she claimed had been caught by hand outside the State Opera House.

Game was plentiful everywhere that year. Even if one didn't actually catch pheasants in Kensington High Street one could buy them very cheaply in the shops. Wild duck, although distinctly fishy some of them, were not more than a shilling apiece. My landlady, living in the flat below mine, was saintly. Not once did she complain about the cooking smells, the garlic, the onions, those eternal bacon bones simmering in the stock . . . About the heating she was, with the best will in the world, powerless. Literally. And gas-less. By mid-January of that year the fire in my sitting room was reduced to a candle-splutter. Impossible to heat the water. My wardrobe, after so long in warm climates, was entirely inadequate. Clothes coupons went nowhere. At this moment somebody put into my head the idea of going to stay, at reduced all-in rates, in a hotel at Ross-on-Wye. You may well ask . . . I didn't. I just went.

I knew little in those days of English hotels. It was many years since I had been exposed to them. This one was adequately warm, and that was miracle enough. There was a fine coal fire in the public sitting room, a maid to bring hot-water-bottles and breakfast in bed. I had friends near by.

In Ross-on-Wye, I was told, there are more public houses to the square yard than in any other town in these islands. There seemed to be some truth in the claim. Many of them were cider pubs. Up and down that steep hill I went, sampling every kind and degree of Hereford cider, most of it rough, some very rough indeed.

On one of these outings I came on an interesting-looking antique shop. A very large shop, with immense windows. These were filled from floor to ceiling with a fantastic jumble of every conceivable kind of antique. Lamps, china, glass, chairs, bedsteads, curtains, Sheffield candlesticks, desks, pictures, books, bookshelves, bronzes, Georgian silver coffee pots, horse brasses, corner cupboards, whole services of dinner plates, soup tureens, sauce boats, statuary. The lady inside the shop was as unusual as her windows. I shall call her Miss D. If you asked to look at something she pulled it out from amid the morass, regardless. A chandelier would come rippling to the ground. A Biedermeier sofa standing on end would topple, upsetting a pile of Wedgwood.

'May I look at that Leeds dish?' Miss D. extracted it from underneath a ship's decanter and an early Peter Jones painted waste paper basket.

'There's a pair to it somewhere. Do you want it?'

'If you can find it.'

'Oh, here it is. Broken with that lot that just came down. Can't be helped.'

I took the bereaved Leeds dish and put it in my basket before Miss D. had a chance to knock it flying. The friend I was with rescued from under the lady's foot, and gave to me, a frail white jug with black transfers of John Wesley's head and a building called the Centenary Hall, dated 1839. As Miss D. took my cheque her elbow jogged the tap of a copper tea-urn perched on top of a model four-masted barque in a heavy box frame. It knocked over a solid silver clock representing General Gordon sitting on a horse, which fell against a scrap screen, a japanned tray and a tortoiseshell and silver-inlaid musical box. The guts of the little musical box cracked out on to the floor. Miss D. was unshaken. 'Take care how you go out,' she said.

Visiting Miss D.'s shop became a compulsive occupation. Before I should myself acquire an abominable taste for cool, passionless destruction, I decided to be gone from Ross-on-Wye. Not so easy. By this time the West Country was devastated by floods. Ross was in the Wye rather than on it. The BBC news announcements had a Shakespearean ring. 'Hereford's under water, Ludlow and Monmouth cut off. Gloucester flooded.' I was intending to go toward Bristol rather than back to London, so I stuck it out. It was an effort. By this time I was finding it very difficult indeed to swallow the food provided in the hotel. It was worse than unpardonable, even for those days of desperation; and, oddly, considering the kindly efforts made in other respects, produced with a kind of bleak triumph which amounted almost to a hatred of humanity and humanity's needs. There was flour and water soup seasoned solely with pepper; bread and gristle rissoles; dehydrated onions and carrots; corned beef toad-in-the-hole. I need not go on. We all know that kind of cooking. It still exists. 'War-time food made with 1963 ingredients' as it was genially put to me by a friend lately returned from a scarring experience in an Eastbourne residential establishment.

It was not feasible, in 1947, to go out and buy food as nowadays I would. When you stayed more than a night or two in a hotel you gave them your ration book, retaining only coupons for things like chocolate and sweets. Those didn't get you far. And of course all that rough cider was inconveniently appetite-rousing.

Hardly knowing what I was doing, I who had scarcely ever put pen to paper except to write memos to the heads of departments in the Ministry which employed me during the war, I sat down and, watched over by John Wesley, started to work out an agonized craving for the sun and a furious revolt against that terrible, cheerless, heartless food by writing down descriptions of Mediterranean and Middle Eastern cooking. Even to write words like apricot, olives and butter, rice and lemons, oil and almonds, produced assuagement. Later I came to realize that in the England of 1947, those were dirty words that I was putting down.

To people who have sometimes asked how it was that in 1949, when such words were still very dubious, I came to be writing them so freely, this is at least partly the answer. Any publisher less perceptive than mine (he was John Lehmann) would have asked me to take them all out when in that year he accepted the cookery book of which those original notes had become a part.

The Spectator, 1 February 1963

Fast and Fresh

It isn't only the expense, the monotony and the false tastes of the food inside most tins and jars and packages which turn me every day more against them. The amount of space they take up, the clutter they make and the performance of opening the things also seem to me quite unnecessarily exasperating. However, even cookery journalists who spend most of their lives with a saucepan in one hand and a pen in the other can't dispense entirely with the kind of stores from which a meal can every now and again be improvised. What I personally require of such things is that there shall be no question whatever of their letting me down or giving me any unwelcome surprise. Out with any product which plays tricks or deteriorates easily. And out also with all the things of which one might say they'll do for an emergency. If something isn't good enough for every day, then it isn't good enough to offer friends, even if they have turned up demanding a meal without notice.

Twenty years ago, during the war years, which I spent in the Eastern Mediterranean, I became accustomed to planning meals from a fairly restricted range of provisions. Now I find myself returning more and more to the same sort of rather ancient and basic foods. They suit my taste and they are the kind of stores which will always produce a coherent and more or less complete meal, which is just what haphazardly bought tins and packages won't do. What happens when you have to open four tins, two jars and three packets in order to make one hasty cook-up is that you get a thoroughly unsatisfactory meal; and the contents of half-used tins and jars have got to be dealt with next day – or left to moulder in the fridge. Or else, like the surburban housewife in N. F. Simpson's *One Way Pendulum*, you've got to pay somebody to come in and eat the stuff up.

The only stores I had to bother about when I lived for a time in a small seashore village on an Ægean island were bread, olive oil, olives, salt fish, hard white cheese, dried figs, tomato paste, rice, dried beans, sugar, coffee and wine.

With fresh fish – mostly small fry or inkfish, but occasionally a treat such as red mullet or a langouste to be obtained from one of the fisher boys, with vegetables and fruit from the garden of the tavern-owner, eggs at about twopence a dozen, and meat – usually kid, lamb or pork – available only for feast days, the diet was certainly limited, but at least presented none of the meal-planning problems which, as I have learned from readers' letters, daily plague the better-off English housewife.

Subsequently, in war-time Egypt, I found, in spite of the comparative plenty and variety and the fact that in Greece I had often grumbled about the food, that the basic commodities of the Eastern Mediterranean shores were the ones which had begun to seem essential. Alexandrians, not surprisingly, knew how to prepare these commodities in a more civilized way than did the Greek islanders. The old-established merchant families of the city – Greek, Syrian, Jewish, English – appeared to have evolved a most delicious and unique blend of Levantine and European cookery and were at the same time most marvellously hospitable. I have seldom seen such wonderfully glamorous looking, and tasting, food as the Levantine cooks of Alexandria could produce for a party. And yet when you got down to analysing it, you would find that much the same ingredients had been used in dish after dish – only they were so differently treated, so skilfully blended and seasoned and spiced that each one had its own perfectly individual character and flavour.

In Cairo the dividing line between European and Eastern food was much sharper. It was uphill work trying to make English-trained Sudanese cooks produce interesting food. Most of them held a firm belief that the proper meal to set before English people consisted of roast or fried chicken, boiled vegetables and a pudding known to one and all as *grème garamel*.

My own cook, Suleiman, was a Sudanese who had previously worked only for Italian and Jewish families. He was erratic and forgetful, but singularly sweet-natured, devoted to his cooking pots and above all knew absolutely nothing of good, clean, English schoolroom food.

I used occasionally to try to teach him some French or English dish for which I had a nostalgic craving, but time for cooking was very limited, my kitchen facilities even more so, and on the whole I left him to his own devices.

So it came about that for three or four more years I lived mainly on rather rough but highly flavoured, colourful shining vegetable dishes, lentil or fresh tomato soups, delicious spiced pilaffs, lamb kebabs grilled over charcoal, salads with cool mint-flavoured yoghurt dressings, the Egyptian *fellahin* dish of black beans with olive oil and lemon and hard-boiled eggs – these things were not only attractive but also cheap and this was important because although Egypt was a land of fantastic plenty compared with war-time Europe, a lot of the better-class food was far beyond the means of young persons living on British Civil Service pay without foreign allowances, and tinned stores were out of the question because there was no room for them in the cave which my landlord was pleased to describe as a furnished flat.

What I found out when I returned to England to another five or six years of the awful dreary foods of rationing was that while my own standard of living in Egypt had perhaps not been very high, my food had always had some sort of life, colour, guts, stimulus; there had always been bite, flavour and inviting smells. These elements were totally absent from English meals.

As imports came slowly back, I found once more, and still find, that it is the basic foods of the Mediterranean world which produce them in the highest degree. And it is curious how much more true variety can be extracted from a few of these basic commodities than from a whole supermarketful of products, none of which really taste of anything in particular.

So long as I have a supply of elementary fresh things like eggs, onions, parsley, lemons, oranges and bread and tomatoes – and I keep tinned tomatoes too – I find that my store cupboard will always provide the main part of an improvised meal. If this has to be made quickly it may be just a salad of anchovy fillets and black olives, hard-boiled eggs and olive oil, with bread and a bottle of wine. If it is a question of not being able to leave the house to go shopping, or of being too otherwise occupied to stand over the cooking pots, then there are white beans or brown lentils for slow cooking, and usually a piece of cured sausage or bacon to add to them, with onions and oil and possibly tomato. Apricots or other dried fruit can be baked in the oven at the same time, or I may have oranges for a fruit salad, and if it comes to the worst there'll at least be bread and butter and honey and jam. Or if I am given, say, forty-five minutes to get an unplanned meal ready – well, I have Italian and Patna rice and Parmesan, spices, herbs, currants, almonds, walnuts, to make a risotto or a pilaff. And perhaps tunny, with eggs to make mayonnaise, for an easy first dish. The countless number of permutations to be devised is part of the entertainment.

The Spectator, 9 December 1960

The True Emulsion

With the mayonnaise season in full blast, once more the familiar complaints about bottled mayonnaise and salad creams are heard in the land. Perhaps there is less cause for grumbling, thanks to the advent of the electric mixer combined with the whackings of the Postgate guide, than there used to be. The defence, when complaints are made, can no longer be that kitchen labour is lacking; it is simply the old one about the majority of customers preferring the synthetic product to the real thing. I am sure that this is very often perfectly true. Why?

Partly, the trouble lies in the characteristic English custom – which in some degree we share with the Swiss – of appropriating the *names* of established French and other foreign dishes, even of our own traditional ones, and attaching to them recipes of our own devising, often with the most carefree disregard of the ingredients and methods of cooking which made these dishes famous. The caterers, the manufacturers and the recipe-hashers employed by public relations firms to help sell factory products may reply that as long as a dish is found acceptable and sells it surely doesn't matter what it is called. Maybe these operators don't realize that what they are doing is fraudulent; legally it isn't. There is no international patent or copyright law to protect the names or the recipes of recognized traditional and classic dishes. While nobody in this country can now, say, label any wine champagne that is not champagne or pass off margarine as butter without risk of prosecution, anybody depraved enough to invent a dish consisting of a wedge of steam-heated bread spread with tomato paste and a piece of synthetic Cheddar can call it a pizza; for that matter they could sell a pizza as a Welsh Rabbit and a Welsh Rabbit as a Swiss fondue or a *quiche lorraine*; they can publish recipes for a soup called vichyssoise containing everything and anything but what its creator actually put into it – leeks and potatoes. At the time the deceptions seem just sad or silly, but the consequences can be far-reaching.

In the case of mayonnaise the damage may have been done by the commercial firms and their bottled products which were already on sale by the mid-1880s, but the cookery advisers and experts certainly helped the public to accept the name 'mayonnaise' as applied to a cooked custard-type sauce made of flour, milk, eggs, and a very high proportion of vinegar. Plenty of relevant recipes are to be found in cookery books and other publications of the period. Two examples will suffice. In the November, 1895, issue of the *Epicure* magazine, under the heading 'New Recipes', Miss Ida Cameron, principal of the Earls Court Cookery School, contributed a recipe for what she called cornflour mayonnaise. The lady explained that in this cooked mixture the cornflour 'does for thickening the sauce instead of salad oil'. Presumably this is what she was teaching her pupils. Herman Senn, a professional of very high standing, at one time chef to the Reform Club, author of countless cookery books, honorary secretary to the Universal Food and Cookery Association, editor of that body's magazine and promoter of a number of commercial products including one called Hygienic Caviar, was employed by Ward, Lock and Co. to edit the gigantic 1906 edition of Mrs Beeton. This edition contains two mayonnaise recipes. (Mrs Beeton's own original formula which had been left untouched for over forty years was dropped, one might think none too soon. It specified four tablespoons of vinegar to six of oil.) One of Senn's recipes was the authentic one, but called for a pint of olive oil to two eggs, an unnecessarily large allowance, tricky to work; and in view of the national English fear and dislike of olive oil, to which every cookery writer of the period refers and which was certainly a factor in the public's easy acceptance of the custard-type dressing in place of true mayonnaise, rather tactless. The second recipe Senn called 'cooked mayonnaise'. With his training he should surely have known that mayonnaise, whatever the origin of the word, had long been accepted in France, Spain and Italy as denoting an emulsion sauce of uncooked egg yolks and olive oil, and that the term 'cooked' used in conjunction with mayonnaise was contradictory.

As things turned out, the recipes from this 1906 edition were the ones which were finally established and accepted as Mrs Beeton's. From 1906 until the mid-1950s they were current – and of course much copied by other writers. During long periods of that half-century it is obvious that desperate shortages made Senn's pint of olive oil (one sees how it was that poor Mrs B acquired her reputation for reckless extravagance) as ordered for the genuine recipe quite unpractical. And then, when even milk was scarce, why bother with the cooked version, which orders a quarter of a pint of vinegar to half a pint of milk when it isn't all that much of an improvement on the mayonnaise or salad cream of commerce? (Although of course the ingredients of these products are not exactly as straightforward as Senn's were.) One has to remember that all this took place at a time when plain English cooks reigned in the majority of English kitchens. They followed plain English recipes and chiefly those from the Mrs Beeton books or their derivatives. Few of them or their employers experimented or questioned what the books said. By the thirties there was already a vast public brought up in the belief that mayonnaise was a sauce which could only be produced in a factory, which contained no olive oil – and tasted mainly of acetic acid. And that is what, by the sixties, when they see mayonnaise announced on a menu, the great majority of people expect. It is not unnatural that they should be suspicious and indignant when confronted with the authentic sauce. Like most tastes, that for olive oil and mayonnaise made with it is an acquired one. Those of us who have acquired it, and hold that the original verion of mayonnaise is the only true one, also feel that we should be entitled to accuse the caterer who offers us something totally different, under the same name, of fraudulent practice. The caterer is the inheritor of the confusions created by our own indifference to the composition of any given dish so long as it bears an attractive name.

The Spectator, 3 August 1962

Lucky Dip

I am going away and it is time for a turn-out of the dresser drawer which houses my supply of tinned goods, emergency division. Underneath the top layer of Arist-o-Kat and Dum-Chum is revealed a modest assortment of products. Some of these have been sent by the manufacturers or their public relations agents, and some of them have been there a long time. The fact is that the emergency in which I find myself obliged to offer a tin of say Walls' Chicken and Veal Pie to that nomadic and marauding tribe known to every reader of magazine cookery as Unexpected Guests, although a recurring dream of mine, is one that has never yet actually come about; and thankful I am for it, because in my dream I can see that those people are beginning to turn ugly as soon as they see me reaching for the tin-opener. I wish a dream-interpreter would tell me how they come to be so sure I'm not going to open a tin of truffled foie gras. True, I did once offer the filling of one of these pies (chicken, veal, flour, edible fats, seasoning, milk powder, flavouring, phosphate. Preheat oven to a hot condition. Remove lid of can) to my cat, and whether it was the chicken and veal or the flavouring or the phosphate, or was it just that I hadn't got the oven to the sufficiently hot condition, she took to it no more than she did to that pair of frankfurters which arrived in the post one early morning after they'd spent a long weekend at the offices of the magazine for which I was then writing, and were thoughtfully packed with a tube of mustard. Come to think of it, it was the mustard they were pushing, not the sausages. That very same post brought, if I remember rightly, a jar of crab paste and a chromium-plated fork for creaming synthetic lard. That was a change, because the postman's load is usually more spread out. The lard to go with the fork arrived, for example, at 8.15 a.m. two days later, and the thermometer for testing frying temperatures for chips had already got me springing out of bed a week previously. Taking delivery of a Christmas card two feet by four from the Amalgamated Cooking Fats Board was a separate treat again – or am I confusing that occasion with the day I abandoned my Béarnaise to admit a package containing photographs of two dishes called Upsidedown Top Hats and Princess Anne's Muff?

*

Now what else is in the bran-tub? A bottle of Horseradish Relish. Fresh horseradish, spirit vinegar, flour, sugar, salt, mustard, skim milk powder, tragacanth, flavouring. Oh, come now, what earthly flavouring could compete with mustard, horseradish, spirit vinegar? Whatever it was, it nearly blew my head off when I unscrewed that cap. I'm just thinking, perhaps if I have that jar handy when I answer the door to the uninvited, the pillaging horde, they will go away quietly . . .

There is a packet of Instant Bread Sauce. What is it doing here? Its place is in the bean jar with the ice-cream powders and the envelopes of Country Vegetable Soup and White Sauce which I've been meaning to try out for years and years. 'Dear Madam,' a Leicestershire manufacturer of poultry stuffings and packet crumbs and herbs wrote to me after an adverse comment of mine on factory bread sauce had been quoted in a Sunday paper, 'you evidently have never made bread sauce, for if you had you would know that to make it *properly* there is a considerable amount of work involved.' There's a juggins for you. If bread sauce is really the product of a kitchen genius with an infinite capacity for taking pains, am I going to be so easily persuaded that it can be produced just as well in a couple of minutes from a bag of shrivelled breadcrumbs and a cup of milk?

Here are some old friends. Half a dozen tins containing divers sorts of mysterious clams called *almejas*, and mussels and inkfish brought to me from Spain; moderately acceptable in an improvised paella or risotto, and so was that tin of the Italian version of clams called *vongole* in brine (and so it could be at 4/6d.), and there is a jar of cranberry sauce named Nora (cranberries, sugar, pectin). Not talkative, Nora; she or it was given to me by some Norwegians and looks rather sparkly and pretty, although I don't know when I shall use it or what for, I don't really think it's good with turkey. And how ever did I acquire that bottle of diluted tomato soup which must be a sauce for prawn cocktails? Was it sent to me on behalf of prawns or tomato soup? Oh, neither, the label says True French Dressing. Well, I never. That packet of English-made spaghetti with a built-in tin of Sauce Bolognese gives me a guilty pang. I would have liked to compare the whole outfit with the Pizza Mix which included a reconstitutable filling, but I gave that away to some children, proper little dustbins they were, they took my cuckoo clock too, sent direct from a Swiss firm and made up of triangles of foil-wrapped processed cheese. Well, it doesn't do to hoard, so perhaps I had better get rid of the whole lot, including that tin of walnut *glyka*, which, I hope, is the kind of syrupy conserve which the Greeks give you as a gesture of hospitality, on a little saucer, with a glass of water and a cup of coffee and which you mustn't refuse. An impulse buy, that walnut jam, it's been there these two years and more. On second thoughts it had better stay. Not that there has been any indication of it in my dreams, but the unexpected guests could quite well have come all the way from Greece, couldn't they?

The Spectator, 29 June 1962

Summer Holidays

August rain swishes down on the leaves of the wild jungly tree which grows, rootless apparently, in the twelve inch strip of gravel outside my London kitchen. I am assured by a gardener that the plant originated in Kamchatka, but now it looks more like something transplanted from the Orinoco. Staring out at it, hunched into her bumble-bee-in-a-black-mood attitude, my cat suddenly jumps up, presses her face to the window, doesn't like what she sees, comes back, wheels round, washes her face, re-settles herself on her blanket, stares out again. I feel restless too. Remembering other rain-soaked Augusts, English holiday Augusts, I am melancholy, I have a *nostalgie de la pluie.* North Cornwall and its leafy lanes dripping, dripping; the walk in a dressing gown and gum boots through long squelching grass to the stream at the end of the field to fetch water for our breakfast coffee. At the nearest farmhouse they can let us have a pint or two of milk every day; no, not cream, and no eggs or butter, these come out on the grocery van from Penzance. Will there be any pilchards? How lovely to eat them grilled like fresh sardines, except we have only a primus in the kitchen, no grill or oven, so I don't know how we'll cook them; in the bent tin frying pan I suppose. The question never arises though, it isn't the season they say, it's too early, too late, too rough, too cold, too warm. Shopping in Penzance we run to earth what we think is a Cornish regional speciality. At Woolworths. Gingery biscuits, bent and soft, delicious, much nicer than the teeth-breaking sort. (Years later, I find tins of biscuits called Cornish Fairings at my London grocers, and buy them, hoping they are the same. They are meant to be, I think, but they are too crisp. I like the squadgy ones, I expect the recipe is secret to the Penzance Woolworths.)

In one of the grey, slatey villages – St. Just in Roseland – we buy saffron buns, dazzling yellow, only the dye doesn't seem to go quite all the way through, and I think it must be anatto not saffron, anyway there is no taste and the buns are terribly dry. Next day the children take up with a fisherman on the beach and he has given them a huge crawfish. How I wish he hadn't. We can't leave the thing clacking round on dry land. Dry – well, everything is relative.

D. says she will take the girls out for the afternoon to look for Lands End (yesterday it was curtained off by rain, she pretends to

think perhaps it will be different today) and leaves me to the grisly task of cooking the crawfish. The only advantage of being the Expedition's cook is that I am entitled to stay indoors. Our largest cooking vessel is an earthenware stew-pot, so I have to boil the lobster in the water bucket. The RSPCA pamphlet says the most humane way to cook lobsters and their like is to put them in cold water, and as it heats the animal loses consciousness and dies peacefully. I never met a fisherman or a fishmonger or a chef who paid any attention to this theory, and few who had even heard of it. I like to believe in it, and also I think that given the right conditions the system produces a better-cooked lobster, less tough than the ones plunged in boiling water, but a bucket of water takes a powerful long time to heat up on a small primus stove, and that animal would be lying in its bath for a good hour before the water boils – and suppose you have to take it off and re-charge the primus in the course of the operation?

*

The year after the Cornish coastguard's cottage, it is a loaned bungalow on the West Coast of Scotland. Rain drumming on the corrugated iron roof makes a stimulating background rhythm for my work on the index of a book about Italian cooking. Thank heaven for these wet Augusts. In what other climate could one do three months' work during a fortnight's holiday? *Gragnano, grancevole, grignolino, gorgonzola, granita, San Gimignano*, no, *Genoa, ginepro*. L. comes in drenched but with a fresh supply of Dainty Dinah toffees and the delicious rindless Ayrshire bacon we have discovered in the village shop, and the information that at high tide the fisherman will be at the landing stage with crabs and lobsters for sale. Must we? Lacrima Cristi, lamb, lampreys, Lambrusco, lasagne . . . All right, on with our Wellingtons and sou'westers. As it turns out the fisherman is *not* selling crabs and lobsters, nobody eats them here, nasty dirty things, they are for despatch to a fish paste factory in Yorkshire. I am relieved. Too soon. He holds out a great rogue crab. Here, take this. Sixpence. 'How shall I cook him? In boiling water or cold?'
  'Boiling.'
  'The RSPCA says –'
  'Don't know about that –'
  '– cruel –'
  'Dirty beast. Let him suffer it out.'

*

On Tory island, off the Donegal coast – two hours off, in an open boat, on what the Irish describe as a nice soft day, the Scots as a bit mixed, and I as a hurricane, a woman tells me that the best way to cook crabs is to pull off their claws and roast them in the ashes and throw the truncated bodies back in the sea. Some evidence of this ancient folk custom was indeed around. After all perhaps I am better off not inquiring too closely into the local cookery lore of these islands. The kind of windfall cookery which comes one's way in London demands a less ferocious spirit. Rapid action is more to the point.

Pale apricot coloured chanterelle mushrooms from sodden Surrey woods have only to be washed and washed and washed until all the grit has gone, every scrap, and cooked instantly before the bloom and that extraordinary, delicate, almost flower-like scent have faded. (As L. was returning to our Scottish bungalow that other year with a damp bundle of these exquisite mushrooms gallantly gathered during a storm, the schoolmaster's wife stopped to look and used the same expression as the fisherman did about the crab – 'You're never going to eat those dirty things?' But she was a kindly woman, and the same evening invited us in for whisky which would dispel the effects of our folly.)

In contrast, a bunch of sweet basil, the kind with big fleshy floppy leaves, fills the kitchen with a quite violently rich spice smell as it is pounded up with Parmesan, garlic, olive oil and walnuts for a *pesto* sauce for pasta. Again, action has to be taken immediately. That basil was wet, and by tomorrow will have begun to turn black. The vine leaves from the wall of a house near Cambridge, now they can wait a day or two, wrapped in a food bag in the refrigerator, then they will make a lining for a pot of baked mushrooms – a recipe of Italian origin intended for big fat boletus and other wild fungi, and which, it turns out, works a notable change in cultivated mushrooms, making you almost believe you have picked them yourself in some early morning field.

The brined vine leaves in tins from Greece work perfectly in the same way too – all that is necessary before using them is a rinse in a colander under running cold water – but fresh ones, a couple of dozen or so if they are small, should be plunged into a big saucepan of boiling water. As soon as it comes back to the boil take them out, drain them, and line a shallow earthenware pot with them, keeping some for the top. Fill up with flat mushrooms, about ½ lb for two, scatter the chopped stalks on top, add salt, freshly milled pepper, several whole small cloves of garlic which don't necessarily have to be eaten but are essential to the flavour, pour in about four tablespoons of olive oil and cover with vine leaves and the lid of the pot and bake in a very moderate oven for about one hour – less or more according to the size of the mushrooms. When the vine leaves are large and tough they do their work all right but are too stringy to eat; little tender ones are delicious (not the top layer, they have dried out) and there is a good deal of richly flavoured thin dark juice; for soaking it up one needs plenty of bread.

The Spectator, 24 August 1962

Big Bad Bramleys

From where I am sitting it looks very much as if this were another apple-glut autumn, like that of 1960. No question here of 'at the top of the house the apples are laid in rows'; they are in bowls and baskets, under the stairs and in the passage and on the kitchen dresser; spotty windfalls, a couple of dozen outsize Bramleys, mixed lots of unidentified garden apples, sweet and sour, red, yellow, brown, green, large and small, from old country gardens where, at any rate in the south, the trees appear to be exceptionally heavily laden this year. Commercial crops of both eating and cooking apples are, I am told, no more than average and, like all our crops this year, have ripened at least a month late; not that that excuses those growers who send their Cox's orange pippins as unripe to market as some I've tasted recently and which make one wonder if the reputation of yet another of our cherished home-grown pro-ducts is on the way to extinction owing to the short-sightedness of the growers.

Those Bramleys now. What to do with them? There are some who say they make wonderful baked apples. Not I. I find them too large, too sour and too collapsible; and in any case I believe there is no more chilling dish in the whole repertory of English cooking than those baked apples with their mackintosh skins and the inevitable fibrous little bits of core left in the centre; and again, because of the way they disintegrate Bramleys are of very little use for the kind of apple dishes which go so wonderfully with pheasant and other game birds and duck. At the Cordon Bleu school in Paris the other day I saw the chef demonstrating quails *à la normande*; roast quails served on a bed of sliced apples, cooked in butter in a sauté pan; they were seasoned with salt *and* sugar, enriched with thick bubbling cream and a good measure of calvados. Delicious; but well-flavoured and aromatically scented dessert apples which keep their shape are essential. I have used those aforementioned unripe Cox's, which make good fried apples; better still, of course, if the apples are ripe. Both Eliza Acton – where fruit cooking of any and every kind is concerned she is unbeatable – and her twentieth-century French counterpart, Madame Saint-Ange,[1] are very insistent about the quality *and* ripeness of apples for cooking, but Miss Acton doesn't mention Bramleys, probably because although they were already known in her time (discovered, it is said, in a garden at Southwell in Nottinghamshire in 1805) they were not commercially cultivated until the 1860s, some fifteen to twenty years after she wrote *Modern Cookery*.

For apple jelly, for example, Miss Acton specifies Nonsuch, Ribstone pippins and Pearmains, or a mixture of two or three such varieties; and for that most elementary of nursery dishes – which can be such a comfort if nicely made and so odious if watery or over-stewed – which we call a purée and the French call a *marmelade*, Madame Saint-Ange demands, as do nearly all French cooks, the sweet apples they call *reinettes*, the pippins of which the old-fashioned russet-brown *reinette grise* is the prototype.

All these are counsels of perfection; Bramleys are our problem now (the apple publicity people tell me that there are three million Bramley trees in England today), so with Bramleys I make my apple purée, and the recipe I use is the one Miss Acton gives for apple sauce. There is nothing much to it except the preparation. Every scrap of peel and core must be most meticulously removed because the purée is not going to be sieved. You simply heap the prepared and sliced apples into an oven pot, jar or casserole and bake them, covered, but entirely without water, sugar or anything else whatsoever, in a very moderate oven (gas no. 3, 330°F) for anything from twenty to thirty minutes. To whisk them into a purée is then the work of less than a minute. You add sugar (according to your taste and whether the purée is to serve as a sauce or a sweet dish) and, following Miss Acton's instructions, a little lump of butter. I think perhaps this final addition provides the clue to the excellence of this

1. *Le Livre de Cuisine de Mme Saint-Ange* (Larousse, 1927).

recipe, and if it sounds dull to suggest the plainest of apple purées (cream and extra sugar – Barbados brown for preference – go on the table with it) as a sweet dish I can only say that there are times when one positively craves for something totally unsensational; the meals in which every dish is an attempted or even a successful *tour de force* are always a bit of a trial.

And how grateful hospital patients would be if such a thing as a good apple purée were ever to be produced in these establishments; it is just the kind of food one needs when not too ill to be interested in eating, but not well enough to face typical hospital or nursing-home cooking.

One point I should add for the benefit of anyone who has no experience of the idiosyncrasies of the Bramley apple: after fifteen minutes the slices may appear nowhere near cooked; five minutes later you find that they have burst into a froth which has spilled all over the oven; so it is advisable to fill your dish no more than half-full to start with.

The Spectator, 26 October 1962

*

The title of this article was less than fortunate. The English Apple and Pear Board which in the person of Robert Carrier, its PR representative, had helped me with information, was not amused. A lady from Todmorden in Lancashire wrote to my editor in ferocious terms about his cookery expert, furiously condemning 'the revolting brown jam-like apology for the real thing' which my Eliza Acton recipe would certainly produce. When some cherished culinary tenet comes under attack from a journalist people do write letters like that. As a matter of fact I had been a bit surprised myself when I opened my Friday Spectator *that week. I had not been conscious of launching a deliberate attack on the Bramley. It can only have been my unflattering remarks about English baked apples – a criticism directed at the method of cooking rather than at the object cooked – which prompted the literary editor or his deputy to give my otherwise fairly mild piece so provocative a title. In weekly journalism naming of articles tends to be rather a last minute affair, so when my proof came in there had naturally not been any hint of bad about my big Bramleys. Anyway, the deed was done, and having apologised as best I could to Robert Carrier, I began to think the little commotion had been rather entertaining. In my household, I regret to say, Bramleys had already become forever big and bad.*

The lady from Todmorden, I should add, on receiving a letter from me explaining that the titles of my articles were beyond my control, wrote to me again, in a kindly and friendly way. It had never occurred to her, she said, that feature writers did not give their own titles to the articles they wrote. What a worry it must be, she thought, what with possible misprints, etc. to be a writer. If only those were the only hazards of the trade . . .

I think it may be of interest to record what my correspondent, a Mrs Dorothy Sutcliffe, had to say about the correct way to produce 'a heavenly fluffy mound of translucent ambrosia which is obtainable only by using Bramleys (no others will do). Put your sliced apples, about 1 lb, in a pan on a good heat, boil up rapidly with a dessertspoon of water and about 3–4 oz of granulated sugar, stirring as you go, and there you are. Easy as pie'. Mrs Sutcliffe also told me that she 'would not consider apple Charlotte, apple Betty, Eve's pudding, or the famous North Country apple pie worth the effort if made with anything other than Bramley apples'. Good Big Bramleys then? But what apple did they use in the North before the birth of the Bramley?

Crackling

A military gentleman I know who used to run a club once told me that one of his clients was asking for the kind of dishes 'which are practically burnt, you know.' After some interrogation I tumbled to what was wanted and it seemed it wasn't so much a question of the breakfast toast as of that method of cooking which is so typically French, the method whereby gelatinous food such as pigs' trotters and breast of lamb is coated with breadcrumbs and grilled to a delicious sizzling, crackling crispness, deep golden brown and here and there slightly blackened and scorched. At the same time the meat itself, usually pre-cooked, remains moist and tender.

To achieve the characteristic and alluring stage of doneness in this kind of dish needs a bit of practice and a certain amount of dash. You have to watch the food while it's under the grill, as if indeed it were toast, and you have to be brave enough to let it go on grilling until you think you've gone just too far – the same applies, incidentally, to the kind of gratin dishes of vegetables or fish in which the top surface is covered with breadcrumbs. For unless the dish has a crisp blistered crust, slightly charred round the edges, it doesn't quite come off.

One of the breadcrumb-grilled dishes I like best is the one called breast of lamb Ste. Ménéhould. It is very cheap (breast of English lamb was 8d. a pound at Harrods last Saturday – one often finds a cheap cut cheaper and of better quality in a high-class butchery than in a so-called cheap one, and 2½ lb was plenty for four), but I am not pretending it is a dish for ten-minute cooks. It is one for those who have the time and the urge to get real value out of cheap ingredients. First you have to braise or bake the meat in the oven with sliced carrots, an onion or two, a bunch of herbs and, if you like, a little something extra in the way of flavouring such as two or three ounces of a cheap little bit of bacon or salt pork, plus seasonings and about a pint of water. It takes about two and a half to three hours – depending on the quality of the meat – covered, in a slow oven. Then, while the meat is still warm, you slip out the bones, leave the meat to cool, preferably with a weight on it, and then slice it into strips slightly on the bias and about one and a half to two inches wide. Next, spread each strip with a little mustard, paint it with beaten egg (one will be enough for 2½ lb of meat), then coat it with the breadcrumbs, pressing them well down into the meat and round the sides. (I always use breadcrumbs which I've made myself from a French loaf, sliced, and dried in the plate drawer underneath the oven. I know people who think this business of making breadcrumbs is a terrible worry, but once the bread is dried it's a matter of minutes to pound it up with a rolling pin or with a pestle – quicker than doing it in the electric blender.)

All this breadcrumbing finished, you can put the meat on a grid over a baking dish and leave it until you are ready to cook it. Then it goes into a moderate oven for about twenty minutes, because if you put it straight under the grill the outside gets browned before the meat itself is hot. As you transfer the whole lot to the grill pour a very little melted butter over each slice, put them close to the heat, then keep a sharp look-out and turn each piece as the first signs of sizzling and scorching appear.

The plates and dishes should be sizzling too, and some sort of sharp, oil-based sauce – a vinaigrette, a tartare, a mustardy mayonnaise – usually goes with this kind of dish. As a matter of fact it can be made with a good deal less fiddling about in a way described to me by M. Kaufeler, the head chef at the Dorchester. No need, he said, for the boning and slicing of the meat once it's cooked. Just grill it whole or in large chunks. He added that in his youth he and his fellow apprentice cooks used to eat this dish frequently. They called it Park Railings. (It's a system of cooking which evidently engenders picturesque names. Once in a Lyonnais restaurant I had a hefty slab of tripe grilled in this way. It was called Fireman's Apron and even to a non-tripe-eater was made delicious by the lovely crackling crust.) I tried M. Kaufeler's method, and although I did not think it as successful as the Ste. Ménéhould one, I found that it did work a treat for the American cut of spare-ribs of pork (not the fore-end joint we call spare-rib, but a belly piece) which Sainsbury's are now selling at about 2s. a pound. Not much meat on these cuts, but what there is, tender and sweet. It needs less initial cooking time than the lamb – about one hour. It's the kind of food you have to pick up in your fingers, and I rather like something of this sort for Sunday lunch. The first cooking is light work for Saturday and the breadcrumbing business is a soothing occupation when you've had enough of the Sunday papers.

The Spectator, 11 August 1961

Your Perfected Hostess

Not so long ago it was *quiche lorraine.* You could hardly go out to a cocktail party without somebody tipping you off about the delicious *quiche* they made in the penthouse restaurant of the new block at the far end of the Finchley Road. At the dinner-table grave discussions would arise as to the proper ingredients of a *quiche* and the desirability or otherwise of putting cheese in the filling.

No doubt it was the recipes put out by the public relations departments of our big food firms and taken up by magazines as editorial backing for advertising which in the end put the *quiche* out of business as a talking point.

By the time our aspiring cooks had absorbed instructions to make this French regional dish with a prefabricated pie-shell, a couple of triangles of processed cheese and a tin of evaporated milk, nothing much of the original remained. The Lorraine part had got away from the *quiche*, and with it its charm and glamour.

A similar fate had already overtaken the Italian *pizza* and the *salade niçoise*, which by the time they'd all finished with it turned out to be nothing more than the time-honoured English mixture of lettuce, tomato, beetroot and hard-boiled eggs. And now it's the turn of a cold soup called *crème vichyssoise*.

This recipe, as evolved some forty years ago by Louis Diat, the French-born chef of the New York Ritz-Carlton, is, basically, every French housewife's potato and leek soup, puréed, chilled, enriched with fresh cream and sprinkled with chives. One of our troubles about reproducing this dish here in England is that leeks go out of season about the beginning, if any, of the summer, and don't normally come into the shops again until the end of it. Which means that if you *must* have vichyssoise during the heat-wave period then it has to come out of a tin. Those people, however, who won't stoop to tinned soups but still want to be in the swim with their vichyssoise, have taken to using cucumber instead of leeks, and watercress or mint instead of chives – which are hard to come by unless you grow them yourself. The mixture is still thick and rich and cold – and what's, after all, in a name?

All this seems to be typical of the uneasy phase which English cooking is going through. As soon as any dish with a vaguely romantic-sounding name (you may well ask why anyone should associate Vichy with romance) becomes known you find it's got befogged by the solemn mystique which can elevate a routine leek and potato soup into what the heroine of a recent upper-class-larks novel refers to as 'my perfected Vichyssoise'. Then a semi-glamour monthly publishes a recipe in which the original few pence-worth of kitchen garden vegetables are omitted entirely and their place taken by cream of chicken soup and French cream cheese. With astounding rapidity the food processors move in, and launch some even further debased version which in a wink is turning up at banquets and parties and on the menus of provincial hotels.

'INGREDIENTS Skim Milk Powder, Edible Fat, Flour, Gelatine, Super-Glycerinated Fats, Whole Dried Egg, Cayenne Pepper, Lemon, Oil, Edible Colour. Immerse unopened bag in boiling water and simmer for ten minutes.' So runs the legend on a packet of boil-in-the-bag hollandaise (cut along dotted line and squeeze into sauceboat) garnered from the deep-freeze in a self-service store in the King's Road, Chelsea.

What I'm waiting for is the day when it's going to be clever to serve some relaxed English dish like cauliflower cheese. It'll be fun to watch it going up in the world, and getting into the glossies (pin a gigantic starched linen napkin round the platter) and the sub-Mitford novels (Jean-Pierre's got a hangover and won't touch a thing except Fortnum's tinned cauliflower cheese), thence into the women's weeklies (Maureen was piping her own very special cheese dip round the cauliflower. The candles were lit . . .), and eventually through all the inevitable transformations and degradations until, dehydrated, double-quick deep-frozen, reboiled and debagged, it finally reaches the tables of our residential hotels and the trays of forty-guinea-a-week nursing homes.

Punch, 6 November 1961

Secrets

Paris isn't the only city where August-stranded inhabitants find themselves bereft of familiar tables to rest their elbows on and nowhere to take the visitors who turn up without warning. In my quarter of London two at least of the better restaurants have been closed for the holidays. Investigation of other local resources has produced the Beau Geste, an establishment situated on the South Kensington-Fulham-Chelsea borders. If this restaurant were listed, which it isn't, in any of the guide books, I think it would be described as of modest aspect. This means that it doesn't have a striped awning or canopy over its doorway and is about the equivalent of any of those restaurants in any French town which you notice only because outside you bump into a cut-out figure representing a waiter proffering a *prix-fixe* menu at 8 N.F. and *poulet rôti cresson* (supp. 4 N.F.). In France you don't go into this restaurant but in London s.w.3/7/10 you do. Inside you find that the walls of the Beau Geste are papered in vandyke brown. On them hang, here and there, a brass sabot or two and a handful of framed reproductions of sketches of picturesque corners of places which might be Montmartre, St Ives or Florence. There are eight tables. At midday only two of them are set with cloths, but such as they are they are clean, cheap and bright. The Beau Geste is not licensed so you have brought your own wine. The waiter takes it away and brings it back five minutes later, and the label looks a trifle damp. You ask him what he has done to the wine. He is Spanish, he does not understand. He fetches the proprietor from behind the match-board partition at the end of the restaurant. M. Pigeon says ah yes, the wine was cold so he has permitted himself to warm it a little. He has been five years with the French navy, *alors vous comprenez madame je connais les vins, moi.* What he doesn't *connait* is that I like my Beaujolais cold, straight from my cellar.

The hors-d'œuvre announced on the yellow menu sheet of the Beau Geste are *piments vinaigrette, rillettes de Tours, pâté maison, salade niçoise, saucisson de Lyon,* egg mayonnaise. There are omelettes, three or four fish dishes including amazingly enough two scampi variations and *truite meunière.* Meat dishes are entrecôtes and veal escalopes, each in three different ways. There is a good line in tinned vegetables such as *petits pois* and *flageolets,* and the routine *pommes sautées.* There is a *salade verte* and a *salade panachée* – the panache consists of tomatoes quartered *à l'anglaise* – a *plateau de fromages* and for dessert three kinds of ice and two sweet omelettes, jam and flambé.

I have already tried the *piments vinaigrette.* They are tinned, but M. Pigeon makes the best of them with a good dressing, slivers of onion and chopped parsley. Today we will have *saucisson de Lyon,* entrecôte maître d'hôtel and a salad without panache. The *saucisson de Lyon* turns out to be Danish salami. As we are picking at it Mme Pigeon, in hat and mackintosh, walks through the restaurant from the street and disappears behind the partition. She re-emerges with an apron tied round her waist, walks past our table, glances to see what wine we have brought. The entrecôtes appear. They are not the best quality Aberdeen Angus meat but they are well and freshly cooked, hot, and served on hot plates. Our green salads are brought, on flat oval hors-d'œuvre dishes. My guest says the salad is delicious. I think she is being polite, because she is herself an instinctive mixer of exquisite green salads. We drink our tepid coffee. M. Pigeon, dressed in his street clothes, bustles out of the restaurant. Madame comes to collect payment. With the tip about £2.10s. Madame says no, no holidays this year. Business has not been famous. It has been a sad summer.

Five days later I take another guest to the Beau Geste, today we will try one of the *plats du jour* announced on the slip of paper attached to the yellow menu sheet. M. Pigeon peers round the partition. Yes, the *veau à la fermière* is an escalope in a *sauce au vin rouge. Il est très bon.* We order it, plus green salads and one portion of pâté *maison* for the more experimental member of the party. The pâté is of M. Pigeon's own confection. It is not discreditable. The red wine sauce with the escalope is. It is a thick brown paste. A fork would stand upright in it. The escalopes could be veal. They could just as easily be the bedroom slippers I threw away last week. My guest says the green salad is the best she has ever had in a London restaurant. I don't doubt that she is telling the truth. The coffee is lukewarm. As we are drinking it (it is 2.20 p.m.) M. Pigeon walks through the restaurant in his street clothes. At 2.25 the waiter also leaves. Madame stays behind to collect the £2 odd for one portion of pâté, two escalopes, two green salads, two coffees.

Four days later I am to be guest at the Beau Geste. It is Saturday and on Saturdays you can park a car in the street right outside the Beau Geste, a circumstance which naturally entrances my hostess. What for a first dish today? The *rillettes*, are they made by M. Pigeon? The waiter shakes his head. We can't make out if this means yes, no, or doesn't know. We will have entrecôtes only, one with tinned pimentos and fried onions, one with a tomato and anchovy garnish; and two green salads. The steaks cost 15s.6d. and 14s.6d. respectively. They are very nice. My hostess is a good cook. She always has a lovely salad with her meals. Nevertheless she says she wishes she could make a salad as good as M. Pigeon's. As we are finishing our tepid coffee M. Pigeon leaves. On Saturdays midday at the Beau Geste is quite lively. At other tables people are sitting over their factory-made sorbets. Madame attends to them. As she passes our table she looks apprehensive. Perhaps we, or the other customers, may stay too long. She turns out the lights. Possibly the Spanish waiter gets overtime on Saturdays. He remains to collect my hostess's £2 odd for two steaks, two salads, two coffees.

On Tuesday an old friend turns up from the country. She wants me to have lunch with her, and to go shopping afterwards. We will take a bottle of wine round to the Beau Geste and eat quickly. The *plats du jour* today are *potage cultivateur* (that's an old familiar I haven't seen on a menu since the days of the London Brighton and South Coast Railway) and *escalope de veau lyonnaise*, and changes her mind when I decide on the Spanish omelette. She says I always get something better than she does. Two omelettes and two green salads then. The Spanish omelettes aren't too bad. The filling contains tinned *petits pois*, tinned pimientos and nicely cooked potatoes and onions. The omelettes are not at all Spanish but also they are not at all stodgy. We enjoy them. Good gracious me, says D., this salad is delicious. Her faith returns. Shall we try the orange sorbet? I deflect her to cheese. The Spanish waiter brings the plateau. On it are a half Camembert, a whole new Camembert, a little log-shaped cheese which might be Neufchatel, and a piece of *tome aux raisins* about one inch square. D. says the Camembert looks a bit shrivelled. The waiter says something we take to mean that that is only because it has been in the fridge. We choose the near-Neufchatel. Perhaps we should have plumped for the sorbet. At least it wouldn't have been any more icy. Today the coffee is not tepid. It is cold. Ten minutes later we get our bill. For two omelettes, two salads, cheese and coffee thirty shillings with tip.

Cherished in our dreams, held close to our hearts in deathless legend is the humble French restaurant, the unpretentious *petit coin pas cher* where one may drop in at any time and be sure always of a friendly welcome, a well-cooked omelette, a good salad, a glass of honest wine. The Beau Geste is the dream made manifest. There are those, and I am one of them, who are so disloyal as to think that thirty shillings for two omelettes, two salads and two coffees accompanied by honest wine of one's own providing is not all that *pas cher*. Like myself they will probably still go back to the Beau Geste and for the same reasons, which are that if M. Pigeon is a rascal, he is at least a cheery one and certainly has a deft hand with an omelette pan and a tin-opener. That he can get away with his prices is partly our own fault, partly that of the local standards of catering. When the alternative is cold sausage rolls and a glass of warm Spanish Sauterne in the local pub we are pleased to get anything eatable at all for two pounds ten shillings. And M. Pigeon's brown wallpaper and even the concierge-type blight cast by his wife are still rather more acceptable than the amateur theatricals of the ex-Eighth Army corporal down the road, whose eating establishment is got up to look like the inside of a saddler's shop and where if you order an omelette as likely as not it will turn up inside a crust of puff pastry, and as for the composition of the dressing on the avocado pear it is a secret, and one you don't want to penetrate. M. Pigeon is at least not revealing much of a secret when, if you can catch him as he hurries to the pub before closing time, he tells you that his salad dressing is made with arrachide oil and malt vinegar. This I have kept from my friends and guests. Where French cooking is concerned they like secrets. They shall have them.

The Spectator, 6 September 1963

Ladies' Halves

What on earth comes over wine waiters when they take the orders of a woman entertaining another woman in a restaurant? Twice in one week recently I have dined in different restaurants (not, admittedly, in the expense-account belt of the West End, where women executives have tables and bottles of 1945 Margaux permanently at the ready, or it's nice to think so, anyway) and with different women friends, on one occasion as the hostess and on the other as the guest. On both occasions, after the regulation lapse of twenty minutes, the wine waiter brought a half-bottle of the wine ordered instead of a whole one. Please don't think I have anything against half-bottles; on the contrary, I find they have a special charm of their own. There are occasions when a half is what one wants, a half and nothing else, in which case I really don't believe one has to be a master-woman to be capable of specifying one's wishes in the matter. I suppose the assumption on the part of wine waiters that women are too frail to consume or too stingy to pay for a whole bottle must be based on some sort of experience, but instead of having to go back to change the order (ten minutes the second time, one is getting edgy by then, and well into the second course; if they held up the food to synchronize with the wine one mightn't mind so much) he could inquire in the first place, in a discreet way. Or even in an indiscreet way, like the steward on the Edinburgh–London express a few years ago who yelled at me across the rattling crockery and two other bemused passengers, 'A bottle, madam? A *whole* bottle? Do you know how large a whole bottle is?'

The Spectator, 13 July 1962

Letting Well Alone

VITAMIN H, JAM reads the last item on the menu of the famous Azanian banquet in *Black Mischief*. I remembered about Seth's dinner ('There is the question of food. I have been reading that now it is called Vitamins') when the proprietor of a village inn in the Var, about twenty-five miles from Aix-en-Provence, brought us bowls of jam as the final course of our delicious lunch. For the English, it's always good for a laugh that the French eat jam for pudding – and jam by itself, jam without bread and butter, without toast or teacakes, or cream or even sponge or roly-poly. Just jam, and the point about this jam, and I can't help how quaint it sounds, was its absolute rightness on this particular occasion. The meal was faultless of its kind, a roughish country inn kind, beginning with tomato salad with chopped onion, the little black olives of the Nyons district, and home-made pâté – the basic hors-d'œuvre in this part of Provence – each item on its own separate dish, and left on the table so we could help ourselves. It was followed by a *gratin* of courgettes and rice. This dish, new to me, was made with courgettes cooked in butter and sieved, the resulting purée then mixed with béchamel and rice, all turned into a shallow dish and browned in the oven. A mixture with delicate and unexpected flavours. Then came a daube of beef, an excellent one, with an unthickened but short sauce of wine and tomato purée, beautifully scented with bayleaf and thyme, brought to the table, and left on it, in a metal casserole in which it kept sizzling hot. Finally, this famous jam – home-made, of green melons, fresh-tasting, not too sweet, a hint of lemons in the background. The wine was coarse red, by the litre. Even the coffee was drinkable, and the bill was very modest.

The English public must be sick and tired of being told that cooking is an art and that the French are the great exponents of it. Or, alternatively, that cooking is not an art but a question of good basic ingredients, which we have more of and better than anyone else (it's surprising how many otherwise quite sane English people really believe this) and so QED we also have the best cooking, while the French, poor things, toil away in their kitchens in a desperate effort to disguise what Lady Barnett, in a speech delivered at a caterers' dinner in the Midlands a few weeks ago, referred to as 'meat not fit to eat and fish without taste'. I don't want to enter into this abysmal argument. I just want to describe that same Provençal meal as it would be if one ordered it in a London restaurant. With the exception of the tomato salad, which can't be made here because tomatoes fit for salad aren't acceptable to the greengrocery trade, there was nothing about that meal which *couldn't* be reproduced by a moderately skilful English cook, professional or amateur.

So here we go. A slab of pâté, smelling powerfully of smoked bacon and rosemary, is brought to your table on a teaplate loaded with lettuce leaves; it is covered with a trellis work of radishes or watercress, interspersed with a tasteful pattern of very large olives, brown rather than black. (Here we can't get the fine black olives of the Nyonsais, the best in Provence, but Italian, Greek, and North African small black olives are quite easy to come by. Those huge brown ones they sell in delicatessens are bitter and over-salt.) For pretty, as American fashion journalists say, there is a spoonful of tinned red peppers, and a couple of gherkins falling off the over-crowded plate. Now, the gratin of courgettes and rice. Well, that doesn't contain fish or meat, so it's not a course by English standards. What about adding a few scampi, or a slice or two of ham, or some little bits of bacon? Or better still, economize on the service or washing up and present it with the meat, plus, naturally, potatoes and a green vegetable. What? The taste of the courgette purée is too fragile to go with that beef and wine? Put plenty of cheese in it then, that'll pep it up. And anyway that daube, it smells all right and it tastes good but there isn't quite enough gravy with it. Add a cupful of the chef's brown sauce to each serving, it'll make it nice and thick and it'll look more shiny and stylish on the plate – it'll be on a plate of course, there'd be chaos if you left a casserole of the stuff on the customers' tables. And now we get to our Vitamin H. Will the customers stand for jam potted in plastic thimbles like they have on British Railways and at Ye Old Sussex Tea Gardens? Going too far perhaps. Better heat up the jam, stir in a little Curaçao, a dash of vanilla essence, some green colouring to cheer it up, and serve it as a sauce with ice-cream. That's more like it. Charge them 8s.6d. for it, it's worth it what with all the trouble it gave the cook. And the wine? This is an expensive meal, so the red plonk won't do. Put a bottle of Château Pont d'Avignon rosé ready in a basket, will you?

And the English customers will pay £3.10s. a head for this version of a meal which in its original form cost about 25s. for two including service. And they will like it, and they will go home and try to reproduce it in their own kitchens – adding of course a little frill here, a trimming there, an extra vegetable, a few mushrooms in the beef stew . . .

It does seem to me that with so much talk about art versus fine ingredients somebody might mention that there is also the art, or the discipline, call it which you like, of leaving well alone. This is a prerequisite of any first-class meal (as opposed to one isolated first-class dish) on any level whatsoever; so is the capacity, among the customers if you are a restaurateur and among your friends if you are an amateur cook, to appreciate well when it *is* left alone. It's a capacity which would make meals a lot cheaper and cooking a great deal easier.

The Spectator, 7 July 1961

*

The London restaurant food described in this article was typical of three or four Belgravia-Knightsbridge-Fulham establishments successful and popular at the time, and subsequently much imitated. Indeed the same type of food, liberally sauced, densely garnished, is to be found in any number of London and provincial restaurants (study the Good Food Guide *and you will see what I mean) and in up-market pubs. Prices have changed. The English attitude to eating out has not. Quantity is all.*

As for the genuine Provençal restaurant which triggered off my Spectator *article, it was just that – genuine and Provençal. It was in a small Varois town called Rians. Last time I went there, in the late nineteen-sixties, road-widening outside and modernization within had made the place difficult to recognize. We did not stop for a meal. The restaurant is called the Esplanade. It is still listed in the* Michelin Guide.

1973

An Omelette and a Glass of Wine

Once upon a time there was a celebrated restaurant called the Hôtel de la Tête d'Or on the Mont-St-Michel just off the coast of Normandy. The reputation of this house was built upon one single menu which was served day in day out for year after year. It consisted of an omelette, ham, a fried sole, *pré-salé* lamb cutlets with potatoes, a roast chicken and salad, and a dessert. Cider and butter were put upon the table and were thrown in with the price of the meal, which was two francs fifty in pre-1914 currency.

But it wasn't so much what now appears to us as the almost absurd lavishness of the menu which made Madame Poulard, proprietress of the hotel, celebrated throughout France. It was the exquisite lightness and beauty of the omelettes, cooked by the proprietress herself, which brought tourists flocking to the mère Poulard's table.

Quite a few of these customers subsequently attempted to explain the particular magic which Madame Poulard exercised over her eggs and her frying pan in terms of those culinary secrets which are so dear to the hearts of all who believe that cookery consists of a series of conjuring tricks. She mixed water with the eggs, one writer would say, she added cream asserted another, she had a specially made pan said a third, she reared a breed of hens unknown to the rest of France claimed a fourth. Before long, recipes for the *omelette de la mère Poulard* began to appear in magazines and cookery books. Some of these recipes were very much on the fanciful side. One I have seen even goes so far as to suggest she put *foie gras* into the omelette. Each writer in turn implied that to him or her alone had Madame Poulard confided the secret of her omelettes.

At last, one fine day, a Frenchman called M. Robert Viel, interested in fact rather than surmise, wrote to Madame Poulard, by this time long retired from her arduous labours, and asked her once and for all to clear up the matter. Her reply, published in 1932 in a magazine called *La Table*, ran as follows:

6 June 1932

Monsieur Viel,
  Here is the recipe for the omelette: I break some good eggs in a bowl, I beat them well, I put a good piece of butter in the pan, I throw the eggs into it, and I shake it constantly. I am happy, monsieur, if this recipe pleases you.

Annette Poulard.

So much for secrets.

But, you will say, everyone knows that the success of omelette making starts with the pan and not with the genius of the cook. And a heavy pan with a perfectly flat base *is*, of course a necessity. And if you are one of those who feel that some special virtue attaches to a venerable black iron pan unwashed for twenty years, then you are probably right to cling to it.

Cookery does, after all, contain an element of the ritualistic and however clearly one may understand that the reason for not washing and scouring omelette pans is the risk of thereby causing rust spots and scratches which would spoil the surface of the pan and cause the eggs to stick, one may still have a superstitious feeling that some magic spell will be broken if water is allowed to approach the precious pan. Soap and water, come not near, come not near our omelette pan . . . (Personally, I keep my old iron omelette pan, the surface protected by a film of oil, for pancakes, and use an aluminium one for omelettes and wash it up like any other utensil. This is not perversity, but simply the ritual which happens to suit me and my omelettes.)

As to the omelette itself, it seems to me to be a confection which demands the most straightforward approach. What one wants is the taste of the fresh eggs and the fresh butter and, visually, a soft bright golden roll plump and spilling out a little at the edges. It should not be a busy, important urban dish but something gentle and pastoral, with the clean scent of the dairy, the kitchen garden, the basket of early morning mushrooms or the sharp tang of freshly picked herbs, sorrel, chives, tarragon. And although there are those who maintain that wine and egg dishes don't go together I must say I do regard a glass or two of wine as not, obviously, essential but at least as an enormous enhancement of the enjoyment of a well-cooked omelette. In any case if it were true that wine and eggs are bad partners, then a good many dishes, and in particular, such sauces as mayonnaise, Hollandaise and Béarnaise would have to be banished from meals designed round a good bottle, and that would surely be absurd. But we are not in any case considering the great occasion menu but the almost primitive and elemental meal evoked by the words: 'Let's just have an omelette and a glass of wine.'

Perhaps first a slice of home-made pâté and a few olives, afterwards a fresh salad and a piece of ripe creamy cheese or some fresh figs or strawberries . . . How many times have I ordered and enjoyed just such a meal in French country hotels and inns in preference to the set menu of *truite meunière, entrecôte, pommes paille* and *crème caramel* which is the French equivalent of the English roast and two veg. and apple tart and no less dull when you have experienced it two or three times.

There was, no doubt there still is, a small restaurant in Avignon where I used to eat about twice a week, on market days, when I was living in a rickety old house in a crumbling Provençal hill-top village about twenty miles from the city of the Popes. Physically and emotionally worn to tatters by the pandemonium and splendour of the Avignon market, tottering under the weight of the provisions we had bought and agonized at the thought of all the glorious things which we hadn't or couldn't, we would make at last for the restaurant Molière to be rested and restored.

It was a totally unpretentious little place and the proprietors had always been angelically kind, welcoming and generous. They purveyed some particularly delicious *marc de Champagne* and were always treating us to a glass or two after lunch so that by the time we piled into the bus which was to take us home we were more than well prepared to face once more the rigours of our mistral-torn village. But even more powerful a draw than the *marc* was the delicious cheese omelette which was the Molière's best speciality. The recipe was given to me by the proprietress whose name I have most ungratefully forgotten, but whose omelette, were there any justice in the world, would be as celebrated as that of Madame Poulard. Here it is.

OMELETTE MOLIÈRE

Beat *one* tablespoon of finely grated Parmesan with 3 eggs and a little pepper.

Warm the pan a minute over the fire. Put in half an oz of butter. Turn up the flame. When the butter bubbles and is about to change colour, pour in the eggs.

Add *one* tablespoon of very fresh Gruyère cut into little dice, and *one* tablespoon of thick fresh cream. Tip the pan towards you, easing some of the mixture from the far edge into the middle. Then tip the pan away from you again, filling the empty space with some of the still liquid eggs. By the time you have done this twice, the Gruyère will have started to melt and your omelette is ready. Fold it over in three with a fork or palette knife, and slide it on to the warmed omelette dish. Serve it instantly.

With our meals in Avignon we generally drank local wine, pink or red, which was nothing much to write home about (the wine of our own village *was* notable though: the worst I have ever consistently had to drink) but what I would choose nowadays if I had the chance would be a deliciously scented Alsatian Traminer or a white burgundy such as the lovely Meursault – Genevrières of 1955, or a Loire wine, perhaps Sancerre or a Pouilly Fume – anyway, you see what I mean. I like white wines with all cheese dishes, and especially when the cheese in question is Gruyère. No doubt this is only a passing phase, because as a wine drinker but not a wine expert one's tastes are constantly changing. But one of the main points about the enjoyment of food and wine seems to me to lie in having what you want *when* you want it and in the particular combination you fancy.

T. B. Layton's *Besides*, September–December 1959

Chez Barattero

From 1956 to 1961 I contributed a monthly cookery article to London Vogue. *In those days cookery writers were very minor fry. Expenses were perks paid to photographers, fashion editors and other such exalted personages. Foreign currency allowances were severely restricted, so cookery contributors didn't come in for subsidised jaunts to Paris or marathons round three star eating cathedrals. They were supposed to supply their articles out of some inexhaustible well of knowledge and their ingredients out of their own funds. At a monthly fee of £20 an article (increased at some stage, I think, to £25) it was quite a struggle to keep up the flow of properly tested recipes, backed up with informative background material, local colour and general chatter. So it was with gratitude that one year I accepted an offer from my editor, the original and enlightened Audrey Withers, to go on the occasional trip to France, provided with £100 from Condé Nast to help cover restaurant meals, hotels, petrol and so on. To be sure, £100 wasn't exactly princely even in those days, but it was double the ordinary currency allowance, and even though those trips were very much France on a shoestring, the knowledge I derived from them was valuable. In French provincial restaurants at that time local and regional dishes weren't always double-priced on a 'menu touristique'. Some, in-credible as it now seems, would be listed as a matter of course on the everyday menus of quite ordinary restaurants. Asked nicely, a* patron *might come up with a speciality based, say, on some local farmhouse pork product, or on a cheese peculiar to the immediate district, perhaps an omelette of the chef's own devising, or a simple fish dish with an uncommon sauce. It was for ideas and stimulus that I was looking, not restaurant set pieces.*

On one trip, however, I came to make the acquaintance of Madame Barattero and her Hôtel du Midi at Lamastre in the Ardèche. Now, a hotel with a Michelin two-star restaurant attached might not seem exactly the appropriate choice for people on a

Madame Barattero and her chef Monsieur Perrier outside the Hôtel du Midi, photograph by Anthony Denney, c1959

restricted budget. As things turned out, that particular two-star restaurant-hotel proved, in the long run, very much cheaper, infinitely better value, and far more rewarding than most of the technically cheap places we'd found. Staying at Lamastre on half-pension terms was restful and comfortable. Every day we drove out to the countryside, usually taking a picnic, or lunching at a small town or village restaurant. In the evening we were provided by Madame Barattero with a delicious dinner made up of quite simple dishes geared to the price charged to pensionnaires. *Prime ingredients and skilled cooking were, however, very much included in our en pension* terms. *That lesson was a valuable one, and seemed well worth passing on to my readers.*

My account of the Hôtel du Midi was published in Vogue *in September 1958. I should add that while much of the material published in* Vogue *as a result of my trips to France in the fifties was incorporated in* French Provincial Cooking, *this was one of several articles which got away. There did not seem to be a place for it in the book, and in fact it was, in its day, unique for a* Vogue *food article in that it included no recipes. It was, again, Audrey Withers who took the decision to publish an article quite unorthodox by the rules prevailing at the time. I appreciated her imaginative gesture. With Madame Barattero I remained on friendly terms for many years, receiving a moving welcome every time I visited her hotel. Two years ago, after a brief retirement, Madame Barattero died. Her declining years had been clouded by increasing deafness, by the withdrawal of one of her Michelin stars, and I believe other untoward happenings. The restaurant of the Hôtel du Midi is now in the hands of the same chef who was in charge of the kitchens all those years ago, and who had long since become a partner in the business. I have not visited Lamastre for several years now, so cannot express any opinion on the cooking. I am glad though to be able to republish my article, as a tribute to Madame Barattero's memory.*

*

Rose Barattero is the euphonious name of the proprietress of the Hôtel du Midi at Lamastre in the Ardèche. Slim, elegant, her pretty grey hair in tight curls all over her head, the minuscule red ribbon of the Legion of Honour on her grey dress, Madame Barattero is an impressive little figure as she stands on the terrace of her hotel welcoming her guests as they drive into the main square of the small provincial town whose name she has made famous throughout France.

Here, in this town, in the modest hotel which stands back to back with her own, she was born. Her parents were hotel keepers, her brother inherited, and still runs, the old Hôtel de la Poste. Her sister has a hotel at St-Vallier down on the Rhône. Her husband, a *niçois*, and a relation of the Escoffier family, started his career as an apprentice at the Carlton in London, and was already making a name for himself as a promising chef when she married him and they set up on their own at the Hôtel du Midi.

When M. Barattero died in 1941 the hotel was already celebrated for its cooking. His young widow took over the running of the hotel and the restaurant, putting the kitchen in the charge of a hard-working and modest chef who had started as Barattero's apprentice. His wife looks after the accounts and the reception work.

During the past fifteen years or so the fame of Barattero's at Lamastre has spread throughout France; Madame Barattero's name is among the most respected in the entire French restaurant industry.

In the fiercely competitive world of the French catering business this is no ordinary achievement. Lamastre is a town of little over three thousand inhabitants. It is not on a main road; the country round about, although magnificent and infinitely varied, is not known to tourists in the way in which, let us say, Provence or the château country of the Loire are known, for there is not very much left in the way of architectural or historical interest for the ordinary sightseer. In other words, a place like Barattero's must rely, not on the local population and the passing tourist, but upon those customers who make the journey to Lamastre expressly for the cooking.

Michelin awards Madame Barattero two stars. Now, although Michelin one-star restaurants are very much on the chancy side, both as regards quality and price, and such of their three-star establishments (there are only eleven in the whole of France) into which I have penetrated, either a little too rarefied in atmosphere for my taste – or, as Raymond Mortimer observed recently of a famous Paris house, the food is too rich and so are the customers – it is rare to find the two-star places at fault. As far as the provinces are concerned these two-star establishments (there are fifty-nine of them in the whole country, about twenty of which are in Paris) offer very remarkable value. I do not mean to suggest that they are places for the impecunious, but rather that while the cooking which they have to offer is unique, the charges compare more than favourably with those prevailing in hundreds of other French establishments where the surroundings vary between the grandiose and the squalid and where the cooking, while probably sound enough, is uneven or without distinction.

I have often heard the criticism that these modest establishments of two-star quality, offering, as most of them do, no more than half a dozen specialities at most, are places whose resources are exhausted after a couple of meals, or alternatively that the accommodation which they have to offer is not up to the standard of the cooking. So tourists make their pilgrimage to eat a meal at a place like the Midi at Lamastre, the Chapon Fin at Thoissey, or the Armes de France at Ammerschwihr and move on without knowing that they could have stayed for several days, not only in comfort and quiet and enjoying a variety of beautifully cooked dishes, but quite often at considerably reduced prices for pension or half-pension terms.

Early last summer we drove from Lyon down the western bank of the Rhône towards St-Péray, and there turned off up the steep and beautiful road which leads to Lamastre and St-Agrève. We had been warned that the forty-odd kilometres from St-Péray to Lamastre would take us twice as long as we expected because of the sinuous road, so we had allowed plenty of time, and arrived in front of the Hôtel du Midi while the afternoon sun was still shining over the little *place*. Our welcome from Madame Baraterro was so warm and the rooms we were shown so airy, light and sympathetically furnished, the bathroom so immense and shining, the little garden below our terrace so pretty and orderly, that we decided there and then to stay several days. We discussed half-pension terms with Madame and then made ourselves scarce until dinner time.

Now it must be explained that chez Barattero there are five special dishes for which the house is renowned. They are *galantine de caneton*, a *pain d'écrevisses sauce cardinal*, a *poularde en vessie*, a *saucisse en feuilletage* and a dish of artichoke hearts with a creamy sauce which they call *artichauts Escoffier*. If you were really trying you could, I suppose, taste them all at one meal (indeed four of them figure on the 1,800 franc menu, the most expensive one, the others being 1,600 and 1,200) but we could take our time and enjoy them gradually. We left the choice of our menus to Madame. Indeed, there was little alternative but to do so. For although she does not herself do the cooking Madame has been studying her guests and composing menus for them for thirty-four years and she neither likes being contradicted nor is capable of making a mistake in this respect. She knew without being told that we didn't want to overload ourselves with food, however delicious; with an unerring touch she provided us night after night with menus which I think it is worth describing if only to demonstrate one or two important points about French restaurant cooking. First, how varied the food can be even in a place where the advertised specialities are very limited; secondly, how well worth while it is eating even the simplest of the routine dishes of French cookery produced in an absolutely first-class manner. ('One does not come here to eat something as ordinary as *œufs en gelée*,' the archbishop-like head waiter in a famous Paris restaurant once said to me. He was wrong. Such simple things are the test of a really good establishment.) And thirdly, how very much a good dish gains by being served quite on its own, without fussy garnish or heaps of vegetables to overfill you and to get in the way of your sauce, to distract from the main flavours of the chicken or the fish and to sicken you of the sight of food long before the end of the meal.

We could have started every meal with soup had we so wished, but in fact we did so only once or twice because they were so good that we should have eaten too much. And the last part of the meal always consisted of a fine platter of cheeses and either strawberries, cherries or an ice, so I will leave those items out of the following account of our menus.

The wines we drank were mostly recent Rhône vintages, the current wines of the house, for many of which, especially the red Hermitages, the Cornas and the Côte Rôtie, I have a particular affection. Among the whites we tried were St-Péray, Chapoutier's Chante Alouette, Jaboulet's La Chapelle Hermitage 1950; for those who prefer, and can afford, old burgundies and bordeaux there is a well-stocked cellar of fine vintages.

Tuesday

Galantine de caneton: The name is misleading to English ears. It is a whole boned duck, its flesh mixed with finely minced pork, truffles, brandy and foie gras, sewn up in the skin of the duck and cooked in the oven; the result resembles a long fat sausage with the feet of the duck protruding at one end. This pâté has a flavour of very great delicacy, and is served sliced and quite unadorned. The lettuce leaves and the little heap of potato salad which, I have an uneasy feeling, would be the inevitable garnish provided by an English restaurateur, is simply unthinkable here.

Sole meunière: Perfectly cooked whole sole with quantities of hissing and foaming butter. Again, no garnish of any kind, and none needed.

Blettes à la crème au gratin: Blettes, or chard, that spinach-like vegetable with fleshy white stalks is, to me, only tolerable when cooked by a master hand, but as the Barattero chef has that hand, and makes a particularly excellent cream sauce, all was well.

Wednesday

After an exhausting day's driving in bad weather, and a good and not expensive lunch at the Cygne (but unsettling contemporary decor in an old hotel) in the rather depressing town of Le Puy, we returned to dinner at Lamastre.

Potage de légumes: The routine vegetable soup of the day, but the mixture of carrots, potatoes and other vegetables was so delicate, so buttery, so full of flavour, that this alone would serve to make the reputation of a lesser restaurant. Note: although so full of flavour this soup was quite thin. I think we make our vegetable soups too thick in this country.

Ris de veau à la crème: I have eaten too many ambitiously conceived but ill-executed dishes of sweetbreads ever again to order them of my own accord, so I was grateful to Madame Barattero for showing me how good they can be when properly done. There were mushrooms in the sauce. Perfect.

Petit pois à la française: A big bowl of very small fresh peas (even in good restaurants it is rare nowadays not to get *petits pois de conserve*) cooked with little shreds of lettuce but without the little onions usually associated with the *à la française* manner of cooking them. The result was very creamy and good. I doubt if I shall ever again put onions with my peas.

Thursday

Pain d'écrevisses sauce cardinal: A very remarkable dish. A variety of *quenelle*, but unlike the pasty *quenelles* one eats elsewhere, even in the much cracked-up Lyon restaurants; as light as a puff of air, with the subtle and inimitable flavour of river crayfish permeating both *quenelle* and the rich cream sauce. The garnish of the dish consisted of a few whole scarlet crayfish and crescents of puff pastry.

Poularde en vessie: A 3-lb Bresse chicken, stuffed with its own liver, a little foie gras and slices of truffle, is tied up inside a pig's bladder and cooked extremely gently in a marmite of barely simmering water for one and a half hours. As Madame Barattero said, a chicken poached in the ordinary way, however carefully, cannot help but be *'un peu délavé'*, a trifle washed out. By this system, which is an ancient one, the chicken, untouched by the cooking liquid, emerges with all its juices and flavours intact. When it is cold, as it was served to us, these juices formed inside the bladder have solidified to a small amount of clear and delicately flavoured jelly. Madame asserted that nothing was easier to cook than this dish – 'What do you mean, why can you not get a pig's bladder in

England? You have pigs, do you not?' – and upheld her point by adding that the chef's eight-year old son already knows how to prepare the *poulardes en vessie*. A green salad with cream in the dressing was the only accompaniment to the chicken.

Friday and Saturday

The most important part of Friday's meal was a sad disappointment. It was a dish of tiny grilled lamb cutlets, obviously beautiful meat, but much too undercooked for our taste.

On Saturday evening, when *épaule d'agneau* was announced, I explained the trouble. The little shoulder appeared cooked to what was, for us, perfection. A beautiful golden brown on the outside and just faintly pink in the middle. It had been preceded by a delicious *omelette aux champignons* and was accompanied by a *gratin* of courgettes and tomatoes, just slightly flavoured with garlic and cooked in butter instead of olive oil as it would have been in Provence. It went admirably with the lamb, and this was a good example of a very nice dinner of quite ordinary French dishes without any particular regional flavour or speciality of the house.

Sunday

Next day was Whitsunday and we stayed in to lunch as well as to dinner, for, as the weekend drew near, we had been observing with fascinated interest the preparations afoot for the large number of customers expected for the *fêtes*. The chef had prepared fifteen of his boned and stuffed ducks and by lunchtime on Sunday dozens of *poulardes* tied up in pig's bladders and scores of *pain d'écrevisses* were ready, all gently murmuring in their respective copper marmites.

Until now the service at meal times had been performed entirely by Marthe and Marie, the two pretty, expertly trained young girls in black frocks and starched white aprons who also brought our breakfasts and looked after our rooms. Now two waiters and Madame's sister from St-Vallier appeared upon the scene. There was no bustle and no panic or noise. Everything went like clockwork. And this I think partly explains what must seem a mystery to many visitors: how these unassuming places, in which the hotel part of the business is only incidental, can manage to maintain, day after day, cooking of a quality which simply could not be found in

England and which is rare even in France. The answer is that they are organized and run in a way which a Guards sergeant-major would envy, and are as well equipped to deal with a banquet for three hundred people or a steady stream of holiday visitors as they are to provide comfort and an intimate atmosphere for a handful of regular guests out of season.

From a peaceful Sunday morning gossip in the charming blue and turquoise and cream tiled *charcuterie* run by M. and Madame Montagne (where there is a good restaurant in a French town or village you may be sure that a good *charcuterie* is not far away), I returned to Barattero's for the promised Sunday feast. Customers were arriving from Valence, from Marseille, from Lyon. A huge shining silver-grey Rolls-Bentley was parked in the square (it was the first English car we had seen). A party of young people flung themselves off their Lambrettas and clattered round a large table. They evidently took the cooking and its reputation for granted, for they hadn't dressed up or put on Sunday voices as we would have here for such an occasion. It was enjoyable to watch them, and all the other customers who were there simply because they were going to enjoy the food, for there was none of that holy hush which to some of us makes the grander eating places such a sore trial.

This was our luncheon menu:

Saucisse en feuilletage: This might be called the apotheosis of the sausage roll. A fresh, pure pork sausage (from the Montagne establishment, as I had already learned), coarsely cut and weighing about ¾ lb, is poached and then encased in flaky pastry, baked, and served hot, cut in slices. Both sausage and pastry were first class. A delicious hors-d'œuvre.

Pain d'écrevisses sauce cardinal: This seemed even better, if possible, than the first time we had eaten it, and this is quite a test, for one is inclined to be more critical when tasting a famous dish for the second time. The chef at Barattero's has been cooking the *pain d'écrivisses*, and the other specialities of the house, almost every day for some thirty years, but even so I suppose it is possible that they might vary.

Artichauts Escoffier: I am always in two minds about dishes of this kind. The cream sauce with mushrooms was very light and did not overwhelm the artichoke hearts, but all the same I wonder if they are not better quite plain; at La Mère Brazier's in Lyon we had had a salad of whole artichoke hearts and lettuce dressed simply with a little oil and lemon, which, in its extreme simplicity, was quite delicious and the best artichoke dish I have ever eaten.

Poulet roti: A *poulet de grain* (the equivalent of a spring chicken) for two people, perfectly roasted in butter, already carved but reconstituted into its original shape, served on a long platter with a nest of miniature *pommes rissolées* beside it. No other garnish.

For dinner that evening we tasted again the wonderful duck pâté, to be followed by a little roast *gigot* and another dish of those tender little *petits pois*. When we told the waiter how much we had enjoyed the lamb, he replied yes, certainly, it must be a treat to us after the mutton boiled with mint of English cookery. Some very quaint notions of English food are current in France.

The last customers were only just leaving as we ourselves said goodbye to Madame Barattero after dinner, for we were leaving early next morning. The place had seemed full to us, but it was the time of the Algerian crisis, and had it not been for *les évènements*, Madame said, there would have been twice as many people. Customers would have come even from Paris. In her long, arduous and successful career as restaurateur and hotel keeper she has learned that you can never be quite sure what to expect, and even with her tremendous experience it is impossible to know how many people to cater for. As she says: 'Thirty-four years in the hotel business, what a stint, hein?'

Vogue, September 1958

*

Since writing my introductory note to the above I have received reassuring news of the food at the Hôtel du Midi. In June 1983 a reader who had stayed at Lamastre as a result of reading about Madame Barattero in French Provincial Cooking *wrote me a charming letter telling me that the dinner had been 'most delicious'. The first course had been a* salade tiède *– 'ce que nous avons ici de la nouvelle cuisine', she was told – but as you would expect subtle and different, followed by the celebrated* pain d'écrevisses, *(the crayfish now come from Hungary), then there were cheeses, and a* chariot de desserts, *stylish, original 'd'un goût tres raffiné'. 'Tout est léger ici' said the maître d'hotel. There was an iced soufflé aux marrons, a pistachio sorbet, oranges in grenadine, tuile tulips filled with a cream of strawberries served with a coulis. Bernard, son of maître Perrier, the chef who became Madame*

Barattero's partner, and inherited from her the restaurant and hotel, of which he is now in charge, has succeeded his father as chef. It was Bernard, I learned, who had added the delicious desserts. The maître d'hôtel had said that they were the only missing elements in the range of dishes in the old days, and they are Bernard's contribution. I remember Bernard Perrier as a small boy, and I remember also how Madame Barattero predicted that in time he would follow in his father's footsteps. It was good to hear that the young man is fulfilling Madame's prophecy and that the Hôtel du Midi continues to flourish.

Dishes for Collectors

A dish of pork and prunes seems a strange one to chase two hundred miles across France, and indeed it was its very oddity that sent me in search of it. The combination of meat with fruit is not only an uncommon one in France, it is one which the French are fond of citing as an example of the barbaric eating habits of other nations, the Germans and the Americans in particular. So to find such a dish in Tours, the very heart of sane and sober French cookery, is surprising, even given the fact that the local prunes are so renowned.

I knew where we would go to look for the dish because I had seen it on the menu of the Rôtisserie Tourangelle on a previous occasion, when there were so many other interesting specialities that it just hadn't been possible to get round to the *quasi de porc aux pruneaux*. But this time I hoped perhaps to find out how the dish was cooked as well as in what manner such a combination had become acceptable to conservative French palates.

Driving out of Orléans toward Tours I observed for the first time the ominous entry in the new *Guide Michelin* concerning the Rôtisserie Tourangelle: '*Déménagement prévu*' it said. Very well, we would get to Tours early, we would enquire upon entering the town whether by some ill-chance the restaurant was at this moment in the throes of house-moving. If so, we would not stay in Tours, but console ourselves by driving on to Langeais, where there was a hotel whose cooking was said to be worth the journey. The evening was to be our last before driving north towards Boulogne, so we specially didn't want to make a hash of it. But we had plenty of time, the afternoon was fine, the Loire countryside lay before us in all its shining early summer beauty. We dawdled along, making a détour to Chenonceaux on the way.

So in the end it was after seven o'clock by the time we had battled into the main street of Tours, found the Office of the Syndicat d'Initiative, and made our enquiry. No, said the pretty and efficient young lady in charge, the house-moving of the Rôtisserie Tourangelle had not yet started. All was well. '*Déménagement prévu*, indeed', said my companion, 'what a fuss. It'll be *prévu* for the next two years'. Fifteen minutes later the car had been man-œuvred into the courtyard of the charming Hotel Central, we had booked our room, the luggage was unloaded. As we were about to get into the lift I returned to the desk and asked the lady in charge if she would be so kind as to telephone *chez* Charvillat and book us a table, for we were already late. As I walked away, I heard her saying into the telephone '*Comment, vous êtes fermé?*'

Yes, the *déménagement* had started that day. Closed for a fortnight. Well, it was hardly the fault of the charming girl at the Syndicat, but . . . anyway, it was now too late to move on to Langeais. We must eat at Tours and make the best of it. By the time I had explained the magnitude of the disaster to Madame at the desk, she and I were both nearly in tears. For she perfectly grasped the situation, and did not think it at all odd that we had driven two hundred miles simply to eat *chez* Charvillat. But all the restaurants in Tours, she said, were good. We would eat well wherever we went. Yes, but would we find that dish of *porc aux pruneaux* which by this time had become an obsession? And in any case what restaurant could possibly be as nice, as charming, as comfortable, as altogether desirable as that of M. Charvillat?

Madame spent the next twenty minutes telephoning round Tours on our behalf, and eventually sent us, somewhat consoled, to a well-known restaurant only two minutes walk from the hotel. I wish I could end this story by saying that the place was a find, a dazzling revelation, a dozen times better than the one we had missed. But it was not as dramatic as that. It was indeed a very nice restaurant, the head waiter was friendly, and we settled down to some entirely entrancing white Vouvray while they cooked our *alose à l'oseille* – shad grilled and served with a sauce in the form of a runny sorrel purée. In this respect at least we had timed things properly, for the shad makes only a short seasonal appearance in the Loire. It was extremely good and nothing like as bony as shad is advertised to be. Then came this restaurant's version of the famous pork dish, which turned out to be made with little noisettes of meat in a very remarkable sauce and of course we immediately felt reproved for doubting for one moment that an intelligent French cook could make something splendid out of even such lumpish-sounding ingredients as pork and prunes.

It *was* worth all the fuss, even for the sauce alone. But, almost inevitably, it was something of an anticlimax. The combination of a long day's drive, the sampling during the day of the lovely, poetical wines of Pouilly and of Sancerre *sur place* (and whatever anyone may say, they *do* taste different on the spot), a hideously ill-advised cream cake at an Orléans patisserie, the alternating emotions of triumph and despair following so rapidly one upon the other, not to mention a very large helping of the shad and sorrel, had wrecked our appetites. By this time it was known throughout the restaurant that some English had arrived especially to eat the *porc aux pruneaux*. The helpings, consequently, were very large. By the time we had eaten through it and learned how it was cooked, we were near collapse, but the maître-d'hôtel and the patronne were just warming up. If we were interested in local recipes, what about their *brochet au beurre blanc* and their *poulet à l'estragon*, and their *dodine de canard*? To be sure, we should have had that duck as an hors-d'oeuvre, but just a slice or two now, to taste, and then at least we would have some local cheeses and a sweet?

Curiosity overcame prudence. We did indeed try their *dodine de canard*, which was not the *daube* of duck in red wine usually associated with this name, but a very rich cold duck galantine, which would have been delicious as an hors-d'oeuvre, but after all that pork . . . Cravenly, we ordered coffee. No salad? No cheese? No dessert?

As we paid our bill, expressed our thanks, and left with the best grace we could muster, I was miserably aware that we had failed these kindly and hospitable people and left them with the feeling that we did not appreciate their food.

It was a long time before I had the courage to set to work on that recipe. When I did, and saw once more the row of little pork noisettes, the bronze and copper lights of the shining sauce, the orderly row of black, rich, wine-soaked prunes on the long white dish, I thought that indeed it had been worth the journey to learn how to make something as beautiful as that. One day, with a better appetite and more stamina, I will go back to that restaurant in Tours and make amends for the evening when justice to their cookery was not done.

Vogue, November 1958

This is one of the pieces omitted from French Provincial Cooking *because my publishers thought the book was too long. I'm sure they were right. Later the piece appeared in Cyril Ray's* Compleat Imbiber *No. 5 under the title* The Day that Justice Wasn't Done. *I believe it was also pirated by some anthologist. The recipes which accompanied the original* Vogue *article were for* noisettes de porc aux pruneaux, *followed by a real collector's dish,* sauce au vin du Médoc. *Both were published in* French Provincial Cooking. *The pork and prune recipe has been one of the most used and most heavily adapted in the whole book. I don't remember hearing much more of the other one, which was passed on to me by Miss Patricia Green via Madame Bernard, wife of a Médoc wine grower. The dish is essentially a peasant one, and consists of a mixture of meats and furred game: rabbit, hare, stewing beef, pork, or any combination of them, with shallots, a bottle of red wine, carrots, aromatics, the sauce thickened and darkened by the addition of a small amount of plain chocolate. This last ingredient dates the dish back as far as the first half of the eighteenth century or even earlier. It may well have originated in the days when Spanish chocolate makers settled in Bayonne, not after all so far away from the Bordelais.*

Eating out in Provincial France
1965–1977

How is it that French restaurant cooking has so notably, so sadly, deteriorated during the past two or three decades? I think there are several reasons. Among them I would say the main one has a good deal to do with the conservatism of the French themselves in matters of eating. In the vast majority of French restaurants, at no matter what level, the order of the menu has remained unchanged for fifty years. The number of courses and the copiousness of the helpings remain undiminished. What has suffered from shrinkage is the quality of the raw materials, of the cooking skills and also, I would say, the critical faculties of the customers.

Lest it be thought that I am basing my observations on two or three isolated experiences, or on a restricted category of restaurant, or on the restaurants of one region only, I must make it clear that between 1965 and 1972 I made yearly and often twice-yearly trips to France on business, spending an average of two to three weeks at a time travelling all over the country, staying in different hotels night after night, eating in every type of restaurant from village inns to the occasional two-star or even three-star establishment. On the whole our journeys did not take us to tourist haunts, and certainly never in the tourist season. We kept away from motorways and motels, staying often in the hotels patronized by commercial travellers. During the subsequent three years my visits to France were less frequent and less extended, and being no longer concerned in any business venture I was free tò pick and choose hotels and restaurants, and to stay in one place for several days if I felt so inclined. So it is with some experience that I record the melancholy fact that during those fifteen years I have eaten far worse meals in France, and more expensively – a bad meal is always expensive – than I would have believed possible in any civilized country.

What has dismayed me as much as anything else has been the complacent attitude of customers and restaurateurs alike. Time and time again we watched the commercial travellers, those *commis voyageurs* of France who are supposed to be so knowledgeable and so critical when it comes to food, swallowing the indifferent stuff put before them without any apparent thought of complaint, criticism or protest. It was we, the traditionally undiscriminating English, who complained when a dish with an honourable regional name turned out to be a disgraceful travesty, when a sauce was indisputably prefabricated, when good fish was wrecked by over-cooking – on one notable occasion the beautiful and exceedingly expensive little scallops we had been shown in their natural state were eventually brought to our table fried to cinders, on another some fresh chanterelles were massacred by the same clumsy treat-ment. Once even a basic *œuf sur le plat* was so badly cooked that it was stuck fast to the dish. (This in a restaurant boasting a Michelin star.) As for the managements of establishments where such things happen, they do not take kindly to criticism. With a shrug indicating that hard-to-please customers are not welcome they return to their television sets. Indeed, the television is another factor which has played its part in the downfall of French restaurant cooking. Come seven o'clock in the evening, the entire staff of many country hotels is to be found clustered round the box. Arriving travellers are a disturbance and if you have not finished your dinner by nine thirty you are a nuisance. In this same context, how is it, I wonder, that English journalists so often give extravagant praise to the *relais routiers* when, nine times out of ten, not only is the food squalid and the wine lethal, but the television blares so loudly and so incessantly that even were Escoffier himself in the kitchen, it would today be impossible to enjoy a meal in a lorry drivers' restaurant unless you were very deaf indeed?

On a less pessimistic note, agreeable surprises do sometimes happen. Last year, returning north via the Bordeaux main road, and still depressed by the recollection of an atrocious midday meal, we stopped for a glass of wine in an auberge scarcely a metre off the road. The proprietor was agreeable. His wine was good. There seemed to be evidence of care and conscientious innkeeping. We were so tired and so discouraged after the disgusting lunch that we decided to stay the night. We had rooms at the back, away from the roar of the traffic. Not that they would have earned a quiet sign in the Michelin guide – in my experience a number of hotels which do have such a sign shouldn't – but the beds were comfortable, the water was hot, the proprietor and his young wife were making a great effort to compensate with welcoming service and decent cooking for the unfortunate situation of their auberge. This is not one of those humble-little-auberge-with-an-unrecognized-genius-in-the-kitchen stories. We didn't eat anything extraordinary, although I remember excellent local sausages cooked by the patron over an open wood fire, making the whole place smell good. There was even – a great rarity nowadays in France – olive oil for the salad. Although the bill was not exactly small, it was fair. We left at daylight feeling, as travellers should, that we had been welcomed, comforted and cheered on our way. It was a good lesson in how the best hospitality is often to be found in the most unlikely of places, and more unlikely than an inn slap on the Bordeaux–Paris auto-route you could hardly find.

I cannot help wondering how much guide books are to blame for both deteriorating standards of cooking and for arousing exaggerated expectations in the minds of tourists. If the French themselves don't complain is it because they don't expect very much and are therefore not disillusioned? It is not, heaven forbid, that one expects a Gastronomic Experience at every meal – although guide books do rather tend to overdo the promises – but simply that one hopes for honest raw materials, honestly cooked at honest prices. That, of course, is asking a great deal. The Michelin guide seems to think it is supplying the answer with those establishments it lists with a red R, indicating that you may expect a copious five-course meal at a fixed fair price. These are the restaurants I avoid. In my experience their cooking is mediocre and their menus are imitations of the over-powering bourgeois family meals of several generations ago. To be sure, such meals still survive in France. I remember one at a *pension de famille* in a village in the Vosges about ten years ago. With my partner I was on a buying trip. We were making, rather unusually, a Saturday morning visit to a factory, a frying pan factory as it happened. We were invited to lunch in the village by the two brothers who ran the factory. Rather reluctantly we abandoned our plan to escape into the delicious countryside – it was early spring, the hedgerows were white with hawthorn blossom – and have a picnic lunch. We were introduced to the three ladies who ran the *pension*. Two were thin and spinsterish, like post office ladies, the third, a niece, was young and graceful. All were quiet and dignified. First, inevitably in the district, came a *quiche lorraine*. It was about fifteen inches across, served on a handsome, flat earthenware platter, the filling risen like a soufflé, supported only by the thinnest layer of pastry. (Note, by the way, that there was not, and in Lorraine there never is, cheese in the filling; it consists simply and solely of bacon, eggs and cream, and it is always baked in a tart tin, never in one of those hideous crinkly-rimmed china dishes which for reasons unclear to me have become fashionable in England as 'quiche dishes'.) With the quiche came a salad of crisp little green leaves. These I have never exactly identified, but in the native habitat of the quiche they are its almost obligatory accompaniment, although in classy restaurants this very appropriate and welcome salad is seldom offered. After the quiche came a mighty platter of hot coarse country sausage, poached with vegetables. So far, so good, and it *was* good. Well fed, we sat back, expecting fruit and coffee. Vain expectation. One of the quiet thin ladies came in apologizing because the river trout she had planned to give us next had not after all been forthcoming. So, *les messieurs et dames* would excuse her if we went straight on to the roast. This turned out to be pigeons, in fact braised rather than roasted, served on another of those spectacular large dishes and surrounded by whole apples, cooked in their skins and by some trick which I have never yet mastered, still rosy red. They were entirely delicious. The pigeons were less interesting. They were followed, with scarcely a pause, by the cheese of the country, a creamy géromé – a milder relation of Münster – flavoured with caraway seeds. Then came another cartwheel of pastry, this time filled with cherries, and served on the huge quiche platter. The brothers now proceeded to drink whisky as a liqueur, while we gratefully enjoyed our coffee (one of our hosts remarking that it was bad for the liver . . .) and a much-needed digestif of the local kirsch.

Such, not forgetting the missing fish course, was the composition of a real country lunch as taken for granted by the ladies who ran that *pension de famille* in the mid-1960s. It was not, I think, anything out of the ordinary in the region. It was the normal meal expected by the factory owners when they invited guests to eat with them. The food was good honest food, honestly cooked. There was no pretention and not the least ostentation about it. All the same, what a misguided meal. The quiche and the salad, both of them delicious and combining perfectly, would alone have been enough. The dishes which followed would have made two more meals.

Reflecting on that extraordinary village lunch, I do wonder – not for the first time – whether rather too much is said and written in praise of the delights of bourgeois French family food and its restaurant equivalent. With what joy and gratitude I remember, in contrast, meals in a pretty and elegant country restaurant which represented – alas that it must be written in the past tense – a very different way of French eating, although one owing just as much to tradition as the bucolic feast in the Vosges. La Mère Brazier's restaurant in Lyon has been famous for decades – I wrote about it in *French Provincial Cooking* – and for many years the same lady had also a lunchtime establishment at the Col de la Luère, a few miles out of the city and high above its notorious fogs and damp. Airy and cool, surrounded by a large garden and much greenery, this was for a time my favourite restaurant in all France. The menu scarcely changed from year to year. With the exception of one dish of fish quenelles with a rather rich sauce, the food was all comparatively plain. There was no showing off, no fireworks. The calm confidence, the certitude that all here would be as it should which one felt upon entering the establishment was somehow communicated to her customers by Madame Brazier herself, invisible though she was in the kitchen, and by her front-of-the-house staff. Her maître d'hôtel was a charming young woman – her daughter-in-law I believe – whose reassuring welcome to two English travellers arriving on a scorching summer day, hot, flustered, extremely late and despairing of lunch after a prolonged tangle with the Lyon motorway, was beautiful to hear. 'But sit down. You have plenty of time. Relax. Shall I bring you some cool white wine? When you are a little rested you can order.'

Seasoned travellers in France will appreciate the rarity of our welcome. In nine hundred and ninety-nine restaurants out of a thousand in the French provinces it is useless to arrive for lunch after 1.30. Even less would one expect to find all the dishes on the menu still available and in prime condition. At the Mère Brazier's the great speciality was her famous *poularde de Bresse*, chicken poached in broth with carrots and leeks – a refined version if you like of the *poule au pot*, the *poule* in the pot being an elderly hen, while the Brazier *poularde* is a young but fully grown chicken, plump and so tender that when she carved it for us, the maître d'hôtel used nothing but an ordinary and rather blunt-looking table knife. This modest little display of showmanship was the sole manifestation of its kind to be seen in this extraordinary restaurant, where everything, the food, the wine, the service, could best be described as of a sumptuous simplicity, but lighthearted and some-how all of a piece. There was a salad, I remember, of artichoke hearts and walnuts, delicate and refreshing. Desserts changed no more than the main dishes. They consisted of *fromage frais à la crème*, an apple tart with pastry as thin as a plate, and the vanilla-flavoured ice cream of the house. I tried this once. It was a beauty. But the soft snowy *fromage frais* with fresh cream poured over it was even better. Whichever sweet one chose, with it there was always offered – and seldom refused – a slice of brioche-like confection, very light and spongey. The Mère Brazier's wines were the young Chiroubles and Brouillys of the Beaujolais region, and their white equivalents from Mâcon and Pouilly Fuissé. To my mind nothing could be more felicitous, in combination with the food and the surroundings and the general mood of the place, than those fresh, youthful, grapey wines. There was a gaiety and grace about lunches at the Col de la Luère which seemed to me to be most essentially French. The restaurant could have been in no country but France, the cooking practised by Madame Brazier and her brigade was the cooking of the French provinces at its best and also its most traditional. While there was no concession to passing fad or fashion, there was also a singular lack of pomp, not a hint of the chill solemnity sometimes to be encountered in places where the cooking has a great reputation. Every dish was offered, it is true, with proper ceremony, and a meal was a serious affair, but in a totally unselfconscious way, and with a quite ungrasping attitude.

At the end of our lunch on that particular day (there was a sizeable party of Lyonnais business men treating themselves to a great deal of wine and cognac and to them perhaps we owed the late hour to which the kitchen remained open) Madame Brazier herself, in immaculate whites from head to foot, came into the dining room and sat down with a customer. She wasn't doing the usual front-of-the-house round, asking for compliments, but as she passed our table I ventured to thank her for the hospitable welcome we had received and for her beautiful food. With a modest smile she said that *en effet* today it had been *pas mauvais*. Her comment reminded me of the anecdote recounted by Henry James concerning the boiled eggs, the bread and the butter he was served for a midday meal at an inn in Bourg-en-Bresse. 'The eggs were so good that I am ashamed to say how many of them I consumed, and as for the butter *nous sommes en Bresse et le beurre n'est pas mauvais*, the landlady said as she placed the article before me. It was the poetry of butter and I ate a pound or two of it.' (*A Little Tour of France*, 1900.) There was, it seems to me, a closer affinity than might be thought between Henry James's boiled eggs and poetry of butter and Madame Brazier's calm, elegant and seemingly effortless cooking. Poetry was surely the apt word for all the food we had eaten that day at the Col de la Luère.

Experiences of such quality are rare anywhere. In France these days they are more likely to be connected with a picnic than with a meal in a restaurant. Picnics in France combine so many joys. First, the buying, to be done as often as possible in a market rather than in shops. At the stalls there is more choice, the produce is fresher and cheaper, buying is quicker, there is the chance of talking to the local people, of finding the country women who have brought in a basket of fresh cheeses, unsalted farm butter, perhaps a few bunches of sorrel, some garden radishes. There is the stimulus of seeing the abundance of produce and its magnificent quality. There is also, unless you are staying in the country on a self-catering basis, the

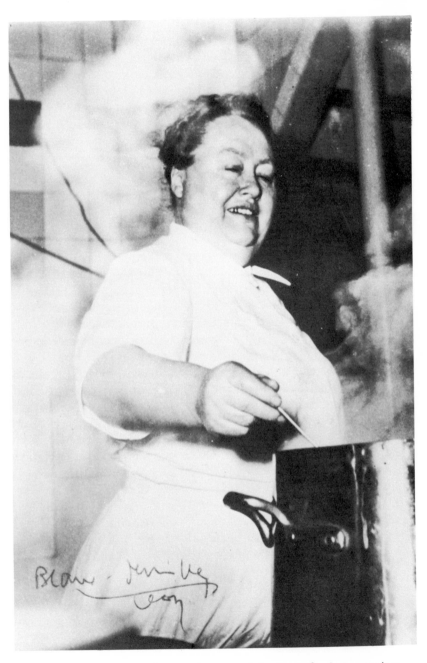

La Mère Brazier, from a photograph in the author's possession

frustration of not being able to take armfuls of it home to cook for yourself. And yet again it must be asked why do the restaurants nowadays so seldom offer a dish of fresh vegetables on their menus? What has become of the homely vegetable soup which used to appear nightly on all country restaurant and hotel menus?

Now, for the pleasure of buying bread. I look, usually, for a bakery selling the big round loaves called *miches* or *boules* or just *pains de campagne*. Those have more character, a more interesting flavour and stay fresher much longer than *baguettes* and *ficelles* and all the rest of the tribe of long loaves. Enticing though these look and smell as they come out of the oven, I find them lacking in savour, although they certainly still compare pretty well with the factory bread which is our own national shame.

When lunchtime approaches, the question is are we near a river or lake? If so, shall we be able to reach its banks? For the ideal picnic there has to be water, and from that point of view, France is wonderful picnic country, so rich in magnificent rivers, waterfalls, reservoirs, that it is rare not to be able to find some delicious spot where you can sit by the water, watch dragonflies and listen to the birds or to the beguiling sound of a fast-flowing stream. As you drink wine from a tumbler, sprinkle your bread with olive oil and salt, and eat it with ripe tomatoes or rough country sausage you feel better off than in even the most perfect restaurant. During one golden September in the valleys of the Corrèze, the Dordogne and the Lot, I enjoyed just such picnics, day after blazing day. The tomatoes that year and in that region were so rich and ripe and fragrant that I shall forever remember their savour. Then, one day in a pastry shop in Beaulieu-sur-Dordogne, we bought a *tarte aux mirabelles* made with yeast pastry. Those little round golden plums of early autumn on their light brioche-like base made an unexpected and memorable end to our outdoor feast. Another year it was Normandy, early autumn again, and daily picnics in the magnificent forests of Mortagne, Brotonne and Bellême, in clearings where foxgloves grew high amid the bracken, and water was always within sight. Once or twice we sat by the banks of the Seine, looking at landscapes and riverscapes which Corot had surely painted.

Petits Propos Culinaires 4, 1980

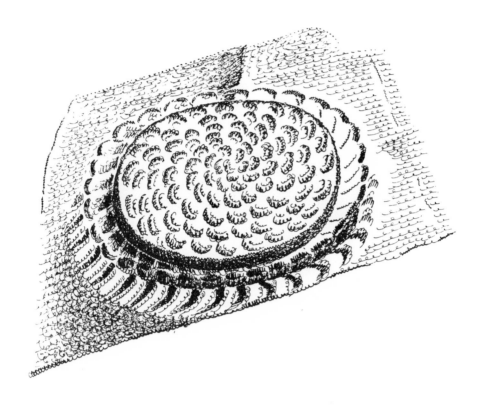

Confort anglais, French fare

This is a 1984 postscript to my 1977 *Eating out in Provincial France*, and is more about eating in than eating out. How gloriously different a matter is French food when you can buy and cook it yourself from that offered at the restaurant meals imposed when you stay in hotels, was brought home to me most forcibly in the early months of 1984. With a friend I was lent, by another and mutual friend, a charming town house in the little south western city of Uzès. With high ceilings, tall windows, comfortable bedrooms, a bathroom for each, blessedly hot water, central heating, simple and appropriate furniture, good lighting, a large kitchen, electric kettles wherever needed, shelves filled with weeks and weeks of reading, plus all the necessary maps and guide books, the whole place was the most engaging possible blend of traditional French building with unaggressive modern English comforts.

Two minutes walk from the house was one of those small town *casinos*, emporiums of modest size and indeed modest content, but efficiently run, open long hours of every day and providing many of the necessities of life, from butter to electric light bulbs, mineral water to toilet paper, a selection of wines, spirits and liqueurs, adequate cheeses, vegetables, fruit and salad stuffs. Next door to this general shop was a Prisunic, another small fairyland offering everything from drinking glasses and crockery to gaudy scarves, cheap envelopes and childrens' exercise books. Across the road were the food shops, a butcher, a charcuterie, a greengrocery, the market place, the Crédit Lyonnais. Three doors down from the house a fine small bakery provided fresh bread six days a week. As well as everyday *baguettes* and other white loaves, we had a choice of four or five different varieties of brown bread, including rye and *pain biologique*, France's version of the loaf made from organically grown whole wheat, in this case a very great improvement on the equivalent product of the English health food shop. As well as good bread the little bakery offered takeaway temptations such as flaky pastry turnovers filled with *brandade de morue*, the creamed salt cod of the region, and an old-fashioned provençal *pissaladière* baked in rectangular iron trays and sold by the slice. They call it *pizza* now. People have forgotten the old name, and will tell you it comes from Italy. I can tell them it comes from no nearer Italy than Marseille where I used to buy it when I lived on a boat tied up in the Vieux Port. That was 1939, before the war started. I used to go ashore every morning and walk up a narrow street to a bakery to buy my *pissaladière* fresh out of the oven. It was a treat to find my anchovy-and-tomato-spread *pissaladière* once again in Uzès, and even handier to the house than the Marseille bakery had been to my boat.

Market day at Uzès is Saturday morning. It was February when I was there, not the most propitious time of year for fresh produce, and on the first Saturday of my stay the mistral was blowing so ferociously that it was difficult to stand up. Even the hardy stallholders were shivering and anxious to pack up and climb into the shelter of their vans. Nevertheless, even on a day like that we could buy quite a good variety of vegetables and salads. Among the greatest pleasures, as always in France, were the good creamy-fleshed firm potatoes. For the thousandth time, why, why, why, I ask, do we, the English, the pioneers of European potato cultivation, now grow such uninteresting potatoes, while the French, who refused to touch them until the Revolution and Parmentier forced them into a reconsideration of the ill-used tuber, and quickly making up for that lost time, took to growing delicate, waxy yellow potatoes, and to making them into wonderful dishes like *pommes Anna* and *gratin dauphinois*, not to mention quite everyday potato salads, no easy matter to achieve with our own all-purpose collapsible English spuds. Then, even in February, there were little round, crisp, bronze-flecked, frilly lettuces, baskets of *mesclun* or mixed salad greens, great floppy bunches of chard, leaf artichokes, trombone-shaped pumpkins which make admirable soup, fat fleshy red peppers, new laid eggs, eight or nine varieties of olives in basins and barrels, thick honey and clear honey, in a variety of colours, in jars and in the comb, and honey soap in golden chunks, bouquets of mixed fresh flowers, tulips, dark purple anemones, marigolds. And then cheeses, cheeses. There are the locally made goats' milk cheeses called *pélardons*, small round and flattish and to be bought in various stages of maturity. Is it for immediate consumption, do you wish to keep it a few days, is it for toasting, roasting, grilling? Try the *magnane à la sarriette*, another goat cheese, strewn with the savory leaves they call *poivre d'âne* across the Rhône in Provence. Or how about the St Marcellin? Or the fresh ewes' milk cheeses? 'They are my own' says the lady on the stall. We buy two. They are delicious, but they are horribly expensive, as anyone who has a taste for roquefort well knows. Given the very small yield of milk, about ½ litre per milking, all ewes' milk cheese is a luxury. Here we are not all that far from the place where that great and glorious roquefort is produced and matured, and in Uzès market, from another cheese stall, we have our pick of three or four grades. Within two or three minutes we have spent £7.00 and have not yet bought our parmesan or gruyère for grating on to the delicate little *ravioles* we have bought from the goat cheese lady. They are tiny, these *ravioles*, filled with a mixture of parsley and comté, the gruyère-like cheese of Franche Comté. They take *one* minute to cook, warns the lady. She imports them from the other side of the Rhône, from Royans near

Romans in the Drôme where *ravioles* have long been a local speciality.

By now we have nearly finished our shopping. We have bought as much as we can carry. But we spend another pound's worth of francs on one of the goat cheese lady's specialities, one of her own. It is something she calls a *tourte à la crème*, or *tourteau*. It is a light, puffy, yeast-leavened *tourte*, round, like an outsize bun, with a layer of subtly flavoured sweet, creamy cream cheese in the centre, and with a characteristically blackened top. It is deliberate, this charred top, and traditional, says the lady. (She turns out to be Finnish, this lady, her husband is Belgian, and everything she sells is of very high quality.)

Lunch is going to be a feast. Our red peppers are to be impaled on the electric spit and roasted until their skins are charred as black as the top of the *tourteau*. Then we shall peel them, cut them in strips, dress them with the good olive oil we have bought direct from the little oil mill at Bédarrides on the Tarascon road out of Fontvieille. Over them we strew chopped parsley and garlic and leave them to mature in their dressing. We shall eat them after we have had our bowls of hot *ravioles*, cooked one minute, according to instructions, in a good chicken broth made from the carcase of a spit-roasted, maize-fed chicken we had a couple of days ago. With fresh brown bread – it always has a good crackly crust – our *sarriette*-strewn *magnane* and a nice creamy little St Marcellin, plus a hunk of that excellent *tourteau* with our coffee, we marvel for the twentieth time in a week that we have such a remarkable choice of provisions here. Pâtés and terrines, large jars of freshly made fish stock, saddle of rabbit rolled and stuffed, ready for roasting or baking, good sausages and *cayettes*, green with the chard so much loved in Rhône Valley cooking, skilfully cut and enticingly trimmed lamb and beef, all the good things from the bakery, the fresh eggs which really are fresh (one stallholder was apologetic because his were three days old), all play their part in making every meal a treat as well as extraordinarily simple to prepare. And in how many towns of no more than 7,500 inhabitants can one choose, on market day, from about seventy different kinds of cheese, at least sixty-five of them French, the rest Italian, Swiss and Dutch?

I must add that Lawrence Durrell, who lives not far away, and whom I hadn't seen for a long while, reminded me that many years ago, about 1950, he and I happened to meet in Nîmes and that I complained angrily about the local food, swearing that I would never go back to the region. The area was indeed then very poor. Now the tourists, foreign residents, enterprising wine-growers, motorways, have made it prosperous. Well, there are worse things than words to eat.

Not surprisingly, with all the good food so easily to hand, we were reluctant to go to restaurants. In three weeks we went to only two. One was the delectable Hièly's in Avignon, a place I had not had the chance of eating at in over twelve years, and which I found, happily, was still offering fine, honest, generous cooking, lovely house wine (a Châteauneuf du Pape *de l'année* from a domaine of very high reputation), basketsful of local goats' milk cheeses and more basketsful of cows' milk cheeses, sumptuous ices, perfect coffee (at £1.00 a tiny cup so it should be but it doesn't necessarily follow) and impeccable service. One of the luxury dishes, by the way, costing a *supplément* of 12.00 francs on top of the 180 franc menu, was a saddle of rabbit with *morilles* in the sauce. In Provence it is quite normal for rabbit to cost more than, say, chicken, and in this case it was without question worth the money. At about £50 for the two of us, with ample wine, our lunch at Hièly's was hardly extortionate. Where in London at that price could you get a comparable meal in a comparably elegant and professional restaurant?

The second restaurant we visited was out in the country, not far from St André-d'Olérargues. We had been shopping in the Thursday morning market at Villeneuve-lès-Avignon – we wanted more of those little *ravioles* and had discovered that the lady selling them would be there – and were prevented from crossing the Rhône into Avignon by the lorry drivers blockade which was disrupting traffic that week. Instead we drove off to try a place with one Michelin star which sounded and indeed looked promising when we had passed it a few days previously. Settled at our table we discovered that the restaurant was run mainly by the chef's wife, assisted by another lady who was perhaps her sister, or some other close relative who was for some reason tied to the place in a subservient capacity. The prix fixe menu seemed to offer decent old-fashioned country cooking. So in a way it did, with a respectable terrine of chicken livers followed by oxtail braised with mushrooms, carrots and onions, a plate of gratiné potatoes and leeks on the side. The oxtail had been substituted for some other dish which was finished. When I had started to explain to Madame that we didn't want the alternative *côte de bœuf* either with or without a supplementary price the lady interrupted me. 'You surely don't imagine I can afford to give you *côte de bœuf* on the fourteen franc menu' she snapped. It wasn't a propitious beginning, but the oxtail was well cooked and so were the vegetables. No complaints. But then we were offered a choice of three fourth-rate commercial cheeses or a dessert of *œufs à la neige* smothered in caramel – a recent development, that tacky caramel, I believe, and one which quite wrecks the innocence of a dish which should be frail and pale as a narcissus, just white meringue and creamy yellow *crème anglaise*. Alternatives were a bought-in gâteau and a tatty-looking apple tart. Turning her back to our table Madame stood over the trolley carefully measuring out the portions of whatever it was we had chosen. Coffee was mediocre. The two women, unprepossessing in their worn tweed skirts and draggy woolies, were anxious to clear away. The chef, who had spent most of the lunch hour sitting at a table reading the paper and smoking, now disappeared, making no attempt to ask the customers if all had been well. Our bill, with a bottle of undistinguished Gigondas, was just half what we had paid at Hièly. Had we enjoyed our lunch half as much as the one at Hièly we should still have had no cause for complaint. Alas, we had not enjoyed it at all. The grasping attitude, the general shabbiness, the brainless parsimony displayed by Madame, the dispirited and dispiriting service, the dreary bread, the absence of a house wine – always a bad sign in a starred restaurant – all added up to yet another of those dozens of unsolved Michelin mysteries of my past travels in France. There was something about the people and the place and the ambiance which took me back to the London of 1963, the Profumo summer, the couple and the restaurant I described in the article called *Secrets* in the present volume. Any restaurant which reminded me so strikingly of that one certainly has no business whatever having a Michelin star. We were lucky that we could shrug off the dispiriting experience, climb back into the car, remember that in the back of it we had a lot of good things bought at Villeneueve that morning, that we had a kitchen to cook and eat them in, that we needn't ever go to another restaurant again for the rest of our stay unless we chose to do so. But I still wonder what the Michelin organisation thinks it is doing. Hièly in Avignon very properly has, and for many years has had, two stars. One star is gravely and grossly overdoing it for a great many of the establishments to which Michelin awards them, and of all the faults which turn me off a restaurant – surely I cannot be alone in this – meanness is just about the most unacceptable. If the Michelin inspectors didn't notice that defect, not to mention others, in the restaurant in question I don't think they can have visited it for a very long time.

*

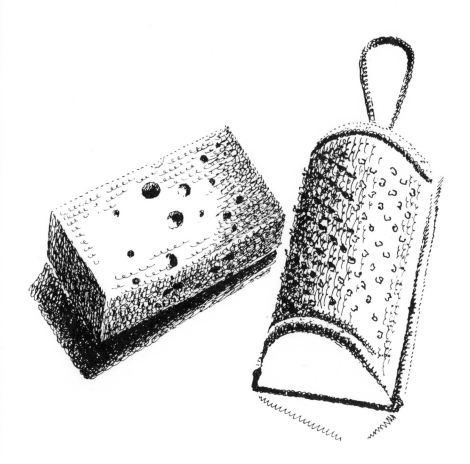

Roustidou

With the exception of ordinary cafés and the *relais routiers*, where you get ordinaries by the litre, few restaurants or hotels in Provence now offer much alternative to fancy-bottled Provençal wines at prices comparing unfavourably with what one would pay for much more classy Alsace, Loire or Beaujolais wines if one were travelling in these districts. One can't have everything, and for me Provence has more than most other provinces of France, so one doesn't complain, and what the local wines may lack in distinction is partly made up for, at least in retrospect, by the evocativeness of their names and the coaxing messages which some of the proprietors send out with – not in – their bottles. In my notebooks of recent Provençal journeys I find Chante-Gorge, Rocmaure, Domaine de l'Aumérade, Castel Roubine, Domaine de Lacroix, Tavel Réserve de St-Estello (*'Pour épousailles et fiançailles, Rien qui ne vaille Ce bon vin vieux, Béni de Dieu'*), Bouquet de Provence, Blanc Coquillages, Château de Fontcreuse, Clos Mireille, Petit Duc, Prince d'Orange, Côtes du Ventoux 1956 (*'Au Pied du Mt Ventoux Je suis né et j'ai vieilli pour vous'*), Clos de les Dames de Baux, Roustidou (now there's a good name for a carafe wine; it tasted uncommonly like Algerian, and made a splendid picnic drink), Château de Beaulieu, Château Rayas, Château Roubaud (a trusty friend, that one), Côtes de Provence BIG, Gigondas Pierre Amadieu (the one I go for when it's on the list), Chante-Perdrix Cornas 1955, red, ravishing with a grilled chicken at the restaurant David (no relation) at Roussillon in the Vaucluse. Cornas is on the west bank of the Rhône near St-Péray and opposite Valence, so it is still a long way north of Provence, but it is round about here, at least if one drives down N8 instead of the terrifying N7, that one begins to sense the Midi; and like the Hermitage from Tain on the other bank, the wines of Cornas and the Côte Rôtie are always associated in my mind with Provence and on my table, when I can get them, with Provençal food.

The Spectator, 13 July 1962

Golden Delicious

As Sunday lunches go in the village hotels of the Vaucluse department of Provence, the meal we had in the Hostellerie du Château at
Beaumes de Venise was far from a bad one. Memorable it was not,
except for two points neither of them relevant to the cooking and
one of which has only now, seven years later, become manifest.

It was the early summer of 1956. The calamitous frosts of the
previous winter and spring had wrought havoc with the countryside
which was fearful to see. The slopes and valleys of the Vaucluse and
of all that country east and north-east of Avignon to Cavaillon, Apt,
Pernes-les-Fontaines, Le Thor and Carpentras, which was once the
papal county of Venaissin, should have been silver and freshly
grey-green in the early June sun. The whole landscape was gashed
with ugly black wounds. Hundreds of olive trees, withered and
blighted by the frosts and the all-blasting mistral winds which
followed them, had been cut down or were standing like ancient
skeletons in that fertile and beflowered landscape which is the heart
and core of Provence. The tall rows of dark cypress trees, windbreaks against the destroying mistral, were unnecessary reminders
that life in Provence is not always quite so idyllic as it may look to
two English visitors driving one Sunday morning in early June from
Malaucène near the foot of the Mont Ventoux toward a village so
irresistibly named Beaumes de Venise. For the odd thing was that
after we had lost our way three times in the identical piece of
country, it dawned upon us that this piece of country *was* idyllic,
almost too good to be true. In this pocket of land apparently
untouched by the ravaging winter were no scars, no dead or
doomed trees. The olives were bright with life and thick with young
leaves. The crippled landscape was here restored and complete.

It was perhaps the sense of relief that somewhere at least in
Provence that year there would be an olive crop and peasant farmers
whose livelihoods had not been utterly destroyed that made
Beaumes de Venise, when eventually we reached it, rather less
interesting than the little piece of country we had passed through on
our way. Subsequent inquiries revealed that the olives and the olive
oil of Beaumes de Venise have a substantial local reputation; and we
did, I remember, remark upon the excellence of the salad and upon
an unusual anchovy-flavoured, oil-based sauce offered with the

routine Sunday roast chicken that day at lunch. Nothing extraordinary about that. In this region, salads with good olive oil dressings, and mayonnaise sauces tasting perceptibly of fruity oil are, or were in the days before the frost destruction, the rule rather than the exception as they are in Northern France. As for the wine, I do not remember what we drank. Probably it was that reliable wine of Provence restaurants, red Gigondas from the vineyards north of Beaumes on the far side of the Dentelles de Montmirail. The wine we did not drink was, as it turned out, the remarkable one. We did not drink it because we had never heard of it, and if it was on the wine list of the hotel – which according to Michelin it now is – we did not notice it.

The wine of Beaumes de Venise is a natural sweet golden wine made from muscat grapes with their own appellation of *Muscat de Beaumes* and unmixed with the Hamburg muscat which coarsens many of the sweet wines of Provence. Nobody, it seems, quite knows when the muscat grapes of Beaumes de Venise were first planted nor how the sweet wine from the vineyards of this tiny area protected by a fold in the hills from the savage north winds acquired its reputation. Certainly that reputation has always been a local one only. There are no more than three or four hectares under vine cultivation, a production of two hundred hectolitres a year and only two growers. From one of these growers, M. Combres, Mr Gerald Asher of the firm of Asher, Storey and Co., 127 Lower Thames Street, EC1, to whose admirable sense of enterprise we already owe the import of so many interesting French regional wines hitherto unknown or unobtainable in this country, has bought the muscat wine of Beaumes de Venise. It is, I believe, the first time this wine has ever been exported. As far as I am concerned its journey was worthwhile.

The custom of drinking a little glass of rich wine with a sweet dish or fruit seems to me a civilized one, and especially welcome to those who do not or cannot swig brandy or port after a meal. The great dessert wines of Bordeaux and the Rhine are rather beyond the reach of ordinary mortals and are in any case wines which demand a certain ceremony. Your meal has to work up to them. The wine of Beaumes, although so rare, seems somehow more within the scope of the simplest or even of an improvised meal. It retails at about 22s. a bottle, which seems reasonable enough since an opened bottle, securely recorked, appears to remain in good condition for some while. A few days ago I shared with a friend the final glasses from a bottle opened before Christmas. With it we ate a fresh apricot tart. The musky golden wine of Beaumes – according to Mr Asher, and I see no reason to quarrel with his judgement, 'its bouquet is penetrating and flower-like, its flavour both honey-sweet and tangy' – and the sweet apricots, vanilla-sugared on crumbly pastry, made an original and entrancing combination of food and wine.

Why Venise? What balm or balsam in conjunction with what lakes, lagoons, canals? Neither and none. The name Venise, they say, has the same origin as Venaissin and Vénasque, that ancient and rather forlorn little village perched on an escarpment overlooking the twisting road between Carpentras and the Forest of Murs. All, it is supposed, stem from *aveniensis* or *avignonnais*. Beaumes is no balm or balsam. In the Provençal language *baumo* is a grotto. The Vaucluse country is honeycombed with caves and grottoes, many of them used for the cultivation of mushrooms. As a spectacle one set of holes in a rock is, I find, much the same as another. So that day we took it on trust from the *Guide Bleu* that the cliffs at the back of the village of Beaumes are *'percées de grottes'*. Still, it is not unpleasing to learn that the meaning of *baumanière*, as in the super-glossy three-star Hostellerie de Baumanière below Les Baux, is really *baume a niero*, in French *grotte à puces*, the grotto of the fleas.

The Spectator, 10 January 1964

*

The dessert wine of Beaumes de Venise is now exported in quantity to Britain and the United States. Sometimes I wish it had not become so popular. At any rate I would advise avoidance of the product of that grower who bottles his wine in very fancy cordial bottles.

A la marinière

Although I lived all my childhood within a few miles of the sea I don't think we ever ate shellfish at home. I don't remember ever seeing a lobster or an oyster until I was grown-up, and as for mussels, I had never heard of them, let alone tasted them, until I went to stay with a Norman family in a farmhouse at Bièville, a village near Caen.

The cooking at Bièville was done by Marie, a local girl hardly older than I was – about seventeen – and her only assistant in the kitchen was her brother, aged about eight. All our food was delicate and delicious, there was always beautiful butter and fresh bread for breakfast, and at midday simply cooked meat and a separate dish of vegetables from the farm's kitchen garden. I had become accustomed to good middle-class French cooking in the same family's Paris household, so none of these things struck me as unusual until, one day, Marie came into the dining-room bearing a big tureen of mussels, cooked in some sort of creamy sauce flecked with parsley and probably other garden herbs as well. The appearance, the smell and the taste of those mussels were to me most fascinating and mysterious. The little black-shelled objects didn't seem like fish at all, they had the same kind of magical quality as mushrooms, the real field mushrooms which, as children, we had so often brought home for breakfast after a dawn search in the fields round our home in the Sussex Downs. Maybe the cream sauce had something to do with the association of sensation, for we had had a Nannie who always used to cook our breakfast mushrooms over the nursery fire in cream, whisked away no doubt, from the kitchen regions before the cook was up and about. As in most households, Nannie and the cook thoroughly disapproved of each other, and had she known this private cookery was going on upstairs in the nursery, the cook would have made a blistering row. We must have been aware of this, as children always are of tension between grown-ups, because Nannie's mushrooms had the charm of the forbidden. We must never be caught eating them. So those Norman mussels which reminded me, for whatever reason, of our secret childhood feasts, became for ever endowed with the mystery of far-off and almost unobtainable things. And to this day the first food I ask for when I land in France is a dish of mussels. Before embarking on the ferry to return home I always try to go to a restaurant where I know there will be mussels, sweet, small mussels, so small in fact that you get about seventy or eighty to a portion, and a London housewife would be indignant if she were asked to clean so many. I have seen, in the market at Rouen, the fishwives selling mussels already cleaned in a gigantic whirling machine – but at the Restaurant La Marée, nearby in the place du Marché, I was told that the machine isn't good enough – the little things must all be cleaned by hand.

The difference between these little mussels of the Norman coast (the best are reputed to come from Yport, although I suspect that a certain quantity are brought over from the English south coast where nobody bothers about them) and the great big Dutch ones we get in London, is just the difference between the field mushrooms of my childhood and today's cultivated mushrooms – the cultivated ones are easy to get and very nice but they lack magic. But that doesn't mean you can't make very excellent dishes out of them if you treat them right, and the same applies to urban fishmongers' mussels – although I must say I try to buy small Welsh or Irish mussels whenever possible, in preference to the huge Dutch ones, which to me seem dry and savourless.

But whichever kind you have, be sure to clean them very meticulously, scraping, scrubbing, bearding and rinsing them in a great deal of cold water and discarding any that are broken or open or abnormally heavy – the latter will probably be full of mud, and one may very well spoil the entire dish.

CROÛTONS À LA MARINIÈRE

For a little first course dish for two people, clean a quart of mussels, put them in a saucepan with a teacup of water and open them over a fairly fast flame. As they open, remove them to a plate, filter the liquid through a muslin, return it to a clean pan, into it put a finely chopped shallot or clove of garlic, a couple of tablespoons of chopped parsley and a small glass of white wine.

Let this boil rapidly until reduced by half. Shell the mussels. (All this can be done in advance.)

Just before serving, fry 4 slices of French bread in butter or olive oil and put them in warmed soup plates.

Heat up the mussels in the prepared sauce – this will take just about 1 minute – pour the whole mixture over the croûtons and serve immediately.

House and Garden, January 1960

Fruits de Mer

Winkles and whelks, cockles and oysters, spider crabs, scallops, shrimps, langoustines, mussels, prawns, the little clams known in France as *palourdes* and in Italy as *vongole*, the big ridged heart-shaped *venus verrucosa,* called by the French *praires* and by Italians *tartufi di mare* – sea truffles – make the open-air market stalls of the Loire estuary port of Nantes a fishy paradise, smelling of iodine, salty, dripping with seaweed and ice.

Of all these small sea-creatures displayed for sale, it is the mussels which interest me most. They are so small that hereabouts a restaurant portion of *moules marinière* must contain seven or eight dozen of the little things. Their shells are so fine they are almost transparent. The mussels themselves are quite unimaginably sweet and fresh. At the restaurant La Sirène in Nantes, an establishment where the cooking is excellently sound and fresh, but which is unaccountably omitted from Michelin, I had an exquisite dish of these little mussels. They are, the proprietress told me, mussels cultivated on those posts called *bouchots* and come from Penesten, on the Morbihan coast of Brittany. They were cooked in their own liquid until they opened; fresh cream was poured over them; they were sprinkled with chopped fresh tarragon; and brought to table piled up in a tureen. Nothing could be simpler; and to us, living so few short miles across the North Sea, not humming birds could appear more magical, nor mandrake root more unlikely.

Mussels we have in plenty, cheap and large. What they make up for in size they tend to lack in flavour and charm. From Holland, Ireland, Wales, Scotland, and from the west coast our mussels come to London, but the little sweet ones are all left behind in the mussel-beds. If they appeared on the fishmongers' stalls nobody would want them. Few would believe they were as good as the big ones. Fewer still would want to go to the trouble of cleaning them. Which is shortsighted, because they are cleaner in the first place and easier to deal with than the monsters covered with barnacles and grit which need such endless scrubbing and rinsing, so much so that one wonders if most of the flavour is not washed out of them, a good deal of the grit still remaining. About this point, the late Henri Pellaprat, teaching chef at the Cordon Bleu School in Paris, has an interesting theory. In *Le Poisson dans la Cuisine Française* (Flammarion, 1954), he writes that most people go about the cleaning of mussels in a way calculated to put sand into them rather than to eliminate it; instead, he says, of first scraping them, one should begin by rinsing them in a quantity of cold water, turning them over and over and whirling them around. One by one you then take them out of the water and put them in a colander. Half of them will be clean already; those which are not must be scraped; as each is done, put it in a bowl, but, and this is the crux of the matter, *without water*. Only when all are cleaned should water be run over the mussels; they should then be kept on the move, the water being changed continually until it is perfectly clear. The explanation given by Pellaprat for this routine is that, put into still water all at once, the mussels start opening; when they close up again, they have imprisoned within their shells the sand already in suspension in the water. In other words, explains M. Pellaprat, the more you keep the mussels moving, the more frightened they are; and the less inclination they will have to open. Ah well, possibly. It is worth paying attention to this theory, but it does mean that the mussels must be prepared only immediately before cooking, which is certainly desirable, but not always practical.

Diminutive size is not necessarily a criterion of flavour in mussels; on the Mediterranean coast, and for that matter in Wales and in the West of Ireland I have had large mussels which were excellent, not as sweet and tender as the little Breton and Norman ones, but full of flavour and with a strong salty tang. It is partly a question, then, of eating them on the spot. But not entirely. Paris is about the same distance from the Breton coast as London is from Cornwall or Conway, and in Paris too one gets delicious mussels. So perhaps it is simply a question of better-organized transport. Last autumn I ate mussels in Paris which tasted just as fresh as those at Nantes – and that was during the freak heatwave of early October.

When it is a question of making the best of what we can get, one dish I had in Paris would be well adapted to London mussels. Medium-sized cooked mussels, on the half-shell (it is of the utmost importance not to over-cook them in the first instance), were spread with a garlic and shallot butter, made in much the same way as for snails or for the Breton *palourdes farcies* (which also, like snails, are sold ready stuffed for cooking on the Nantes fish stalls), and were arranged on snail dishes, the mussels and the butter protected by a layer of breadcrumbs, an addition of fresh, unthickened cream and a sprinkling of coarsely grated Gruyère. Quickly cooked in a hot oven, this is a sizzling, bubbling, richly flavoured dish.

The proprietress of the restaurant, Chez Maria in the rue du Maine, is half-Norman, half-Breton; very likely she is the cousin or the sister-in-law of the lady in charge of the left-luggage office at the Gare Montparnasse who had directed me to the little restaurant; perhaps, arriving by train from her native shores, she never travelled much farther than the station. There are many such people running just such restaurants or cafés in Paris. Anyone who wants to eat French regional specialities in the capital without paying the high prices of the fashionable Burgundian, Provençal, Auvergnat, Breton, Alsatian or Savoyard restaurants (in which three out of every five people eating are going to write the place up for a guide book or are begging recipes from the understandably blasé owners) could do worse than search round about, or inquire at, the main-line stations serving these provinces. There is always a sprinkling of small places owned by people like Maria; they can afford to provide their clients with a few genuine regional products at reasonable prices because they receive them direct by rail – by-passing the markets, the wholesalers, the double transport bills – from relations who are growers, poultry breeders, charcutiers, wine producers, fish-dealers (Maria had spanking fresh sardines the day I was there, served grilled and with a half-kilo of Breton butter on the table). The cooking in these places, although on the rough side and limited in choice, is likely to have a more authentically country flavour than that in the well-known bistros and restaurants where the proprietor has sophisticated his recipes to suit chic Parisian taste. By this I do not mean that these re-created dishes are necessarily any the worse; they are just more evolved, less innocent. Take, for example, another mussel dish, this one from an elegant, typically Parisian and rather expensive establishment called the Berlioz, in the rue Pergolèse, not a specifically regional restaurant, but one in which a number of provincial dishes are cooked – and well cooked. Here I ordered, from the menu, *moules marinière*. When they came, the mussels were those same delicious little Breton creatures, a great tureen of them. The sauce was yellow, just barely thickened, very light and subtle. It was, the patron told me, the result of mixing the mussel liquid with *sauce hollandaise*. It was delicious. It was perfection. What it was not was the primitive *moules marinière* known in every seaport café and to every housewife around the entire coastline of France.

The Spectator, 4 January 1963

Waiting for Lunch

On page 96 of *French Country Cooking* is a four line description of *el pa y all*, the French Catalan peasant's one-time morning meal of a hunk of fresh bread rubbed with garlic and moistened with fruity olive oil. When the book first appeared in 1951, one reviewer remarked rather tartly that she hoped we British would never be reduced to breakfasting off so primitive a dish. I was shaken, not to say shocked – I still am – by the smug expression of British superiority and by the revelation, unconscious, of the reviewer's innocence. Believing, no doubt, that a breakfast of bacon and eggs, sausages, toast, butter, marmalade and sweetened tea has always been every Englishman's birthright, she ignored countless generations of farm labourers, mill workers, miners, schoolboys, whose sole sustenance before setting off for a long day's work was nothing more substantial than a crust of coarse bread or an oatcake broken up in milk, buttermilk, or when times were good, in thin broth, when bad in water. The bread and olive oil of the Southern European peasant was simply the equivalent of those sparse breakfasts of our own ancestors.

Recording some of the older recipes and meals of the country people of rural France was an exercise I had found most stimulating and instructive. There were ideas which often proved helpful in those days of shortages and strict rationing. It was not my intention to imply that we should copy those ideas to the letter – to do so at the time would hardly have been possible – but rather that we should learn from them, adapt them to our own climate and conditions, and perhaps benefit from increased knowledge of other people's diets and food tastes.

During the twenty-five years odd since this book was first published, we have indeed taken to imported dishes and cookery in a way which in 1951 would have seemed entirely in the realm of fantasy. One obvious example is the Neapolitan pizza – or rather, a tenth-rate imitation of it – now big business and familiar in every commercial deep freeze and take-away shop in the land. And the original pizza, after all, was nothing more complicated than a by-product of the days of household bread-baking, when a few pieces of dough were kept back from the main batch, spread with oil and some kind of savoury mixture – onions usually – baked in the brick oven after the bread was taken out, and devoured by hungry children and farm workers. That that pizza was not so far removed from the French and Catalan *pa y all* (the cookery of Catalonia was at one time closely related to that of Southern Italy and Sicily) was demonstrated by a recent incident in a very ordinary restaurant in the town of Vendrell, a few miles across the Spanish frontier. Stopping one autumn morning in 1976 for an early lunch, we saw the people at a neighbouring table devouring some very appetizing-looking, aromatically-smelling thick slices of warm bread spread with tomato and oil. We asked for the same. It was, of course a version of *pa y all*. Those slices of garlic-scented oil-saturated bread, just lightly spread with a little cooked tomato turned out to be the best item on the menu. You might think that doesn't say much for the restaurant's cooking, and that could be a fair criticism. What was interesting was that, not only were the local people eating it, but that it was also the most expensive dish on the menu. The story is familiar. The necessity of the day-before-yesterday's peasant has become the prized speciality of today's middle-class restaurant.

I don't think, however, that *el pa y all* will ever achieve popularity in England, at any rate not popularity on the scale reached by the pizza. We must be thankful for that, although for reasons rather different from those clearly in the mind of my reviewer of so long ago. As a nation we have a curious distrust of the primitive and simple in food, and so carefree a way with the specialities of other countries that while retaining names, we have no inhibitions about complicating, altering, travestying and degrading the dish itself. It is not difficult to visualize the fate of the *pa y all* if translated into English restaurant terms. It would become chopped garlic on toast made from factory bread, spread with salad cream and crowned with a pimento-stuffed olive (that is the Catalan part, we should be told). In time, a very short time probably, this creation would find its way into the nation's deep-freeze. There would be a curry version and a cheese variation and a super gigantic one with bacon, lettuce, onion rings and radishes. Before long it would be more like an imitation Scandinavian open-face sandwich than the Mediterranean agricultural labourer's early morning breakfast.

*

This piece was written in 1978 for a projected revised edition of French Country Cooking *which never materialised.*

In March 1984, as I was putting together the articles and essays which make up the present volume, I received a reminder of the pa y *all I remembered so vividly at Vendrell in 1976. A postcard written from Spain by my friend Gerald Asher, wine merchant and wine writer now resident in San Francisco, informed me that before business meetings on Monday he had been spending a restful weekend at Sitges in Catalonia. 'Waiting for lunch', Gerald wrote, 'one is given a basket of hot grilled bread, a clove of garlic, a tomato, salt and olive oil.'*

April 1984

Para Navidad

It is the last day of October. Here in the south-eastern corner of Spain the afternoon is hazy and the sun is warm, although not quite what it was a week ago. Then we were eating out-of-doors at midday, and were baked even in our cotton sweaters. The colours of the land are still those of late summer – roan, silver, lilac, and ochre. In the soft light the formation of the rock and the ancient terracing of the hills become clearly visible. In the summer the sun on the limestone-white soil dazzles the eyes, and the greens of June obscure the shapes of the ravines and craggy outcroppings. Now there are signs of autumn on the leaves of some of the almond trees. They have turned a frail, transparent auburn, and this morning when I awoke I devoured two of the very first tangerines of the season. In the dawn their scent was piercing and their taste was sharp. During the night it had rained – not much, nothing like enough to affect the parched soil – but all the same there was a sheen on the rose bricks and grey stones of the courtyard. The immense old terra-cotta oil jar in the centre was freshly washed, and over the mountains a half-rainbow gave a pretty performance as we drank our breakfast coffee.

At midday we picked small figs, dusty purple and pale jade green. On the skins is a bloom not to be seen on midsummer figs. The taste, too, is quite different. The flesh is a clear garnet red, less rich and more subtle than that of the main-crop fruit, which is of the *vernal* variety, brilliant green. Some of the figs have split open and are half dried by the sun. In the north we can never taste fruit like this, fruit midway between fresh and dried. It has the same poignancy as the black Valencia grapes still hanging in heavy bunches on the vines. These, too, are in the process of transforming themselves – from fresh grapes to raisins on the stalk as we know them. Here the bunches have been tied up in cotton bags.

The two ancients who tend the almond trees (this is Valencia almond country, and it has been a bad season. If the rain fails, next year's crop may prove to be another disaster) and who have known the estate of La Alfarella all their lives, were hoping that the grapes could be cut late and hung in the storeroom until Christmas. Their plans have been foiled by the wasps. This year there has been a fearsome plague of the persistent and destructive brutes. They have bitten their way through the protecting cotton, sucked out the juice of the fruit, and left nothing but husks. Here and there where a bunch has escaped the marauders, we have cut one and brought it back to the house in a basket with the green lemons and some of the wild thyme that has an almost overpowering scent, one that seems to be peculiar to Spanish thyme. It is perhaps fanciful, but it seems to have undertones of aniseed, chamomile, hyssop, lavender.

My English host, who has re-created this property of La Alfarella out of a ruin and is bringing its land back to life after twenty years of neglect, is at the cooking pots. He seizes on the green lemons and grates the skins of two of them into the meat mixture he is stirring up. He throws in a little of the sun-dried thyme and makes us a beguiling dish of *albóndigas*, little *rissoles* fried in olive oil. He fries them skilfully and they emerge with a caramel-brown and gold coating reflecting the glaze of the shallow earthenware *sartén*, the frying dish in which they have been cooked and brought to the table. All the cooking here is done in the local earthenware pots. Even the water is boiled in them. They are very thick and sturdy, unglazed on the outside, and are used directly over the Butagaz flame, or sometimes on the wood fire in the open hearth. As yet there is no oven. That is one of next year's projects.

Surprisingly, in an isolated farmhouse in a country believed by so many people to produce the worst and most repetitive food in Europe, our diet has a good deal of variety, and some of the produce is of a very high quality. I have never eaten such delicate and fine-grained pork meat, and the cured fillet, *lomo de cerdo*, is by any standard a luxury worth paying for. The chicken and the rabbit that go into the ritual paella cooked in a vast burnished iron pan (only for paella on a big scale and for the frying of *tortillas* are metal pans used) over a crackling fire are tender, possessed of their true flavours. We have had little red mullet and fresh sardines *a la plancha*, grilled on primitive round tin grill plates made sizzling hot on the fire. This is the utensil, common to France, Italy, Spain, and Greece, that also produces the best toast in the world – brittle and black-barred with the marks of the grill.

To start our midday meal we have, invariably, a tomato and onion salad, a few slices of fresh white cheese, and a dish of olives. The tomatoes are the Mediterranean ridged variety of which I never tire. They are huge, sweet, fleshy, richly red. Here they cut out and discard the central wedge, almost as we core apples, then slice the tomatoes into rough sections. They need no dressing, nothing but salt. With the roughly cut raw onions, sweet as all the vegetables grown in this limestone and clay soil, they make a wonderfully refreshing salad. It has no catchy name. It is just *ensalada*, and it cannot be reproduced without these sweet Spanish onions and Mediterranean tomatoes.

In the summer, seventeen-year-old Juanita asked for empty wine bottles to take to her married sister in the village, who would, she explained, preserve the tomatoes for the winter by slicing them, packing them in bottles, and sealing them with olive oil. They would keep for a year or more, Juanita said. Had her sister a bottle we could try? No. There were only two of last year's vintage left. They were to be kept *para Navidad*, for Christmas.

Yesterday in the market there were fresh dates from Elche, the first of the season. They are rather small, treacle-sticky, and come in tortoiseshell-cat colours: black, acorn brown, peeled-chestnut beige; like the lengths of Barcelona corduroy I have bought in the village shop. Inevitably, we were told that the best dates would not be ready until *Navidad*. That applies to the oranges and the muscatel raisins; and presumably also to the little rosy copper medlars now on sale in the market. They are not yet ripe enough to eat, so I suppose they are to be kept, like Juanita's sister's tomatoes, and the yellow and green Elche melons stored in an *esparto* basket in the house, for *Navidad*. We nibble at the candied melon peel in sugar-frosted and lemon-ice-coloured wedges we have bought in the market, and we have already torn open the Christmas-wrapped *mazapan* (it bears the trade name of El Alce, 'the elk'; a sad-faced moose with tired hooves and snow on its antlers decorates the paper), which is of a kind I have not before encountered. It is not at all like marzipan. It is very white, in bricks, with a consistency reminiscent of frozen sherbet. It is made of almonds and egg whites, and studded with crystallized fruit. There is the new season's quince cheese, the *carne de membrillo*, which we ought to be keeping to take to England for *Navidad* presents, and with it there is also a peach cheese. How is it that one never hears mention of this beautiful and delicious clear amber sweetmeat?

There are many more Mediterranean treats, cheap treats of autumn, like the newly brined green olives that the people of all olive-growing countries rightly regard as a delicacy. In Rome, one late October, I remember buying new green olives from a woman who was selling them straight from the barrel she had set up at a street corner. That was twelve years ago. I have never forgotten the fresh flavour of the Roman green olives. The *manzanilla* variety we have bought here come from Andalucía. They are neither green nor black, but purple, rose, lavender, and brown, picked at varying stages of maturity, and intended for quick home consumption rather than for export. It is the tasting of familiar products at their point of origin (before they are graded, classified, prinked up, and imprisoned in bottles, tins, jars, and packets) that makes them memorable; forever changes their aspect.

By chance, saffron is another commodity that has acquired a new dimension. It was somewhere on the way up to Córdoba that we saw the first purple patches of autumn-flowering saffron crocuses in bloom. On our return we called on Mercedes, the second village girl who works at La Alfarella, to tell her that we were back. Her father was preparing saffron – picking the orange stigmas one by one from the iridescent mauve flowers heaped up in a shoe box by his side and spreading them carefully on a piece of brown paper to dry. The heap of discarded crocus petals made a splash of intense and pure colour, shining like a pool of quicksilver in the cavernous shadows of the village living room. Every night, during the six-odd weeks that the season lasts, he prepares a boxful of flowers, so his wife told us. The bundle of saffron that she took out of a battered tin, wrapped in a square of paper, and gave to us must represent a fortnight's work. It is last year's vintage because there is not yet enough of the new season's batch to make a respectable offering. It appears to have lost nothing of its penetrating, quite violently acrid-sweet and pungent scent. It is certainly a handsome present that Mercedes' mother has given us, a rare present, straight from the source, and appropriate for us to take home to England for *Navidad*.

An even better one is the rain. At last, now it is real rain that is falling. The ancient have stopped work for the day, and most of the population of the village is gathered in the café. The day the rain comes the village votes its own fiesta day.

The Spectator, 27 November 1964

Pizza

From the stuffy and steaming little bakers' shops of Naples and Southern Italy, where it still costs a few lire for a portion large enough for a horse, the Pizza Napoletana has travelled the world. In Paris restaurants, in Shaftesbury Avenue milk bars, in South Kensington coffee shops the pizza has become acclimatized. In the latest paperback thriller[1] to come my way it figures as a delicate exchange of compliments, a token of esteem, between one hoodlum and another. The cheese-covered pizza arrives from Chicago by hand of hired killer, in a foot square wooden box, packed in dry ice. 'It's from Antonio's Cellar, ready for the oven.' The gangster is misty-eyed. 'Damn, this was a sweet thing for Sylvester to do – what a sweet guy.' He turns to his cook-valet. 'Get some Chianti tomorrow morning and we'll have a real Ginny lunch.'

Whatever there may be about a pizza which tugs at the heart-strings of a big shot of the Philadelphia underworld, to law-abiding British citizens I suspect that its chief charm is that thick layer of sticky melting cheese on the top. Whether it's on toast, or macaroni, or cauliflower, nearly everyone loves a nice top dressing of chewy bubbling cheese. But for those who may share my preference for one of the many versions of the pizza made without that rubbery cheese, such as the Provençal *pissaladière* or the beautifully named Ligurian *sardenara*, here is a recipe. Not for the hefty slab of dough thinly spread with onions or tomatoes and cooked on a huge iron sheet which you buy from the bakeries and which is food only for the really ravenous, but for a more polite, a household or *casalinga* version. In Italy many such recipes for the pizza have been evolved by chefs and household cooks; they use a basis of simplified brioche dough, or short crumbly pastry, or thin, miniature rounds of enriched bread dough no larger than a coffee saucer.

SARDENARA CASALINGA

5 oz plain flour; 1½ oz butter; 1 egg; ½ oz yeast; salt; a little water.

Cut the softened butter in little pieces and rub it into the flour. Add a good pinch of salt. Make a well in the centre, put in the egg and yeast dissolved in about 2 tablespoons of barely tepid water.

---

1. *The Big Heat* by William McGovern, Penguin.

Mix and knead until the dough comes away clean from the sides of the bowl. Shape into a ball, put on a floured plate, cover with a floured cloth and leave in a warm place to rise for 2 hours.

For the filling: 1 lb onions; ½ lb tomatoes; a dozen anchovy fillets (in San Remo, home of the *sardenara*, salted sardines are used); a dozen small, stoned black olives; pepper; salt; dried oregano or basil; and olive oil.

Heat 4 tablespoons of olive oil in a heavy frying pan. Put in the thinly sliced onions and cook them very gently, with the cover on the pan, until they are quite soft and pale golden. They must not fry or turn brown. Add the skinned tomatoes, the seasonings (plus garlic if you like) and the basil or oregano. Continue cooking until the tomatoes and onions are amalgamated, and the water from the tomatoes evaporated.

When the dough has risen sprinkle it with flour and break it down again. Knead once more into a ball, which you place in the centre of an oiled, 8½- to 10-inch (21- to 25-cm) removable-base flan tin. With your knuckles press it gently but quickly outwards until it is spread right over the tin and all round the sides. Put in the filling. Make a criss-cross pattern over the top with the anchovies, then fill in with the olives. Leave to rise another 15 minutes. Stand the flan tin on a baking sheet and cook in the centre of a pre-heated oven at gas no. 6, 400°F, for 20 minutes, then turn down to gas no. 4, 350°F, and cook another 20 minutes.

Alternative pizza or *pissaladière* filling: 1 onion; 2 cloves of garlic; 1 lb fresh tomatoes; 4 to 6 Italian tinned tomatoes and their juice; ½ coffee cup olive oil; dried basil or marjoram, seasonings, olives and anchovies.

A PROVENÇAL PISSALADIÈRE

This used to be spread with a brined fish product called *pissala*, peculiar to the Mediterranean coast between Nice and Marseille. It is now a thing of the past, and the *pissaladière* is made mainly with stewed onions and anchovies. There is also a version in which a tomato sauce figures. This one is excellent.

It is made as follows: spread the dough, prepared as for Ligurian pizza, with a mixture of 6 tablespoons of the onion and tomato sauce (also made as for the Ligurian version), the contents of a 50-gr tin of anchovy fillets and 2 cloves of garlic pounded up together, almost to a paste. Bake as before. This anchovy-flavoured filling is my own favourite.

The Sunday Times, 1 December 1957

Sweet Vegetables, Soft Wines

Why is it that Italian wines are so seldom featured on the wine lists of restaurants other than those which serve specifically Italian food? Italy produces a great variety, as well as a very large quantity of wines, and it does seem rather unimaginative to confine them to drinking entirely with Italian food. In the repertory of French regional and country cooking there are surely scores of dishes with which an authentic Italian wine would make a most refreshing change from the inevitable Beaujolais, and in fish restaurants especially, the too familiar and usually unidentifiable Chablis. Personally, I would welcome the occasional offer of a Verdicchio with the mussels, a fresh, light Frascati with the sole and spinach. And as far as the red wines are concerned, the lighter ones of Verona and Garda harmonize uncommonly well with pâtés, the fuller ones of Piedmont and Tuscany with *daubes* of beef, hot cheese dishes, rich ox-tail stews, game birds, herb-flavoured chickens.

Then for that matter, why not Italian wines with English food? We are, after all, more practised than are the people of wine-growing countries at the game of matching our dishes to appropriate wines. I have found that roast duck and a bottle of Piedmontese Barolo make a most excellent combination. And I think that a Barbera from the same region should do particularly well with a steak, kidney and mushroom pudding, or a jugged hare, while a Chianti Classico is a wine for roast lamb or a handsome joint of pork, as indeed it is in its native country, where the whole roast pigs, marvellously aromatic with wild fennel and whole garlic cloves roasted golden and translucent, are one of the most splendid features of Tuscan food markets. Impaled on a huge pole, the pig is carved to order, hefty slices, each with a portion of the golden garlic cloves scooped out from the inside, are handed to you with a big hunk of bread and wrapped in a paper napkin. The local house-wives are buying it for the midday meal, but we are tourists, so we go off to another stall to buy cheese, perhaps a good big piece of Parmesan, finest of all cheeses with red wine. And we drive off, up into the beautiful Tuscan hills to find a picnic place in the warm autumn sun. We are worlds away from the baked lasagne, the veal with ham and mushrooms, the standard caramelized oranges and Bertorelli ices of everybody's Italian trattoria down the road. And although here in England we cannot hope to reproduce anything very close to true Italian country food (the ingredients are so elusive – where is the veal, where the good Parmesan, where the sweet, pale rose Parma ham, the fish straight out of the sea, the fruity Tuscan olive oil?) we can at least enjoy Italian wines and an increasingly large variety of them, without going to the local pizza house or trattoria, and with food of our own cooking and choosing. I do suggest too that these wines will benefit by being served with a shade less of that careless abandon which characterizes the Italian trattoria wine waiter. Open the red wines well in advance, don't chill the whites until they are as frozen as a sorbet.

For the pork dish, which I have chosen as being a good one with Italian red wine, I would settle for a flask of Chianti Classico Montepaldi, a very typical Chianti, clean and bright, not too heavy. A lighter wine, the delicious estate-bottled Lamberti Valpolicella from the Verona district would also be a happy choice. This wine incidentally is one which I would fancy for the Christmas turkey, while the full and fragrant red Torgiano from Umbria would be lovely with a roast fillet of beef, should anyone be rich enough for such a luxury this year. And for everyday drinking nobody should despise the much cheaper Tuscan red wine. It seems to me to offer remarkable value. But this wine too will improve noticeably if given an hour or two to breathe. At normal room temperature. NOT, please not, in front of the fire. And the corner of the Aga is the place for the kettle, not for the red wine.

STUFFED AND ROLLED PORK

A dish of Italian origin, and, properly, made with veal. But since in England veal is so hard to come by, so expensive, and so different in quality from Italian veal, I have found that it is best to make the dish with pork which is very successful cooked in this manner.

Buy a piece of loin of pork boned by the butcher and weighing after boning 2½ to 3 lb. The joint should also have the rind removed. Other ingredients are 2 whole eggs, 2 thin slices of mild cooked ham, parsley, about 1 oz. of grated Parmesan, a small onion, ¾ pint of milk, butter and olive oil, seasonings of salt, freshly ground pepper, grated nutmeg, a clove of garlic.

Put the meat upon a board and flatten it out with a rolling pin; season it. Cut the peeled garlic clove into little slivers and set them neatly over the surface of the meat. With the eggs, chopped ham and parsley (about 2 tablespoons), and the cheese and seasonings make an ordinary omelette but don't fold it. It is to be spread flat upon the meat, which you then roll up and tie as neatly and securely as possible into a nice fat sausage, not, however, tying the string too tightly, or the stuffing will burst out during the cooking.

In a small oval cocotte, braising pan, or other utensil in which the meat will fit without too much room to spare, melt 1 oz. of butter and a couple of tablespoons of olive oil. In this melt the chopped onion until it turns yellow. Put in the meat, let it gently brown on both sides. Pour in the *heated* milk. It is important that the milk be scalding hot. Let it just come back to simmering point. Cover the pot with foil or paper and a lid. Transfer it to a slow oven (gas no. 2, 310°F.) for 2 to 2¼ hours, then remove the meat and keep it warm in the oven. Transfer the pan containing the sauce to the top of the stove and let it cook fairly fast, stirring it continuously until the thin part of the liquid has reduced by about half. Press the sauce quickly through a fine wire sieve and pour it over and round the meat (having first removed the string). Sprinkle some parsley over the top, and your dish is ready to be served with a few plain, new potatoes. And it is just as good cold as hot. There should be ample for six people.

The pork rind and the bones should not be wasted. They will make very good stock.

*

Now for two dishes which should really bring out the charms of the sweeter white table wines of Italy. One of the recipes is for Florentine fennel, and perhaps it sounds freakish to suggest a sweet wine with a vegetable dish. But consider a moment. When the experts make a big production of choosing food to go with their wines, I wonder how often it is remembered that many vegetables are very sweet, that they quarrel badly with the claret chosen for the lamb, distort the burgundy with the game? Who stops to think that chestnuts, parsnips, peas, carrots, turnips, celery, Belgian endives, onions, even to a certain extent potatoes have potent overtones of sugar in their make-up which are intensified by the so-called *classic* French methods of cooking them to an almost caramelized state of sweetness. Think, for instance, of *navets glacés, carottes Vichy*, and those small golden, syrupy onions which accompany so many French meat and chicken dishes. Delicious, but they don't help the red wine. Try these same vegetables as a separate course *after* the meat or fish, and you find that they almost take the place of a sweet or pudding. *Mangetout* peas are a good example. Their alternative name of sugar peas should provide sufficient indication of their qualities, and to me it is all wrong to muddle these exquisitely delicate and sweet vegetables with meat and potatoes, sauce and gravy. They should always be eaten as a separate course. With them try one of the naturally sweet wines of Italy, the ones they call *amabile* (soft rather than luscious or rich). They make a most interesting partnership with sweetish vegetables, perhaps even better than they do with a dessert dish proper for which they are not full enough. In fact the Lacrima Christi del Vesuvio, a wine which in the past I have not much appreciated, has proved quite a revelation to me when I have drunk it with a *gratin* of Florentine fennel. The two have a real affinity. This wine – which should be drunk chilled, but not with all the fragrance frozen out of it – is also very successful with dishes based on white cream cheese, either sweet or savoury. Italian cooking offers a rich variety of such dishes, the savoury ones often mixed with spinach, the sweet ones with cloves, nutmeg, cinnamon.

Orvieto amabile (the one in the flask) to my mind far more attractive and somehow more natural and right than the dry version, is a little sweeter than the Lacrima Christi, and makes a happy partnership with cooked dessert apples, or provides a nice finish to a meal when served with delicate little biscuits or cakes such as French madeleines. This wine should be well chilled.

FLORENTINE FENNEL WITH PARMESAN

This is a simple and refreshing vegetable dish; it is surprising that it is not better known; it consists of the bulbous root stems of the Florentine or sweet fennel – this form of fennel now arrives in England from Israel, Kenya, Morocco and sometimes from France and Italy, during the late summer and again in the very early spring. The sweet, aniseed-like flavour of the plant is not to everybody's taste, but to those who do like it, it is quite an addiction.

For this dish, allow a minimum of one large fennel bulb – for want of an alternative short name, that is what everyone calls these root stems – per person. Other ingredients are butter, grated Parmesan cheese, and breadcrumbs. Trim the bulbs by slicing off the top stalks, the thick base, and removing all the stringy outer layers of leaves. There is a good deal of waste. Slice the bulbs in half, longitudinally. Plunge them into a saucepan of boiling salted water. According to size they should cook for 7 to 10 minutes. When tender enough to be pierced fairly easily with a skewer, drain them.

Have ready a buttered *gratin* dish or the appropriate number of individual dishes. In this arrange the fennel halves, cut side down. Strew breadcrumbs over them (approximately 1 tablespoon per bulb) then grated Parmesan (again, 1 tablespoon per bulb) and finally a few little knobs of butter. Put the *gratin* dish in a medium oven (gas no. 4, 350°F.) and leave for 10 to 15 minutes until the cheese and breadcrumbs are very pale gold, and bubbling.

APPLES WITH LEMON AND CINNAMON

A cool and fresh sweet dish to serve after a rich or heavy meat course.

Core, peel and slice (as for an apple flan) some good eating apples, preferably Cox's, allowing two apples per person. Put the cores and peel into a saucepan with a heaped dessertspoon of sugar and a slice of lemon, peel included, for each apple. Cover amply with water and cook to a syrup. This will take about 7 minutes' rapid boiling.

Put the sliced apples into a skillet, sauté pan, or frying pan. Over them strain the prepared syrup. Cover the pan and cook over moderate heat until the apples are soft but not broken up. Add more sugar if necessary.

Arrange the apples in a shallow serving dish, with a few lemon slices on the top – for decoration and for the scent. These apples can be eaten hot or cold.

An alternative method of cooking this dish, much easier when you are making a large quantity, is to arrange the sliced apples in an oven dish, pour the prepared syrup over them, cover the dish (with foil, if you have no lid) and cook in a moderate oven (gas no. 3 to 4, 325 to 340°F.) for 25 to 35 minutes. Serve the apples in the dish in which they have cooked, not forgetting the final sprinkling of cinnamon.

An alternative flavouring for those who do not care for cinnamon is a vanilla pod, cut in half and put in with the apples before cooking. The lemon slices are still included in the flavouring of the syrup.

Wine Mine, 25 November 1973

Bruscandoli

One fine morning early in May, 1969, with my sister Diana Grey and her husband, I arrived at the island of Torcello to lunch at Cipriani's lovely little Locanda, famous both for its cooking and its charm. I knew the place of old, so did the fourth member of our party. To my sister and brother-in-law it was new. This was their first visit to Venice. For all of us the trip was a particularly magical one.

When we had settled at our table and ordered our food – the jugs of house wine were at our elbow as we sat down – I became aware of a couple at a neighbouring table exclaiming with rapture over their food. They were a handsome and elegant pair. I wondered what was so special about the rice dish which was giving them such pleasure. They in turn noticed my curiosity. With beautiful Italian manners they passed some across to me, explaining that it was a risotto unique to Venice and unique to this particular season. It was made with a green vegetable called *bruscandoli*, or *brucelando*. Wild asparagus, so they explained. It was so good that I called the waiter and changed my order. A most delicate and remarkable risotto it was. The manager of the restaurant told me that only during the first ten days of May can this particular wild asparagus be found in the Venetian countryside.

Next day, we all went to another of the lagoon islands, to lunch at Romano's on Burano. Surprise. There were our friends again, and again the green risotto was on the menu. They had of course ordered it. So did we. This time they told me I might find some *brucelando* in the Rialto market if I went early enough in the morning. Hurry though. The season ends any day now. When the charming and splendid pair had left, I asked the proprietor of the tavern who they were. Ah, you mean the Isotta-Fraschini? The inheritors of the name of that wonderful and glamorous automobile of the twenties and thirties, no less. No wonder they carried about them the aura of romance, and, he especially, of the authentic Italian magnifico. So, to me, the name of Isotta-Fraschini is now indissolubly linked with the memory of those extraordinary and subtle risotti of the Venetian lagoons.

We went again to Torcello to eat *bruscandoli*, I went to the Rialto market, found an old woman selling a few bunches of it – it's the last of the year, she said – took it back to my hotel, stuck it in a glass so that I could make a drawing of it. When I came back in the evening the zealous chambermaid had thrown it away. No, next morning there was no old lady selling *bruscandoli* in the market. For once it was true, that warning 'tomorrow it will be finished'.

I searched the cookery books and the dictionaries for more details of the wild asparagus. I could find no descriptions, no references. Months later in a little book about Venetian specialities I discovered the following sentence: '*le minestre piu usate sono quelle di riso:*

con bruscandoli (luppolo) kumo (finocchio selvatrico) ...'[1] So *bruscandoli* is Venetian for *luppoli*. And *luppoli* or *cime di luppolo* are wild hop-shoots.

It is of course well known that hop-shoots have a flavour much akin to that of asparagus, and the confusion is a common one. All the same, it was curious that neither the local Venetians to whom I talked, nor the knowledgeable Isotta-Fraschini couple should have known that hop-shoots rather than asparagus were used in those famous risotti. Maybe they did but didn't know the alternative word (in the Milan region they have yet another name, *loertis*) and thought that wild asparagus was a near enough approximation. The truth is, that when I bought the *brucelando* in the market, it didn't look much like any kind of asparagus, so I was suspicious. But it didn't look like hops either. And wild hop-shoots I had never before seen.

Research has yielded various other regional Italian dishes made with *bruscandoli* or *luppoli*. In her little book *La Cucina Romana* dealing with the old specialities of Roman cooking, Ada Boni gives a recipe for a *zuppa di luppoli*, and I have heard of a *frittata* or flat omelette with hop-shoots in Tuscany and also in the more northerly region of Brianza. In Belgium hop-shoots are equally a speciality. They are called *jets de houblon*.

Of the virtues of hops

As we know, hops were introduced into England only during the reign of Henry VIII. Fifty years later, by the latter part of his daughter Elizabeth's life, the shoots of the cultivated plant were evidently accepted as a delicacy resembling asparagus. Dr Muffet, author of *Health's Improvement*, written during the 1590s but published only in 1655, fifty-one years after the author's death, even calls them *lupularii asparagi*. 'Hop-shoots', he says, 'are of the same nature with Asparagus, nourishing not a little, being prepared in the like sort, though rather cleansing and scouring of their own nature.' In other words, hop-shoots were yet another of the precious blood-purifying herbs of spring, so welcome and so necessary in the days when the winter diet was predominantly one of salt meat, dried pulses, bread.

1. 'The most popular *minestre* are those based on rice: with wild hops, wild fennel...', Ugo Azzalin, *Di Alcune Minestre Venete e Particolarmente Vicentine con le Buone Norme per preparatare i Soffriti* (Editore Neri Pozza, Vicenza 1968).

An Italian doctor, Baldassare Pisanelli of Bologna, went a great deal further than his contemporary Dr Muffet in praise of hops and their health-giving properties. Pisanelli's *Trattato della Natura dei Cibi, et del Bere*, or *Treatise on the Nature of Foods and Beverages*, was first published in Rome in 1583. It was evidently a popular and influential book, for it was continuously in print for the next two hundred years. Hops, declared Dr Pisanelli, 'are the best of all edible herbs' . . . 'they refresh the blood and cleanse it . . . they are also efficacious in cleansing the stomach organs in particular the liver, and the wonder is that with so many virtues they are so little used, for in truth the benefits they confer are most marvellous, and immediate. They are much esteemed in Germany and other northern countries . . . the shoots are eaten cooked, in salad . . . they loosen the bowels and move obstructions, the decoction of flowers and leaves clears bad smells and cures the itch. The syrup is miraculous in choleric fevers and the plague.'

The only breath of criticism the good doctor has to make of hops is that if gathered with their tendrils and hard stalks they are of difficult digestion, and even the tender ones are still slightly windy. The defect however, is remedied by cooking and 'the shoots are then of blameless virtue, and of great benefit to those who eat them dressed with oil and vinegar.'[1]

In no way qualified to comment on Dr Pisanelli's eulogy of the hop's healthful and healing properties, I can confirm only that wild hop-shoots, at least as cooked in the famous risotto of the Venetian lagoons, are certainly very delicious. It comes, therefore, as no great surprise to discover from Rupert Croft-Cooke's entertaining book *Exotic Food* (Allen & Unwin, 1969) that there are gardeners in Kent who grow hops especially for the shoots, although Mr Croft-Cooke says that he himself learned of their excellence through his association with gypsies.

TO PREPARE HOP-SHOOTS

The following advice comes from a Belgian chef, author of *La Cuisine et la Pâtisserie Bourgeoises*, 2nd edition (J. Lebègue & Cie, Paris and Brussels, 1896).

'They are obtained by earthing up the plants with light soil, as for asparagus. The shoots used as a vegetable should be of the greatest

---

1 Some while after writing my hop-shoot article I came across an interesting mention of *lupoli, cioè bruscandoli* in Scappi's great *Opera* of 1570. He lists them in the third service of a Good Friday dinner (p 393 of the 1643 edition). Scappi was private cook to Pope Pius V.

freshness, if possible picked on the day of use. Take each shoot by its earthy extremity between the thumb and index finger of the left hand; slide the same fingers of the right hand down the shoot, bending it and pulling it down towards the point; the straight part of the broken shoot is edible; what remains in the left hand is fibrous and should be discarded.

'Rinse the shoots thoroughly in ample cold water. As soon as they are washed, cook them in plenty of boiling water lightly acidulated with lemon juice or vinegar; keep them on the firm side. Drain them. The slightly bitter taste of the shoots, which for connoisseurs constitutes their special quality, is lost if they are overcooked.

'Plunge them into cold water for a second, to arrest the cooking. The hop-shoots are now ready for eating with olive oil and lemon juice or with melted butter, or in any other of the ways appropriate to the asparagus sprue they so much resemble.'

The *risotto al bruscandoli* of Torcello and Burano I have never had the opportunity to cook for myself, so I shall not attempt to give a recipe here. Indeed a Venetian risotto is a dish notoriously difficult to reproduce anywhere else. The finest quality of round-grained risotto rice from the Po valley, essential to the success of the dish, is hard to come by nowadays, and few English people appreciate its importance or are willing to accept the fact that long-grained pilau rice simply will not cook to the subtle, rich creaminess of texture characteristic of the refined and aristocratic *risotti* of the Veneto. So here instead are a few interesting recipes for other dishes which may be of interest to anyone who has access to hop-shoots, wild or cultivated.

BUDS OF HOPPES

'Seeth them with a little of the tender stalke in faire water: and put them in a Dish over coales with Butter, and so serve them to the Table.'

> J. Murrell, *A New Book of Cookerie. Set forth by the observation of a Traveller. J.M. London. Printed for John Browne, and are to be solde at his shop in S. Dunstanes Church-yard 1615*

ZUPPA DI LUPPOLI (hop soup)

'Hop-shoots, which have a distant point of contact with asparagus are called lupari in Rome and are sold by street vendors, who cry them with the characteristic chant 'lupari, lupari'. They make a good soup in the following manner.

'You clean and rinse the shoots and put them in a pan with oil, a little garlic and a few small pieces of raw ham. Leave them to cook a little, season them with salt and pepper and cover them with plenty of water. Cover the pan and let them finish cooking very gently. When cooking is complete there should be enough broth to make the number of bowls of soup you need. In the soup tureen put some slices of toasted bread, over them pour the hop-shoots and their liquid. Leave to soak a moment or two and then take to the table.

'This is the simplest method of making hop-shoot soup, but it is general usage to enrich the soup with a few eggs. In this case, you beat the eggs as for an omelette, pour them directly into the pot allowing one egg for each bowl, and stir well. Leave the soup in its pot away from the heat for a minute or two before transferring it to the soup tureen.'

Ada Boni, *La Cucina Romana* (Edizioni Della Rivista *Preziosa*, Rome, 1947)

It seems curious that Ada Boni, author of Italy's most famous twentieth-century cookery book *Il Talismano della Felicita* should have found that hop-shoots had only so distant a relationship with asparagus. Could it be that she was applying the highly critical standards of a Roman accustomed to the true wild asparagus, those incomparably flavoured little *asparagi del campo* of Rome beside which all other asparagus seems insipid?

Here is an alternative hop-shoot soup, an English recipe unusual in our eighteenth-century cookery literature.

HOP-TOP SOUP

'Take a large quantity of hop-tops, in April, when they are in their greatest perfection; tie them in bunches twenty or thirty in a bunch; lay them in spring-water for an hour or two, drain them well from the water, and put them to some thin pease soup; boil them well, and add three spoonfuls of the juice of onions, some pepper, and salt; let them boil some time longer; when done, soak some crusts of bread in the broth, and lay them in the tureen, then pour in the soup.

'This is a plain soup, but very good; the French pour in some cray fish cullis.'

Mrs Charlotte Mason, *The Lady's Assistant* (a new edition, 1786; first published 1775)

FRITTATA CON I LOERTIS (hop-shoot omelette)

'The *loertis* or wild hop-shoots are cut into small pieces, and so long as they are really tender (this omelette should be made only in the spring) they are not cooked but mixed into the beaten eggs just before the frittata is made.'

    Ottorina Perna Bozzi, *Vecchia Brianza in Cucina* (Martello Editore, 1968)

The Brianza is the Montevecchio-Como-Monza region of Lombardy, the countryside of Manzoni's famous novel *The Betrothed*. And, for those not already familiar with Italian cookery, a *frittata* is a flat omelette, rather thick and solid, usually cooked in olive oil rather than butter.

Herbal Review, Spring 1979

*

Following the publication of my article, a Mr G. Amory of Nevers, France wrote to The Herbal Review *expressing doubts as to my identification of* bruscandoli *with hop shoots. 'By May in the Veneto wild hops would be a tough tangle' Mr Amory wrote. In addition he provided a fine red herring in the shape of a surmise that my* bruscandoli *was really a plant called* ornithogalum pyrenaicum, *in England called Bath asparagus.*

The ornithogalum *theory was easily disposed of. The identity of* bruscandoli *as* luppolo *is beyond question. I supplied detailed evidence for my statement, starting with a check in the great Venetian–Italian dictionary of 1876 (there is a copy in the reference room of the London Library) and this was published in the 1979 Summer number of* The Herbal Review. *There was still, however, the point made by Mr Amory concerning the apparent lateness of the season during which I had eaten wild hop shoots in Venice, and I felt that it was worth enlarging upon this. My published notes on the strictly seasonal aspect of the* minestra *and the* bruscandoli *risotto were as follows:*

'The minestra *can be made only in the month of April, at which period all the vegetable stalls of the famous Rialto market have it for sale. The traditional and characteristic* minestra *is still much in use in Venetian households ... the taste of* bruscandoli *is midway between spinach and asparagus' wrote a Venetian author, Mariu Salvatori de Zuliani in* A Tola Co i Nostri Veci *(At Table with our Ancestors) published in 1971 by Franco Angeli, Milano. It was*

perhaps misleading that the opening sentence of my article had been 'One fine morning in early May'. Well, it certainly was fine, and it certainly was May. But the operative word was early. To be precise it was May 3rd. And three or four days later, as I wrote, bruscandoli had vanished from the market.

In our English world of produce imported all the year round from all parts of the globe – strawberries from Mexico, asparagus from California, lichees from Israel, courgettes from Kenya – it is from time to time an intense pleasure to rediscover, as in Venice one does, the delicate climatic line dividing the vegetables and salads and fruit of spring from those of summer. Because of that dividing line, because they were so very much there one day and vanished the next, bruscandoli became a particularly sharp and poignant memory. In England, incidentally, wild hop shoots can be found as late as the first week of June, but I hope that those who may find them will keep the information to themselves. Were the fussy fashionable restaurants whose proprietors boast that they serve such delicacies as 'wild' mushrooms, smoked wild rabbit and wild seaweed to start featuring wild hop shoots on their menus the species would very soon become extinct.

Mafalda, Giovanna, Giulia

Mafalda

In the early 1950s, Mafalda and her husband ran a small restaurant in the village of Anacapri and willingly gave me several of their recipes for Southern Italian dishes. But when it came to the bottled pimentos it was a different matter. These pimentos were rather a speciality of Mafalda's, and they were by far the best I had ever tasted; she used to serve them as an antipasto: beautiful, brilliant scarlet strips of tender sweet peppers lightly sprinkled with olive oil and parsley and chopped garlic. 'Come back in the summer', Mafalda would say, 'and I will show you.' So I went back in the summer, and by the end of August the market stalls near the Piazza in Capri were loaded to bursting with the most magnificent red and yellow peppers. 'Shall I bring you back some peppers from the Piazza tomorrow morning?' I would say hopefully to Mafalda. 'Oh, no, it is too soon; on Thursday perhaps.' On Thursday Mafalda would observe that the pimentos were not just quite ripe enough – another twenty-four hours and no doubt they would be ready. This went on for nearly a month, while my host and hostess on the island must have been wondering if I was ever going to leave. At last Mafalda relented: the weather was fine, the moon no doubt was in the right quarter, the peppers were fat and fleshy, the price was as low as was compatible with the goods still being in their prime. It would drop again, but then it would be too late; there might be a risk of getting one or two which were not quite sound.

As it turned out, it was well worth waiting, because year after year I have used Mafalda's method of bottling peppers with great success. A number of people, however, have questioned whether it is possible to do this preserve without oil. The answer is, yes it is, and I think it is because of this that they are so good, for the addition of oil tends to make the peppers soggy.

It is difficult to say exactly when in the autumn the season for bottling peppers will arrive, since this depends not only on where you are but also on the weather conditions each year. Indeed, here in England I have sometimes waited until November for peppers in the condition prescribed by Mafalda.

CONSERVA DI PEPERONI (preserved pimentos)

Having obtained a number of the above described large, ripe and fleshy red sweet peppers, and some screw-top preserving jars, you impale the peppers on a long-handled toasting fork and hold them right in the gas flame of your cooker, or immediately under the grill if it is an electric cooker. (Mafalda cooked on a charcoal stove, and the peppers were placed directly on the glowing embers.) Turn them round and round until the skin is completely charred and blackened.

As soon as each pepper is cool enough to handle peel off all the blackened skin, rinsing them in cold water from time to time to facilitate the process. Every speck of black skin must be removed, and it is a tedious process. The stalks and cores and all seeds must also be discarded. It is at this stage of the proceedings that one appreciates the reasons for waiting until the peppers are very fat and fleshy, because if they are unripe it is difficult to remove the skins and there would be very little of the flesh left by the time you had done so.

Each skinned pepper is now sliced into strips about half an inch wide and these are packed into preserving jars. Pound-size jars are best for a small household because once opened this preserve must be fairly quickly eaten up. (Mafalda used wine bottles, still a common practice in the country in Italy where it would be thought wasteful to buy special preserving jars; she tied the corks with a piece of string with that deft manipulative skill which appears to be instinctive to all Italians.)

Having filled your jars, add a teaspoon of salt to each, and, if possible, a couple of basil leaves. Screw down the tops, and wrap each jar in a cloth or in several sheets of newspaper – this is a precaution to prevent the jars touching each other during the next stage of cooking. The jars are now to be laid flat[1] in a large pan and completely covered with cold water. Bring to the boil and continue boiling for 15 minutes. When quite cold, remove from the pan and make sure that the tops are screwed as tight as they will go.

I have kept jars of peppers preserved in this way in the autumn until well into the following summer; but, as for all preserves, a dry airy larder or cupboard is essential.[2]

Giovanna

SPAGHETTI WITH CHICKEN LIVERS AND LEMON

This is an unexpected combination of flavours and textures. I haven't seen the recipe in print before. It was given to me some years ago by Giovanna, the young Tuscan girl who cooked it in a country restaurant, now alas vanished, in a remote part of the Chianti district of Tuscany. Far from any town or village, lost among the trees on a gentle hill overlooking a man-made reservoir, the restaurant didn't even have a name. We called it 'the lake place'. There was no telephone. If we wanted to make sure of a table we would drive up the previous day to order our meal, but sometimes we would take a chance, arriving at midday and hoping that Giovanna would have some of her freshly-made pasta for us. We were never disappointed. Giovanna was a most original and gifted pasta cook, and it was on a day when we had turned up without warning that she first gave us this delicious dish. Her pasta, by the way, was made with 7 eggs to the kilo of flour, the more normal allowance being 5.

Ingredients: for 500 gr. of spaghetti, 5 eggs, 3 large chicken livers (about 100 gr. in all – Tuscan chickens are well fed and their livers

1. If you have a deep enough pot, the jars can be stood upright. Obviously, using bottles, it was necessary for Mafalda to lay them flat in the pan.

2. This is an extract from an article which originally appeared in the August 1958 number of London *Vogue*.

are large), 100 gr. of Italian raw lean ham or *coppa*, 4 or 5 cloves of garlic, 1 lemon, 200 gr. of grated Parmesan or pecorino cheese, seasonings of salt, pepper and nutmeg, 150 gr. of olive oil.

Cook the spaghetti *al dente*, in the Italian way. While it is cooking prepare the sauce. Put the olive oil in a sauté pan. Clean the chicken livers, cut them in small pieces. Peel the garlic cloves and crush them with salt on a board. (You must use your judgement about the amount of garlic. You may find that just one or two small cloves are sufficient. It would be a mistake, though, to leave it out altogether.) Cut the ham into fine strips.

Warm the olive oil, throw in the chicken livers, add the ham, the garlic, salt, freshly milled pepper, and the coarsely grated lemon peel. The cooking of all these ingredients should take scarcely three minutes. The chicken livers will be spoiled and tasteless if they are overcooked.

Now, in a big bowl beat 1 whole egg and 4 yolks. Add the grated cheese and a sprinkling of nutmeg.

When your spaghetti is ready, drain it (see Note 1 below), turn it into a big, deep, heated dish.

Quickly, pour the egg and cheese mixture into the sauté pan containing the hot olive oil and chicken livers, garlic and ham. Mix all together very thoroughly, but away from the heat. Now amalgamate the sauce with the pasta, turning it over and over, as if you were mixing a salad. The eggs cook in the heat from the pasta. You must have warm deep plates ready. Your guests must be ready too. Tepid pasta is as dismal as a fallen soufflé. 500 gr. of pasta should be ample for 4 to 5 people, 100 gr. per person being the usual Italian allowance.

Notes

1. It is a mistake to drain pasta too thoroughly. A little of the water it has cooked in should always go into the dish with it. This helps to keep it moist and retain the heat.

2. Enormous quantities of chickens are eaten in Tuscany. Hence the regional cooking provides many ways of using up the livers. One of the most popular of these dishes is called *crostini*. The livers are quickly cooked in butter or olive oil, well-seasoned, mashed to a rough purée and spread on oven-toasted, French-type bread. These hot *crostini* are invariably served as part of an *antipasto* or hors-d'œuvre, usually with a fine big dish of locally cured salame and raw ham. Anyone who would like to try the chicken liver and lemon

mixture without the pasta and eggs will find that it makes an excellent little spread for *crostini*. They are good as an accompaniment to scrambled eggs.

3. At the lake, as at many other Tuscan country restaurants, the meals always followed much the same pattern: a platter of locally cured raw ham (the lake family produced their own) and various salame, accompanied by hot *crostini* spread with fresh chicken liver or sometimes anchovy paste; a gigantic dish of pasta; meat or birds or rabbit – or all three – cut into chunks and roasted on a narrow spit in front of a wood fire; fried vegetables such as aubergines, sliced leaf-artichokes in batter, tomatoes, fruit, and another big platter of very thin light crisp *cenci*, strips or, more literally, rags and tatters of a sweet pastry batter deep-fried to a crackly pale gold in olive oil, and dusted with icing sugar. With these, a bottle of the local sweet white wine, called *vin santo*, was put on the table in one of the old, now fast-vanishing, straw-covered flasks.

Giulia

Giulia Piccini was Tuscan. She came from a hill village near Florence, and during the fifties she cooked for Derek Hill, the English painter, who at that time occupied the *villino* in the garden of I Tatti, Bernard Berenson's villa at Settignano. Giulia's cooking was like herself, elegant and delicate – in bearing she was more the fastidious aristocrat than the sturdy peasant – subtly seasoned, but with unexpected contrasts, as in a cold, uncooked tomato sauce which she served with hot dry rice. Conversely, *riso ricco*, or rich rice, consists of plain white rice left to cool until barely more than lukewarm, when a hot cheese sauce resembling a *fonduta* is poured over it. Not an easy dish to get right, but when it comes off, glorious.

GIULIA'S RISO RICCO

This is Giulia's own recipe written out by her husband, Emilio.
'For 500 gr. of rice: put 3 litres of water in a large boiling pot, and when it boils throw in the rice and a little salt, and cook it for about 15 to 17 minutes, stirring so that it doesn't stick. Turn it into a colander, and then into a buttered mould and leave it to cool. (The mould can be plain or with a central tube).

'Meanwhile prepare the sauce: into ½ litre of barely tepid milk put 250 gr. of Gruyère cut in small thin slices; then leave them for about an hour in this tepid bath, until the cheese has softened and melted and is forming threads. At this point add 4 egg yolks, whisking them in to obtain a cream which you then cook over a very slow fire.

'The sauce made, turn the rice into a serving dish and pour the sauce over it, first putting little flakes of butter over the rice.'

Notes

The only point Giulia doesn't make quite clear is that the milk and Gruyère should be held 'barely tepid' during the hour it takes for the cheese to melt, so a bain-marie or a double saucepan is indicated. Provided the water underneath or surrounding the milk is hot when you add the cheese, there should not be any necessity for further cooking at this stage. But keep the milk and cheese covered.

When it comes to adding the egg yolks and the final cooking of the sauce to a smooth custard-like cream I find it necessary, for the sake of speed, to have recourse to the blender, giving the yolks and the milk-cheese mixture a quick whirl, then returning them to the saucepan to thicken over very gentle heat. The sauce is not supposed to be thicker than double cream.

Both for flavour and melting property I prefer the Italian Fontina cheese to Gruyère which in England is of such variable quality, and inclined to turn into rubbery knots when heated. The rice should be Italian round-grained risotto rice. Giulia reckoned 500 gr. for 6 people.

GIULIA'S TOMATO SAUCE AND DRY RICE

With a dish of dry rice cooked in the manner of a pilau, Giulia used to serve the simplest possible tomato sauce. She sliced ripe tomatoes into a bowl (I don't think she skinned them. I do, but that's a matter of choice), mixed them with olive oil, wine vinegar, salt, pepper and a scrap of onion. The important points are to prepare the mixture two hours in advance, and immediately before serving to stir in a pinch of sugar.

For the *riso secco* use long-grain rice. Put half a small onion in a deep saucepan or casserole with olive oil and butter. When the onion turns pale gold, extract it, throw in 500 gr. of rice (for 6 people) and let it cook until it turns a pale blond colour; now pour in salted water or broth, and cook, covered, for 20 minutes. 'Take care that the rice is not too liquid; it is sufficient for the water to cover it by one finger's depth or less; when cooked turn it on to a serving dish and on top put, here and there, some flakes of butter and some grated cheese.'

The tomato sauce is served separately. '*Riso secco* may sound dull,' says Derek Hill, 'but the contrast of the hard hot rice and the cold tomato "salad" is absolutely delectable. It's most important I remember that the rice should not be shaken about or disturbed.'

Another Tuscan cook – Lina by name – from whom I learned several excellent dishes, used to serve a very similar uncooked tomato sauce with *riso in bianco*, plain boiled rice, but she skinned the tomatoes and chopped them almost into a purée. In Piedmont, just such a sauce is often offered with *bollito misto*, that splendid dish of mixed boiled meats. Indeed I wonder if Lina's method was not the very first way the Italians knew of making a tomato sauce. Not so long ago I came across almost the same recipe in Antonio Latini's *Lo Scalco alla Moderna*, or *The Modern Steward*, published in Naples in 1692. Latini, a native of Colle Amato di Fabbriano in the Marche, was steward to Don Stefano y Salcedo, Spanish Prime Minister of Naples. He called his recipe *Salsa di Pomadoro, alla Spagnuola*. Half a dozen ripe tomatoes were to be roasted in the embers and diligently skinned, then finely chopped with onions *a discretione*, also minutely chopped, pepper and creeping thyme or *piperna*[1] in small quantity. 'Mix all together, season it with a little salt, olive oil, vinegar, and it will make a most excellent sauce for boiled meats, or other.' The basis, it will be seen, of the modern Spanish gazpacho.

Although it is fortunately not true, as is so often asserted, that modern Italian cooking has foundered in tomato sauce, it is difficult not to regret the days when the tomato was treated with caution, and kept in its place. But it is also agreeable to recall, in savouring a simple sauce such as Latini's, something of the shock of surprise and pleasure some of his contemporaries must have experienced when they first tasted those cool, sweet-acid tomatoes in the heat of a Naples summer.

Petits Propos Culinaires No. 9, 1980

1. *Piperna* in this context may have been intended by Latini to mean *erba pipiritu*, one of several colloquial names for *Thymus vulgaris*, common thyme. (Battista & Giovanni Alessio. *Dizionaria Etimologico Italiano*. Firenze 1954.) Latini could equally have meant *piperite*, to which, according to Florio's *Worlde of Words* 1611, *piperna* was an alternative. The English for *piperite* was 'Ginny, Indian or Calicut pepper'. Ginny or Guinea pepper, also called Malagueta pepper and grains of Paradise, is the seed of *amomum melegueta*, a plant related to cardamom. What the tomato sauce required, clearly, was a mildly peppery seasoning, and in seventeenth century Italian cooking thyme was one of several herbs used in that context.

Have It Your Way

'Always do as you please, and send everybody to Hell, and take the consequences. Damned good Rule of Life. N.' I think we must both have been more than a little tipsy the evening Norman wrote those words on the back page of my copy of *Old Calabria*. They are in a pencilled untidy scrawl that is very different from the neat pen-and-ink inscription, dated 21 May 1940, on the flyleaf of the book, and from the methodical list of 'misprints etc.' written on the title page when he gave me the book. 'Old-fashioned stuff, my dear. Heavy going. I don't know whether you'll be able to get through it.'

I have forgotten the occasion that gave rise to Norman's ferociously worded advice, although I fancy the message was written after a dinner during which he had tried to jolt me out of an entanglement which, as he could see without being told, had already become a burden to me. And the gentleman concerned was not very much to his liking.

'You are leaving with him because you think it is your duty. Duty? Ha! Stay here with me. Let him make do without you.'

'I can't, Norman. I have to go.'

'Have it your way, my dear, have it your way.'

Had I listened to Norman's advice I should have been saved a deal of trouble. Also, I should not, perhaps, have seen Greece and the islands, not spent the war years working in Alexandria and Cairo, not have married and gone to India, not have returned to England, not become involved in the painful business of learning to write about food and cookery. And I should not now be writing this long-overdue tribute to Norman Douglas. Was he right? Was he wrong? Does it matter? I did what I pleased at the time. I took the consequences. That is all that Norman would have wanted to know.

When I met him first, Norman Douglas was seventy-two. I was twenty-four. It was that period in Norman's life when, exiled from his home in Florence and from his possessions, he was living in far-from-prosperous circumstances in a room in the place Macé in Antibes.

Quite often we met for drinks or a meal together in one or another of the cafés or restaurants of the old lower town, a rather seedy place in those days. There was little evidence of that bacchanal existence that legend attributes to all Riviera resorts.

*Norman Douglas, © photograph by Islay Lyons, reproduced by kind
permission of the photographer*

The establishment Norman chose when he fancied a pasta meal was in a narrow street near the old port. 'We'll meet at George's and have a drink. Then we'll go and tell them we're coming for lunch. No sense in letting them know sooner. If we do, they'll boil the macaroni in advance. Then all we shall get is heated-up muck. Worthless, my dear. We'll give them just twenty minutes. Mind you meet me on the dot.'

At the restaurant he would produce from his pocket a hunk of Parmesan cheese. 'Ask Pascal to be so good as to grate this at our table. Poor stuff, my dear, that Gruyère they give you in France. Useless for macaroni.' And a bunch of fresh basil for the sauce. 'Tear the leaves, mind. Don't chop them. Spoils the flavour.'

Now and again Norman would waylay me as I was buying provisions in the market. 'Let's get out of this hole. Leave that basket at George's. We'll take the bus up toward Vence and go for a little stroll.'

The prospect of a day in Norman's company was exhilarating; that little stroll rather less so. A feeble and unwilling walker, then as now, I found it arduous work trying to keep up with Norman. The way he went stumping up and down those steep and stony paths, myself shambling behind, reversed our ages. And well he knew it.

'Had enough?'

'Nearly.'

'Can you tackle another half kilometre?'

'Why can't we stop here?'

'*Pazienza*. You'll see.'

'I hope so.'

At that time I had not yet come to understand that in every step Norman took there was a perfectly sound purpose, and so was innocently impressed when at the end of that half kilometre, out in the scrub, at the back of beyond, there was a café. One of those two-chair, one-table, one-woman-and-a-dog establishments. Blessed scruffy café. Blessed crumbling crone and mangy dog.

'Can we deal with a litre?'

'Yes, and I'm hungry too.'

'Ha! You won't get much out of *her*. Nothing but bread and that beastly ham. Miserable insipid stuff.' From out of his pocket came a hunk of salami and a clasp knife.

'Do you always carry your own provisions in your pocket?'

'Ha! I should say so. I should advise you to adopt the same rule.

Otherwise you may have to put up with what you get. No telling what it may be, nowadays.'

Certain famous passages in Norman Douglas' work, among them Count Caloveglia's dissertation in *South Wind* on the qualities necessary to a good cook, in *Siren Land* the explosive denunciation of Neapolitan fish soup, in *Alone* the passage in which he describes the authentic pre-1914 macaroni, 'those macaroni of a lily-like candour' (enviable phrase – who else could have written it?), have led many people to believe that Norman Douglas was a great epicure in matters gastronomical, and so he was – in an uncommon way; in a way few mortals can ever hope to become. His way was most certainly not the way of the solemn wine sipper or of the grave debater of recipes. Connoisseurship of this particular kind he left to others. He himself preferred the study of the original sources of his food and wine. Authenticity in these matters was of the first importance to him. (Of this, plenty of evidence can be found by those who care to look into *Old Calabria, Together, Siren Land, Alone,* and *Late Harvest*.) Cause and effect were eminently his concerns, and in their application he taught me some unforgettable lessons.

Once during that last summer of his life, on Capri (he was then eighty-three), I took him a basket of figs from the market in the piazza. He asked me from which stall I had bought them. 'That one down nearest to the steps.'

'Not bad, my dear, not bad. Next time, you could try Graziella. I fancy you'll find her figs are sweeter; just wait a few days, if you can.'

He knew, who better, from which garden those figs came; he was familiar with the history of the trees, he knew their age and in what type of soil they grew; he knew by which tempests, blights, invasions, and plagues that particular property had or had not been affected during the past three hundred years; how many times it had changed hands, in what lawsuits the owners had been involved; that the son now grown up was a man less grasping than his neighbours and was consequently in less of a hurry to pick and sell his fruit before it ripened . . . I may add that it was not Norman's way to give lectures. These pieces of information emerged gradually, in the course of walks, sessions at the tavern, apropos a chance remark. It was up to you to put two and two together if you were sufficiently interested.

Knowing, as he made it his business wherever he lived and

travelled to know, every innkeeper and restaurant owner on the island (including, naturally, Miss Gracie Fields; these two remarkable human beings were much to each other's taste) and all their families and their staff as well, still Norman would rarely go to eat in any establishment without first, in the morning, having looked in; or if he felt too poorly in those latter days, sent a message. What was to be had that day? What fish had come in? Was the mozzarella cheese dripping, positively dripping fresh? Otherwise we should have to have it fried. 'Giovanni's wine will slip down all right, my dear. At least he doesn't pick his grapes green.' When things did not go according to plan – and on Capri this could happen even to Norman Douglas – he wasted no time in recriminations. 'Come on. Nothing to be gained by staying here. Can you deal with a little glass up at the Cercola? Off we go then.'

Well-meaning people nowadays are always telling us to complain when we get a bad meal, to send back a dish if it is not as it should be. I remember, one bleak February day in 1962, reading that a British Cabinet Minister had told the hotel-keepers and caterers assembled at Olympia for the opening of their bi-annual exhibition of icing-sugar buses and models of Windsor Forest in chocolate-work, 'If the food you have in a restaurant is lousy, condemn it . . .'

At the time Norman Douglas was much in my mind, for it was round about the tenth anniversary of his death. How would he have reacted to this piece of advice? The inelegance of the phrase would not have been to his taste, of that much one can be certain. And from the Shades I think I hear a snort, that snort he gave when he caught you out in a piece of woolly thinking. 'Condemn it? Ha! That won't get you far. Better see you don't have cause for complaint, I'd say. No sense in growling when it's too late.'

Gourmet, February 1969

South Wind through the Kitchen

'A venerated Queen of Northern Isles reared to the memory of her loving Consort a monument whereat the nations stand aghast.' Thus Norman Douglas on the Albert Memorial. All Norman's friends must, as did I, have stood aghast when they saw what had been perpetrated on his posthumously published *Venus in the*

Kitchen.[1] 'Decorations by Bruce Roberts' announced the title-page. Decorations? Defacements would have been a more accurate description. Had not any director or editor at Messrs Heinemann's ever glanced at so much as a paragraph of even one of the Douglas books before publishing *Venus in the Kitchen*? Did they simply take it on trust from Mr Graham Greene (whose brief, moving and purposeful introduction to the book would, had anyone in the publishing house taken the trouble to study it, have provided all the necessary clues) that Norman Douglas was a rather famous writer and that they would be lucky to get his final work? Did they hand a typescript or a set of galley proofs to their illustrator? Or did they think it sufficient to commission him to provide 'decorations' for what they innocently supposed was a cookery book which would sell on a title and illustrations with an erotic twist? If so, then their intentions were cruelly foiled by Mr Roberts. Anything more anaphrodisiac than his simpering cupids (in bathing trunks), his bows and arrows and hearts, his chefs in Christmas cracker hats, his amorphous fishes and bottles and birds, his waiters in jocular poses, his lifeless, sexless couples seated at tables-for-two, it would be hard to envisage. One would not dwell upon the dismal blunder were it not that these so-called decorations (where was the necessity for decorations?) have given to *Venus in the Kitchen* an image of Valentine-card mawkishness so absurdly alien to the author's intentions that potential buyers of the book (now reissued in an American paper-back[2] with, intact, alas, the English illustrations plus a gigantic scarlet heart on the cover thrown in for good measure) should be warned that the contents of the little book have nothing whatsoever to do with its appearance.

Cupids in the kitchen? Whatever next? The book is no more, and also no less, than an instructive and entertaining little collection of recipes mainly (as was to be expected from an author who had spent some forty years of his life in Italy, who was rather more than familiar with the Greek and Latin classics and had written a treatise dealing with every bird and beast mentioned in the Greek Anthology) of ancient Mediterranean lineage. To those even a little versed in the history and literature of cookery the recipes are unastonishing. In varying versions they are to be found in a number of books in French, Italian, Spanish, Latin, English, Greek. What makes this

1. Heinemann, 1952.
2. McGraw Hill, 14s. Available from Sandoe Books, 11 Blacklands Terrace, London, s.w.3, and Johnson & Son Paperbacks, 39 Museum St., w.c.1.

particular little anthology notable is not the recipes. It is the characteristically irreverent Douglas spirit which imbues them, and the style in which they are presented; a style which gives the impression that they were written not with a pen, but with a diamond-cutter; and then, appended to many of them – and they are the ones to be looked for – the typical deflating comment. There is nothing erotic here, much less anything with the slightest sniff of the sentimental. It is as plain as the nose on your face that at the age of eighty-two or thereabout, Norman Douglas was back at his old game of mocking at superstition and the superstitious. He regarded the whole business of aphrodisiac recipes as comical and bawdy. And to be frank, he did not know, nor pretend to know, very much about the practical aspects of cooking. Many of the recipes were, I believe, collected by Pino Orioli, the bookseller who was Norman's great friend and, at one time, his partner in the Florentine publishing venture which produced some of Norman's own books; and in the postscript to his preface he acknowledges technical assistance received from one of his oldest friends, the late Faith Compton Mackenzie, and from that magical writer, Sybille Bedford. What Norman Douglas did know about, and better than most, was the importance of the relationship between the enjoyment of food and wine and the conduct of love affairs, and for that matter of most other aspects of life.

I was, myself, once inducted onto a panel, somewhat uncertain and disorganized, of ladies and gentlemen thought to be capable of presiding over a kind of gastronomes' brains-trust at a certain English country food festival. Among the more resourceful worthies on the platform upon that memorable occasion was Mr Osbert Lancaster. A member of the audience demanded to be informed whether the panel considered good food to be possessed of aphrodisiac properties. And if so, what food in particular. A tricky question. The panel was silent. From the audience came shouts and derisive taunts. The whole meeting looked like breaking up in pandemonium. With faultless timing Mr Lancaster rose to his feet and boomed, in authoritative tones, that while he did not feel empowered to pronounce upon what food might or might not be prescribed for those in need of an aphrodisiac, he was prepared to commit himself to the point of declaring that if anyone wanted a sure-fire *an*aphrodisiac then it would be badly cooked food presented with a bad grace. An opinion with which Norman Douglas would have concurred.

'Indigestion and love will not be yoked together.' 'No love-joy comes to bodies misfed, nor shall any progress in knowledge come from them.' 'A man's worst enemy is his own empty stomach.' 'Be sober; let the loved one drink.' 'Good intentions – no . . . Gastritis will be the result of good intentions.' 'I have been perusing Seneca's letters. He was a cocoa-drinker, masquerading as an ancient.' 'The longer one lives, the more one realizes that nothing is a dish for every day.' 'The unseemly haste in rising! One might really think the company were ashamed of so natural and jovial a function as that to which a dining-room is consecrated.' 'To be miserly towards your friends is not pretty; to be miserly towards yourself is contemptible.'

That last maxim of Norman's was one he was particularly fond of enlarging upon when it came to a question of whether we could or should afford an extra treat in a restaurant or a more expensive bottle of wine than usual. It was a lesson from which I have derived much benefit. Eating alone in restaurants, as I have often in the pursuit of gastronomic researches been obliged to, I never fail to recall Norman's words (a recollection which has resulted in a surprise for many a haughty maître d'hôtel and patronizing wine waiter, expecting a lone woman to order the cheapest dish and the most humble wine on the list). More important, to treat yourself to what you want, need, or are curious to taste, is the proper, and the only way, to learn to enjoy solitary meals, whether in restaurants or at home.

And let nobody waste his time looking into *Venus in the Kitchen* for advice on love-potions. Not once in the entire book does Norman suggest that he regards the idea of aphrodisiac recipes as anything more than a jovial diversion. A certain artichoke dish is 'appetizing, even if not efficacious'. Salad rocket is 'certainly a stimulant'. A 'timid person is advised to sustain himself' with 'leopard's marrow cooked in goat's milk and abundant white pepper'. Pork chops with fennel seeds (an interesting dish. I know it well. Fennel seeds figure frequently in the country cooking of Tuscany) makes 'a stimulant for sturdy stomachs'. A piece of loin of pork simmered in milk (a method of meat-cooking well known in certain parts of central and northern Italy) is 'a good restorative'. Restoratives, stimulants, sustaining dishes, one notes. Why are they restorative, stimulating, sustaining? Because this is good cooking; interesting, well-seasoned, appetizing, fresh, unmonotonous. Nothing is a dish for every day . . . Certainly not that concoction of the intestines of a sucking pig stuffed with pieces of eel, peppercorns, cloves and plenty of sage (evidently an uncommonly grisly form of chitterling sausage) concerning which Norman is at his most teasing: 'This is an extremely appetizing and stimulating dish. The eel goes very well with pork, because it is among fish what the pig is among quadrupeds.' A simultaneous right and left to certain religious observances and to inherent prejudices with which he had no patience.

'Anchovies have long been famed for their lust-provoking virtues' is the piece of information appended to a recipe for anchovy toast. Ha! This recipe, which sounds a good one, consists of an emulsion of four ounces of butter and the yolks of four eggs plus one tablespoon of anchovy sauce and a seasoning of Nepal pepper. Hardly enough anchovy to provoke a mild thirst, let alone a lust. Anyone who hopes that *Venus in the Kitchen* is going to provide a roll on the dining-room floor would do well to reconsider. And to buy the book for a different kind of fun. For the fun, that is, of reading about the spices and wines and herbs, the fruit and flowers, the snails, the truffles, the birds, animals and parts of animals (the crane, the skink, the testicles of bulls) which went into the cooking pots of ancient Rome and Greece and of Renaissance Europe; for a glimpse, just enough to send us looking for more of the same kind, of the cinnamon and ginger and coriander flavoured game dishes, of the rose- and saffron-spiced sauces and meats, of the pistachio creams, the carnation conserves, the gentian and honey-flavoured wines, the Easter rice, the Sardinian pie of broad beans, the rolls of beef marbled with hard-boiled eggs and ham, the fennel and the almond soups which have all but vanished from European cooking.

To students of *Venus in the Kitchen* it may come as a disappointment to learn that Norman Douglas did not himself go in for the little extravaganzas he was fond of describing. Authentic food (if you can lay hands on a copy, see the passage in *Alone* describing his search in wartime Italy for genuine *maccheroni*, those *maccheroni* of a lily-like candour made from the correct hard fine white wheat flour), wine properly made, fruit from the trees he knew to have been well tended and grown in the right conditions – such things were his concerns. Gourmets' solemnities and sippings were not for him.

His tastes in food, in his last years, had become more than a trifle idiosyncratic. His explosive denunciations concerning the fish of the Mediterranean waters were familiar to all his friends (and to readers of *Siren Land*). 'Mussels? Of course, if you *want* to be poisoned, my dear. You know what happened to the consul in Naples, don't you? *Palombo?* No fear. But have it your way, my dear, have it your way. If you *care* to eat shark . . .' Then there was that business of the saffron. 'Liz, now take another glass of wine, and go into the kitchen; just see that Antonio puts enough saffron into that risotto. A man who is stingy with the saffron is capable of seducing his own grandmother.' From his pocket would come a brilliant yellow handkerchief. 'When the rice is that colour, there's enough saffron.' Enough! I should say so. For me the taste of saffron was overpowering long before the requisite colour had been attained. Just another of Norman's kinks, like his mania for hard-boiled eggs, of which he ate only the whites. How many discarded hard-boiled egg yolks did I consume in those weeks spent with him on Capri during the last summer of his life?

'For Liz. Farewell to Capri,' Norman wrote in the copy of *Late Harvest*[1] which he gave me when I said goodbye to him on 25 August 1951. For me it was not farewell to Capri. It was farewell to Norman. On a dark drizzling London day in February 1952 news came from Capri of Norman's death. When, in the summer of that year, I spent six weeks on the island all I could do for Norman was to take a pot of the basil which was his favourite herb to his grave in the cemetery on the hill-road leading down to the port. I went there only once. I had never shared Norman's rather melancholy taste for visiting churchyards. A more fitting place to remember him was in the lemon grove to be reached only by descending some three hundred steps from the Piazza. It was so thick, that lemon grove, that it concealed from all but those who knew their Capri well the old Archbishops' palace in which was housed yet another of those private taverns which appeared to materialize for Norman alone. There, at a table outside the half-ruined house, a branch of piercingly aromatic lemons hanging within arm's reach, a piece of bread and a bottle of the proprietor's olive oil in front of me, a glass of wine in my hand, Norman was speaking.

'I wish you would listen when I tell you that if you fill my glass before it's empty I shan't know how much I've drunk.'

To this day I cannot bring myself to refill somebody else's glass until it is empty. A sensible rule, on the whole, even if it does mean that sometimes a guest is obliged to sit for a moment or two with an

---

1. Lindsay Drummond, 1946.

empty glass, uncertain whether to ask for more wine or to wait until it is offered.

In the shade of the lemon grove I break off a hunch of bread, sprinkle it with the delicious fruity olive oil, empty my glass of sour white Capri wine; and remember that Norman Douglas once wrote that whoever has helped us to a larger understanding is entitled to our gratitude for all time. Remember too that other saying of his, the one upon which all his life he acted, the one which does much to account for the uncommonly large number of men and women of all ages, classes and nationalities who took Norman Douglas to their hearts and will hold him there so long as they live. 'I like to taste my friends, not eat them.' From his friends Norman expected the same respect for his privacy as he had for theirs, the same rejection of idle questioning, meddling gossip and rattling chatter. From most of them he knew how to get it. The few who failed him in this regard did not for long remain his friends. Habitually tolerant and generous with his time, especially to the youthful and inexperienced, he had his own methods of ridding himself of those who bored him. I once witnessed a memorable demonstration of his technique in this matter.

In the summer of 1951 there was much talk on Capri, and elsewhere in Italy, of a great fancy-dress ball to be given in a Venetian palace by a South American millionaire. The entertainment was to be on a scale and of a splendour unheard of since the great days of the Serene Republic. One evening Norman, a group of young men and I myself were sitting late at Georgio's café in the Piazza. Criticism of the Palazzo Labia ball and the squandered thousands was being freely expressed. Norman was bored. He appeared to be asleep. At a pause in the chatter he opened his eyes. 'Don't you agree, Mr Douglas?' asked one of the eager young men. 'All that money.' He floundered on. 'I mean, so many more important things to spend it on . . .'

'Oh, I don't know.' Norman sounded far away. Then, gently: 'I like to see things done in style.'

And he stomped off. Evaporated, as he used to put it. The reproof had been as annihilating as any I ever heard administered.

In Graham Greene's words 'so without warning Douglas operates and the victim has no time to realize in what purgatorio of lopped limbs he is about to awaken, among the miserly, the bogus, the boring, and the ungenerous'.

It was when Norman Douglas was in his very early fifties that, one night after a convivial dinner, he 'was deputed or rather implored' by those of his companions who had been bemoaning their lost vigour, 'to look into the subject of aphrodisiac recipes and the rejuvenating effects of certain condiments and certain dishes'.

Some twelve years later Norman put his collection of recipes together in book form and wrote a preface signed 'Pilaff Bey'. (On the spine of the present American edition 'Bey' appears as the author's name. A circumstance which may lead to some confusion among booksellers and their customers.) As a frontispiece for the book Norman still had in his possession a drawing done some years previously by D. H. Lawrence. The spasmodic friendship, doomed, one would suppose, from the first, between these two men of almost ludicrously opposed temperaments, had ended in the pillorying in print of each by the other. The illustration Lawrence had done for the aphrodisiac book was so perversely hideous, so awful an example of Lawrence's gifts as an artist that Norman thought it a good joke. He decided to use it. When, eighteen years later, the book at last was published Messrs Heinemann did at least respect their lately dead author's wishes in the matter. In juxtaposition to the febrile drawings commissioned by the publishers the frontispiece looked startling enough. For those who had eyes to see it indicated also something of the tone of the book and of the intentions of the author. The preface, left as it was written 'not later than 1936' told them the rest. The book had originated as an exposition of the absurdities, the lengths 'to which humanity will go in its search for the lost vigour of youth'. In spirit it was a send-up, a spoof. As such Norman intended it to remain. He was reckoning, for once in his life, without his publishers. He was reckoning, perhaps, without Death. With the present American publishers he could hardly be expected to have reckoned. In what spirit of prudery one can only guess, these worthies have relegated the Lawrence frontispiece (there would appear to be matter in it to interest the Warden of All Souls and other students of Lawrence-Mellors-Lady Chatterley mythology) to the last page of the book, facing the index. That, at least, Norman would have found a capital joke.

*

Recipes

YELLOW SAUSAGES

'For every ten pounds of chopped lean meat of pork, take one pound of grated cheese, two ounces of pepper, one of cinnamon, one of ginger, one of cloves, one of grated nutmeg, and a good pinch of saffron. Season with salt. Put everything in a mortar and pound well. Now put it in a saucepan with a glass of old white wine and cook over a gentle fire till the wine has been absorbed. Have ready some pigs' guts which you have washed first in hot water and afterwards in wine, fill them in with the above, tie them well at both ends, and when you want to eat them, just put them in boiling water for five minutes and serve hot.

'Could not be better.'

Venus in the Kitchen

OYSTERS IN WINE

'Heat the oysters in their shells. Open them, take them out, and collect their liquid in a pot. Put the oysters in a frying pan with butter, a sprig of garlic, mint, marjoram, pounded peppercorns, and cinnamon. As soon as they are lightly fried add their liquid and a glass of Malmsey or another generous wine. Serve them on toast.'

Venus in the Kitchen

PHEASANT À LA HANNIBAL

'Choose a not too tender pheasant, put it in an earthenware pot with a veal marrow bone. Add water to cover it up to three fingers, and put also a whole piece of cinnamon, some pieces of dried apricots, prunes, cherries, pine nuts, saffron, cloves, and some chopped mushrooms. Boil with the cover well sealed, but before covering it add a glass of white wine, a little vinegar and sugar, and cook.

'Simply delicious!'

Venus in the Kitchen

ON THE AUSTRIAN FOOD OF THE VORARLBERG

'Prolonged and confidential talks with the innkeeper's wife – his third one, a lively woman from the Tyrol, full of fun and capability – have already laid down the broad lines of our bill of fare. I must devour all the old local specialities, to begin with, over and over again; items such as *Tiroler Knödel* and *Saueres Nierle* and *Rahm-*

schnitzel (veal, the lovely Austrian veal, is scarce just now, but she means to get it) and brook trout *blau gesotten* and *Hasenpfeffer* and fresh ox-tongue with that delicious brown onion sauce, and *gebaitz-ter Rehschlegel* (venison is cheap; three halfpence a pound at the present rate of exchange); and first and foremost, Kaiserfleisch, a dish which alone would repay the trouble of a journey to this country from the other end of the world, were travelling fifty times more vexatious than it is. Then: cucumber salad of the only true – i.e. non-Anglo-Saxon – variety, sprinkled with *paprika*; no soup without the traditional chives; beetroot with cummin-seed, and beans with *Bohnenkraut* (whatever that may be); also things like *Kohlrabi* and *Kässpatzle* – malodorous but succulent; above all, those ordinary, those quite ordinary, *geröstete Kartoffeln* with onions, one of the few methods by which the potato, the grossly overrated potato, that marvel of insipidity, can be made palatable. How comes it that other nations are unable to produce *geröstete Kartoffeln*? Is it a question of Schmalz? If so, the sooner they learn to make *Schmalz* the better. Pommes Lyonnaise are a miserable imitation, a caricature.'

Together, 1923. Penguin Books, 1945

RED MULLET

'Of those sauces and pickles for fish so beloved of antiquity there is no mention save in two enigmas (14, 23 and 36) and who would guess that the following means a fish served up in a sauce consisting of the blood of other fish? "Bitter is my life, my death is sweet, and both are water. I die pierced by bloodless spears. But if anyone will cover me, dead, in a living tomb, I am first drenched in the blood of kinsmen." This strange and excellent recipe survives today in the islands where, if the fishermen cook a number of common fish together, squeeze the juice out of their bodies and then boil you, in this liquid, a red mullet.'

Birds and Beasts of The Greek Anthology, Chapman & Hall, 1928

Wine and Food, Autumn 1964

*

The Englishman's Food

The Englishman's Food: Five Centuries of English Diet, by J. C. Drummond and Anne Wilbraham; revised and with a new chapter by D. F. Hollingsworth (Cape, 36s.).

The Arcadian picture of long-lost peace and plenty, of a land overflowing with wholesome home-grown food, which we like to evoke when exasperated by today's hygienically processed and synthetically flavoured food-stuffs, is singularly absent from the late Sir Jack Drummond's detailed study of the Englishman's food during the last 500 years.

Lucidly, with great learning and a nice dry wit, he analyses the diets and the eating habits of our ancestors. Our own complaints, however justifiable, move into a slightly different perspective as Sir Jack recreates a past in which the adulteration, often injurious, of nearly every kind of food and drink was common practice and could not be prevented owing to the lack of reliable tests; in which food prejudices and superstitions hampered medical learning for centuries; in which salt meat was so hard that sailors could use it for making carved snuff boxes, and in which, according to Smollett, unspeakably dirty milk was hawked in the streets of London by verminous drabs masquerading under the 'respectable denomination of milkmaid'. There is no reason, Sir Jack adds, to suppose that Smollett was exaggerating.

Butter was certainly cheap, but nearly always rancid, at any rate until towards the end of the seventeenth century; although it was thought by many to be injurious to health it was eaten in large quantities by the poorer classes, while the rich used it only for cooking. By the time the value of green vegetables came to be understood the wheel had turned and butter was a luxury. English cooks grew accustomed to boiling all their vegetables in water, and to this circumstance Sir Jack attributes the deplorable methods which have made our vegetable cookery a byword.

This absolutely engrossing book has been a valuable work of reference for food historians and students of the science of nutrition ever since it first appeared in 1939. It should now find a much bigger public, for there is an immense amount in it for everyone seriously concerned with what they eat, and why.

The Sunday Times, 1958

Home Baked Bread

In the summer of 1955, following the publication of Summer Cooking, *Leonard Russell, the then Literary Editor of the* Sunday Times, *offered me a weekly cookery column in the paper. In 1956, when I had been writing for the paper for about a year (it was in those far-off days before the Colour Supplement), Leonard asked me if I would review a little book called* Home Baked, *written by George and Cecilia Scurfield, published by Faber. I declined, on the grounds that I knew little about bread-making, even less of book-reviewing. Leonard proceeded to cajole, coax, persuade. Although it is difficult to describe an editor's technique when he has made up his mind that a contributor will do something which that contributor would prefer not to do, every journalist will recognise it, and will appreciate that in the end I applied myself to studying the book and writing the review.*

The book was a sympathetic one, and a little research into the history of English bread-making proved instructive.

On the Sunday fortnight following the appearance of my review, the paper's Atticus *column contained an item headed 'Who sells books?' from which it emerged that within the two weeks my notice had sold 1,000 copies, half the first print order of* Home Baked. *This news item, it turned out, was a retort to the rival Sunday paper, which had made, apparently, a claim that its reviewers sold more books than those of any other national newspaper.*

Now the book in question was a cheap one – 6/6 at the time – my review, written in perfect innocence, was enthusiastic, it had been given space which in the ordinary way such a book would not have been accorded, and the subject was one which as my Literary Editor well knew – although at that time I did not – never fails to touch a sensitive spot in the minds of English newspaper readers. It would have been foolish to resent unduly the little confidence trick which had been played upon me. It was a good example of something right done for the wrong reason. The book's success was deserved, it has gone into many editions since, is still in print as a paper-back, and must have helped thousands of readers to learn how to make their own bread. For me, the book eventually opened up a whole new field of study and of cookery.

Reproduced below is that Sunday Times *review.*

*

Home Baked, by George and Cecilia Scurfield (Faber, 6s. 6d.).

For at least 250 years the bad quality of English bread has been notorious. Throughout the eighteenth and early nineteenth centuries, long before the invention of roller mills put white flour within the reach of all, the bakers and the millers were periodically accused of almost every possible fraud upon the community.

The adulteration of flour with alum to make it white was a common practice. One pamphleteer even went so far as to accuse the bakers of mixing their flour with ground-down human bones. According to Smollett the bread in London was 'a deleterious paste, mixed up with chalk, alum, and bone-ashes; insipid to the taste and destructive to the constitution' (*Humphry Clinker*, 1771). '*Que votre pain est mauvais*,' said a French friend to Eliza Acton, who observed in her *English Bread Book* (1857) that our bread was noted, 'both at home and abroad, for its want of genuineness and the faulty mode of its preparation'. Some thirty years later we have Sir Henry Thompson, an eminent doctor and writer on diet, complaining that bakers' bread was unpalatable and indigestible; he did not suppose any 'thoughtful or prudent consumer would, unless compelled, eat it habitually'.

The authors of this new book on breadmaking at home are even more blunt. 'We got fed up with shop bread.' Who has not? But it is useless to rage against the bakers and the bread manufacturers. So long as our ancient obsession with ever-whiter and whiter bread persists, the bakers will be delighted to sell it to us steam-baked, sliced, and hygienically wrapped. The only remedy for those who want genuine wholesome bread, and surely the wish is not a cranky one, is the same as it has always been. It must be made at home. And why not? In one of the most reassuring sentences to be found in any cookery book Mr and Mrs Scurfield sweep away all misgivings. 'The great thing about baking with yeast,' they say, 'is the difficulty of failure.' Exact measurements are not important, a draughty kitchen is no deterrent. No mystery is attached to the kneading of dough.

It is elsewhere that the rub lies. To get the full benefit of home-made bread it should be made with stone-ground wholemeal flour. You may have to go to some trouble or to some distance to find it. Quite apart from the extra burden of heavy bags of flour in the shopping basket, it will be expensive unless bought in large quantities. City dwellers scarcely have the space to keep 'a small dustbin' (mouse-proof) in which to store five stone of flour. Yeast is not always easy to come by, either. But the difficulties are not insurmountable.

Even bread made at home with ordinary white flour from the grocer is superior to manufactured white bread. The brown scone meal sold under the name of Scofa doesn't even need yeast to turn it into an excellent loaf. The Scurfields give recipes for a half white and half wholemeal loaf and for sourdough rye bread which should be useful, and I shall certainly try their method for French bread; but I wouldn't myself care for a fresh-baked Swedish coffee twist for breakfast, a fresh-baked cinnamon ring with coffee after lunch, and fresh-baked fruit and nut buns for tea, all made from the same batch of dough.

We have become a very food-conscious people during the past few years. Ever more cookery books pour from the presses, *millefeuille* pastry and shark fin soup, *crêpes suzette* and *bœuf Stroganoff, quiche lorraine* and *bouillabaisse* and *Linzertorte* no longer hold any mysteries for us. How about putting the horse in front of the cart and having a crack at baking a decent loaf of bread?

The Sunday Times, 25 March 1956

West Points

In 1952 we were still in the grip of rationing in this country. Few cookery writers or publishers had the nerve to tantalize the public with recipes calling for steaks and wine, joints of pork and veal, pheasants and cream, chickens cooked in butter, sauces made with eggs and olive oil, and meat stock for soups and stews. The flow of new cookery books which in the late fifties turned into a flood had barely started, and I suppose this explains the fact that while during the past few years some really very pointless American publications have been taken up over here – and often launched on the English market without the slightest acknowledgement of their transatlantic origin – one of the most entertaining and illuminating of cookery books from the United States was overlooked.

Helen Brown's *West Coast Cook Book*, now in its fourth printing, was first published (by Little, Brown & Co., Boston) in 1952, and I wish it had come my way long before now, for Mrs Brown throws light on scores of points about American ingredients and American cooking which, in my ignorance of the American continent, have always to me seemed most mysterious. The recipes, says the author, are the regional ones of the three Pacific States – California, Oregon, and Washington. Some, brought from all over Europe, originated with the early settlers, and proving suitable to the new world, settled in as native dishes. There were the foods and the recipes introduced by the Spaniards and the Mexicans; others were brought across the plains by the pioneers of the Oregon Territory and have, Mrs Brown says, a Yankee flavour. In many of the dishes there are Chinese, Italian or French influences; and dishes one often reads about in cookery books without being given a clue as to their origin – Cioppino (a sea-food ragoût), Olympia pan roast (olympia is an oyster) and Green Goddess dressing (created at the Palace Hotel, San Francisco, in honour of George Arliss) – turn out to be entirely local inventions.

Nearly all the recipes make convincing reading and probably delicious eating; Mrs Brown makes short work of substitutes, makeshifts and synthetics and her lists of ingredients, easy on the eye and the mind, are very far removed from those interminable recipes of American magazine cookery which call for one half-cup or one quarter-teaspoon of everything but the washing-up water. For English readers, though, the most valuable parts of the book are the notes on West Coast ingredients, the fish, the flora, the fauna. Mrs Brown explains abalone, albacore, barracuda, white sea bass and black sea bass which 'grows as large as six hundred pounds so we seldom cook it whole', tells us that there are thirty-five kinds of clam on the West Coast and describes the razor, the pismo, the mud, the gaper, the empire and butter clams, and also a gigantic freak called geoduck – about which it seems there are aspects not entirely polite so that 'ladies of an earlier day stayed at a discreet distance when their men went hunting them'. With one of quite a few poker-faced digs at her own compatriots' passion for gimmicky names and their carefree debasing of recipes, Mrs Brown remarks of a dish called Coos Bay Clam Cakes that 'this could be stuck in a split buttered bun and called a clamburger, but let's not.'

Reading of the extraordinary variety of the wild berries and fruits of the West – Oregon crab-apples, wild cherries, plums, elderberries, blackberries, barberries, grapes, gooseberries, huckleberries, cranberries – one begins to understand the origin of the preponderance of recipes for pies and fruit desserts which one finds in

American cookery books, and also the American taste for eating fruit jellies and preserves with meat and poultry.

As for those mixed-up fruit, vegetable and cheese salads which many people, excusably, appear to think form the staple diet of America, Mrs Brown doesn't bother too much about them; her explanation of the tendency to fling all and sundry ingredients into the salad bowl is that 'this everlasting green salad tossing is becoming something of a bore. So – to vary it – we make it in the classic manner but toss in other ingredients at will – nuts, cheese, olives, croûtons, slivers of orange peel or anchovies . . .' I don't altogether agree that a plain green salad ever becomes a bore – not, that is, if it's made with fresh well-drained crisp greenstuff and a properly seasoned dressing of good-quality olive oil and sound wine vinegar. But I do agree that all this *talk* about 'tossed salads' is a bore; it seems to me that a salad and its dressing are things we should take more or less for granted at a meal, like bread and salt; and not carry on about them.

But when you go, as a friend of mine did last week, to the restaurant of a big West End department store, order something called an egg salad costing 3s. 9d. which turns out to consist of outside lettuce leaves laid on a flat plate with a little dollop of grated carrot, two of diced beetroot and two halved hard-boiled eggs, and quite devoid of seasoning or dressing but plus – separately – a teeny pottikin containing two teaspoonfuls of what appeared to be slightly thinned-down commercial salad cream – well, boring though it may be, how can we *stop* going on about salads?

The Spectator, 8 December 1961

If You Care to Eat Shark

'I think I will try some of that *palombo*'.
'Of course my dear. If you *care* to eat shark'.

I wish that at the time I'd known more about that so-called shark. The place was a Capri tavern, my informant, up to his favourite trick of warning one off almost any fish which happened to be on the menu of the day by recounting something untoward about its feeding habits and the way it was caught, killed or cooked, was Norman Douglas.

'Don't say I didn't warn you. Let me tell you what happened to the vice-consul's wife in Naples. Ha!'

Before he had had time to invent some preposterous tale of how the vice-consul's wife in Naples had discovered a human nose inside a *palombo* I had found out for myself that there is nothing extraordinary about that fish except its dullness. Dogfish, that's all that shark turns out to be, and smooth dogfish at that, but at least not a man-eater. It feeds, I learn, upon 'crabs, lobsters etc.' (ha! Norman would scarcely have missed the opportunity of making something of that *etcetera*) 'its smooth pavement-like teeth being adapted for crushing shells rather than for seizing and holding active fish . . . the Irish call it stinkard, Devon fishermen Sweet William'.

This beguiling information I find almost on the very first page of a publication called *Seafish of Tunisia and the Central Mediterranean*, which is further described as a handbook giving the names of 144 species in five languages (actually six, Latin, English, French, Italian, Tunisian Arabic and modern Greek), with a list of molluscs, crustaceans and other marine creatures, and notes on cooking. The compiler is Alan Davidson, an official at the British Embassy in Tunis, who as an entirely unofficial activity, has made a serious attempt to classify and illustrate the local edible fish, a task originally undertaken, as he explains in his introductory note, simply to enable his own household, newly arrived in Tunisia, to use both the fish and their cookery books to the greatest advantage. Now as any amateur who has ever attempted to identify so many as a couple of dozen varieties of the fish for sale in any Mediterranean market from Barcelona to Alexandria, and from Marseille to Malta, Genoa, Venice and the Piraeus will know, Mr Davidson could, working on his own, have gone quickly and quietly raving mad – or have produced a volume adding to rather than clearing up the existing confusion in the minds of all those who deal in and buy, sell, or write about fish for the kitchen. Fishermen naturally suffer much less from this confusion. They see the fish in life, understand their habits and know the small differences in characteristics between several varieties of one fish. By the same token it is often the fishermen who have helped to create the confusion by bestowing their own private and local names upon each one of a tribe of fish to them possessed of obvious differences very often not easily distinguishable by the time the fish reach the buyers, let alone the cooking pots. Names then get transferred from one fish to another and confusion is rampant.

To help him sort out the appalling problems attendant upon his search Mr Davidson sensibly sought professional assistance and found it – he could scarcely have found better – chiefly in the person of Professor Georgio Bini, compiler of the marvellous *Catalogue of the Names of Mediterranean Fish* issued in 1960 by the General Fisheries Council for the Mediterranean, attached to the UN Food and Agricultural Organisation in Rome. (This impressive work of research, carried out primarily with a view to the establishment of one standard nomenclature for each fish in every Mediterranean language – and also in English – is at present unobtainable. Professor Bini's work is the model on which, as Mr Davidson makes clear, he has based his own. His diagrammatic drawings and much of the material come, indeed, straight from the FAO publication, and none the worse for that.

As we know, a great number of Mediterranean fish are by no means unique to the Mediterranean. We could do with knowing much more than we now do about creatures such as the delicious John Dory, a fish often dismissed as wasteful and expensive because of its huge head. Of course it is wasteful if you throw away that head, and the carcase; keep these pieces of fall-out for fish broth or soup for which they are especially good and suitable, and the John Dory becomes an economical proposition. Brill, another fish which to my taste is much superior to the absurdly over-rated sole, the mullets red and grey and the gurnards ditto, the rays, the inkfish tribe, the bass, and even I believe the angler fish, the *lotte* or *baudroie* of the French, of which again only the tail is eaten could all be more generally available in England if only people were not frightened to buy fish with which they are not familiar. The simple remedy is for us to become familiar with them, and if eventually works such as Mr Davidson's could be published here we should be getting somewhere. In any case Mr Davidson has a gift for conveying memorable information in a way so effortless that his book makes lively reading for its own sake. Who could not find it entertaining to know that there is a fish called, in Latin, *boops boops* or *box boops*, that *boops* signifies big eyes – well of course Betty Boops – that in English and French this fish is known as bogue, and that alas 'bogue is not particularly good'. Or that in Venice you may insult someone by calling him a picarel-eater, and that this same picarel, a fish of the *centracanthidae* family is known at Port-Vendres as the *mata-soldat* or kill-soldier? One is glad too to find out at last that the *dentice* so beloved of the Italians is identical with the *synagrida* equally beloved of the Greeks, that the English name for *brème de mer* is Ray's bream, that it is a deep water fish, and uncommon, that its face is that of a petulant old baby, that the fish we call sea-bream the French call *pagre* (I know it as *pagel* – or is that another one?) and that the *daurade* or Italian *orata* should properly be called in English the gilt-head bream, and that, en passant, it is a hermaphrodite.

Of the *mérou*, called in English grouper, in Italy *cernia* and of which one hears so much from under-water fishermen (they too would perhaps find this book illuminating) Mr Davidson thinks highly, mentioning a sauce to serve with cold poached grouper steaks in which is incorporated some Bresse Bleu. Tantalising, that. Perhaps more details of this recipe will appear in the next edition, for which Mr Davidson is asking from his readers co-operation in the form of corrections, amplifications, authentic Mediterranean recipes.

The Spectator, 26 April 1963

Moorish Recipes

Moorish Recipes, collected and compiled by John, fourth Marquis of Bute, K.T., Oliver & Boyd, 7s. 6d.

A cookery book concerned more with the authenticity of the dishes than with what the English housewife may make of them is a rarity. Indeed this book was not originally intended for the public at all, and we are fortunate to get it. It is a collector's find. The technicalities of *kuskusu* and of that remarkable papery Arab pastry are beautifully propounded. The use and composition of spices is explained; there are English and Arabic indexes.

I can testify that a Moorish dish of pigeons stuffed with raisins, almonds, cinnamon and sugar and cooked in a quantity of olive oil does wonders with those intractable birds. The fine free style in which the recipes are written and set out is most pleasing, and how elegant are the Moorish cookery pots and serving dishes shown in the illustrations. Some illuminating facts emerge. A plate of honey containing a lump of butter, in which bread is dipped, may be placed upon the table, salt never; it is up to the cook to add salt according to the *smell* of the dish when it is half cooked. Only one of the fifty-nine recipes contains garlic. *Ras el hanoot*, literally meaning 'head of the shop', is a tantalizing compound of pepper, cinnamon, curry, bird's tongue, saffron wood (I should like to know more of this) and two kinds of aubergine to be used chiefly in the cooking of game. Anyone who wants to taste locust bread, a delicacy available only when the locusts make their visitation every nine years, may start planning now, for they are due next year.

The Sunday Times, 1955

Fine Bouche

Fine Bouche: A History of the Restaurant in France, by Pierre Andrieu (Cassell, 31s. 6d.).

Until the second half of the eighteenth century there were no restaurants in France – only taverns, wine shops, cafés, dealers in cooked meat or poultry, pastries, pies and so on. The rules as to

what each dealer might sell were clearly defined. Or so it was thought until one Boulanger, a dispenser of high-class restorative broths or *restaurants*, appeared upon the scene.

He acquired quite a reputation for the *pieds de mouton sauce blanche*, with which he provided the customers along with the soups; so his rivals declared that he had no licence to sell cooked meats. An action was brought to restrain him. With resounding publicity the affair ended in victory for Boulanger, and the ancestor of the restaurant was born.

Some twenty years later, Beauvilliers, ex-Royal cook, opened the Grande Taverne de Londres, and there established the attitude of the successful restaurateur as we know him today. From this point on it would have been of real interest to learn something of how a great restaurant works. But M. Andrieu gives us instead a bewildering chronicle of the vicissitudes of most of the famous restaurants and their owners, waggish tales of private rooms and princely wit.

We must take M. Andrieu's word for it that on these high altars of gastronomy the food was never less than superb, the wines perfection, the service faultless, the décor invariably the last word in luxury. But the more modest establishments, both of Paris and the provinces, come out of it more convincingly.

There is some engaging information in the book, such as the true origin of *Homard à l'Américaine*, and the fact that Weber's in the rue Royale made its name by serving Welsh Rabbit, cold roast beef, and marrow bones prepared with English mustard and served with chips.

The Sunday Times, 4 November 1956

How Bare is Your Cupboard?

Pot-Luck Cookery; original cooking with what you have in hand, in the cupboard or refrigerator Beverly Pepper (Faber & Faber, 18s.).

Pantry Shelf Fishbit: Turnip-Tomato Patty Casserole: Lentil Cheese Cassoulets: Ham-wiches: Fantastic Belgian Meat Balls: Veal-odds-and-ends-Casserole: Salem Fish'n Chutney Tarts: Festa Turkey-nut Logs: Mixed Beet Ring Mould: Gnocchi Semolina (pronounced Knee Oh'-Key): Chocolate Bread Custard: Curried Pea Spoon-fritters. These haunting names are chosen for their sheer vivid descriptiveness from a newly published book dealing with cookery 'for a roomful of unexpected guests – or perhaps just that awkward moment when the larder seems completely bare'. But not completely bare, as it turns out. Because there is a whole thoughtful chapter telling you how to make out in what might seem to many of us even more awkward moments than having only the ingredients of Knee-Oh'Key to hand; those in fact when there is Nothing in the House but Processed Cheese or even, if you can imagine it, Nothing in the House but Cream-Style Corn, Cream-Style Corn, Nothing in the House but Cream-Style Corn.

Now, I know as well as anybody that it's hard work writing cookery books and very easy for others to mock. The author of this work has conscientiously, not to say with almost frenetic zeal, compiled a volume of recipes dealing with what he, or she, thinks you might have in the Cupboard or Refrigerator. No doubt the public at which it was originally directed does have fifteen 2 inch lengths of leftover broccoli or 'at least' 1½ cups leftover cooked kidneys, thinly sliced, in its Cupboard or Refrigerator, and it is not for me to quarrel with Mr or Miss Pepper about what should be done in such situations. He or she has done his or her, work with a view to his or her audience which lives, loves, and one must believe, eats, *Veal-odds-and-ends-casserole* on the other side of the Atlantic. My bone of contention is with her or his English publishers. They've got, frankly, a dashed nerve to try and foist this stuff on us without so much as the courtesy of acknowledging where and when it was originally published and with not the slightest apparent attempt to change a single word for the benefit of the English public. And if a reputable firm of publishers can confidently put out a book purporting to be one of technical instruction (which is, after all, what a cookery book is supposed to be) so totally unrelated to life as it is lived in these Islands that it might as well be written in Swahili, hideously produced into the bargain, and at the fancy price of eighteen shillings, then the publishing business can hardly be as pushed as it's always making out.

Myself, I'd prefer to spend my eighteen shillings on food. I wouldn't care to face a roomful of hungry guests with nothing in the house but *Pantry shelf fishbits*. They might cut up rough. And I don't know whether, in such an event, one would be entitled to send the bill for damages to the publishers.

*

This review was written for The Sunday Times *sometime in the summer of 1957, but never published. Recently I unearthed a letter from Leonard Russell, the paper's then Literary Editor, dated September 18th, 1957, explaining that during his absence on holiday the book in question was recommended, among a number on wine and food, to appear among 'our gourmet advertisements' in a special panel. Leonard said he didn't know how this contretemps happened. 'But it would have been too absurd to have recommended the book in one issue and to have had you exposing it utterly in the next.'*

Referring to the affair as 'somebody's misconceived enterprise' Leonard said he had asked the Cashier to send me a cheque for seven guineas. Yes, well.

Chez Gee-Gee

The Gun Room, the Garrison, the Saddle Room, the Stable; a flavour of far off cantonments and safe frontier wars, a wistful feeling for the rude soldiery, fond memories of childhood loves for girl grooms and stable boys, a heady scent of manure mingled with salmon snatched straight from the tin in the harness room have come seeping these last few months through the restaurant and entertainment-after-dark columns of the weekly magazines.

If the Minister of Transport[1] has his way and succeeds in abolishing the few surviving horse-drawn commercial vehicles in the London area then one does not need to be a professional clairvoyant to predict that the disappearance of the last brewers' drays and costers' flower carts will intensify our nostalgia for the urban horse and all its manifestations; and that before long half of our Belgravia and Hampstead, South Kensington and Golders Green bistros now called Le Casserole d'Abondance, La Sole Vierge, Au fils de ma Grand-Mère, La Nappe Tachée and La Poubelle will change their names to La Bouche de mon Cheval, Au Sac d'Orge, Le Horse Sexy, The Well-Served Mare, The Bit between the Teeth, the Drench, the Hock's on the Hoof.

Tourists will stray into the Cavalry Club supposing it to be a French auberge recently acquired by Harvey's of Bristol, the Chinese Lily Pond chain will cash in on the boom by translating the Fantang Crispy Noodles on their menus into Eight Precious Mares' Nest No. 63; Paul Hamlyn alias Books for Pleasure will discover and publish only seventy five years out of date and for only four guineas a 4,000 page encyclopaedia entitled *La Cuisine Chevalline* illustrated with three hundred full colour reproductions of oil paintings by Sir Alfred Munnings. Three weeks later, broken down into six half-crown paperbacks the book will be bought by eight million people. The entire conclave of Rump Rooms and Grill Pans will, as one, turn into Knacker Parlours.

By then a new wave will be starting, derived from sources more purely domestic than those of the barracks and the nosebag. Mr E. S. Turner's *What the Butler Saw*, a book revealing and entertaining in a way quite other than the implication of the title, and

---

1. The late Ernest Marples.

Anthony Powell's wonderful recreation of a pre-1914 upper mid-dle-class military family's more eccentric and lugubrious servants in *The Kindly Ones* will surely engender fresh yearnings for a vanished below-stairs world of plain cooks, soldier servants, trays for the governess and the nursery, dressing gongs, and the scrape of Monkey Brand on stone sinks.

In terms of eating-boutiques and clubs, this will mean establish-ments called The Scullery, The Flue, The Servants Hall, The Stewed Prune, the Suet Room, Chez Cronin, The Knife Box (a little more moisture in the cabbage would have won Mr Stalleybrass his third star, as one of our earnest eating guides will be writing by 1964), the Dripping Bowl (to do full justice to Mrs Bravo's cooking you should start with the sophisticatedly served Spotted Dog; but what a pity in a place of this quality to find such a short tinned-soup list), The Batman (this restaurant is something of an enigma. You are served delectable Swiss cuisine in genuine English surroundings. The day I was there the litter bins were quite overflowing. But perhaps on days other than August Bank Holiday they may not be so bustling. Mr Lavender's early training is revealed by the superb polish on his chocolate éclairs. The coffee is traditionally made with water and coffee but could have been a little drier. The home-made toast was included in the price of this soigné meal, four pounds ten for two.)

*

The above was published in the Spectator *in December 1962. Some twelve months later Sam White, in his weekly* Evening Standard *report from Paris, remarked that at least four restaurants with names like The Stables or the Rubbish Bin or The Swill exist in Paris and 'that it is now without any doubt the definitely established fashionable trend to eat as badly as possible, and as expensively as possible'.*

In London, 1963 saw the opening of restaurants with the self-consciously down-beat names of La Gaffe *and* Grumbles, *situated respectively in Hampstead and Pimlico. In the summer of 1964, the neighing of* The Hungry Horse *was heard right down the Fulham Road, and the creature hoofed it straight home into the very first issue of the Daily Telegraph's colour supplement.*

*

Carrots a la Kazbek

It is a bit soon, even now, for the world of paw-paw cocktails, breakfasts on the verandah and Royals alighting on the tarmac to return to us through the names of airport motels and the menus of manor-house country clubs. But it will have its turn (what will the decorators make of the plumed hats?) and when it comes, students will find a great deal of unique material in Sir Harry Luke's *The Tenth Muse*, first published in 1954 and now re-issued in a revised edition (Putnam, 25s.). During a lifetime spent – and uncommonly well-spent, one deduces from this book – in the Colonial Service, Sir Harry has collected recipes from British Residencies and Government Houses, from their châtelaines, their cooks – cooks Maltese and Cypriot, Hindu and Persian and Assyrian, cooks Goanese and Polynesian, cooks naval, military and consular, cooks in Union Clubs in South American capitals, cooks of French princes and Brazilian countesses, of Turkish Grand Viziers and Patriarchs of the Syrian Orthodox Church – and in setting down his recipes Sir Harry has acknowledged the source of each and every one: Government House, Springfield, St Kitts; Government House, Fiji; St Anton Palace, Malta; the Goanese cook at the Residency, Bahrein; Government House, Wellington, New Zealand; Count Haupt Pappenheim, Sao Paulo, Brazil; Lloyd, the butler at Kent House, Port of Spain.

Sir Harry must be a gratifying guest. Everything interests him. The wife of the British Resident in Brunei prefers to mix her own curry powders, so off he goes with her to market, noting that she buys, separately and in varying quantities, black pepper, aniseed, cardamom, chillies, cinnamon, cloves, coriander, cumin, mace, nutmeg, poppyseed, saffron, tamarind, turmeric ... As British Chief Commissioner in the Trans-Caucasian Republics of Georgia, Armenia and Azerbaijan, he attends a banquet (it is 1919) at Novo Bayazid; there he eats a species of salmon trout unique to Lake Sevan and called *ishkan*, the prince; it is served 'surrounded by its own amber-coloured caviare, accompanied by a sauce made of the cream of water-buffalo's milk, mixed with *fresh* peeled walnuts ... with somewhere a touch of horseradish ... the dish was subtly and incredibly delicious.' Delicious it sounds too; so does goose steeped in salt and sugar brine as it is done in the South Swedish province of Scania (recipe from the British Vice-Consul at Malmö); we get enticing information about how medlar and guava jellies to be served with meat and game are vastly improved by the inclusion of a little Worcester Sauce and fresh lemon juice in their composition; and how a lady who lives at Dramia, below the mediæval castle of Buffavento in Cyprus, uses the leaf of the *persica* or wild cyclamen instead of vine leaves for her dishes of rice-stuffed dolmas.

In the sense that they are not technically very expert Sir Harry's recipes are not for the beginner. Indeed he is himself the very first to warn the reader that he is not a practising or practical cook. In the sense that his descriptions, directions and notes are possessed of the essential quality of arousing the urge to get into the kitchen to cook something new, then they are for everyone, beginners and collectors especially. Sir Harry has the beginner's enthusiasm and fresh eye, the collector's madness. One of the things I like best in his book is his own admission to a lifelong pursuit, world-wide and slightly manic, of the strawberry grape. From California to Kenya, from Malta to an English vicarage garden he has carried this particular vine, advocating its cultivation and propagation. Does he know that oddity, one of the sweet syrupy and picturesque Greek confections called 'spoon jams', made from the strawberry-grape?

Few authors are as modest as Sir Harry Luke (naive he is not) and fewer still provide the stimulus, the improbable information, the travellers' tales, the new visions which to me make his book a true collectors' piece.

The Spectator, 7 December 1962

Franglais

Just two leaves of tarragon, two and no more, are to go into the butter and herb stuffing for a dish called *poulet au réveil*. 'I say two leaves only', wrote Benjamin Renaudet, the author of this lovely recipe, 'because although they are very small, in adding more the taste of the stuffing might be distorted.' That is the kind of observation Renaudet makes often in his book. It is called *Les Secrets de la Bonne Table*, is undated, and is concerned with post-1870, pre-1914 household cookery in the provinces of France. Renaudet's book is one I have used and quoted often, read over and over again. Even so, it is only recently that I have paid close attention to the handful of English recipes which appear in the book and of which Renaudet says that they were evolved from notes made on the spot in England.

Renaudet was a selective collector and meticulous recorder of little-known French provincial recipes. On English cooking his views should therefore be worth hearing. So they are. Noting that the English kitchen 'in which roast beef plays so important a part' supplies also some interesting methods of using the left-overs, he gives a recipe for *ragoût de bœuf rôti*, in English, says M. Renaudet, called roast-beef stew. A French version of cottage pie? Nothing of the kind. It is basically a *bœuf miroton*, the time-honoured dish of every Frenchwoman who ever had to deal with boiled beef left over from the *pot-au-feu*. The essential difference is that Renaudet's recipe calls for roast instead of boiled meat. The sliced beef, re-heated in stock, with bacon, onions, bay leaves and whole small potatoes 'all as much of a size as possible' is arranged in a pyramid in the centre of the serving dish, the little potatoes disposed in a circle around the meat. Now if there is anything more typical of an old-fashioned French household dish than Renaudet's little whole potatoes all of a size and his description of the manner of serving of his roast-beef stew then I should like to hear of it. (In all fairness he does add that in England it is more usual to serve the meat within a border of boiled rice. Was it? Is it?) For the next of the interesting methods with left-overs as promised by M. Renaudet, invention seems to take over and we get *pudding de rosbif*, or cold beef boiled for three hours in a pudding crust.

Now we get to our muttons. A *gigot bouilli à l'anglaise*, it surprises me only mildly by this time to learn from dear M. Renaudet, is 'très délicat' and retains 'tout son jus'. So it may be and so it might had it been or were it ever cooked as M. Renaudet claims it is. He envelops his leg of mutton entirely in a flour-and-water paste two centimetres thick and covering every inch of the joint, shank bone included. The paste-wrapped gigot is then sewn securely in a cloth, lowered into a pan of *boiling* water and simmered extremely gently – 'no faster than for our *pot-au-feu*' – for five hours. It is at this point that M. Renaudet throws caution as well as the entente cordiale to the winds and suggests that his French readers may prefer to serve a Villeroy or Béarnaise sauce with their *gigot* instead of the 'usual English mint or Cumberland sauce'.

The suggestion that Cumberland sauce (no mention of caper sauce) goes with boiled mutton does rather confirm my suspicion that Renaudet was borrowing at least some of his English cookery lore not from the 'Mrs Holly of Blackheath' or the 'Mrs Allingham of Turtle Cottage near Oakham in the Rutland', the ladies to whom he attributes some quite plausible English recipes, but from Alfred Suzanne, author of *La Cuisine Anglaise*, published in 1898 and still freely quoted as a responsible French authority on English cookery.

At any rate Renaudet gives, in a footnote, a recipe for Cumberland sauce which is certainly Suzanne's, and one for which we have cause to be grateful, even if we do not eat it with boiled mutton. (It is curious that this sauce, originally German, appears to have entered the English kitchen via three French chefs – Alexis Soyer, Alfred Suzanne and Auguste Escoffier.) Other aspects of Suzanne's book are less enchanting. 'All fruits are made into pies' . . . plum cakes are as French as possible and English in name only . . . plum pudding is the English national dessert . . . bacon is an unbeatable English speciality . . . it is cooked in the following way. Cut it into thin slices like veal birds, then split them on small skewers and grill them over a hot fire or in a very hot oven. Serve on toast . . . 'Haddock; this smoked fish is very common in England. The English bake or boil it and fill it with a forcemeat called veal stuffing.'

Two of M. Suzanne's employers were the then Duke of Bedford and the Earl of Wilton. Making every allowance for aristocratic eccentricity, it is still hard to envisage those Victorian noblemen eating breakfast bacon dished up in genteel little rolls, demanding that their smoked haddock be stuffed and boiled, and ordering plum pudding every other day for luncheon. If, in the 1960s, Suzanne's book is still the only one on English cooking available to

French gastronomic researchers (the English dishes in Flammarion's recently translated and loudly trumpeted *Art of Cookery* are all based on Suzanne) then it would seem to be high time for somebody to provide them with an authoritative exposition of the subject.

It is not so much that anyone would want to convert the French to English food – although there are those timid souls who transport their own English bread across the Channel, and many more who are horribly disillusioned when they order roast beef in France and find it cooked to a rare red rather than to English Sunday lunch grey – as that it would be so interesting to see what French housewives would evolve from authentic English recipes. We should see our own cooking with fresh eyes. We should also see, I think, that the Englishness of many of our dishes lies not so much in the basic treatment of the raw materials as in the finishing touches and presentation of the dish.

Those whole small potatoes for example, of Renaudet's – unless we were making super-human efforts to be French, we should never incorporate them in the dish with the meat. We should have them boiled separately and served separately, and probably there would be cauliflower or sprouts and green peas as well, whereas a French-woman, however English she wanted to pretend to be, would find it going too much against the grain to provide three boiled vegetables with one meat dish, let alone offer a steak and kidney pudding – a dish which much fascinates French cooks – accompanied by mashed potatoes and a boiled pease pudding. This classic combination is offered, so I learn, at Flanagan's restaurant in Baker Street. Perhaps this would be the place to take French visitors in search of authentic English food, although it must be said that I have myself always found it safe enough to take Paris friends to London-French restaurants. Whatever the efforts made by the proprietors and cooks to produce true French cooking, nothing will persuade my French friends that what they are eating is anything but typically English. They might be right.

It is no doubt our taste for extraneous unrelated flourishes and garnishes which to the French makes our attempts at their cooking amusing, original (*inattendu* I think is the correct word), and characteristically English.

It must have been a French cook more observant than his contemporary Alfred Suzanne but still not quite observant enough, who decided that to please the English gentlemen of the Turf who frequented the old Café Weber, originally the Taverne Anglaise, in the rue Royale, he would add a flourish or two to the grilled marrow bones which were one of the specialities (others were cold roast beef, York ham, and Welsh Rabbit), on which Weber's reputation was founded. By serving English mustard and chips with their marrow bones, Weber's were no doubt making a graceful concession to English taste. Which only goes to show, marrow bones being one of the rare dishes that no Englishman would want chips with, how difficult it is to get quite precisely under the skin of another country's cookery.

The Spectator, 22 February 1965

Exigez le véritable Cheddar français

'The Comté

'Privileged heir of the Gruyère's great and noble family, it is made in the Franche-Comté and its surroundings. The paste is coloured like pale yellow ivory, when it is cut, holes appear well shared exactly, like a hazelnut, sometimes, at most, like a cherry.'

'The Beaufort

This Gruyère is made in the high alpine mountains, the paste is soft and supple, the cut shows not any hole like butter.'

'The Emmental

This Gruyère, from the Savoy is like a settler who knew to put himself forward leaving off the East countries for other lands. The mosaic of the cut looks like a great distribution of attractive holes.

'As soon as one enters "Jura" and the whole region centred on this French Department, one is aware of the respect which is due to French Gruyère cheese. Public opinion has long remained wrongfully ignorant of what the French Gruyère cheeses really are.'

The above extracts are from a leaflet issued for the American and English markets by the French manufacturers of Le Creuset fondue sets. Under the signature of Raymond Oliver, the Parisian gastrono-

— 156 —

mic publicist and owner of the Grand Véfour restaurant in the Palais Royal, is appended the information that 'you will always find your dairyman has one of the great vintages of French Gruyère'.

This instructive leaflet also supplies three recipes for fondue, one to be made with Emmental, one with Comté, one with Beaufort. None of the versions differs in any notable respect from the rustic Swiss cheese fondue. That famous dish of cheese stewed with white wine and flavoured very expensively, but very necessarily, with kirsch, has of late years received so much publicity that you can find a recipe for it in almost any cookery book or magazine you pick up. What to me seems surprising is that M. Oliver, who presumably supplied the recipes for the Le Creuset leaflet, does not give what is said to be the old and traditional fondue of Franche-Comté, a dish in every respect superior to its primitive Swiss counterpart, having both greater finesse of flavour and texture and far less brutally indigestible qualities.

Like Brillat-Savarin's famous fondue and the *fonduta* of Piedmont, the fondue of Franche-Comté is really a cream of eggs and cheese (not, be it noted, scrambled eggs and cheese) and has been rejected, I fancy, as being unauthentic either because it is more difficult to cook correctly than the Swiss version or because it is the cheese purveyors rather than the egg-marketeers who have been on the job. Since Raymond Oliver's assertion to the effect that your dairyman always has one of the great vintages of French Gruyère[1] cannot be said to apply to any of *my* dairymen both the questions of authenticity and of relative skill with the fondue set are academic.

All the same, just for the record, here is the version of the fondue of Franche-Comté given by Pierre Dupin in *Les Secrets de la Cuisine Comtoise* (Ed. Nourry, Paris, 1927).

FONDUE DE FRANCHE-COMTÉ

'Into a saucepan you pour 2 decilitres (approximately 7 fluid oz.) of white wine, you add a large clove of garlic, chopped, and you boil the wine until it is reduced by half and the garlic is cooked. Strain the wine and leave it to cool.

---

1. It is difficult enough to lay hands on genuine Swiss Gruyère, let alone the Comtois version; but Bartholdi's, the Swiss shop at 4 Charlotte Street, London, w.1, can usually supply the authentic Swiss article, and I have bought the delicious Beaufort cheese from Paxton and Whitfields' in Jermyn Street. Fontina, the Val d'Aosta cheese required for the Piedmontese *fonduta*, is sometimes to be found at Soho shops such as Lina's in Brewer Street, and King Bomba's and Parmigiani Brothers of Old Compton Street.

'In a bowl mix 10 well-beaten eggs with 60 gr. (2 oz.) of Gruyère cut into very tiny pieces, 60 gr. of butter, pepper and a little salt. You add the wine, and mix it with the eggs and cheese, pour the mixture into a flameproof casserole and put it to cook immediately, but you do not leave it for an instant: you stir ceaselessly until you have a homogenous cream, and you serve it sizzling in the recipient in which it has cooked.'

Well, that is the authentic recipe. One of them anyhow. At a period when I kept house in France and could lay hands on the Gruyère of the Comté I used on occasion to cook a similar version. When it comes off it is a very fine dish indeed. But in addition to great patience it does demand a little advance planning; the business of adding the already garlic-flavoured and cooked but cooled wine to the cheese and eggs and putting the whole mixture together into the cooking pot is important. Then, as M. Dupin stresses more than once in his book, all types of genuine Gruyère cheese should be cut into little pieces for cooking, never on any account grated, a procedure which causes it to form sticky masses rather than the long creamy threads which constitute one of its essential characteristics – a characteristic considered especially important when it comes to the *soupe au fromage* of the eastern French provinces, that same soup which transmogrified into the onion soup of the Paris all-night bistros has now found its way into packets labelled *la soupe au fromage instantanée*. (Ingredients: dehydrated Gruyère cheese, potato-starch, spices, salt.) Which would seem to reduce the whole matter of authenticity to the level of farce. If the word Gruyère on the packet can induce people to buy the product in question (I have tasted it; and it seems only fair to say that of its kind it is of a matchless ignobility) then it becomes clear that it is a too innocent belief in authenticity and the efficacy of the ancient formula which has made us such easy victims of the purveyors of the farmyard-fresh Surrey chicken from the battery house, the mountain-brook trout from the breeding tank, via the deep-freeze, the hedgerow-ripened blackberry pie-filling out of the cardboard box.

When the original ingredients of a dish become obsolete or so debased as to be unrecognizable radical change is preferable to make-believe replacements. By accepting changes and variations on the ancient recipes we can achieve a different kind of authenticity, one which has at least some semblance of reality. In the matter of genuine Gruyère, for example, a great deal sold in this country turns out, on close inspection, to be German Emmental. This is a cheese which is expensive, smells of drains – it is marketed in wrapped wedges so you do not find this out until you get it home – and in consistence is more suitable for mending tyres than for the cooking pot. (One longs for the Germans to give up trying to make facsimiles of other people's cheeses. They are terrible duffers at it. It is, I am told, German settlers in County Wexford who are responsible for the Irish Brie called St Edi now being peddled in this country; the assault of its ammoniac smell brought back to me with terrible force a twenty-two-year-old memory of the Camembert of war-time Egypt which, I now realize, could have been none other than the handiwork of a German fifth column active in Alexandria.)

Among newly-invented cheese dishes which seem to me worth a trial are a French Welsh Rabbit and an Anglo-Irish fondue. These recipes are being currently hawked around by, respectively, the publicity agents of Guinness and of the Trappist monks who own the Port-du-Salut cheese factory in North-Western France. Recipes disseminated by such bodies – one does appreciate that in the case of the Trappists a spokesman is essential – are bound to be suspect, but not all the public relations cookery experts are as cruelly anti-humanitarian as the lady who publicized the traditional Welsh trifle for St David's Day to be made with one tin of fruit salad and one packet of Birds Pineapple Instant Whip, a leek confected from angelica, piped cream, cocoa powder and desiccated coconut adding the finishing festive touches. Insults so ferocious as the recipe for Sussex Layer Pancakes – why pick on Sussex? Was it directed at the restaurants of Chichester or Glyndebourne? – calling for two 16-oz. cans of spaghetti in tomato sauce, 9 oz. of plain flour and 6 oz. of shredded suet (put about by the Atora Suet Bureau) are also uncommon.

Even the recipe for George Washington's mother's gingerbread allegedly found 'in an old worn cookery book' dated 1784, of which the first item on the list of ingredients is ½ cup of margarine, could be said to be honest in the sense that it is candidly admitted that margarine is what is actually now used in the kitchens at Claverton Manor, the American Museum near Bath where both the ginger-bread and the leaflet giving the recipe are purveyed to the public. After all, one feels, Mrs Washington was surely a thrifty housewife; had the invention of margarine occurred a century sooner than it did, no doubt she would have taken advantage of the development. And we must not forget that it is to a Public Relations expert that we owe the invention of traditional Irish coffee laced with Irish whiskey, which nobody will deny is a very great improvement on Irish coffee *tout court*.

I have not, by the way, yet tried the Guinness fondue recipe, but I do know from past experience that stout is an excellent and enriching alternative to wine for a number of meat and game dishes. Why not also for cheese?

CHEESE AND GUINNESS FONDUE (makes one pint)

2 lb. grated Cheddar cheese; ½ pint Guinness (good measure); 6–8 teaspoons Worcestershire Sauce; salt; pepper; Cayenne pepper; 1 level tablespoon cornflour.

Put grated cheese into a 7-inch fondue dish or enamelled iron casserole and melt gently, stirring continuously. Add remaining ingredients and stir until the fondue thickens slightly.

For dipping use chunks of French bread or toast.

Note

If a normal 7-inch or bigger dish is used, one pint of fondue is the right quantity. For half the quantity, a smaller dish must be used.

Canadian Black Diamond Cheddar (the straightforward one, not the wine-cured variety) is without question by far the best Cheddar now generally available to the British public. There is also the point that it has in fact so excellent a flavour that I doubt if a fondue made with it would need 6 to 8 teaspoons (which is an awful lot) of Worcestershire sauce. It might even not need the Guinness. Then there is the matter of the French Cheddar (not to be confused with an unidentified English cheese known for generations to the French public as Chester) now being made down at Castres in the Tarn department of the Languedoc. I do not know if Guinness is imported by the French on anything like the scale on which Scotch whisky pours into France. If not, this recipe, plus French Cheddar – by no means an uninteresting cheese (French Dairy Farmers Ltd, 17 Bentinck Street, w.1 are importing it into England) – should help; and a new French regional dish will have come into being.

For that matter, why not a Scottish fondue made with the Orkney Cheddar distributed under the auspices of the North of Scotland Milk Marketing Board? For eating purposes Orkney Cheddar is pretty soapy and bears no resemblance whatever to a cheese actually brought from the Orkneys which I once tasted in the house of Edinburgh friends of mine. Still, in the cooking pot, and enlivened let's say with a dash of Cutty Sark or Christopher's Finest Old Scotch, I don't see why it shouldn't make out pretty well.

As for Welsh Rabbit, over the years it seems to have evolved from primitive toasted cheese into a dish not all that different from the fondues of France and Switzerland. An authentic Welsh version was, according to Lady Llanover's *Good Cookery* (1867) once upon a time made with ewe's milk cheese (Lady Llanover lived in Monmouthshire for about ninety years), now presumably obsolete. Double Gloucester and new Lancashire are the more conventionally accepted cheeses – vintages which your dairyman *can* usually supply – for toasting or for English Welsh Rabbit.

FRENCH WELSH RABBIT

(Recipe by the Comtesse Mapie de Toulouse-Lautrec for a leaflet publicizing Port-Salut cheese.)

'For 2 people: 2 large slices of bread, 4 oz. of Port-Salut, 1 large glass of beer, ½ a glass of kirsch, 2 oz. of butter, Cayenne pepper.

'Melt the butter in a frying pan and put the bread slices in it so that they are golden coloured on both sides. In a large saucepan, pour the beer that you warm for 5 minutes. Then add the Port-Salut, minced as thinly as possible, the kirsch and a pinch of Cayenne pepper. Stir with a wooden spoon until the cheese is quite melted. Put the bread slices in an oven dish, buttered beforehand, cover them with cheese cream and leave in the oven to brown.'

A mixture of beer and kirsch? H'm. Not quite as Cambrian as the Pineapple Instant Whip. But perhaps the Comtesse's fried bread is better than the toast which traditionally accompanies Welsh Rabbit. And, in passing, it is worth noting that French (I have not tried the Danish imitation) Port-Salut makes an excellent cooking cheese with a low melting point, which means that it turns creamy but not rubbery. The other day I put it into a fondue made according to the Franche-Comté method. It gave the dish a very subtle flavour, that Port-Salut. There is, of course, no temptation to take the quick way out by grating it. You can't grate Port-Salut. And myself, I do not find the creamy threads formed by melting Gruyère all that beguiling. In my experience creamy threads are all too often elastic bands with knots in.

Dutch Gouda, by the way, makes just as good Welsh Rabbit as French Port-Salut; and there is always Caerphilly from Somerset, not to mention the Caerphilly (it may, I think, have now vanished) made by Irish nuns – not I fancy in this case German parachutists. It was a delicious cheese, as good as the true Glamorgan Caerphilly used to be.

Wine and Food, Summer 1964

Having Crossed the Channel

THE WORK OF X. MARCEL BOULESTIN

A refugee from the Colette-Willy ménage of the early nineteen hundreds, from what promised to be a long stint of sterile work as Willy's secretary and as yet another among the throng of that extraordinary man's unacknowledged collaborators, the young Marcel Boulestin fled the malicious gossip, the dramas and scandals in which these two now legendary figures were for ever involving each other and their friends. Avoiding the recriminations which he knew would ensue should he inform Willy of his decision, Boulestin slipped away from Paris while his employer was absent. Thenceforth he made his life in England.

As a result of two previous visits to London, Boulestin had already gone through a period of serious anglomania which extended even to our food, and an attempt to make his father's household in Poitiers appreciate the beauty of mint sauce with mutton, the fascination of Sir Kenelm Digby's Stuart recipes for hydromel and mead, and the anglo-oriental romance of curry as served at Romano's. In Paris he bought mince pies and English marmalade, took Colette to tea at the British Dairy, shared a blazing plum pudding with her at Christmas, drank whisky instead of wine at a dinner party at Fouquet's, spent two summer holidays in Dieppe because it was so English, and there made friends with Walter Sickert, William Nicholson, Reggie Turner, Ada Leverson, Marie Tempest and Max Beerbohm. As a result he did a French translation of *The Happy Hypocrite* which was published in 1904 by the *Mercure de France*, illustrated with a caricature of Boulestin by Max (Boulestin had some difficulty in convincing the *Mercure*'s editor that Max Beerbohm actually existed and was not an invention of his own).

At the time of the Beerbohm translation Boulestin was already a writer and journalist of some experience. Before his Colette-Willy period he had contributed a weekly column of musical criticism to a

Marcel Boulestin, by Gromaire, London, 1925, reproduced in Myself, My
Two Countries

Bordeaux newspaper. Willy was an astute talent-spotter. The young men who made up his troupe of ghosts were seldom nonentities. I have been told by Mr Gerald Hamilton that Boulestin's novel called *Les Fréquentations de Maurice*, published about 1910, is highly entertaining. In France the book had quite a *succès de scandale*. Dealing with the life of a gigolo it was considered altogether too fast for the English public.

It was not until after the 1914 war and nearly five years with the French army – although domiciled in England for some thirty years he never at any time entertained the idea of becoming a naturalized British subject, considering it highly improper for a Frenchman to renounce his country – and following the failure of his London decorating business, which before the war had been successful, that Boulestin turned to cookery writing.

In the first years of the twenties Boulestin had been dabbling, in a small way, in picture dealing, starting off promisingly with a Modigliani bought in Paris for £12 and sold in London for £90. Returning to interior decorating he imported French wallpapers and fabrics designed by Poiret and Dufy. He found his English customers unready for such innovations. Before long he was broke. During the course of negotiating the sale of some etchings by his friend J. E. Laboureur to Byard, a director of Heinemann's, Boulestin asked if a cookery book would be of any interest at that moment. It would, said Byard. On the spot a contract was produced and signed. An advance of £10 was paid over.

Boulestin's writing still seems so fresh and original that it comes as a shock to realize that these happenings occurred over forty years ago, and that his first cookery book *Simple French Cooking for English Homes* appeared in 1923. On the plain white jacket of the little book, and as a frontispiece, was a design, enticing, fresh and lively, by Laboureur. The book, priced at 5s., was reprinted in September of the same year, again in 1924, 1925, 1928, 1930 and 1933. In the meantime Boulestin had written cookery articles for the *Daily Express*, the *Morning Post*, *Vogue*, the *Manchester Guardian* and the *Spectator*; in February 1925 *A Second Helping* was published, also with a Laboureur jacket and frontispiece. It was uncommon in those days, and still is, for publishers to commission artists of such quality to illustrate cookery books, and a little of the success of Boulestin's early books must be acknowledged to his publishers who, no doubt under the guidance of their author, produced them in so appropriate a form, in large type, on thick paper: chunky, easy little books to handle, attractively bound. (To the general reader such matters may appear trifling. From the point of view of a book being lastingly used and loved the effect of the rightness and appropriateness as a whole is enormous.)

A Second Helping is perhaps the least successful of Boulestin's books. A certain proportion of 'amusing' recipes and chic asides 'get your rabbits sent from Dartmoor' give it a distinct sniff of the fashion-magazine hostess style. Later the same year appeared, for 3s. 6d., *The Conduct of the Kitchen*. In that year also the first Boulestin restaurant was opened in Leicester Square. Again, artists and innovators in the decorating business collaborated with Boulestin. Allan Walton, the enlightened owner of a prosperous textile firm in the Midlands, produced a friend who produced the capital for the restaurant, and supplied also the fabrics (he was employing artists of the stature of Cedric Morris, Vanessa Bell and Duncan Grant to design for him) with which the restaurant was furnished.

In 1930 Boulestin collaborated with Jason Hill on *Herbs, Salads and Seasonings*, illustrated with unique grace by Cedric Morris. In 1931 came *What Shall We Have Today?* (5s. and in paper covers 3s.), the most popular of all the Boulestin books, containing a large selection of recipes plus a sample luncheon and dinner menu for each month of the year. In 1932, in collaboration with Robin Adair, appeared three little volumes at 2s. each, dealing with *Savouries and Hors-d'Œuvre, Eggs* and *Potatoes*. Reprinted by Heinemann in 1956, these little books are still (or were last year) available at 2s. 6d. each. The grotesquely inappropriate and anti-food coloured board covers have presumably hampered their sales even at what is today a give-away price.

In 1934 came *Having Crossed the Channel*, a lighthearted record of a journey through the Vendée, the Landes, the Bordelais, a pilgrimage back to his native Périgord and into his youth, a drive across central France, down to the coast, into Italy and Southern Germany and back via Belgium and Holland. This little nugget of a book (but all Boulestin books are nuggets) contains some of Boulestin's best writing about his own province and about the food of obscure country inns of a type now all but vanished. In this book also are the best illustrations Laboureur ever did for Boulestin, one being of the archetype of the French small-town restaurant, the wide, shuttered window, the tree in a tub on the pavement, the façade which has not changed and which still promises decent and genuine country cooking at modest prices. That you may find neither when you get inside is another matter. The evocation is there.

In 1935 Boulestin's *Evening Standard Book of Menus* was published by Heinemann. This book is in its way a *tour de force*. It contains a luncheon and dinner menu for every day of the year, plus every relevant recipe. It was directed at an audience to which a man of lesser wit and native grace might have been tempted to talk down (it has to be remembered that by this time Boulestin and his restaurant had already become almost legendary) but this was a trap into which he was at the same time too subtle and too naturally courteous to fall. What he produced was a volume for which he really should have kept his title *The Conduct of the Kitchen* – a title borrowed incidentally from Meredith – because that was just what the book of menus was about: the logical and orderly conduct of a kitchen as related to daily life and seen not through the medium of a few isolated menus for special occasions, but as part of the natural order of everyday living. Given time, Boulestin could perhaps with his book of menus have opened the door to organized cooking for thousands of young women who in the thirties were finding themselves on their own in flats and bed-sitting rooms knowing nothing more about how to make a meal than that it ought to taste nice and should not be a bore. As things turned out, time was something not just then at our disposal. Very soon we were to be concerned with matters less peaceful than the conduct of our kitchens.

In the summer of 1939 Boulestin left as usual to spend his holidays in the house he had built for himself in the Landes. Caught by the outbreak of war he and Robin Adair lingered, not knowing what to do. Boulestin's services, offered to the British Ministry of Food and to the Army Quartermaster General, were refused. When France fell Adair was too ill to flee and Boulestin of course stayed with him. Arrested and interned by the Germans, Adair was eventually moved from Bayonne to Fresne. Boulestin went to live in occupied Paris to be near his friend. There, on 22nd September 1943, he died, aged, so Adair tells us, sixty-five.

*

M. André Simon, Boulestin's compatriot and contemporary, writing two years ago of Boulestin's rule that all wines young or old, red or white must be served in a decanter, recorded that 'he never liked the shape and colour of wine bottles standing on the table: they were of the greatest use, of course, but their right place was the cellar or pantry'. 'He was a born artist,' says M. Simon of Boulestin, 'and he was right.'

*

Quotation is my only means of conveying something of that artistry, of the essence of Boulestin's writing, of his intelligence, sense and taste, of his ease of style, un-scolding, un-pompous, un-sarcastic, ineffusive, and to so high a degree inspiriting and creative.

The handful of extracts, words of kitchen advice, recipes, menus, and descriptive passages I have chosen to quote are none of them to be found in *The Best of Boulestin*, the American-selected anthology published in England by Heinemann in 1952 and still available at 21s. This volume does indeed contain many of Boulestin's best recipes, but not one single one of the delicious menus in the composition of which he excelled; and it was a mistake for the editors to suppose that they understood French syntax better than their author. Boulestin was no illiterate peasant: when he called a recipe *sauce moutarde* he did so because that is correct French. There was no call to make him look like an Anglo-Saxon writing in schoolboy French by altering it to *sauce de moutarde*. For that matter little seems to have been gained by the translation of *gâteau petit duc* into Little Duke Cake and *crêpes normandes* into French pancakes Normande. At any rate anybody who buys *The Best of Boulestin* should be warned to pay no attention to the announcement on the jacket which informs us that the book contains a selection of the best recipes of a 'World-Famous Chef'. A chef in the professional sense of the word is just exactly what Boulestin was not and certainly did not pretend to be. The implications of that piece of grandiloquence would not have been at all to his taste, as anyone can see from reading a paragraph or two of any of his books. It would be a mistake for anyone to infer that Boulestin was a man who had no more sense than to attempt amateur cooking in his own restaurant. He hired an experienced French chef (his name was Bigorre. He came from Paillard's in Paris), but not one who would substitute an arid classicism for personal taste and character in his cooking. Boulestin was not out to emulate Escoffier. He was creating something new, as much in his restaurant as in his cookery writing. In his very first book his admonitions about the indiscriminate use of stock, even of fine stock, were news, and good news:

– 167 –

Do not spoil the special taste of the gravy obtained in the roasting of beef, veal, mutton or pork by adding to it the classical stock which gives to all meats the same deplorable taste of soup. It is obvious that you cannot out of a joint get the sauceboat full which usually appears on the table.

Simple French Cooking for English Homes

The chief thing to remember is that all these soups – unless otherwise specified – must be made with plain water. When made with the addition of stock they lose all character and cease to be what they were intended to be. The fresh pleasant taste is lost owing to the addition of meat stock, and the value of the soup from an economical point of view is also lost.

What Shall We Have Today?

That commodities such as simple sardine or anchovy butter which we had hitherto regarded as sandwich fillings, egg dishes which belonged to the breakfast table, the bed-sitting room or the night club, and little hot dishes which were ordinary English family supper savouries were valuable resources which could be quite differently deployed and offered as party dishes were ideas which had occurred to few people in pre-Boulestin days:

SARDINE BUTTER

'Take a tin of sardines, carefully remove the skins and bones and pound well. Add same quantity of butter, salt and pepper. Mix thoroughly so that it becomes a smooth paste. Serve very cold. Quite ordinary sardines will do for this.'

The Evening Standard Book of Menus

Boulestin's idea was that while you were at it you made – as in a great many of his recipes – enough of this mixture (he treats smoked cod's roe and anchovy fillets in precisely the same manner) for two meals: you serve it as a first course, with toast, for two very differently composed lunches. On a Friday in January it is followed by Irish stew and cheese (not for me, that menu, but Boulestin had something for everybody), on Saturday by cold ham and pressed beef, a hot purée of leeks with croûtons as a separate course, and fruit. On an August Thursday he thinks of it again. It precedes a sauté of liver and bacon, potato croquettes and fruit salad. On the Saturday it is followed by a Spanish omelette, cheese and fruit. And bless him, it is delicious, his sardine butter, and marvellously cheap and quick. You allow, or at any rate, I allow, an ounce of butter per Portuguese sardine. Pack the paste into a little terrine, chill it – and you will never again feel it necessary to go to the delicatessen for bought liver pâté or any such sub-standard hors d'œuvre.

From the same book come these two menus for September luncheons:

Salad of Tunny Fish and Celery
Risotto Milanaise
Fruit

———

Scrambled Eggs with Haddock
Vegetable Salad
Creamed Rice.

In those days only Boulestin thought of actually inviting people to lunch to eat scrambled eggs. It goes without saying that he did not serve scrambled eggs *with* smoked haddock, he cooked the haddock first, flaked it, and mixed it with the beaten eggs before cooking them. He added a little cream to the finished scrambled eggs and put fried croûtons round them. In January the same breakfast dish appears as a first course before the cold turkey and salad, the meal to be ended with English toasted cheese.

BRAISED VEAL WITH CARROTS

'Take a good piece of veal, about three pounds in weight, brown it both sides in butter. Put in a fireproof dish eight carrots cut in round pieces, about half an inch thick, half a dozen small onions, parsley, salt and pepper and a rasher of bacon cut in small pieces, add a tablespoon of water, cover the dish and cook on a slow fire for about three and a half hours. Shake the dish occasionally, but do not remove the lid.'

The Conduct of the Kitchen

This recipe must have been one of Boulestin's favourites. It appears over and over again in his books. His omission of detail was deliberate. It is impossible, he was in the habit of saying, to give precise recipes. And certainly precision – unless carried to the ultimate degree, as in Madame Saint-Ange's *Livre de Cuisine*[1] or Julia Child's *Mastering the Art of French Cooking*[2] – can be more misleading than vagueness. Boulestin was impatient of written detail. When he does specify precise quantities or times he is often

1. Flammarion 1927: an English translation of this marvellous cookery book was planned ca. 1965 but did not come to fruition.
2. Cassell, London, 1963, Knopf, New York, 1961.

wrong. His special gift was to get us on the move, send us out to the butcher to buy that good piece of veal, into the kitchen to discover how delicate is the combination of veal, carrots, little onions, a scrap of bacon, seasonings and butter all so slowly and carefully amalgamated – and all done with butter and water alone. Three and a half hours for a three-pound piece of veal – and on top of the stove too – is an awful long time. At minimum heat and in a heavy well-closed pot stood on the floor of the oven rather than on a shelf, the timing would be however just about right. Most of us know enough about absentee cooking these days to work out such details for ourselves. Those who do not would I think be well advised to use Boulestin recipes in conjunction with a fully detailed work such as one of those mentioned. Where Boulestin never falters or misleads is in the sureness of his taste and the sobriety of his ingredients even when his recipes are new inventions. Anglophile he may have been. Not so much as he thought he was. His recipes could never be mistaken for anything but the recipes of an educated Frenchman.

It was, I think, Boulestin who introduced the English public to the Basque *pipérade*. A recipe for it or a description of this beguiling dish of peppers, onions, tomatoes and eggs appears in every one of his books, even down to the booklet commissioned from him by the Romary biscuit firm and which sold for sixpence. The briefest *pipérade* recipe is the one recorded in *Having Crossed the Channel* as it was blurted out by a tipsy smuggler one morning in a Basque inn on the Bidassoa. '*Vous faîtes cuire vos piments et vos tomates et vous . . . foutez vos œufs dedans.*' (This was later translated by Adair as 'shove in your eggs'.)

In the same little volume Boulestin gives us an explanation of the old-fashioned French custom of serving a vegetable before the roast – an explanation which contains also some sound gastronomic advice:

We had at Aurillac, where we avoided the two main hotels, a delicious meal in a quite ordinary inn full of market people. Trout was on the menu, done in a rather unusual way, and a cabbage which was almost a revelation, firm, white, and beautifully seasoned; the meat was well-flavoured and tender, and the cheese perfection.

. . . There they still serve the vegetable course before the roast. This is constantly done, especially in small, old-fashioned towns; but the foreigner must not think that this is provincial lack of knowledge.

It is simply due to the fact that these little hotels have remained faithful to habits dating from 1840 or so. In those days dinners were much longer, and there was always an entrée and a roast. It became the rule to serve the vegetable – a fairly plain dish – as a pleasant change after the usually rich taste of the entrée, as a kind of diversion after the sauce, and, so to speak, to clean the palate for the roast to come, the roast being always (it still is) accompanied by a green salad.

Having Crossed the Channel[1]

As can be seen even from these brief extracts Boulestin did not by any means invariably advocate traditional French bourgeois or regional cooking. He was nothing if not open-minded, adapting English ingredients to his own purposes and forever exercising his gift for fantasy. A dish he calls Maltese curry – an unlikely and most interesting mixture of onions, tomatoes and fruit with eggs mixed in at the end of the cooking, rather in the *pipérade* manner – was another recipe he repeated in several of his books. It is given in *The Best of Boulestin* and was a feature of his restaurant menu. Another of his favourites seems to have been a tomato jam; this he uses for a sweet called Peaches Barbara with cream and kirschwasser and pistachio nuts. One may and one does read plenty of freakish recipes in cookery books. To dismiss them out of hand is a sign either of defective knowledge or lack of imagination on the reader's part or of the author's incapacity to convince. In the case of writers whose taste is to be trusted the very oddness of a recipe often means that here is something worth special investigation. It turns out that the tomato jam has great finesse of flavour and emerges as a most beautiful translucent cornelian-red preserve, delicious for a jam served in the French manner as a sweet with plain cream or fresh cream cheese. Fantasies these little dishes may be. Again we see that in their subtlety and the manner in which they are presented they are still French fantasies.

One indication of the effect produced by Boulestin's recipes is that whenever a second-hand copy of one of his books turns up – and that is not often – one finds it scarred with pencil marks against the recipes which have been cooked by the previous owner and often, slipped somewhere among the pages, a list of dishes noted for future trial. One I commend to your attention is a *mousse de laitues*, a kind of soufflé of cooked lettuces, given in *The Finer Cooking* and reproduced in *The Best of Boulestin*. Another is a pickled ox-tongue, plain-boiled and served hot with a very smooth purée of white turnips enriched with butter and slices of hard-boiled egg. This was one of the original and unique specialities of the Boulestin

1. Heinemann, 1937.

restaurant. The recipe which, under the name of *langue savoyarde* again appears in several of his books, is to be found in *The Best of Boulestin*. So is the formula for the famous cheese soufflé which so wonderfully conceals melting whole poached eggs, an old dish of French cookery and one served by Boulestin at a luncheon given at his restaurant to celebrate the publication by Cassells on 26 September 1936, of the autobiography entitled *Myself, My Two Countries*. An uncommonly good lunch it must have been that day. The wine was a Cheval Blanc 1925 and the sole liqueur was Armagnac. A modest show as press luncheons given by famous restaurateurs go. So was the luncheon given at Boulestin's by a party of American journalists in honour of M. Aristide Briand. Somehow Boulestin contrived to persuade these gentlemen that the great statesman, surfeited with political banquets and pompous food, would appreciate something simple and at least one dish and one wine from his native Nantais country. Where today, one wonders, would a visiting celebrity be allowed so unceremonial a ceremonial meal, and one with so much character? Less than perfect, such a meal could indeed be a memorable flop. That Boulestin recorded the menu and the occasion indicates, one deduces, that it was no such thing:

Hors d'Œuvre
Omelette au crabe
Chou farçi
Fromages et Fruits
Vins:
Muscadet 1928
Château Gruaud Larose 1923

The Finer Cooking[1]

At the premises in Southampton Street, Covent Garden, to which the Boulestin Restaurant moved from Leicester Square there exists still today an establishment which bears Boulestin's name. The Dufy panels and some of the original decorations still exist. Its founder, was, I think, the first amateur to venture on a London restaurant and certainly the only one to acquire an international reputation for his food. In *Ease and Endurance*,[2] the continuation of the autobiography which Boulestin wrote in French under the title of *A Londres Naguère* and which was published after his death in a somewhat harum-scarum translation by Robin Adair (at one point

1. Cassells.
2. Home and Van Thal, 1948.

MENU. *Galanis*

Soufflé aux Oeufs

·:·

Entrecôte Maître d'Hôtel
Pommes Frites

·:·

Entremet
Crêpes Verlaine

Cheval blanc 1925
Armagnac

Boulestin
Restaurant
Français
London
26.9.36

*A 1936 menu for the Boulestin restaurant in London, in the possession of
the author*

Adair has Boulestin exploring the Cecil Hotel in a taxi), he tells how the place was crammed night after night with customers from the Savoy, Ritz and Carlton belt, stage stars, artists, writers, royalty and High Bohemia. His prices were reputed to be the highest in London. And still the restaurant did not pay. Boulestin had found, like so many before and since, that in England the price of perfection is too high. During most of the fourteen years that he was running his restaurant he found it necessary to supplement his earnings by articles, books – heaven knows how he found the time to write them – cookery classes, lectures and the television demonstrations which were the first of their kind.

*

One final passage from *Myself, My Two Countries* vividly evokes the influences which formed Boulestin's tastes in food and implanted in him that feeling for the authenticity which alone is true luxury. Here he remembers the kitchen quarters of his grandmother's house at St Aulaye in the Périgord:

> In the store room next to the kitchen were a long table and shelves always covered with all sorts of provisions; large earthenware jars full of *confits* of pork and goose, a small barrel where vinegar slowly matured, a bowl where honey oozed out of the comb, jams, preserves of sorrel and of tomatoes, and odd bottles with grapes and cherries marinating in brandy; next to the table a weighing machine on which I used to stand at regular intervals; sacks of haricot beans, of potatoes; eggs, each one carefully dated in pencil.
>
> And there were the baskets of fruit, perfect small melons, late plums, under-ripe medlars waiting to soften, peaches, pears hollowed out by a bird or a wasp, figs that had fallen of their own accord, all the fruits of September naturally ripe and sometimes still warm from the sun. Everything in profusion. It is no doubt the remembrance of these early days which makes me despise and dislike all primeurs, the fruit artificially grown, gathered too early and expensively sent, wrapped in cotton wool, to 'smart' restaurants.
>
> The garden could hardly be called a garden; it was large, wild and not too well kept. There were fruit trees amongst the flowers, here a pear tree, there a currant bush, so that one could either smell a rose, crush a verbena, or eat a fruit; there were borders of box, but also of sorrel and chibol; and the stiff battalion of leeks, shallots, and garlic, the delicate pale-green foliage of the carrot, the aggressive steel-grey leaves of the artichokes, the rows of lettuce which always ran to seed too quickly.

Wine and Food, Spring 1965

Pomiane, Master of the Unsacrosanct

'Art demands an impeccable technique; science a little understanding.' Today the mention of art in connection with cookery is taken for pretention. Science and cookery make a combination even more suspect. Because he was a scientist by profession, making no claims to being an artist, Docteur de Pomiane's observation was a statement of belief, made in all humility. Vainglory is totally missing from de Pomiane's work. He knew that the attainment of impeccable technique meant a lifetime – in de Pomiane's case an exceptionally long one – of experiment and discipline. Out of it all he appears to have extracted, and given, an uncommon amount of pleasure.

Docteur Edouard de Pomiane's real name was Edouard Pozerski. He was of purely Polish origin, the son of emigrés who had fled Poland and settled in Paris after the Revolution of 1863. Born and brought up in Montmartre, he was educated at the Ecole Polonaise – an establishment described by Henri Babinski, another celebrated Franco-Polish cookery writer, as one of ferocious austerity – and subsequently at the Lycée Condorcet. Pomiane chose for his career the study of biology, specialising in food chemistry and dietetics. Before long he had invented a new science called Gastrotechnology, which he defined simply as the scientific explanation of accepted principles of cookery. For a half-century – interrupted only by his war service from 1914 to 1918 – de Pomiane also made cookery and cookery writing his hobby and second profession. After his retirement from the Institut Pasteur, where he lectured for some 50 years, he devoted himself entirely to his cookery studies. He was 89 when he died in January 1964.

De Pomiane's output was immense – some dozen cookery books, countless scores of articles, broadcasts, lectures. In France his books were best-sellers; among French cookery writers his place is one very much apart.

Many before him had attempted to explain cookery in scientific terms and had succeeded only in turning both science and cookery into the deadliest of bores.

De Pomiane was the first writer to propound such happenings as the fusion of egg yolks and olive oil in a mayonnaise, the sizzling of a potato chip when plunged into fat for deep-frying, in language so straightforward, so graphic, that even the least scientifically minded could grasp the principles instead of simply learning the rules. In cooking, the possibility of muffing a dish is always with us. Nobody can eliminate that. What de Pomiane did by explaining the cause, was to banish the *fear* of failure.

Adored by his public and his pupils, feared by the phoney, derided by the reactionary, de Pomiane's irreverent attitude to established tradition, his independence of mind backed up by scientific training, earned him the reputation of being something of a Candide, a provocative rebel disturbing the grave conclaves of French gastronomes, questioning the holy rites of the 'white-vestured officiating priests' of classical French cookery. It was understandable that not all his colleagues appreciated de Pomiane's particular brand of irony:

'As to the fish, everyone agrees that it must be served between the soup and the meat. The sacred position of the fish before the meat course implies that one must eat fish *and* meat. Now such a meal, as any dietician will tell you, is far too rich in nitrogenous substances, since fish has just as much assimilable albumen as meat, and contains a great deal more phosphorus . . .' Good for Dr de Pomiane. Too bad for us that so few of his readers – or listeners – paid attention to his liberating words.

It does, on any count, seem extraordinary that thirty years after de Pomiane's heyday, the dispiriting progress from soup to fish, from fish to meat and on, remorselessly on, to salad, cheese, a piece of pastry, a crème caramel or an ice cream, still constitutes the standard menu throughout the entire French-influenced world of hotels and catering establishments.

Reading some of de Pomiane's neat menus (from *365 Menus, 365 Recettes*, Albin Michel 1938) it is so easy to see how little effort is required to transform the dull, overcharged, stereotyped meal into one with a fresh emphasis and a proper balance:

Tomates à la crème
Côtelettes de porc
Purée de farine de marrons
Salade de mâche à la betterave
Poires

An unambitious enough menu – and what a delicious surprise it would be to encounter such a meal at any one of those country town

Edouard de Pomiane, courtesy of Bruno Cassirer (Publishers) Ltd

Hôtels des Voyageurs, du Commerce, du Lion d'Or, to which my own business affairs in France now take me. In these establishments, where one stays because there is no choice, the food is of a mediocrity, a predictability redeemed for me only by the good bread, the fresh eggs in the omelettes, the still relatively civilised presentation – which in Paris is becoming rare – the soup brought to table in a tureen, the hors d'œuvre on the familiar, plain little white dishes, the salad in a simple glass bowl. If it all tasted as beguiling as it looks, every dish would be a feast. Two courses out of the whole menu would be more than enough.

Now that little meal of de Pomiane's is a feast, as a whole entity. It is also a real lesson in how to avoid the obvious without being freakish, how to start with the stimulus of a hot vegetable dish, how to vary the eternal purée of potatoes with your meat (lacking chestnut flour we could try instead a purée of lentils or split peas), how to follow it with a fresh, bright, unexpected salad (that excellent mixture of corn salad and beetroot – how often does one meet with it nowadays?) and since by that time most people would have had enough without embarking on cheese, de Pomiane is brave enough to leave it out. How much harm has that tyrannical maxim of Brillat Savarin's about a meal without cheese done to all our waistlines and our digestions?

For a hot first dish, de Pomiane's recipe for *tomates à la crème* is worth knowing. His method makes tomatoes taste so startingly unlike any other dish of cooked tomatoes that any restaurateur who put it on his menu would, in all probability, soon find it listed in the guide books as a regional speciality. De Pomiane himself said the recipe came from his Polish mother. That would not prevent anyone from calling it what he pleases:

TOMATES À LA CRÈME

'Take six tomatoes. Cut them in halves. In your frying pan melt a lump of butter. Put in the tomatoes, cut side downwards, with a sharply-pointed knife puncturing here and there the rounded sides of the tomatoes. Let them heat for five minutes. Turn them over. Cook them for another ten minutes. Turn them again. The juices run out and spread into the pan. Once more turn the tomatoes cut side upwards. Around them put 80 grammes (3 oz. near enough) of thick cream. Mix it with the juices. As soon as it bubbles, slip the tomatoes and all their sauce on to a hot dish. Serve instantly, very hot.'

The faults of the orthodox menu were by no means the only facet of so-called classic French cooking upon which de Pomiane turned his analytical intelligence. Recipes accepted as great and sacrosanct are not always compatible with sense. Dr de Pomiane's radar eye saw through them: '*Homard à l'américaine* is a cacophony . . . it offends a basic principle of taste.' I rather wish he had gone to work on some of the astonishing things Escoffier and his contemporaries did to fruit. Choice pears masked with chocolate sauce and cream, beautiful fresh peaches smothered in raspberry purée and set around with vanilla ice seem to me offences to nature, let alone to art or basic principles. How very rum that people still write of these inventions with breathless awe.

De Pomiane, however, was a man too civilised, too subtle, to labour his points. He passes speedily from the absurdities of haute cuisine to the shortcomings of folk cookery, and deals a swift right and left to those writers whose reverent genuflections before the glory and wonder of every least piece of peasant cookery-lore make much journalistic cookery writing so tedious. By the simple device of warning his readers to expect the worst, de Pomiane gets his message across. From a village baker-woman of venerable age, he obtains an ancestral recipe for a cherry tart made on a basis of butter-enriched bread dough. He passes on the recipe, modified to suit himself, and carrying with it the characteristically deflating note:

'When you open the oven door you will have a shock. It is not a pretty sight. The edges of the tart are slightly burnt and the top layer of cherries blackened in places . . . It will be received without much enthusiasm for, frankly, it is not too prepossessing.

'Don't be discouraged. Cut the first slice and the juice will run out. Now try it. A surprise. The pastry is neither crisp nor soggy, and just tinged with cherry juice. The cherries have kept all their flavour and the juice is not sticky – just pure cherry juice. They had some good ideas in 1865.'

Of a dish from the Swiss mountains, Dr de Pomiane observes that it is 'a peasant dish, rustic and vigorous. It is not everybody's taste. But one can improve upon it. Let us get to work.' This same recipe provides an instructive example of the way in which Dr de Pomiane thinks we should go to work improving a primitive dish to our own taste while preserving its character intact. Enthusiastic beginners might add olives, parsley, red peppers. Dr Pomiane is scarcely that simple. The school-trained professional might be tempted to superimpose cream, wine, mushrooms, upon his rough and rustic dish. That is not de Pomiane's way. His way is the way of the artist; of the man who can add one sure touch, one only, and thereby create an effect of the pre-ordained, the inevitable, the entirely right and proper:

TRANCHES AU FROMAGE

'Black bread – a huge slice weighing 5 to 7 oz., French mustard, 8 oz. Gruyère.

'The slice of bread should be as big as a dessert plate and nearly 1 inch thick. Spread it with a layer of French mustard and cover the whole surface of the bread with strips of cheese about ½ in. thick. Put the slice of bread on a fireproof dish and under the grill. The cheese softens and turns golden brown. Just before it begins to run, remove the dish and carry it to the table. Sprinkle it with salt and pepper. Cut the slice in four and put it on to four hot plates. Pour out the white wine and taste your cheese slice. In the mountains this would seem delicious. Here it is all wrong. But you can put it right. Over each slice pour some melted butter. A mountaineer from the Valais would be shocked, but my friends are enthusiastic, and that is good enough for me.'

This is the best kind of cookery writing. It is courageous, courteous, adult. It is creative in the true sense of that ill-used word, creative because it invites the reader to use his own critical and inventive faculties, sends him out to make discoveries, form his own opinions, observe things for himself, instead of slavishly accepting what the books tell him. That little trick, for example, of spreading the mustard on the bread *underneath* the cheese in de Pomiane's Swiss mountain dish is, for those who notice such things, worth a volume of admonition. So is the little tomato recipe quoted above.

All de Pomiane's vegetable dishes are interesting, freshly observed. He is particularly fond of hot beetroot, recommending it as an accompaniment to roast saddle of hare – a delicious combination. It was especially in his original approach to vegetables and sauces that de Pomiane provoked the criticism of hidebound French professional chefs. Perhaps they were not aware that in this respect de Pomiane was often simply harking back to his Polish origins, thereby refreshing French cookery in the perfectly traditional way.

De Pomiane gives, incidentally, the only way (the non-orthodox way) to braise Belgian endive with success – no water, no blanching, just butter and slow cooking.

The English public knows little of de Pomiane's work and it is missing something of great value. Although his *Cooking in Ten Minutes* (Bruno Cassirer, distributed by Faber, 15s.), a lighthearted treatise on how to make the most of charcuterie or delicatessen food – first published in England in 1948 – has proved a great favourite, there exists a much more representative book, a collection of lectures, radio talks, recipes and articles, called *Cooking with Pomiane* (Bruno Cassirer, distributed by Faber, 18s.). It is most adroitly put together and translated into English cookery usage by Mrs Peggie Benton. Published four years ago and still relatively unknown, the book is modest in appearance and in size, its jacket is the reverse of eyecatching, there are no colour photographs, no packaging. It is just a very good and immensely sane book.

The Sunday Times Colour Supplement, 22 January 1967

✳

Many a time, in the years since the explosion of nouvelle cuisine, *I have wanted to write more of Dr de Pomiane and his unorthodox approach to classic French cookery. I wonder how many of the younger of today's professional chefs realise that the origins of their great rebellion of the late 1960s and early 1970s stem, at least in part, from the days of Dr de Pomiane and his protests against illogical and harmful eating habits. At any rate, some of those rebel chefs must surely know, even if they don't acknowledge as much, that some of their most publicised inventions were not their inventions at all, but were derived, however indirectly, from the Polish and Jewish recipes published or described by Pomiane in his books and radio talks of the 1930s. That* confiture d'oignons, *for instance, for which the recipe appeared in Michel Guérard's* Cuisine Gourmande *and which has since made the* tour du monde *surely derived from Pomiane's dish of sweet-sour onions in which the sweetening elements were sultanas and* pain d'épices, *the spiced honey cake of central Europe, and which Pomiane had in turn borrowed from the*

Jewish cookery of his native Poland.[1] *True, Guérard uses sugar rather than* pain d'épices, *adds red wine, sherry vinegar, and grenadine syrup 'to warm up the purple colour', and suggests that as well as sultanas, prunes or little pieces of dried apricot may be added. Again, Guérard gives a recipe for saddle of hare with hot beetroot which differs only in minor respects from the one Pomiane published two or three times and which I myself used often in the fifties, and eventually quoted, with acknowledgements, in* French Provincial Cooking. *As I mentioned in the* Sunday Times *article, Pomiane was fond of hot beetroot, and used it often, mixing vinegar and cream with it, a very un-French combination, and by no means the only one of his unconventional suggestions in the domain of vegetable cookery to arouse the scorn of reactionaries.*

In the days when Pomiane was writing, chefs did not dream of braising vegetables – lettuces, leeks, Belgian endives, for example – without a preliminary blanching. That rule was immutable, and woe betide anyone who disregarded it. Dr de Pomiane bypassed it, and I adopted his method, particularly his recipe for cooking Belgian endives in butter and entirely without a prior water baptism. That sort of unorthodoxy got one into trouble. I have referred, in my Introduction, to the venerable French chef who in the fifties pursued me and my Sunday Times *cookery articles with a zeal worthy of a Spanish inquisitor. One of his more intemperate outbursts, I recall, concerned a recipe for dipping sliced young fennel bulbs, mushrooms and scallops in batter and deep frying them in oil to make a* fritto misto *in the Italian manner. That idea was already red rag enough to the old gentleman. Worse was my omission of any mention of the essential ordeal by blanching of the vegetables, and of course of the scallops. In those days a French chef simply did not serve vegetables crisp. They had to be soft and woolly. (I have remembered for many years the* patronne *of a restaurant in the little Norman port of Barfleur who refused to cook artichokes for dinner that night – it was then 6.30 p.m. – on the grounds that they required two hours boiling. I'm afraid she meant it.) As for the idea that scallops might be cooked in one minute and no more, that old chef was genuinely outraged by it. There was just one way he, as a man who had risen to eminence in his profession, had learned to do things. It was the classical French way. There was*

1. He had made a study of that cookery, published as *Cuisine Juive, Ghetto Modernes*, Albin Michel, 1929.

*no other. It did not occur to him that there might be. Today's chefs
have very properly outlawed that preliminary blanching which
spelled ruin to so many vegetables – of course there are still those
such as celeriac and turnips which may need it – and one of their
most fiercely held tenets concerns the brief cooking of fish, in
particular of the fragile scallop. Heaven knows it was not before
time that reformation in that respect came about. I hope it has
penetrated the middle and lower échelons of French restaurant
chefs. How many times have I nearly wept at the destruction of
delicate little scallops at the hands of ignorant or insensitive chefs?*

*The uninformed criticism of the narrow-minded, whether it came
from members of the cooking profession or from old-fashioned
gourmets among his own colleagues, did not worry Dr de Pomiane
one jot. His own unorthodox approach extended to his study of
historical cookery and even to his choice of words when describing
an ancient recipe he wanted to revive. That particular trend, now a
flood, was something of a novelty in Pomiane's day. A sauce he
adapted from* Les Dix Livres de Cuisine d'Apicius, *of which a
French translation by the cookery historian Bertrand Guégan
appeared in 1933, providing the starting point of the new trend, was
one containing dates, almonds and a very large amount of chopped
parsley. The way Pomiane chose to convey the necessary quantity to
his listeners – he must have been a compelling radio talker – and
later to his readers was in terms of 'a bunch as large as a bunch of
violets'. Everybody in Paris and indeed in all France knows what a
flower seller's bunch of violets looks like, but whoever heard of such
a cookery direction, let alone of a sauce containing a mixture of
dates and parsley? To the conventional, whether professional cooks
or serious gourmets, this sort of thing was at best perverse and
eccentric, at worst a blasphemous crime committed on the sacred
body politic of* la cuisine française. *To me, and to the hundreds of
ordinary French housewives who listened to his talks and read his
books, his ideas and his attitude to cookery were stimulating and
liberating. Now that we have become accustomed to reading about,
if not to eating, such unconventional combinations of foods as duck*
foie gras *with turnips in a sweet-sour sauce composed of wine
vinegar, sugar, sherry and port, plus the odd 30 grammes of truffles;
paupiettes of crayfish garnished with leaves of Brussels sprouts;
lobster mould with a sauce of carrots and port blended in turn with
a* sauce américaine, *Pomiane's innovations don't sound very auda-
cious. Nobody is surprised by the idea of spirals of black Spanish*

radish, forerunners of the Troisgros serpentins *de légumes, as part of an hors d'œuvre, or lettuce dressed with orange juice as well as oil and vinegar. Turnip salad with capers is no shock today and raw choucroûte salad, an idea Pomiane had picked up in Moscow – buy very fresh choucroûte from the charcutier and stop at the village pump to wash it thoroughly, he told those of his French readers who went in for picnics on canoeing and automobile excursions*[1] *– should be the joy of vegetarians. Even apples filled with honey, spiced with cumin or dried mint and baked in pastry, another adaptation from Apicius, seems timid in comparison with Michel Guérard's* Ali baba, *two fantasy babas made with* 120 *grammes of mixed candied fruits and sultanas to only* 250 *grammes of brioche batter. The cooked babas are hollowed out, filled with confection-ers' custard, sugared,* gratinés *in the oven, chilled in the refrigerator, and ultimately served with a* coulis *of raspberries or caramelised peaches. Altogether more of a Second Empire kind of guzzle than a Roman treat, that invention.*

A long time ago, in 1956, *I published a little review of a new edition of Pomiane's delightful and much loved* Cooking in Ten Minutes *in my* Sunday Times *cookery column. He wrote me a touching letter of thanks. 'J'ai été très heureux d'avoir été compris par une si aimable Anglaise', he said, and ended 'if you were French I should give you a kiss. But I believe in England that is not done'. If I have really understood Dr de Pomiane aright, I fancy that while an extravaganza such as Maître Guérard's* Ali Baba *would not have met with his unqualified acclaim, with many of the nouvelle cuisine innovations he would surely have been in sympathy. I think he would have been amused rather than otherwise at finding his own dishes reappearing as specialities of the starry restaurants of the* 1970s, *and pleased that reforms in the matter of lighter meals and more logical sauce and vegetable cookery which he had preached in the* 1930s *have at last been put into practise. If there are lapses, obsessions, aberrations – and few would deny that there are – in the practise of the new style chefs, well, Pomiane was a man with a sense of humour and without a sense of self-importance. He would have smiled and said those are the foibles of innovators, they must be excused, and you are not after all obliged to mop up all those pools of* beurre blanc *which appear on your plate in such quantity. Nobody forces you to consume the equivalent of half a dozen eggs*

---

1. *La Cuisine en plein air,* 1934.

at one meal, but it is very easy to do so, so if you have eaten a mousseline *of scallops, red mullet, and* écrevisses *floating in a lake of* sabayon *sauce, then do not follow it with a honey ice cream or one of those* ali baba *affairs nor with a peach charlotte containing five egg yolks, but rather with a* tarte fine chaude aux pommes acidulées, *which is nothing more outlandish or richer than an old-fashioned apple tart made on a base of puff pastry.*[1] *Come to think of it, myself I would just as soon have a try at Doctor de Pomiane's honey-filled and cumin-spiced Apician apples. The recipe may be found on p.203 of* Cooking with Pomiane, *of which a paperback version was published by Faber in* 1976. *If obtaining a copy of either version should entail a search, I do not think anyone will regret the time spent on it.*

May 1984

Table Talk

If we are to believe late nineteenth- and early twentieth-century etiquette writers (which I don't altogether) this was a period when it was thought gross to talk about food except to your cook and in bad taste to discuss your host's wine. What did provide a fruitful source of conversation at dinner was the table setting. No drinks were served before dinner, so some form of ice-breaking equipment in the way of elaborate and festive flower decorations which everybody could remark upon must have been invaluable weapons in the hands of a conscientious hostess.

If we are to believe the cookery contributor (are we to? It's early to tell yet) to a recent number of one of the fashion monthlies, the wheel has turned just about half-circle and arrived at the point where it is almost essential to talk about the food and drink, because they have been chosen mainly with a view to distracting attention from the table decorations.

The idea is that while your guests are chattering happily away about the fabulous cottage pie, you, the host, are making subtle

1. The recipe is to be found in Michel Guérard's *Cuisine Gourmande.*

changes in the dining-room décor. Cool and fresh it's to be for the fish, more studied and solid for the main course; for the dessert, fragile and delicate. Skilfully thought out, this writer says, such transformations can be effected *without anybody noticing.* This is splendidly unlike the early thirties, when Lady Mendl published her *Recipes for Successful Dining.* 'In the year 1929 I used two rock-crystal vases in which were branches of white orchids, but those days are gone I fear for ever, and a few white carnations have to suffice now . . . at Christmas time 1931 I had a table of gold, hoping that it might in some way draw us all back to the old gold standard again . . . gold lamé tablecloth, old white Mennecey china, many yellow roses.'

Now Lady Mendl was after all a highly successful professional decorator, and whatever her sumptuous simplicities in the matter of table decoration – a little white Ming rabbit at each guest's place, a remnant of sixteenth-century French green silk brocade used as a tablecloth, one flawless magnolia on the tea tray (the photograph of her butler carrying this same tray alone makes a copy of the book worth searching for) – she certainly didn't seriously intend playing them down. Not for her, one feels fairly sure, would have been sables worn as a chemise, nor Savonnerie carpets used as underfelting. Had she arranged for the sets to be changed three times during a dinner party, she would have seen to it that everybody noticed. So, quite certainly, would Mrs Brooks, a journalist of the turn of the century who thought that the flowers, the food and the wine should be chosen to match the hostess's dress, and her contemporary, Mrs Alfred Praga, who believed, on the contrary, that the hostess's dress should be chosen to harmonize with the food and décor.

The style of Mrs Praga's book, *Dainty Dinner Tables and How to Decorate Them* (published in 1907), may be archaic, but something about the tone and even the context is curiously familiar. 'Have you ever tried a great bunch of ruddy brown-red wallflowers in an old majolica vase? Blue larkspur against a table-slip of faded mauve velvet, oh! how unutterably delicious it is to tired eyes . . . For half-a-crown, one of those gigantic glazed brown earthenware jugs (filled with cream) and for 5½d. each half a dozen tiny ones to match. When the cream has gone fill them with daffodils, set them on a table centre of tawny orange silk with a bordering of asparagus fern. Hey! how one's pen flies! . . .'

Keeping up with that galloping pen of hers, Mrs Praga one day devised 'a scheme based on deep orange-hued carnations', the table-slip to be of deep sunset yellow satin edged with écru lace (sunset yellow, she tells us elsewhere, was a Liberty colour – in fact most of her inspiration came from Liberty's). At each corner, satin ribbon bows. A squat Nuremberg bowl for the centrepiece and eight or ten specimen glasses of the same ware to be filled with orange carnations and silver grasses, each guest's place was to have a boutonnière to match and each finger bowl a floating full-blown orange carnation plus a few drops of orange flower water. Menu cards of sunset yellow lettering on deep orange, salt-sticks tied with ribbons to match, table glass of brown Nuremberg throughout, liqueurs to be yellow Chartreuse and old cognac. Candles deep yellow, shades orange silk, place cards written in orange on a yellow background, ices coloured yellow with saffron or turmeric and served in paper baskets of a deep orange colour. The sweets to be deep orange and the coffee served in deep brown and orange Wedgwood cups. 'If the hostess happens to be a brunette she can wear an orange gown ... to heighten and complete the illusion.'

Really, it's too bad of her, that last line. Is it all illusion, then? Is that what the decorator-hosts and hostesses are trying to tell us? The cool, fresh fish, the fragile dessert, the gold lamé, the gigantic brown earthenware cream jugs, the tawny orange silk? Didn't any of it ever exist? Not even the turmeric-flavoured ices?

The Spectator, 22 December 1961

Whisky in the Kitchen

Two or three years ago a friend of mine who is a publisher applied to me for help in dealing with a complaint from a man who had bought one of his cookery books. The recipe which was causing a minor commotion was for a lobster set ablaze with whisky. What, the gentleman would like to know, did a reputable publisher mean by allowing his author to suggest such a preposterous concoction? Whisky! Merciful heavens, what next? Surely everybody knew that cognac was the correct, and the only correct, spirit to use in conjunction with lobster. Do let us have some regard for the classic recipes ... not mislead the public ... irresponsible chatter ... a

French cook would never . . . barbaric mixture . . . I shudder to think . . . the great Escoffier said . . .

As it happens, the offence on this occasion was not mine, but I am familiar – what cookery writer is not? – with the tone of voice and with the gale force of the feelings expressed. Quite often something one had thought perfectly uncontroversial or even almost too insultingly obvious to include in one's cooking instructions arouses readers to a pitch of rage and scorn which strikes one as very much out of proportion to the offence committed.

The truth, I fancy – and the discovery that letters of this kind tend to be written in oddly similar terms (the writer invariably shudders to think, the mixtures are always revolting or barbaric) does something to bear out my theory – is simply that reference to some particular ingredient has, subconsciously, touched off a painful nerve in the reader. (Unworkable or downright fatuous recipes and real howlers often get by unchallenged. Once, owing to a printer's understandable failure to decipher my proof corrections, a book of mine appeared with a recipe which called for the whisked whites of 123 eggs . . . no reader has ever written to me demanding an explanation of this recipe.)

The clue to the whisky affair is not entirely obvious. Had the complainant been a woman it would have been easier to spot. Whisky is still, to many Englishwomen, a man's drink, tough masculine tipple. Advice to splash it into the sauté pan strikes a rough rude note. Cognac, being foreign and French, is altogether more glamorous and elegant-sounding, therefore more appropriate to the refinements of good cooking. I wonder if deep down that peppery gentleman's irritation might perhaps have been due to fear that once the gaff about whisky not being suitable for the kitchen was blown the master's bottle would no longer be quite sacrosanct. The little woman, instead of having to explain the spending of twenty-five shillings of the housekeeping money on a half bottle of 'cooking' brandy, would be at liberty to raid the Scotch for a few tablespoonsful at any time, and nobody the wiser.

In France, whisky was once a very smart and snob drink; it is now astonishingly popular. In 1961, it is estimated, 682,000 gallons of whisky were consumed by the French, and that was twice as much as in 1960. How many hundreds or thousands of those gallons were tipped into the saucepans the report does not reveal, but certain it is that in these days it is not at all uncommon to find dishes of chicken, langouste or lobster *flambé au whisky* on the menus of French provincial and Parisian restaurants. (For chapter and verse without going to France look at the lists of specialities given by the starred restaurants in the guide books.) An establishment at Arras even serves a speciality of *andouillettes flambées au whisky* – a faint echo of the haggis ritual . . .?

I find the French development encouraging, for I have myself for years been experimenting with whisky in the cooking pots. One of the circumstances which drove me to these experiments will be familiar to most home cooks. It was simply that a bottle of brandy, even of the kind intended only for the kitchen (by which I don't mean something not fit to drink, I mean something one *prefers* not to drink), somehow always turns out in fact to have been drunk by somebody just when it is needed for cooking and hasn't been replaced, while whisky is a supply which is more or less automatically re-ordered as soon as it runs out. And not only have I found whisky successful as an alternative to cognac and armagnac in many fish and poultry dishes, but it has frequently had to do duty instead of Calvados in Norman dishes of veal, pork, pheasant and apples. Calvados isn't always easy to come by in this country and such as we can get is usually one or other of the commercial brands which in spite of their high prices are pretty crude. So, for that matter, are all too many three-star-quality cognacs.

Obviously, the flavour which whisky gives to a sauce differs from that produced by cognac, armagnac or Calvados; certainly the aromas coming from the pot while the whisky is cooking are also very different; but by the time the alcohol has been burned and cooked away I wonder how many people would spot what precisely the difference is.

Not that that is quite the point. There should be no attempt to deceive. To take the simplest example, *faisan à la normande* would be understood, by anybody who knew a little about French regional cooking, to imply a dish of pheasant with a cream sauce and apples, blazed with Calvados. If the dish is blazed with whisky instead it is possible that nobody will know the difference; but a point of principle is involved; once the wedge is in how long before the apples have been replaced with carrots and peas, and the cream with tomato purée or pineapple juice? So all the restaurateur has to do (in the privacy of one's own kitchen one can, after all, call one's inventions what one pleases; until they leave the house one's guests are in no position to pass remarks) is to follow the French example and describe his dish as *faisan flambé au whisky* or alternatively pheasant *au Scotch*. And if he feels that the French have an unfair advantage in that to them the words 'whisky' and 'scotch' are good selling points whereas to us they are just rather blunt or evocative in the wrong way then he can invent some totally new name.

The whisky hurdle cleared, one quickly finds the way open to the successful use of all kinds of supposedly unorthodox spirits and wines in the kitchen. Not only have I used whisky instead of the brandy usually specified in pork and liver pâté recipes, which is a question of only about two, but two important, tablespoons to 1 ½ lb. of the mixture, but I have resorted also to rum (white rum is especially useful in the kitchen) and to gin for the same purpose, and the results have been excellent. Gin, we are told, is one of the purest spirits made, and juniper berries, the *baies de genièvre* or *ginepro* from which Geneva or gin derived its name, provide the characteristic flavouring which everyone who ever drank a glass of gin in their lives would recognize when he tastes the juniper-berry flavour in Provençal game terrines and certain Northern Italian sauces and stuffings for partridge and pheasant; and *eau de vie de genièvre* is a spirit used in French and Belgian Ardennais regional cooking, so it seems extraordinary that people blanch at the suggestion that gin should go into the casseroles. At least, before shuddering or crying 'barbarism!' and 'Escoffier never said . . .' look up – and cook – the delicious recipe for veal kidneys *à la liégeoise* given by Mr Ambrose Heath in his *Good Food* (Faber & Faber). The kidneys are cooked whole in butter and just before serving them you 'throw in a wineglassful of burnt gin and a few crushed juniper berries. This is quite wonderful . . .'

Then there is that recipe for a sauce for lobster which I came across in a French dictionary of cooking of the 1830s. Among the collection of outlandish ingredients called for were anisette liqueur and soy sauce. In those days cookery writers weren't just filling out their recipes with ingredients they were being paid to sell. There must be some basis in reason for that sauce. Why not try it? I did, and came to the conclusion that it was the best sauce for lobster ever invented; and it is extraordinary that it has remained for so long buried in the cookery books. In a moment I will produce the recipe – and please, will readers do their best to suspend disbelief until they have tried it? – but one of the main points about this recipe is that it taught me (for after all, one does not buy lobsters all that often) that anisette is, improbably but incontrovertibly, a quite magical ingredient in fish dishes and sauces. You rarely need more than a teaspoonful, you add it at the absolute final moment of cooking, you do not blaze it (at least I do not), you treat it simply as a seasoning. To a creamy sauce for white fish such as John Dory, brill, and sole, to dishes of molluscs such as mussels and scallops, its concentrated, pungent-sweet and aromatic qualities give a lift such as could hardly be achieved with a mountain of fennel stalks or seeds used in the preparation of the initial stock (anise is a close relation of fennel, caraway and dill), and this in turn gives one ideas as to the use of many other liqueurs, aromatic vermouths, country wines, even drinks such as Pernod and Pastis in the cooking of fish and white meat and poultry dishes.

LOBSTER COURCHAMPS

For one freshly boiled, medium large (about 1½ lb.) hen lobster or langouste (if you are boiling the creature at home, you can always add the large goblet of Madeira called for in the original recipe), the ingredients for the sauce are 2 small shallots, a heaped teaspoon of tarragon leaves, 2 tablespoons of chopped parsley, salt, pepper, a scant teaspoon of strong yellow French mustard, 24 to 30 drops of soy sauce, approximately 6 tablespoons of mildly fruity Provence olive oil, the juice of half a rather small lemon, 1 teaspoon of anisette de Bordeaux.

From the split lobster extract all the red and creamy parts. Pound them in a mortar. Mix with the finely chopped shallots, tarragon and parsley. Add the seasonings and the soy sauce, then gradually stir in the olive oil; add lemon juice. Finally, the anisette. Divide the sauce into two portions, and serve it in little bowls or squat glasses placed on each person's plate, so that the lobster can be dipped into it. The lobster meat can be cut into scallops and piled neatly back into the shells.

Apart from its sheer deliciousness (most cold lobster sauces, including mayonnaise, are on the heavy side for what is already rich and solid food) this sauce has other points to recommend it. Anisette is not a liqueur which, speaking at least for myself, one has a great compulsion to swig down in quantity; in my cupboard a bottle lasts for years. A half-crown's worth of soy sauce also tends – unless you are keen on Chinese cooking – to remain an old faithful among the stores; and although nothing can quite compare with fresh tarragon, it is perfectly possible to use the excellent Chiltern Herb Farm dried version. The makings of your sauce, then, are always with you. All you need is the freshly boiled hen lobster . . . And, as it is not a classic regional or other recognized traditional dish, you can call it what you please. It has no name of its own. I have named it after the Comte de Courchamps, author of the first of the three books[1] in which I found the recipe. The others were by Dumas the Elder[2] and the Baron Brisse.[3] Highly imaginative as they were, all three gentlemen called it Sauce for Boiled Lobster.

The Compleat Imbiber 4, 1963

A Gourmet in Edwardian London

The last years of Queen Victoria's reign and the beginning of the Edwardian era saw the rise to fame and prosperity of the great London hotels we know to-day; the Savoy, the Ritz, the Carlton, the Berkeley, Claridges (even then known as 'the home of kings'), the Piccadilly, the Hyde Park and – the only one which has since disappeared – the Cecil. At that time Romano's was at the height of its glory; Mr Lyons and Mr Salmon were presiding at the Trocadero; and at Simpson's in the Strand a fish luncheon for three, consisting of turbot, stewed eels, whitebait, celery and cheese, with two bottles of Liebfraumilch, cost £1.1s.3d.

The restaurant world of that period was described in detail by the Edwardian gourmet, Colonel Newnham-Davis, the gastronomic correspondent of the Pall Mall Gazette. The Colonel made a habit of inviting to dinner certain of his friends whom, in his subsequent reports, he would disguise under discreet pseudonyms. A regular guest of his was Miss Dainty, an actress. One evening she dined with him at, curiously it seems to us, the Midland Hotel. A railway hotel dinner in those days seems hardly to have been the dread experience

1. *Néo-Physiologie du Goût par Ordre Alphabétique: Dictionnaire Général de la Cuisine Française Ancienne et Moderne ainsi que de l'Office et de la Pharmacie domestique*, Paris, Henri Plon. Published anonymously in 1839, reprinted 1853 and 1866. Vicaire asserts that the book was the work of Maurice Cousin, Comte de Courchamps. In the preface to the book it is claimed that a number of the recipes came from unpublished papers of Grimod de la Reynière. The recipe in question might well be from his hand.
2. *Grand Dictionnaire de Cuisine*, Alexandre Dumas, 1873.
3. *Les 366 Menus de Baron Brisse*, 2nd edition 1875, first published *c.* 1867.

Colonel Newnham-Davis. Photograph from Le Carnet d'Epicure Janvier
1914 and restored by Hawkley Studio Associates Ltd

'it would be to-day. The Colonel and Miss Dainty ate oysters, soup, sole, a fillet of beef cooked with truffles and accompanied by *pommes de terre soufflées*, wild duck *à la presse*, a pudding and an ice-cream (*bombe Midland*). With a bottle of wine this meal cost 28s. for the two of them.

Miss Brighteyes was a debutante who, to her host's grief, drank lemonade with her caviare and gossiped of dresses and weddings while she ate *terrine de foie gras*. The Colleen – what a tiring girl she sounds – prattled incessantly of horses. The little Prima Donna was an American taken by the Colonel to the Star and Garter at Richmond. They had a pleasant drive down there (Goodwood was over and London deserted) and arrived at sunset; on this occasion the food was not a great success. There was *petite marmite* and, not for the first time, the Colonel is at a loss to understand why some restaurant managers seem unaware of the existence of any other soup. The mullet was not fresh – 'I guess it has not been scientifically embalmed,' said the Prima Donna.

I should like to think that the Colonel's sister-in-law (the daughter of a dean) to whom he gave dinner at the Café Royal, the Aunt whom he entertained at the Walsingham, and the Uncle whom he nicknamed the Nabob, were really his relations and not figments of his humorous imagination. Alas, they are just a trifle over life size.

The dean's daughter did not care for shell-fish, so they were forced to start dinner with caviare. The inevitable clear soup followed (*pot au feu* this time); the sole was served in a delicate sauce almost imperceptibly flavoured with cheese, and the dean's daughter appreciated it so much that the Colonel's initial peevishness began to wear off. The lamb which followed the sole was tough. Foie gras came next, then quails *en cocotte*. The ice which ended the meal was christened *Pôle Nord* and consisted of a soft cream encased in ice-cream, resting on an ice pedestal carved in the shape of a bird sitting on a rock. This creation cost 2s. 6d. the foie gras 4s. Champagne Rosé was what they drank and, with liqueurs and coffee, the total bill came to £2.4s.6d.

The maiden aunt who was invited to Walsingham House arrived in a four-wheeler. She wore a stiff black silk dress, a lace cap and an expression of disapproval – 'I hope they won't take me for one of your actress friends,' she boomed. The Walsingham was in Piccadilly, on the site now occupied by the Ritz; from the Colonel's description of the panelling of inlaid woods, the white pillars and cornices touched with gold, the curtains of deep crimson velvet, the ceiling of little cupids floating in roseate clouds, the dining-room must have been every bit as ravishing as the pink and white Louis XVI restaurant which succeeded it and which, under the direction of César Ritz, became synonymous with all that was elegant, rich and glamorous in the early years of this century.

Mrs Tota and her husband George were friends from the Colonel's Indian Army days. George, it has to be faced, was a bore; he grunted and grumbled and refused to take his wife out to dinner on the grounds that the night air would bring on his fever. So the Colonel gallantly invited Mrs Tota, a maddeningly vivacious young woman, to a select little dinner for two. She was homesick for the gaieties of Simla, the dainty dinners and masked balls of that remarkable hill station. 'We'll have a regular Simla evening,' declared the Colonel, and for this nostalgic excursion he chose to dine in a private room at Kettner's, which still exists to-day, in Romilly Street, Soho; after dinner they were to proceed to a box at the Palace Theatre, return to Kettner's, where they arranged to leave their dominos, and thence to a masked ball at Covent Garden. The meal, for a change, began with caviare, continued with *consommé, filets de sole à la Joinville, langue de bœuf aux champignons* accompanied by spinach and *pommes Anna* (how agreeable it would be to find these delicious potatoes on an English restaurant menu to-day), followed by chicken and salad, asparagus with *sauce mousseline*, and the inevitable ice. They drank a bottle of champagne (15s. seems to have been the standard charge at that period, 1s. each for liqueurs). Mrs Tota was duly coy about the private room decorated with a gold, brown and green paper, oil paintings of Italian scenery and gilt candelabra ('very snug', pronounced the Colonel); she enjoyed her dinner, chattered nineteen to the dozen and decided that Room A at Kettner's was almost as glamorous as the dear old Châlet at Simla.

Although he was strictly fair in his reports and seldom expressed a particular preference, it is clear that one of the Colonel's favourite restaurants was the Savoy. It was D'Oyly Carte, of Gilbert and Sullivan fame, who invited César Ritz, then at the Grand Hotel, Monte Carlo, to come to London and take charge of his recently opened Savoy Hotel. With him Ritz brought Escoffier to supervise the kitchens, and Echenard, proprietor of the famous Hôtel du Louvre, Marseille, to assist him as manager in the restaurant – a formidable combination indeed; no wonder the Savoy soon became the favourite haunt of stage celebrities, industrial magnates, Indian princes (there was a well-known curry cook attached to the Savoy kitchens) and, in fact, of all classes of the rich, the great, the greedy. Escoffier's *mousse de jambon*, served on a great block of ice and melting like snow in the mouth, was recognised as a masterpiece; and the *bortsch*, with cream stirred into the hot strong liquid, was declared by Colonel Newnham-Davis to be the best soup in the world.

Joseph, who succeeded the Ritz-Escoffier partnership, had an almost unique devotion to his art. On one occasion, when Sarah Bernhardt was the guest of honour at a Savoy dinner, he cooked the greater part of the meal at a side table under her very eyes; his carving of the duck was a flamboyant display of swordsmanship; when asked if he ever went to the theatre he replied that he would rather see six gourmets eating a perfectly cooked meal than watch the finest performance of Bernhardt or of Coquelin.

A few years later, the Savoy became the scene of all manner of fabulous banquets. At one of these the courtyard was flooded to represent a Venetian canal, tables were arranged all round, and Caruso sang to the guests as he floated in a gondola.

What, I wonder, would our reactions be to-day to these junketings? What of the long menus and, the everlasting sameness of the food? With stupefaction one thinks of the wholesale slaughter of ducks and chickens, of pheasant and quail, the shiploads of Dover sole and the immense cargoes of foie gras from France, of caviare from Russia, the crates of champagne and the tons of truffles, which went to make up a single day's entertainment in the great hotels of Europe. By present day standards the prices were, of course, absurd, although the cooking was luxurious and the service impeccable.

The *petite marmite*, the *pot au feu*, the *croûte au pot* were made with rich beef, veal and chicken stock; the fillets of sole were invariably cooked with truffles and cream or with mushrooms and lobster sauce, with artichoke hearts or with white wine and grapes; *noisettes d'agneau*, from the finest baby lamb, made such frequent appearances on the menu that one wonders how any sheep has survived; the chicken was stuffed with a *mousse de foie gras*; the little birds which followed – quail, ortolan or snipe – were again presented with truffles; asparagus, in and out of season, were always accompanied by hollandaise sauce; and the *bombe glacée*, indispensable, it seems, to a good dinner, was the signal for all the display of which the confectionery chef was capable.

The wines were probably better than anything we shall ever drink again in England, and served in the proper manner. What on earth would the Colonel have said to the waiter at a world famous hotel, who the other day brought a bottle of Chambertin to the table in a bucket of ice? What, for that matter, would he have done, when confronted with the pile of chips and mass of Brussels sprouts heaped onto a plate containing an alleged *sole meunière*, in a restaurant where they ought to know better?

Even so, a course of Edwardian dinners might well prove a sore trial to-day. Although Colonel Newnham-Davis consistently pleaded for more varied menus and shorter meals, this did not prevent him from ordering and eating, with evident enjoyment and approval, what seems to-day a perfectly astounding meal. On this occasion, his uncle, the peppery old Nabob, was bidden to dine at the Cecil Hotel, in order that it might be proved to him that a respectable curry could be had outside the portals of the East India Club. This is the menu as recorded by the Colonel and solemnly consumed down to the last *friandise*:

> *Hors-d'œuvre variés*
> *Consommé Sarah Bernhardt*
> *Filet de sole à la garbure*
> *Côtes en chevreuil: Sauce poivrade*
> *Haricots verts à la Villars*
> *Pommes Cecil*
> *Mousse de foie gras et Jambon au champagne*
> *Curry à l'indienne*
> *Bombay duck, etc., etc.*
> *Asperges*
> *Bombes à la Cecil*
> *Petites friandises choisies*

By the time they reached the curry, which was accompanied by a whole battery of poppadoms, chutneys and relishes, it was hardly surprising that the Nabob's resistance had almost given out. He was only able to murmur, 'Good, decidedly. I don't say as good as we get it at the Club' – there was still a spark of spirit left in him – 'but decidedly good.' It should be added that the dinner, with champagne, liqueurs and cigarettes, cost £2.8s.6d., and that the *bombe à la Cecil* appeared with an electrically illuminated ice windmill as a background.

Go, 1952

'I'll Be with You in the Squeezing of a Lemon'

Oliver Goldsmith

In 1533 the Company of Leathersellers offered Henry the Eighth and Anne Boleyn a great banquet to celebrate Anne's coronation on Whit Sunday in Westminster Hall. Among the princely luxuries which graced the feast was one lemon, one only, for which the Leathersellers had paid six silver pennies.

Now that in England we pay an average of six copper pence per lemon, I think I would still find them almost worth the silver pennies which in 1533 must have represented a pretty large sum.

It is hard to envisage any cooking without lemons, and indeed those of us who remember the shortage or total absence of lemons during the war years, recall the lack as one of the very worst of the minor deprivations of those days.

Without a lemon to squeeze on to fried or grilled fish, no lemon juice to sharpen the flatness of the dried pulses – the red lentils, the split peas – which in those days loomed so largely in our daily diet, no lemon juice to help out the stringy ewe-mutton and the ancient boiling fowls of the time, no lemon juice for pancakes, no peel to grate into cake mixtures and puddings, we felt frustrated every time we opened a cookery book or picked up a mixing bowl. In short, during the past four hundred years the lemon has become, in cooking, the condiment which has largely replaced the vinegar, the verjuice (preserved juice of green grapes), the pomegranate juice, the bitter orange juice, the mustard and wine compounds which were the acidifiers poured so freely into the cooking pots of sixteenth- and seventeenth-century Europe. There are indeed times when a lemon as a seasoning seems second only in importance to salt.

To Mediterranean cooking the juice of the lemon is vital. It is the astringent corrective, as well as the flavouring, for olive-oil-based dishes and fat meat. By English cooks this point is not and has never been sufficiently appreciated. For example a home-made brawn or pig's-head cheese seasoned with a generous amount of lemon juice (squeezed in after cooking and when the meat is shredded or chopped ready for potting or moulding) transforms an often insipid dish into a delicacy. And to me a lentil soup or purée is unthinkable without the complement of lemon and olive oil; then, just try to imagine lamb kebabs without lemon . . .

In scores of English and French creams, ices, cakes, soufflés, sweet omelettes and preserves, it is the aromatic oil contained in the peel or zest, rather than the juice, which is the operative part of the lemon. For these dishes choose thick-skinned fruit.

One of the best of lemon graters is lump sugar, although Hannah Glasse (*The Art of Cookery Made Plain and Easy*, 1747) who was perhaps partial to a pun, directed her readers to grate lemon skins with a piece of broken glass. Possibly in her day that practical little utensil known as a lemon zester had not yet been invented. And the lump sugar business, called for in so many recipes, is often exasperating because it is unexplained. When however it is remembered that sugar was bought in loaves, the whole procedure becomes logical. You simply hacked off a sizeable lump, and with this big piece, rasped off the skin of the lemon, thus releasing the essential oil of the zest which is so important to the flavour of creams, ices, and particularly of that uniquely English speciality, lemon curd. This lovely dish does of course also include the juice of the lemons. So do all the lemon recipes which I have chosen for this article. There is something especially satisfactory about using the whole of the fruit in one dish. Even more satisfactory are the beautiful flavours and scents of these dishes authentically made and eaten when fresh. (Lemon curd has been one of the most painfully travestied and ill-used of all our true English preserves. No commercially-made version gives so much as a hint of its true nature.)

ENGLISH LEMON CURD

To make 1 lb. approximately, ingredients are: 2 large lemons, preferably thick-skinned; ½ lb. loaf sugar; 4 whole large eggs; ¼ lb. of unsalted or slightly salted butter.

Rub sugar lumps on to the peel of the lemons, holding them over a bowl, until each lump starts crumbling, then start on another. About four lumps will rub sufficient outside peel and oil out of each lemon. Put all the sugar together into the bowl.

Squeeze the lemons, and strain the juice. Whisk the eggs very thoroughly with the strained juice.

Cut the butter into small cubes.

Set the bowl in, or over, a pan of water. When the sugar has dissolved add the eggs, then the butter. Stir until all ingredients are amalgamated and the whole mixture looks rather like thick honey, with about the same consistency. Remove the bowl (older cooks still find an old-fashioned stoneware jam jar the best vessel for making lemon curd. I prefer an open bowl. I like to see what's happening) and stir until the curd has cooled. Turn into small jars and cover with good quality kitchen parchment such as Bakewell, to be bought at W. H. Smith and other stationers.

To the straightforward lemon curd, a couple of sponge fingers, broken up, are sometimes added. They thicken the curd, giving it extra body and making it more stable when spread into flan cases or flat, open plate pies. A richer alternative is a small proportion of ground almonds. Allow up to 2 oz. for the quantities given.

Writers of old recipes often claimed that lemon curd keeps for years. Perhaps it does. I would say that three months is about the maximum, and that long before this period is up the confection, like a fresh fruit sorbet stored in the deep freeze, has lost its exquisite flavour and the edge has gone from the sharp scent.

Use lemon curd to make a delicious filling for little brown bread sandwiches to eat with ices, to spread on brioche or currant bread, or as a sauce for little yeast pancakes as well as for the traditional lemon curd pie made with rich, sweet short crust.

SHORT CRUST FOR LEMON CURD PIE OR LEMON CHEESE-CAKE

Proportions for the crust, which is rich, sweet, and crumbly, are easy to remember. They are 3 oz. of sugar, 6 oz. of butter, 9 oz. of flour, 1 whole egg plus a little iced water for moistening the dough, which should be mixed and rolled out, very quickly and lightly, and cooked at once. The 3, 6, 9, formula makes enough for two 7-inch tins. It is easy enough to halve the quantities and use only the yolk of the egg, but easier still to remember the recipe in its original formula.

The pastry cases are cooked blind (do not forget to prick the base with the tip of a sharp little knife) protected with paper (it burns easily, like all pastry containing sugar) and filled with dry beans or rice. Put it into the centre of a hot oven, gas no. 6 or 7, 410°F. to 440°F., and bake for 20 minutes, then lower the temperature to gas no. 4, 370°F., and cook for another 15 minutes. This seems a long time. It is intentional. So much English pastry is spoiled by timid cooking and under-baking.

While still hot remove the beans and the paper. Fill with lemon curd – about 6 to 8 tablespoons – and put back into the oven for 5 minutes, just enough time for the filling to warm through, no more. The effect to aim at is a crisp, sugary crust with the contrast of a smooth, delicately aromatic and refreshing filling.

CURATIVE PROPERTIES OF LEMONS

It was during the last years of the reign of Anne Boleyn's daughter Elizabeth that the curative effects of lemon juice on scurvy victims was observed, although neither cause nor effect were understood. Only as late as 1918 was it established – by a woman doctor – that the juice of lemons is more than twice as rich in anti-scorbutic vitamins as that of the lime, for long thought to be as or more effective than lemon juice in the prevention of scurvy. The lime juice myth was so firmly entrenched that it is still commonly believed.

TO PRESERVE LEMONS IN CLOVES

Finally, here is a beautiful little lemon recipe from the MS. *Receipt Book of Anne Blencowe*, dated 1694, and printed by Guy Chapman, the Adelphi, in 1925. The segments of lemon embedded in clear apple jelly must have made a ravishing little dessert dish:

'You must pare them very close. Part ye cloves, then scrape all ye white off, but have a care not to break ye cloves when you scrape them. Take out all ye seeds, then weight them and take their weight in sugar. To a pound of sugar half a pint of water. Sett all on a slow fire and keep them covered with syrup & paper, but let them not boyl. So sett them by till ye next day; then heat them again as you did before, & when you think their sowrness is pretty well out, they are enough. Then make a Jelly with pipins & put them in. So let them have one boyl Then glass them. They must not stand upon the fire above an hour att a time. The cloves of ye Lemon must be taken clean from ye syrup to put to ye jelly.'

Wine and Food, February/March 1969

Pleasing Cheeses

In food-song and travel-story the scene, the characters, and the opening dialogue are familiar enough: the inn is humble and is situated close to the banks of the radiant Loire. (In legend the Loire is always radiant. Quite often it actually is radiant. On this particular day it is super-radiant. The inn, ever-humble, of French cookery fables is, on this occasion, archi-humble.) The cook-proprietress is where she should be, in the kitchen, cooking lunch. Her own lunch, not ours. Frying-pan in hand, she is saying she has nothing for us, she hadn't been expecting customers; at this time of year there are visitors only at weekends. The customers reply never mind about lunch, they will drink a carafe of wine and perhaps Madame has some bread and sausage? Oh, if that is all monsieur and madame wish, would they be seated? One will attend to them.

Enter the cross-eyed daughter, bearing wine, plates and cutlery. She sets the oilcloth-covered table. Couldn't we eat out of doors? On such a beautiful day it seems sad to sit in the dank, scruffy room. The girl looks scared. She does not answer. We repeat our request. She shakes her head. Deaf as well as cross-eyed.

Oh well. We were thirsty and hungry. Not to make a palaver. Bread, butter, sausage and sliced raw ham were put before us. The loaf was very large, flat, brown-crusted, open-textured, a *pain de ménage*, the real household French bread such as is rarely produced nowadays in restaurants and inns. That bread alone was well worth the journey. We ate so much of it, it was so marvellous, that we hardly wanted the sausage and the ham, noticed only in passing that the wine wasn't up to much, and that the eggs in the omelette which presently appeared were spanking fresh and buttercup yellow – in the French countryside one takes that for granted. And anyway, by now the son of the house had come in for his midday meal, turned on the television, created havoc out of the quiet day. Like his sister, the young man was cross-eyed, deaf and simple. His mother came in from the kitchen to ask if we'd like cheese or fresh cheese with cream. The two, please. We need not have bothered with the cheese proper. The fresh cheese with cream was all we, or at any rate I, wanted.

The telly faded, the shoddy oilcloth vanished, the beautiful sunshine we were missing was forgotten. There it was, the big glass bowl half-filled with soft, very white, very fresh milk cheese with its covering of fresh thick cream. It was just as I had remembered it for over thirty years, it was just as it used to appear at least once a week at lunch in the Paris household where I spent two years of my youth with a greedy Norman family: two years of study interspersed with the most trying of family meals, endless and infinitely to be dreaded but for the blessed beauty of the food. It was first class, not at all, as I later understood, ambitious or opulent, but of consistent quality, very fresh and, in effect, just very good French bourgeois food, carefully bought, traditionally cooked, presented with much visual taste. Sorrel soups we used to eat, and lettuce soups, delicate vegetables such as salsify and celeriac, golden melting potatoes, a nutmeg-flavoured rice salad with tomatoes, apricot soufflés, and the famous *fromage frais à la crème* invariably presented in a glass bowl with sugar and more cream, Norman cream (well, I said they were greedy), on the table.

So what did she mean, the proprietress of the lugubrious little *estaminet* on the banks of the lovely Loire, what could she have meant when she said she had nothing in the house for lunch? She had that astonishingly good bread, did she not, and she had the freshly made fresh cream cheese – goat's milk cheese and cow's milk cream, not too thick, not rich, not yellow, appearing cream coloured only because the cheese it half-concealed and half-revealed (you see the point of the glass bowl) was so muslin-white and new.

Where did all our own home-made cream and milk cheeses go? Time was when we had scores of versions of them. Every English cookery book and manuscript collection from the fifteenth to the early twentieth century gave recipes for fresh milk cheeses, cream cheeses, whey cheeses, cream curds, bandstring curds, rush cheeses, napkin cheeses, snow cheeses.

Some of these cheeses were eaten the day they were made, with cream and sugar, some were for almond cheesecakes, some for the fillings of covered pies called Florentines, some for spiced cheese loaves baked in stoneware porringers. Some were salted and stored in brine in stoneware jars, some were laid between rushes and turned daily until ripe for eating. Some were whipped up with egg whites, lemon peel, and extra cream, some were served with raspberry, strawberry, redcurrant, apple, quince or medlar jelly. Once these cheeses were known collectively as green cheeses – green in the sense of being unripened, unmatured. Now they are all cream cheeses even if they're made only of milk. (Cottage cheese seems to be a term now applied almost entirely, and characteristically, in our looking-glass culinary language, to the thin and acid skim-milk product of big dairy factories. It is popular with slimmers but not much good in cooking.)

Possibly, somewhere along the line, green became corrupted into cream and hence the confusion of nomenclature. 'Take yolkys of Eyroun and putte ther-to a gode hepe, and grene chese putt ther-to,' directs a fifteenth-century recipe which includes chopped pork, minced dates, ginger, cinnamon, and hard-boiled eggs baked in an open pie. Although real cream cheese may be made from real cream it isn't real cheese, since it is not a curd but simply ripened cream, semi-solidified and drained of its fluid content. Cheeses of this kind used to be known in country-house and home-farm dairy cookery as napkin cheeses. The following recipe from *The Cookery Book of Lady Clark of Tillypronie* (1909) is a typical one:

OSBORNE CREAM CHEESE

'Take 1 pint of very thick cream, and put it into a fine damask cloth, previously dipped in strong salt water, and tie up. At the end of 2 hours, turn it into a clean cloth, and repeat the process every 2 hours throughout the day, when the cheese will be ready for use. The cheese will generally be of the right consistency in 12 hours if the cream is thoroughly good and the weather not too warm.'

For such cream cheeses moulds are not strictly necessary, although the cheese looks more presentable if it has been pressed in a muslin-lined basket, a heart-shaped mould, a cake tin pierced with holes, even an expendable carton or a flower pot – always provided that the essential lining is not forgotten. For cooking purposes, this rich cream cheese, mixed with Parmesan and chopped walnuts, makes a lovely sauce for pasta, similar to the one the Italians make with their own *mascarpone* cheese. On home-baked brown bread it takes the place of butter.

To make a fresh milk cheese at home is the simplest of processes. Like bread-making, any mugwump can do it. In the same way, it is uncommonly satisfactory in that it is a simple basic skill with great possibilities of expansion and variation of which the full exploration does suppose a certain creative intelligence and deductive wit. For example, although many people hold that pasteurized milk won't make acceptable cheese of any kind, the Italian-owned

Milkflower factory which produces such delicious fresh *ricotta* cheese – a traditional Italian whey cheese – right here in the centre of London (in Percy Mews, w.1, to be exact) uses ordinary Marketing Board milk. In that case so can you or I. The next point is that the special rennet that professional cheese-making demands is available only in bulk, and therefore – since only a teaspoonful or so per half-gallon of milk is required – of little use for making cheese at home. So we have to use junket rennet.

There is nothing wrong with this, and in fact soft milk cheese is little more than an extension of junket. (Our word derives from the French *jonches* or rushes, one of the numerous old French names for freshly made milk cheese drained in rushes or a rush basket.) But whereas junket is made with great rapidity and is eaten almost as soon as the curd has set and without being drained, soft cheese takes longer to turn because less rennet must be used and the milk is barely heated, too much rennet and/or too much heat producing a leathery and acid curd. Once drained, which takes anything from four to eight hours, the cheese can be eaten immediately, with or without the addition of fresh cream; or it can be left draining until it is all but dry, when it can be kept for cooking, or salted and flavoured for consumption as a mild cheese.

FRESH MILK CHEESE

To make a good pound of cheese, ingredients are 4 pints of ordinary full cream milk, 2 teaspoons of junket rennet (liquid, *not* powder) and a little salt. Implements and utensils are a gallon-size pan, a long-handled cooking spoon, a cloth, a colander, a skimmer or flat perforated slice, a 24 to 28 inch square of muslin or cheesecloth, a big basin and a pierced mould.

Pour the milk into your large pan. Heat it very gradually until it is little more than tepid. Put in the rennet, measuring it carefully and remembering about too much making a tough and acid curd; stir it well into the milk. Cover the pan with a cloth – to prevent steam from condensing on the cover of the pan and falling back on the curd – and the lid, and leave it for two to four hours, until the curd is fairly firm.

Have ready a colander standing in a deep bowl, and lined with the dampened muslin or cheesecloth. With the skimmer or perforated slice, break up the curd, spoon it into the lined colander. As the whey runs out and the curd sinks, add more, until all the curd is taken from the pan. Knot the corners of the cloth, hang it up on a hook with the basin underneath to catch the whey. Leave it for an hour, until the bulk of the whey has drained off, and transfer the curd, still in its cloth, to the mould. If this is an improvised one such as a pierced cake tin, without feet to raise it from the plate on which it drains, set it in the top of a basin, mixing bowl, saucepan, wide jar, or any vessel in which it will fit without actually resting on the bottom. There must be space underneath for the whey to drain. A curd which has been soaking in its own whey makes an acid cheese (which explains the often sharp taste of Eastern Mediterranean white cheeses which are sometimes stored in whey).

In about eight to twelve hours the cheese will be firm enough to be turned into a deepish glass dish or large soup plate. Pour fresh cream over the cheese, covering it completely; serve caster sugar separately. Alternately, having made the cheese as above, leave it draining for an extra six to eight hours. Turn it out on to a plate. Now, and not before, sprinkle it with salt on both sides (a teaspoonful for each side is enough), put it into a clean cloth and leave it draining until it is to be used. For cooking, the cheese should be dry. Any substantial quantity of moisture forced out of the cheese when it is subjected to heat may spoil the consistency of a dish, making it watery. In the case of cream cheese fillings for pies and flans, the risk is that the moisture may sink into the pastry, making it soggy.

CREAM CHEESE CROÛTONS

Mash 3 to 4 oz. of soft-curd milk or cream cheese or demi-sel with 4 tablespoons of grated Cheddar, Gruyère, Parmesan, or any other hard cheese you have to hand. Add plenty of freshly milled black pepper and lots of herbs – chopped fresh parsley, or dried basil, or chopped celery leaves. Then stir in one whole well-beaten egg.

Spread this mixture on not too thick slices of white, brown, or French bread from which you have cut the crusts. There is enough for 12 croûtons. On top of each put little pieces of anchovy fillet (or anchovy paste squeezed from a tube) and/or halved, stoned black olives. Put the croûtons on a baking sheet and cook them near the top of the oven for 15 minutes at gas no. 3, 330°F.

Incidentally, this cream cheese mixture, spread on little fingers of bread and cooked in just the same way, is extremely good for a cocktail party as a change from those eternal sausages. The egg in the mixture makes it stay put, instead of running all over the place as most cheese mixtures do.

Nova, October 1965

Sweet Aristo

The enormous ridged tomatoes were cored with a little sharp knife, cut round roughly into sections, thrown into a shallow bowl, mixed with thickly sliced raw onions, mild and very sweet. Salt, a sprinkling of olive oil and wine vinegar were the only seasonings.

In the little white house in the almond and lemon country of South-Eastern Spain where I stayed last summer every midday meal started with the tomato and onion salad. It has no regional or picturesque name. It is just *ensalada*. In all the restaurants down on the coast they offer you very much the same salad, sometimes with a few olives, cucumber slices and cos lettuce all prettily arranged on a flat dish, a mixture not unlike the *salade niçoise* of Southern France. I prefer the basic tomato and onion salad. It is so rich in flavour, so sweet, so cool, fresh – and so entirely appropriate to the high summer of the Mediterranean.

Every day, with the first taste of that lovely fresh salad came also the reminder that the tomato at its best is a luxury and should be treated as such. The trouble is that in England a tomato good enough to be eaten raw and unadorned is becoming a good deal more of a rarity than a ripe avocado, and nearly as elusive as a perfect fresh peach or purple fig. Only during the brief summer season of English out-of-doors tomatoes can we count on a tomato worth eating. Mass-grown Channel Island and Canary tomatoes are a sore disappointment to anyone familiar with native Spanish tomatoes.[1] The Spanish growers may be doing their best to provide tomatoes acceptable to the English market but evidently English varieties and the Spanish soil and climatic conditions just don't suit each other. Dutch tomatoes lack character. French tomatoes we seldom get nowadays. Some five years ago a few growers in the Nîmes district of Southern France made an attempt to raid the English market by cultivating Moneymaker, a favourite high-yield English commercial tomato. The experiment was not an unqualified success. In the summer of 1961 the Board of Trade clamped down on imported tomatoes early in the season. The French growers were

---

1. Written in 1965. Friends living in Spain now (1984) tell me that the old ridged, sweet-tasting tomatoes have all but vanished. You may see them in Spanish still-life paintings, but not in the markets. The so-called beefsteak tomatoes we now buy in England are hot-house grown in Holland, and I believe, in Guernsey.

landed with hundreds of tons of English-type tomatoes unacceptable in the local cooking and unsuitable for canning or preserving. In the wholesale markets of Provence the customers wouldn't even take English-type tomatoes as gifts. English importers and wholesalers on the other hand stubbornly refuse to touch either the little pear-shaped Roi Humbert variety of tomatoes grown in Provence and Italy for sauce and for canning, or the big meaty, untidy tomatoes which are so important to Mediterranean cookery for salads and fresh tomato sauces.

It is the same old story. Whether it's potatoes or plums, lettuces or leeks, mushrooms or mangoes, the English greengrocery trade is reluctant to handle any produce which does not conform to a given size, a given number to the pound. Five years ago it was announced in a communiqué issued from Agriculture House that tomatoes 'which are smallish, about 7 to the pound, round, red all over, and firm are the best and command the highest prices'. In other words – in, to be precise, the words of the public relations bureau of the Cucumber and Tomato Marketing Board – the tomato which commands the highest price is an all-purpose (or is it non-purpose?) product; 'not every mouth' and I quote 'can afford to choose caviare instead of kippers or an aristocratic difficult low yielding variety of tomato rather than a less fastidious tomato with a heavy yield.'

Ah, that difficult, aristocratic, fastidious tomato, what's the betting that quite a few mouths would go for it were it on offer? (Harbinger and Ailsa Craig are, according to gardeners, the aristocrats of the English tomato world.) The Tomato Marketers might be interested to know that back in the twenties, when grapefruit was making its way in France, so highly reputed an establishment as the old Café de Paris listed that novelty in the special corner of the menu normally reserved for caviare alone. Maybe we should reassess the tomato. These days it is the authenticity of a product, not its basic price, which spells luxury.[1]

Along with the Israeli melons, the Swaziland avocados, and the

1. Was it optimism or naïvité on my part which made me express such a belief? Look at the Chinese gooseberry or Kiwi fruit. It is a pretty colour, but not a very interesting fruit. The moment the French restaurant chefs took it up, it became a luxury, now sells at absurdly inflated prices, and figures in every other new style dessert recipe and often with duck, with game birds, even with fish. It is not its merit which dictates its presence in those dishes. It is its known high price. The same could be said of the out of season imported asparagus three pieces of which appear in every *salade tiède* and on every plate of *noisettes d'agneau au sabayon de poireaux*.

Kenya asparagus of present-day classy restaurants there might well be a place for Mediterranean tomatoes. Some four or five years ago one of our gastronomic columnists wrote of a Leicester Square bistro called Chez Solange that an advance telephone call would ensure production of an 'authentic *salade de tomates*'. The makings of a quite substantial tomato salad mystique are scattered around waiting to be gathered up by some enterprising buyer who will get the produce flown in from Barcelona or Marseilles, Naples, Valencia or even possibly from Portugal, where the tomatoes are as good and plentiful as anywhere in Mediterranean lands. It was after all from the Portuguese that the French took the hint about the rightness of fresh tomato sauce with eggs, fish and rice; *à la portuguaise* signifying, in French cookery, a dish in which the tomato figures. And our own early recipes for tomato soups thickened with rice or bread were derived from Portuguese rather than American, French or Italian cookery.

*

A world devoid of tomato soup, tomato sauce, tomato ketchup and tomato paste is hard to visualize. Could the tin and processed food industries have got where they have without the benefit of the tomato compounds which colour, flavour, thicken, and conceal so many deficiencies? How did the Italians eat spaghetti before the advent of the tomato? Was there such a thing as a tomato-less Neapolitan pizza? What were English salads like before there were tomatoes to mix with lettuce? Did Provençal cooking exist without *tomates provençale, salade niçoise* and *ratatouille*? Then there is that warmed red billiard ball with its skin slit round the middle, so oddly known as a grilled tomato. (I believe the official name for this dish is dressed tomatoes.) Without it could the British landlady's and railway dining-car breakfast ever have become what it is? How many people would accept baked beans innocent of tomato sauce? And many of us still remember that among the food shortages of the war years and after, the scarcity of fresh tomatoes was a privation on the same level as the lack of lemons, onions and butter.

Incredible though it now seems, the tomato, brought by the Spaniards from Peru to Spain at the close of the sixteenth century and shortly afterwards planted in France, Portugal, Italy and England, was well known to us as an ornamental plant for two hundred years before its culinary possibilities were perceived. The first English cookery book recipes for tomatoes appear only at the beginning of the nineteenth century. They were for ketchup-type sauces. Since the tomato, being a member of the Solanacae tribe which includes also the poisonous nightshades, was long regarded as a dangerous if not actually deadly fruit (the potato and the aubergine, also of the Solanacae family, have in their time suffered from the same associations) presumably the mixture of vinegar and spices used in the early sauces were regarded as safety-devices against the possibly toxic effects of the fruit itself. By the end of the nineteenth century, when tomatoes had become an upper-class luxury and tomato soup was well on its way, a new legend had become attached to the tomato. It was reputed to induce cancer. It was also, wrote Miss Anne Buckland, the anthropological scholar and author of an entertaining book called *Our Viands* (1893), too expensive to be generally popular, and was regarded with suspicion by the poor who 'despise and dislike it'. Adding that a splendid show of numerous varieties of outdoor tomatoes at the Crystal Palace had recently caused some stir among market gardeners, Miss Buckland remarks that while awaiting cheaper and more plentiful fresh tomatoes 'the tinned tomatoes from America and France answer fairly well for cooking purposes'.

In the seventy years which have elapsed since the publication of Miss Buckland's book the tomato has taken its revenge for three centuries of neglect. What we need now is a tomato antidote or at least a little of the restraint implicit in the observation made in a French book of *Dissertations Gastronomiques* (1928) by Ernest Verdier, owner of the Maison Dorée, a restaurant celebrated in the Paris of the Belle Epoque. 'The tomato', says M. Verdier, 'imparts its delicious taste, at the same time acid and slightly sweet, to so many sauces and dishes that it can fairly be classed among the best of condiments. Happy are those who understand how to use it judiciously.' Those of us who remember the food shortages of the war years and after learned the lesson the hard way. Lacking fresh tomatoes and meat we tried to compensate by piling tomato paste into all our stews and soups and sauces. In the end the taste of tinned concentrated tomato became all-pervading and deadly. So, for a start, be miserly about tomato paste in meat sauces for pasta. Used in conjunction with fresh tomatoes a teaspoonful will be enough to give extra colour and body to a sauce for four people. Covered with a sealing layer of olive oil the paste in an opened tin will keep in the refrigerator for a week or more.

Italian and Bulgarian canned peeled tomatoes are terrific value.[1] Used occasionally and in very small quantities they work wonders for chicken and fish stocks and soups, pizza fillings and sauces made from insufficiently ripe tomatoes. Used to excess they become monotonous and sickly. Two to three tablespoons of tinned tomatoes are enough for a sauce made from 2 lb. of the fresh fruit or for 3 pints of stock.

Cookery book instructions to 'de-seed' tomatoes or squeeze out the watery parts before cooking are unrealistic; the water content of tomatoes is 94 per cent and the sole effective way to get rid of it is by evaporation. On the degree of evaporation or reduction to which the tomatoes are subjected the flavour of the sauce very largely depends. A tomato sauce can be completely changed by two or three minutes more or less of reduction or concentration by steady simmering. Demonstration of this point makes an illuminating cookery/chemistry lesson. As for the ideal consistency of a tomato sauce to go with, or to be incorporated in, any given dish, a cookery-student's thesis could be written on the subject, and for all I know already has been.

When the potentialities of the tomato were first being explored in the nineteenth century, it was nearly as often used for sweet dishes as for sauces and soups. French cookery books of the period nearly all include recipes for tomato jam. Escoffier gives a couple, and in England an eight-volume *Encyclopedia of Practical Cookery*, published in 1899, gives a formula for candied tomatoes, several for jam, and another for green tomatoes to be stewed in a sugar syrup and eaten cold with cream. Evidently even tomato soups were heavily sweetened. A booklet put out in 1900 by the Franco-American Food Company of Jersey City made the point that its canned tomato soup was a spiced rather than a sweet one, 'and our increasing sales of this variety show that it suits the taste of the majority. Sugar could be added "when desired".'

Although slightly strange, tomato jam is a most delicate and attractive preserve, with the charm of the unfamiliar. It is worth trying, even if only in a very small quantity.

*

First published in Nova, *July 1965. The second half of the article reappeared in my* Spices, Salts and Aromatics in the English

1. In 1965 Bulgarian canned tomatoes were easily available, but it is now many years since I have seen them in English shops.

Kitchen, *1970, so did the recipes which followed the introductory essay. These I do not repeat here, but my version of Boulestin's sweet tomato conserve, which I had intended to include in the same book and which is indeed indexed as appearing in it, somehow got away. The recipe is neither long nor complicated. For those who grow their own tomatoes or can buy from the market when the fruit is cheap, here it is:*

TOMATO PRESERVE

This may sound freakish but is a delicate and beautiful preserve. Evidently it was one of Marcel Boulestin's favourite sweetmeats; a recipe for tomato jam or preserve appears in every one of his cookery books.

2 lbs. of very ripe and sweet tomatoes, 2 lbs of sugar, a vanilla bean, ½ pint of water.

In a wide preserving pan boil the sugar and water to a syrup. Add the tomatoes, skinned and sliced. Boil steadily, stirring fairly often, for about 35 minutes. Put in the vanilla bean (vanilla essence will not do). Cook for approximately 10 to 15 minutes longer or until setting point is reached. Remove the vanilla pod, skim the jam, and let it cool for a few minutes before turning it into small jars.

Tomato jam is particularly good when eaten in the French way, as a sweet,[1] with fresh cream cheese or plain pouring cream.

TOMATA HONEY

This is a recipe I tried in 1973 and found excellent. It is of American origin and comes from *Miss Leslie's Complete Cookery*, Philadelphia, 1837.

'To each pound of tomatoes, allow the grated peel of a lemon and six fresh peach leaves. Boil them slowly till they are all to pieces; then squeeze and strain them through a bag. To each pint of liquid allow a pound of loaf-sugar, and the juice of one lemon. Boil them together half an hour, or till they become a thick jelly. Then put it into glasses, and lay double tissue paper closely over the top. It will be scarcely distinguishable from real honey.'

Be sure to use really juicy tomatoes for this preserve, or the yield of juice will be very small, and at best will not be more than 1 pint from 2½ lb. of fruit. Peach leaves being unavailable in my strip of London back garden, I used instead a few drops of real almond

---

1. See *Letting Well Alone*, p. 46 and *Foods of Legend*, p. 249.

essence, towards the end of the cooking, when the juice and sugar are on the boil.

Tomato honey is excellent with pork, especially the salted or pickled variety, and goes nicely too with lamb, as a change from redcurrant or mint jelly.

Escoffier and the canned tomato industry

It is interesting to learn that Escoffier played an important part in the creation of the canned tomato industry. According to his own testimony, when he was Chef de Cuisine at the Petit Moulin Rouge restaurant in the Champs Elysées in the mid 1870s[1] he had had the idea of preserving tomatoes in such a way that they would replace fresh ones at any season. At the time tomato purée for the restaurant was preserved in champagne bottles which were then sterilised (a method which was demonstrated to me by the cook at a pensione in Anacapri where I stayed during the summer of 1952, and which I described in Italian Food. *The same method was used by country people in Spain in the 1960s and probably still is. The bottles didn't have to be champagne bottles. Any wine bottles would do).*

To Escoffier the disadvantage of the bottled purée was that it could only be used for sauces, so he set about evolving a method which would ensure a supply of crushed tomatoes – by which he meant tomates concassées *– for any dish which required them whenever the fresh fruit was unobtainable. Having experimented to his own complete satisfaction – he does not say what method he used – he contacted various firms of food manufacturers, among them La Maison Gilbert at Lambesc in the Bouches-du-Rhône, and La Maison Caressa at Nice. Finding that neither firm was interested, and that further attempts to get the idea taken up had failed, Escoffier dropped the matter until after he had taken charge of the Savoy Hotel kitchens. In August one year he spent a few days holiday at Saxon-les-Bains in the Rhône Valley, where he had an interest in a fruit preserving factory. It so happened that the summer was an exceptionally hot one, the yield of tomatoes in the region was unusually high, and 'taking advantage of this wonderful opportunity, two thousand 2 kilo cans of crushed tomato were manufactured and despatched at once to the Savoy Hotel.'*

1. Escoffier remained at this restaurant from 1873 to 1878.

Still recounting his own story, Escoffier reported that the follow-ing year the factory at Saxon, all set to manufacture a quantity of the canned crushed tomatoes, was obliged to abandon the project because of the loss of the tomato crop owing to periods of intense cold that summer. Escoffier was not the man to let go easily. Returning to the Maison Caressa at Nice, he persuaded the factory which had turned down the project fifteen years earlier to manufac-ture 'a certain quantity' of 2 kilo cans of crushed tomato according to his own specification. The new product was an immense success, its fame spread rapidly, the following year the Maison Caressa canned 60,000 kilos of tomatoes and the director thanked Escoffier – as a friend – for his advice.

The story of the Escoffier canned crushed tomatoes is told in

George Auguste Escoffier *by Eugène Herbodeau and Paul Thalamas, published by the Practical Press Ltd, London, 1955 (pp.99–104). The authors do not acknowledge the source of Escoffier's account, but recount that it was during his days as an army chef de cuisine at the siege of Metz in 1870 that he had first grasped the necessity of improving the techniques of canning food. Again, according to Escoffier himself, a Paris factory, the Maison Fontaine, took up the canned tomato industry, the whole department of the Vaucluse started to specialise in the same business, and it was only after the events recorded by him that Italy and America introduced their own versions of canned tomatoes. Escoffier's story is entirely credible. He was not one to make exaggerated claims, and scarcely needed to. He was in any case always an innovator. But what happened to the crushed tomatoes which had been such a success? Were they abandoned in favour of whole canned tomatoes?*

English Potted Meats and Fish Pastes

In the late forties and the early fifties, every new member of the Wine and Food Society received, together with a copy of the current number of the Society's quarterly magazine and a membership card, a pamphlet entitled *Pottery, or Home Made Potted Foods, Meat and Fish Pastes, Savoury Butters and Others*. The little booklet was a Wine and Food Society publication, the author's name was concealed under the whimsical pseudonym of 'A Potter', and the date was 1946.

The Wine and Food Society's propaganda in favour of home-made potted meats and fish was premature. In those days of rationing and imitation food we associated fish paste and potted meat with the fearful compounds of soya bean flour, dried egg and dehydrated onions bashed up with snoek or Spam which were cheerfully known as 'mock crab paste' and 'meat spread'. By 1954, when fourteen years of rationing came to an end none of us wanted to hear another word of the makeshift cooking which potted meats and fish pastes seemed to imply.

It was not until ten years later that we began to see that in fact these very English store-cupboard provisions, so far from being suited to the cheese-paring methods necessitated by desperate shortages, demand first-class basic ingredients and a liberal hand with butter. It is indeed essential to understand that the whole success of the recipes described in this booklet depends upon these factors, and upon the correct balance of the ingredients.

Hungry as we are today for the luxury of authenticity and for visual elegance, we find that the Potter's work makes enticing reading: 'How delicious to a schoolboy's healthy appetite sixty years ago, was a potted meat at breakfast in my grandmother's old Wiltshire home. Neat little white pots, with a crust of yellow butter suggesting the spicy treat beneath, beef, ham or tongue, handiwork of the second or third kitchenmaid . . .'

The Potter whose grandmother employed the second and third kitchenmaids in question was, M. André Simon tells me, Major Matthew Connolly (father of Mr Cyril Connolly); and with his felicitous evocation of a mid-Victorian country breakfast table and those second and third kitchenmaids pounding away at the ham and tongue for potting he makes a number of points, most relevant of which concerns the kitchenmaids. What but the return of these handmaidens to our kitchens in the re-incarnated form of electric mixers, blenders and beaters[1] has made the revival of one of our most characteristic national delicacies a feasible proposition? Then, the neat little white pots, the crust of yellow butter, there is something fundamentally and uniquely English in the picture evoked by Major Connolly. It is a picture which belongs as much to the world of Beatrix Potter (Major Connolly would no doubt have appreciated the coincidental pun) as to that of the military gentleman from Bath, making it doubly an insult that the mass-produced pastes and sandwich spreads of the factories should go by the honourable names of potted meat, potted ham, tongue, lobster, salmon, shrimp and the rest. Potted shrimps alone remain as the sole representative of these products to retain something of its original nature, although a few smoked haddock pastes are beginning to appear on London restaurant menus. These are usually somewhat absurdly listed as haddock pâté, or pâté de haddock fumé. In an expensive Chelsea restaurant I have even seen − and eaten − a mixture called *rillettes écossaises* or 'pâté of Arbroath smokies with whisky'. The dish was good, but to label such a mixture *rillettes*

---

1. Of these machines by far the most effective for potted meats, as also for raw pâté ingredients, is the recently introduced French Moulinette Automatic Chopper. This device does the job of chopping and pounding without emulsifying the ingredients or squeezing out their juices.

when this is a word applicable exclusively to potted fat pork, or pork with goose or rabbit, does seem to touch the fringe of restaurateur's lunacy. For that matter, I find it sad that Arbroath smokies, the most delicate, expensive and rare of all the smoked haddock tribe, should be subjected to such treatment. Simply heated through in the oven with fresh butter, smokies are to me one of the most exquisite of our national specialities.

That crust of yellow butter so important to the true English potted meats and pastes as opposed to the Franglais and the factory-produced versions, does perhaps need a little more explanation than the late Major Connolly, who refers to it throughout his little work as 'melted butter', thought necessary to clarify. Clarified in fact is what it is, or should be, that butter. And since for the successful confection and storage of many, although not all, potted meats and fish, clarified butter is a necessary adjunct, it seems only fair to warn readers that the process does involve a little bother, although a trifling one compared to the services rendered by a supply of this highly satisfactory sealing, mixing, and incidentally, frying ingredient.

Storage of Potted Foods

Concerning the keeping qualities of home-potted foods, there are some essential points to make. First, all juices and liquid which come from fish or meat to be potted, whether especially cooked for the purpose or whether left-over from a joint, *must be drained off before the food is pounded or packed up for potting.* Because stock or gravy from salmon, game or beef, let us say, happens to look rich and taste delicious, that does not mean it will not go bad if it separates from the meat or fish in question and settles to the bottom of the pot. We all know what happens when jellied gravy and sediment is left at the bottom of a bowl of dripping or lard.

It is also important to eliminate as far as possible any air pockets in pots of meat and fish. This means that the pots must be packed very full and the contents pressed and pressed until they are as tightly packed as possible.

Finally, make sure that the layer of melted clarified butter with which the pots are covered is sufficiently thick to seal the contents completely. Given these conditions there is no reason why potted meat and fish should not keep, in a correctly ventilated larder, for several weeks. 'Game to be sent to distant places', wrote Meg Dods, long before the advent of the refrigerator 'and potted without cutting up the birds will keep for a month.' Once broached, the contents of a pot should be stored in the refrigerator and quickly consumed. For this reason, potted meats and fish are essentially delicacies to be packed into small pots. Failing the old-fashioned neat white pots described by Major Connolly use miniature white china soufflé dishes or ramekins, small straight-sided glass jars, foie gras or pâté terrines, or white, covered pots such as those associated with Gentleman's Relish – still a favourite fish paste. Apart from the dimensions and shape of the pot, an important point to remember is that whatever the colour or decoration on the *outside* of the pots·or jars used for potted meats, the *inside* should be of a pale colour and preferably white, so that the delicate creams and pinks of the contents with their layer of yellow butter look fresh and appetizing against their background.

When and How to Serve Potted Foods and Pastes

'A noble breakfast,' says George Borrow of the morning meal offered him at an inn at Bala in North Wales, 'there was tea and coffee, a goodly white loaf and butter, there were a couple of eggs and two mutton chops – there was boiled and pickled salmon – fried trout . . . also potted trout and potted shrimps . . .' A few weeks later he returns in search of more country delicacies. He is not disappointed. 'What a breakfast! Pot of hare; ditto of trout; pot of prepared shrimps; dish of plain shrimps; tin of sardines; beautiful beef-steak; eggs, muffins, large loaf, and butter, not forgetting capital tea . . .'

George Borrow was writing of *Wild Wales* in the eighteen-fifties. When you come to analyse his splendid breakfasts you find that with slight changes he might almost be describing a nineteen-sixties, chop-house revival period, West End restaurant lunch. The potted shrimps, the trout, the steak, the pot of hare (now the chef's *terrine de lièvre*), the mutton chops (now lamb cutlets), the salmon, now smoked rather than pickled, are very much with us still. The March of Progress has alas transformed the goodly white bread into that unique substance, restaurateur's toast, while tea and coffee are replaced by gin-and-tonic or a bottle of white wine, and for my part I would say none the worse for that. Tea with a fish breakfast or coffee with beefsteaks have never been my own great favourites in the game of what to drink with what.

Here we are then with plenty of ideas for an easy and simple English lunch; potted tongue or game followed by a simple hot egg dish; or smoked salmon paste with butter and brown bread to precede grilled lamb chops, or oven-baked sole, or fillet steak if you are rich. For a high-tea or supper meal spread smoked haddock paste on fingers of hot toast and arrange them in a circle around a dish of scrambled eggs. For cocktail parties, use smoked salmon butter, fresh salmon paste, sardine or tunny fish butter, potted cheese, as fillings for the smallest of small sandwiches. Fish, meat and cheese pastes do not combine successfully with vol-au-vent cases, pastry or biscuits, but in sandwiches or spread on fingers of coarse brown bread they will be greeted as a blessed change from sticky canapés and messy dips. Stir a spoonful or two of potted crab or lobster (minus the butter covering) into fresh cream for eggs *en cocotte*, into a béchamel sauce to go over poached eggs or a *gratin* of sole fillets. And as Mrs Johnstone, alias Meg Dods, author of the admirable *Housewife's Manual* of 1826 wrote, 'What is left of the clarified butter (from potted lobster or crab) will be very relishing for sauces' while 'any butter from potted tongue or chicken remaining uneaten will afterwards be useful for frying meat and for pastry for pies'.

Recipes

CLARIFIED BUTTER

In a large frying or sauté pan put a slab of butter (I use a good quality butter and find that it pays to prepare 2 lb. at a time since it keeps almost indefinitely and is immeasurably superior to fresh butter for frying bread, croquettes, rissoles, fish cakes, veal escalopes, fish *à la meunière* and a score of other tricky cooking jobs). Let the butter melt over very gentle heat. It must not brown, but should be left to bubble for a few seconds before being removed from the heat and left to settle.

Have ready a piece of butter muslin wrung out in warm water, doubled, and laid in a sieve standing over the bowl or deep wide jar in which the butter is to be stored. Filter the butter while it is still warm. For storage keep the jar, covered, in the refrigerator.

The object of clarifying butter is to rid it of water, buttermilk sediment, salt and any foreign matter which (a) for purposes of frying cause the butter to blacken and burn, and (b) render it susceptible to eventual rancidity. The clarification process also expels air and causes the butter to solidify as it cools, making it a highly effective sealing material. In French cookery clarified beef suet, pigs' lard and goose fat are used in precisely the same way to seal pâtés and home-preserved pork and goose. These are the famous *confits* which are the French equivalents of our eighteenth and nineteenth century potted meat, game and poultry. The delicious pork and goose *rillettes* and *rillons* of Western France are also close relations of English potted meats – in other words cooked and shredded or pounded meat packed into pots *after* cooking, as opposed to the pâtés and terrines which are made from raw ingredients cooked directly in the pots or the crust in which they are to be stored and served.

POTTED TONGUE

To my mind this is the best and most subtle of all English potted meat inventions. My recipe is adapted from John Farley's *The London Art of Cookery* published in 1783. Farley was master of the London Tavern, and an unusually lucid writer. One deduces that the cold table at the London Tavern must have been exceptionally good, for all Farley's sideboard dishes, cold pies, hams, spiced beef joints and potted meats are thought out with much care, are set down in detail and show a delicate and educated taste.

Ingredients and proportions for potted tongue are ½ lb. each of cooked, brined and/or smoked ox tongue and clarified butter, a salt-spoonful of ground mace, a turn or two of black or white pepper from the mill.

Chop the tongue and, with 5 oz. (weighed after clarifying) of the butter, reduce it to a paste in the blender or liquidizer, season it, pack it tightly down into a pot or pots, smooth over the top, cover, and leave in the refrigerator until very firm. Melt the remaining 3 oz. of clarified butter and pour it, tepid, over the tongue paste, so that it sets in a sealing layer about one eighth of an inch thick. When completely cold, cover the pot with foil or greaseproof paper. The amount given will fill one ¾ to 1 pint shallow soufflé dish, although I prefer to pack my potted tongue in two or three smaller containers.

Venison can be potted in the same way as tongue, and makes one of the best of all sandwich fillings. Salt beef makes another excellent potted meat.

TO POT HAM WITH CHICKENS

Readers interested in more than the bare formula of a dish will appreciate the charming, simple and well explained recipe below. Apart from the eighteenth-century country house atmosphere evoked by the writing, we get also a very clear picture of the manner in which these potted meats were presented and a substantial hint as to the devising of other permutations and combinations of poultry, game and meat for potting:

'Take as much lean of boiled ham as you please, and half the quantity of fat, cut it as thin as possible, beat it very fine in a mortar, with a little oiled butter, beaten mace, pepper and salt, pot part of it into a china pot, then beat the white part of a fowl with a very little seasoning; it is to qualify the ham, put a lay of chicken, then one of ham, then chicken at the top, press it hard down, and when it is cold, pour clarified butter over it; when you send it to the table cut out a thin slice in the form of half a diamond, and lay it round the edge of your pot.'

Elizabeth Raffald, *The Experienced English Housekeeper*, 1769

POTTED CHICKEN LIVERS

This is a recipe which produces a rich, smooth and gamey-flavoured mixture, rather like a very expensive French pâté, at a fraction of the price and with very little fuss.

Ingredients are 4 oz. of chicken livers (frozen livers are perfectly adequate); 3 oz. of butter; a tablespoon of brandy; seasonings.

Frozen chicken livers are already cleaned, so if they are being used the only preliminary required is the thawing-out process. If you have bought fresh livers, put them in a bowl of tepid, slightly salted water and leave them for about a couple of hours. Then look at each one very carefully, removing any yellowish pieces, which may give the finished dish a bitter taste.

Heat 1 oz. of butter in a small heavy frying pan. In this cook the livers for about 5 minutes, turning them over constantly. The outsides should be browned but not toughened, the insides should remain pink but not raw. Take them from the pan with a perforated spoon and transfer them to a mortar or the liquidizer goblet.

To the buttery juices in the pan add the brandy and let it sizzle for a few seconds. Pour it over the chicken livers. Add a teaspoon of salt, and a sprinkling of milled pepper. Put in the remaining 2 oz. of butter, softened but not melted. Pound or whizz the whole mixture to a very smooth paste. Taste for seasoning. Press into a little china, glass or glazed earthenware pot or terrine and smooth down the top. Cover, and chill in the refrigerator. Serve with hot crisp dry toast.

If to be made in larger quantities and stored, seal the little pots with a layer of clarified butter, melted and poured over the chilled paste.

Rum (white, for preference) makes a sound alternative to the brandy in this recipe. Surprisingly, perhaps, gin is also very successful.

N.B. Since this dish is a very rich one, I sometimes add to the chicken livers an equal quantity of blanched, poached pickled pork (*not* bacon) or failing pickled pork, a piece of fresh belly of pork, salted overnight, then gently poached for about 30 minutes. Add the cooked pork, cut in small pieces to the chicken livers in the blender.

POTTED GAME

Grouse 'potted whole, stowed singly into pots with clarified butter poured over' as described by Professor Saintsbury[1] (the old boy didn't miss much) are infinitely enticing, exceedingly extravagant with butter and not very practical for these days, but you can make one young cooked grouse or partridge go a very long way by the simple method of chopping the flesh, freed from all skin and sinew with about one quarter of its weight in mild, rather fat, cooked ham. You then put the chopped grouse and ham in the electric blender with 4 tablespoons of clarified butter to every ½ lb. of the mixture. Add salt if necessary, a few grains of cayenne, a few drops of lemon juice. Reduce the mixture to a paste or purée. Pack it in to small straight-sided china, glazed earthenware or glass pots. Put these into the refrigerator until the meat is very cold and firm. Then seal the pots with a layer of just-melted clarified butter.

Potted game is most delicious and delicate with hot thin crisp brown toast for tea or as a first course at lunch.

It goes without saying that old birds can, equally, be used for potting, but they are much less delicate, need very long slow and

1. In one of the *Fur, Feather and Fin* series of volumes published in the 1890s by Longmans, Green.

thorough cooking, a larger proportion of fat ham (or pickled pork but *not* smoked bacon), and must be carefully drained of their cooking juices before they are prepared for chopping and pounding, otherwise sediment seeps through, collects at the bottom of the little jars and causes mould.

RILLETTES OR POTTED PORK IN THE FRENCH MANNER

This very famous charcutiers' or pork butchers' speciality is native to Southern Brittany, Anjou and Touraine. It could be described as the French equivalent of our potted meat – although it is very different in texture and taste.

2 lb. of a cheap and fat cut of pork such as neck or belly; 1 lb. of back pork fat; salt; 1 clove of garlic; 2 or 3 sprigs of dried wild thyme on the stalk; a couple of bay leaves; freshly milled black pepper.

Ask your butcher to remove the rind and the bones from the piece of pork meat (the bones can be added to stock and the rind will enrich a beef dish for the next course) and if he will, to cut the back pork fat into cubes.

Rub the meat with salt (about a couple of tablespoonsful) and let it stand overnight or at least a few hours before cutting it into 1½-inch thick strips – along the grooves left by the bones. Put these strips, and the fat, into an earthenware or other oven dish. In the centre put the crushed clove of garlic, the bay leaf and twig of thyme; mill a little black pepper over the meat and add about half a pint of cold water. Cover the pot. Place it in a very cool oven, gas no. 1, 290°F., and leave for about 4 hours.

Now place a sieve over a big bowl. Turn meat and fat out into the sieve, so that all the liquid drips through. With two forks, pull apart the meat and fat (which should be soft as butter) so that the *rillettes* are shredded rather than in a paste. Pack the *rillettes* lightly into a glazed earthenware or stoneware jar of about ¾ pint capacity (or into two or three smaller jars). Taste for seasoning. Pour over the rillettes (taking care to leave the sediment) enough strained fat to fill the jar. Cool, cover and store in the refrigerator until needed.

Rillettes should be soft enough to spoon out, so remember to remove the jar several hours before dinner. Serve with bread or toast, with or without butter, as you please.

Potted Fish and Fish Pastes

POTTED SALMON

Any woman who has salmon-fishing relations or friends will appreciate the point of this dish. Evolved at a time when salmon was comparatively cheap, and before the days of the tin and the refrigerated larder, potted salmon provided one method (pickling in wine and vinegar, salting, drying, kippering and smoking were others) of preserving surplus fish. Even today there will be readers who will be glad to know of a formula for dealing with a salmon or a piece of one received as a present, too big to be consumed immediately and likely to prove wearisome if eaten cold day after day.

For this recipe, evolved from instructions given in Elizabeth Raffald's *Experienced English Housekeeper* (an admirable book first published in 1769) all you need, apart from fresh salmon, are seasonings of salt, freshly milled white pepper, nutmeg, fresh butter and clarified butter.

Cut the salmon into thinnish steaks, arrange them in one layer in a well-buttered baking dish, sprinkle them with salt and seasonings, add about 1 oz. of fresh butter, cut in pieces, for every pound of salmon, cover the dish with buttered paper and a lid, and put to cook in the centre of a moderately heated oven, gas no. 3, 330°F. In 45 to 50 minutes – a little more or less according to the thickness of the steaks – the salmon will be cooked. Lift the steaks, very carefully, on to a wide sieve, colander, or wire grid placed over a dish so that the cooking butter drains away.

Pack the salmon steaks into a wide dish or pot with the skin side showing. The dish or pot should be filled to capacity without being so crammed that the fish comes higher than the rim of the pot. I make my potted salmon in a shallow round white pot decorated on the outside with coloured fish. It is one of the old dishes especially made for potted char, the freshwater fish once a celebrated delicacy of the Cumberland lake district. Cover with a piece of oiled foil or greaseproof paper and a board, or the base of one of the removable-base tart or cake tins now to be found in many kitchen utensil shops, to fit exactly *inside* the dish. Weight the board. Next day pour in clarified butter to cover the salmon and seal it completely.

Serve potted salmon in its own dish with a cucumber or green salad and perhaps jacket potatoes. A good luncheon or supper dish – and very decorative looking when cut at the table, into the cross-slices of which Elizabeth Raffald notes that 'the skin makes them look ribbed'.

SALMON PASTE

A more ordinary version of potted salmon can be made using cooked salmon and clarified butter in similar proportions and the same manner as for potted tongue (page 221). A salmon steak weighing about 7 oz. will make a pot of salmon paste ample for four people, so it is a quite economical proposition.

POTTED CRAB

Extract all the meat from a freshly boiled crab weighing about 2 lb. Keep the creamy brown body meat separate from the flaked white claw meat. Season both with salt, freshly milled pepper, mace or nutmeg, cayenne, lemon juice.

Pack claw and body meat in alternate layers in small fire-proof pots. Press down closely. Pour in melted butter just to cover the meat.

Stand the pots in a baking tin of water, cook uncovered on the bottom shelf of a very low oven, gas no. 2, 310°F., for 25 to 30 minutes.

When cold, seal with clarified butter. Serve well chilled.

Potted crab is very rich in flavour as well as in content, and is best appreciated quite on its own, perhaps as a midday dish served only with crisp dry toast, to be followed by a simple lettuce salad or freshly cooked green beans or purple-sprouting broccoli eaten when barely cold, with an oil and lemon dressing.

Those who find crab indigestible may be interested in the advice proffered by Merle's *Domestic Dictionary and Household Manual* of 1842, to the effect that after eating fresh crab it is always advisable to take 'a very small quantity of good French brandy, mixed with its own bulk of water'.

POTTED·LOBSTER

Make in the same way as potted crab. Meg Dods (*The Cook's and Housewife's Manual*, 1826) instructs that if this is to be kept as a cold relish the white meat and the coral and spawn should be packed 'in a regular manner, in layers, or alternate pieces, so that when sliced it may have that marbled appearance, that look of mosaic work which so commends the taste of the cook'.

SMOKED HADDOCK PASTE

Smoked haddock on the bone or in fillets, fresh butter, cayenne pepper, lemon.

Pour boiling water over the fish, cover it, leave 10 minutes. Pour off the water, skin and flake the fish. (Taste it at this stage. If it is very salty, pour a second lot of boiling water over it.) Weigh it. Mash it or purée it in the blender with an equal quantity of fresh unsalted butter. Season with plenty of lemon juice and a very little cayenne. No salt. Press into pots, cover, and store in the refrigerator.

I do not advise frozen haddock fillets for this paste. The false flavours of dye and chemical smoke are all too perceptible in the finished product.

There are restaurateurs and cookery journalists who like to call confections such as haddock and kipper paste by the name of pâté. I find this comical and also misleading.

KIPPER PASTE

As for smoked haddock. Smoked trout, mackerel and smoked cod's roe paste (not to be confused with the Greek *taramasalata* in which the cod's roe is mixed with olive oil and garlic) are also made in the same way, except that the boiling water treatment is superfluous.

SARDINE BUTTER

For this wonderfully simple little delicacy the sole requirements are good quality sardines in oil, fresh butter, lemon, and cayenne pepper. No clarified butter seal is necessary.

Drain off the oil. Skin and bone the sardines. To each large sardine allow a scant ounce of butter, ½ oz. if the sardines are small. Mix butter and sardines very thoroughly, mashing them with a fork until you have a smooth paste. Season with a few drops of lemon juice and a sprinkling of cayenne pepper.

Pack the sardine butter into small pots, cover, store in the refrigerator, serve well chilled, with thin, crisp brown toast.

SMOKED SALMON BUTTER

Make this in the same way as sardine butter, using the same proportions of fish and butter. It is an excellent way of turning a second-grade smoked salmon, i.e. imported Canadian or Norwegian, or a few slices cut from the end of a side (sometimes sold cheaply by fishmongers and delicatessen merchants) into a real delicacy. If possible, use unsalted or only very slightly salted butter. A good deal of lemon juice will be needed.

For a first course for four, 6 oz. each of salmon and butter is a plentiful allowance.

Have lemons and a pepper mill on the table and toast as for sardine butter.

TUNNY FISH BUTTER

Same again. But pick your brand of tunny carefully. It isn't worth wasting butter or work on coarse dark tunny. About the best English-packed brand is Epicure. The Portuguese *Nice* is better.

COD'S ROE PASTE IN THE GREEK MANNER

Cheap, easy, made in advance, an admirable standby. What you can do with a two-ounce jar of smoked cod's roe, a few spoonfuls of oil and a potato is quite a revelation to many people.

For a 2-oz. jar of smoked cod's roe the other ingredients are about 4 tablespoons of olive oil, a medium sized potato, lemon juice, cayenne pepper, and water; and, optionally, a clove of garlic.

An hour or two before you are going to make the paste, or the evening before if it's more convenient, turn the contents of the jar into a bowl, break it up, and put about 3 tablespoons of cold water with it. This softens it and makes it much easier to work. Drain off the water before starting work on the making of the dish.

Pound the garlic and mash it with the cod's roe until the paste is quite smooth before gradually adding 3 tablespoons of the oil. Boil the potato without salt, mash it smooth with the rest of the oil, combine the two mixtures, stir again until quite free from lumps, add the juice of half a lemon and a scrap of cayenne pepper. Pack the mixture into little pots or jars. Serve chilled with hot dry toast. Enough for four.

This little dish, or a similar one, is now listed on the menus of scores of Cypriot-Greek taverns and London bistros under the name of *taramasalata*. It is indeed very much akin to the famous Greek speciality, except that true *taramasalata* is made from a cod's roe much more salty, more pungent, and less smoked than our own. There is also a great deal more garlic in the Greek version, and very often bread instead of potato is used as a softening agent.

Booklet published by Elizabeth David, 1968

*

English Potted Meats and Fish Pastes *first appeared in article form in the April 1965 issue of* Nova. *Rearranged, revised and slightly augmented, the original article was turned into a booklet in 1968, price 2/9. I did not choose to reprint it, but the material has been freely drawn on by others, sometimes in all but word for word form. The recipes, I was happy to notice, rapidly found favour with restaurateurs. That was as it should have been. I am pleased to have the opportunity of reprinting the material from the original booklet here. It may be found useful to a new generation of cooks, professional and amateur.*

Syllabubs and Fruit Fools

Syllabub

It was Herbert Beerbohm Tree's wedding day. His half-brother had been called in to act as best man in place of his real brother who had vanished to Spain. At the celebration breakfast there were syllabubs. Herbert was beguiled by the biblical rhythm of the name. 'And Sillabub, the son of Sillabub reigned in his stead,' he intoned. His stepbrother, half-scandalized and wholly impressed by Herbert's levity, never forgot the episode. He had been ten years old at the time of Herbert's wedding; his name was Max Beerbohm; the story is recounted in Lord David Cecil's *Max, A Biography*;[1] the date was 1882, and sillabub,[2] added Max, was then his favourite dish.

Max Beerbohm's generation must have been the last to which the delicious syllabub was a familiar childhood treat. Already for nearly a century the syllabub had been keeping company with the trifle, and in due course the trifle came to reign in the syllabub's stead; and before long the party pudding of the English was not any more the fragile whip of cream contained in a little glass, concealing within its innocent white froth a powerful alcoholic punch, but a built-up confection of sponge fingers and ratafias soaked in wine and brandy, spread with jam, clothed in an egg-and-cream custard, topped with a syllabub and strewn with little coloured comfits. Came 1846, the year that Mr Alfred Bird brought forth custard powder;

1. Published by Constable, 1964.
2. The spelling is Max Beerbohm's.

and Mr Bird's brain-child grew and grew until all the land was covered with custard made with custard powder and the Trifle had become custard's favourite resting-place. The wine and lemon-flavoured cream whip or syllabub which had crowned the Trifle had begun to disappear. Sponge cake left over from millions of nursery teas usurped the place of sponge fingers and the little bitter almond macaroons called ratafias. Kitchen sherry replaced Rhenish and Madeira and Lisbon wines. Brandy was banished. The little coloured comfits – sugar-coated coriander seeds and caraways – bright as tiny tiddlywinks, went into a decline and in their stead reigned candied angelica and nicely varnished glacé cherries.

Now seeking means to combat the Chemicals Age, we look to our forbears for help. We find that the syllabub can replace the synthetic ice cream which replaced the trifle which replaced the syllabub in the first place. The ingredients of a syllabub, we find, are simple and sumptuous. The skill demanded for its confection is minimal, the presentation is basic and elegant. Swiftly, now, before the deep-freezers, the dehydrators and the emulsifiers take the syllabub away from us and return it transformed and forever despoiled, let us discover how it was made in its heyday and what we can do to recapture something of its pristine charm.

In the beginning then, in the seventeenth and eighteenth centuries, there were three kinds of syllabub. There was the syllabub mixed in a punch bowl on a basis of cider or ale and sometimes both, sweetened with sugar and spiced with cinnamon or nutmeg. Into the bowl the milkmaid milked the cow so that the new warm milk fell in a foam and froth on to the cider. The contents of the bowl were left undisturbed for an hour or two, by which time a kind of honeycombed curd had formed on the top, leaving alcoholic whey underneath. Sometimes, on top of the milk curd, a layer of thick fresh cream was poured. This syllabub was more a drink than a whip, a diversion for country parties and rustic festivals.

Co-existing with the syllabub of pastoral England was one made with wine and spirits instead of cider and ale, and with cream instead of milk. This mixture was a more solid one. It was about four-fifths sweetened whipped cream, to be spooned rather than drunk out of the glasses in which it was served, and one-fifth of wine and whey which had separated from the whip, and which you drank when you reached the end of the cream. Then, at some stage, it was discovered that by reducing the proportions of wine and sugar to cream, the whip would remain thick and light without separating.

This version was called a solid or everlasting syllabub. One eight-eenth-century author, E. Smith, whose *Complete Housewife*, pub-lished in 1727, was also the first cookery book to be printed in America, claimed that her Everlasting Syllabubs would remain in perfect condition for nine or ten days, although at their best after three or four.

Not all syllabubs were necessarily made with wine. Sir Kenelm Digby, whose book of recipes collected from his contemporaries and friends has provided posterity with a graphic record of Stuart cookery, notes that he himself made a fine syllabub with syrup left over from the home-drying of plums; being 'very quick of the fruit and very weak of sugar' this syrup 'makes the Syllabub exceeding well tasted' says Sir Kenelm. He adds that cherry syrup may be used in like manner. In the eighteenth and nineteenth centuries, syllabubs were sometimes made with the juice of Seville oranges, and in these days we can devise cream and wine or cream and fruit-syrup syllabubs to suit ourselves.

Before venturing on new formulas, however, it is as well to have an idea of what the old recipes were like and to know in what quantities, approximately, the ingredients were portioned out. From the following cross-section of recipes, chosen from cookery books written by professional and practising cooks and from household receipt books of the seventeenth, eighteenth and nineteenth centuries, emerges a fairly clear picture of the ways in which the cooks of the Stuart, the Georgian and the Victorian eras made and served their syllabubs. Historical and documentary interest apart, some of the old recipes are remarkable for the beauty and the clarity of the English in which they are written.

The Seventeenth Century

AN EXCELLENT SYLLABUB

'Fill your Sillabub pot half full with sider, and good store of sugar, and a little nutmeg, stir it well together, and put in as much cream by two or three spoonfuls at a time, as hard as you can, as though you milk it in; then stir it together very softly once about, and let it stand two hours before you eat it, for the standing makes it curd.'

Robert May, *The Accomplisht Cook*, 1660

The author of this celebrated Stuart cookery book was a pro-fessional cook whose father, also a professional, apprenticed him to

Arthur Hollingsworth, cook and caterer to one of the City Guilds during the last years of the sixteenth century. Since May was seventy-two when his book was published, it is clear that many of his recipes must date back to the days of Queen Elizabeth 1st.

A SYLLABUB

'My Lady Middlesex makes Syllabubs for little glasses with spouts, thus. Take three pints of Sweet Cream, one of quick white wine (or Rhenish)[1] and a good wine glassful (better the ¼ of a pint) of Sack:[2] mingle with them about three quarters of a pound of fine Sugar in Powder. Beat all these together with a whisk, till all appeareth converted into froth, and let them stand all night. The next day the Curd will be thick and firm above, and the drink clear under it. I conceive it may do well, to put into each glass (when you pour the liquor into it) a sprig of Rosemary a little bruised, or a little Limon-peel, or some such thing to quicken the taste; or use Amber-sugar, or spirit of Cinnamon, or of Lignum-Cassie,[3] or Nutmegs, or Mace, or Cloves, a very little.'

The Closet of the Eminently Learned Sir Kenelme Digby Kt. Opened,
Published by his Son's Consent, 1669

Sir Kenelm Digby, philosopher-scientist, soldier-diplomat, ardent royalist, lifelong friend and confidant of Charles the First's widow, Queen Henrietta Maria, was born in 1603 and died in 1664. His recipes, some his own and many collected from his friends and contemporaries, were put together in the form of a private note-book rather than for publication. They provide us with a first-hand and unique record of cooking as it was understood and practised in the kitchens and still-rooms of aristocratic houses of the first half of the seventeenth century.

The Eighteenth Century

TO MAKE WHIPT SYLLABUBS

'Take a quart of Creme and a pint of rhenish wine and the juice of 4 lemons sweeten it to your taste and put in some leamon peele then whip it up with a small rod and put it with a spoone into syllabub glasses.'

1. Rhine wine.
2. Sherry.
3. Cassia bark, an alternative to cinnamon, cheaper and less pungent.

The MS. receipt book of Judith Frampton of Morton House, nr Dorchester, Dorset. 1708. Quoted in *Dorset Dishes of the 18th Century*, edited by J. Stevens Cox, published by the Dorset Natural History and Archaeological Society, Dorchester, 1961

TO MAKE LEMON SYLLABUB

'To a pint of cream put a pound of double-refined sugar, the juice of seven lemons, grate the rinds of two lemons into a pint of white wine, add half a pint of sack, then put them all into a deep pot, and whisk them for half an hour, put it into glasses the night before you want it: it is better for standing two or three days, but it will keep a week if required.'

Elizabeth Raffald, *The Experienced English Housekeeper*, 1769

Elizabeth Raffald was a Yorkshire woman, housekeeper in the Cheshire household of Lady Elizabeth Warburton. She married Lady Elizabeth's head gardener, left her service to run a catering establishment in Manchester, bore sixteen daughters, and managed the kitchens in two different Manchester inns. Her book, substantially as she wrote it, was still in print, and selling, a hundred years after its original publication.

A FINE SYLLABUB FROM THE COW

'Sweeten a quart of cyder with refined sugar, grate a nutmeg over it; and milk the cow into your liquor. When you have added what is necessary, pour half-a-pint of the sweetest cream over it.'

Barbara Young, Steyning, Sussex. MS. receipt book, 1781. From *Dorset Dishes of the 18th Century*, already quoted above.

The Nineteenth Century

SOMERSETSHIRE SYLLABUB

'Sweeten a pint of port, and another of Madeira or sherry, in a china bowl. Milk about three pints of milk over this. In a short time it will bear clouted cream laid over it. Grate nutmeg over this, and strew a few coloured comfits on the top if you choose.'

Mistress Margaret Dods, *The Cook's and Housewife's Manual*, 4th edition, 1819

The copious footnotes to the recipes in this book were believed by his contemporaries to have been written by Sir Walter Scott. Margaret or Meg Dods is a character in Scott's *St Roman's Well*. It was also the pseudonym used by Christine Isobel Johnstone, wife of an Edinburgh publisher. Her cookery book is still one of the two main sources of authentic Scottish recipes. The other is *The Scots Kitchen*, a fine book by a living writer, Marian McNeill.[1] *The Scots Kitchen* was first published by Blackie and Son in 1929.

The Twentieth Century

My own version of Everlasting Syllabub:

One small glass, or 4 oz. of white wine or sherry, 2 tablespoons of brandy, one lemon, 2 oz. of sugar, ½ pint of double cream, nutmeg.

The day before the syllabub is to be made, put the thinly pared rind of the lemon and the juice in a bowl with the wine and brandy and leave overnight. Next day, strain the wine and lemon mixture into a large and deep bowl. Add the sugar and stir until it has dissolved. Pour in the cream slowly, stirring all the time. Grate in a little nutmeg. Now whisk the mixture until it thickens and will hold a soft peak on the whisk. The process may take 5 minutes, it may take as long as 15. It depends on the cream, the temperature and the method of whisking. Unless dealing with a large quantity of cream, an electric mixer can be perilous. A couple of seconds too long and the cream is a ruined and grainy mass. For a small amount of cream a wire whisk is perfectly satisfactory and just as quick as an electric beater. An old-fashioned wooden chocolate mill or whisk held upright and twirled between the palms of both hands is also a good implement for whisking cream. The important point is to learn to recognize the moment at which the whisking process is complete.

When the cream is ready, spoon it into glasses, which should be of very small capacity (2 to 2½ oz.) but filled to overflowing. Once in the glasses the cream will not spoil nor sink nor separate. As suggested by Sir Kenelm Digby, a tiny sprig of rosemary or a little twist of lemon peel can be stuck into each little filled glass. Keep the syllabubs in a cool place – not in the refrigerator – until you are ready to serve them. They can be made at least two days before they are needed. The quantities given will fill ten small syllabub or custard cups or sherry glasses and will be enough for four to six people. Though circumstances are so changed it is relevant to remember that in their heyday syllabubs were regarded as refreshments to be offered at card parties, ball suppers and at public

1. Miss McNeill has since died.

entertainments, rather than just as a pudding for lunches and dinners, although they did quite often figure as part of the dessert in the days when a choice of sweetmeats, fruits, jellies, confectionery and creams was set out in a formal symmetrical array in the centre of the table. This seems to have been particularly the case in aristocratic Scottish houses in the early decades of the eighteenth century. In *The Household Book of Lady Grisell Baillie 1692–1733*, edited, with Notes and Introduction, by Robert Scott-Moncrieff, W.S. Edinburgh, 1911, many of the bills of fare for dinners and suppers recorded between 1713 and 1728 featured syllabus, regardless of the season. On Christmas Day 1715 'w^t 9 of our frinds 14 at table in all' Lady Grisell's dessert consisted of ratafia cream, two dishes of butter and cheese, jacolet [chocolate] walnuts and almonds, apples, stewed pears, chestnuts, 'sillibubs and jellys'. On May 26th 1718 'at Mr Johnstons' the dessert was 'cherries, sillibubs with strawberries, sweetmeats, oranges', and four dishes of milk. The dessert for Lord Anadall's dinner guests on January 29th 1719, '10 at table' was a specially fine affair. The way it was arranged was indicated by Lady Grisell:

Desert

a salver with sweet meats

stewed pears   pistosenuts

butter   cheese

sillibubs and jellies   a lagere salver   sillibubs and jellies

wt sweet meats

cheese   butter

pistache nuts   stweed aples

a salver with sweet meats

At Lord Anadall's supper that night there was lobster and roast lamb (obviously cold) 'a ring w^t wild foull collops and pickles etc' brawn, a cold tart, 'two salvers of silibubs and jellies', and two dishes of confections.

On December 14th 1719 'Super at Mr Cockburn 11 at table 22 persons in al' there were 'eating poset in cheana [china] high dish at the head of the table, at the foot a haunch of venison, 'in the middle of the table a pirimide sillibubs and orang cream in the past, above it sweet meets dry and wet', on the sides black pudding, partridge, larks, celery salad 'made and unmade', veal collops white sauce, '2 boyld pullets w^t persley sauce, in the midle pickles of other sort than the comon ones.'

It was at about this time that the epergne, a standing centre-piece with branched supports for the dessert was coming into fashion. At the Princess of Wales's at Richmond on July 15th 1720 Lady Grisell noted that the 'Deseart' was 'a big dish in the Midle with connections and frute only', and on April 12th 1725, at the Duke of Chandos' magnificent house at Canons, near Edgware, with 'A Duson at Table' there was 'ane Eparn in the Midle.[1] Again in 1727 'We was eight days at Twitenham. We had always an Eparn in the middle'. It is interesting to note that when an epergne stood on the table, there were no creams, jellies, or syllabubs in glasses mentioned in the dessert course, but Lady Grisell herself did not possess such an ornament and for her own dinners still served 'sweetmeats and jelly and sillibubs', curds and cream, pears and apples, 'pistaches and scorcht almonds, Bisket round the milk' in the old way in separate dishes, in glasses on footed salvers, and in sweetmeat glasses.[2]

For those interested in tracing the evolution of our national dishes, the brief recipe on page 245 shows how the syllabub and the trifle were eventually amalgamated to make one glorious sticky mess. Then, looking back into the old recipes for English fruit fools, we find that trifles, syllabubs, creams and fools have all at some point merged one with the other. In the history of cookery nothing is conveniently consistent.

English Fruit Fools

'Our frailties are invincible'. Robert Louis Stevenson

Soft, pale, creamy, untroubled, the English fruit fool is the most frail and insubstantial of English summer dishes. That at any rate is how it should be, and how we like to think it always was. Here the old cookery books interrupt the smooth sequence. The seventeenth- and eighteenth-century writers do describe a number of fruit fools, fools made from gooseberries, raspberries, strawberries, redcurrants, apples, mulberries, apricots, even from fresh figs; but few of these dishes turn out to be the simple cream-enriched purées we know today. Some were made from rather roughly crushed fruit (the French word *foulé*, meaning crushed or pressed must surely

1. The editors of the 1971 OED missed Lady Grisell Baillie. Their earliest mention of an epergne is quoted as 1775.
2. For the syllabub, sweetmeat glasses and glass epergnes of the eighteenth century see Therle Hughes *Sweetmeat and Jelly Glasses*. Lutterworth Press, Guildford 1982.

have some bearing on the English name), often they were thickened with eggs as well as cream, sometimes they were flavoured with wine and spices, perfumed sugar and lemon peel.

Two hundred years ago it was those recipes listed under the heading of creams which were much more like the fruit fools of today. Evidently, at some stage, it came to be appreciated that the eggs and the extra flavourings were unnecessary, that they even distort the fresh flavour of the fruit. This is especially true of berry fruits and of apricots. Gradually the delicacy now regarded as the traditional English fruit fool came to be accepted as a purée of fruit plus sugar, fresh thick cream, and nothing more.

Like the syllabub, the fruit fool was almost always served in glasses or custard cups, although Susannah MacIver, an Edinburgh cookery teacher and author of an excellent little book called *Cookery and Pastry*, 1774, directs that her gooseberry cream be served on an 'asset', the old Scots word for platter.

From the following few recipes it is easy to see that there was never any *one* method of making English fruit creams and fools, and that over the past three centuries the two have fused. In the process some charming variations have disappeared. Some of these would be worth reviving, for example Elizabeth Hammond's gooseberry or apple trifle quoted on page 240 and Robert May's beautiful 'black fruit' mixtures.

In this selection of old and modern recipes I give precedence to those dishes made from the gooseberry, because green gooseberry fool is – to me at any rate – the most delicious as well as the most characteristic of all these simple, almost childlike, English dishes.

GOOSEBERRY FOOL

This is my own method of making gooseberry fool.

2 lb. of green gooseberries; ½ lb. of sugar; a minimum of ½ pint of double cream.

Wash the gooseberries. There is no need to top and tail them. Put them in the top half of a double saucepan with the sugar, and steam them (or if it is easier bake them in a covered jar in a low oven) until they are quite soft. Sieve them through the mouli having first strained off surplus liquid which would make the fool watery. When the purée is quite cold add the cream. More sugar may be necessary.

Later in the season when gooseberries are over, delicious fools can be made with uncooked strawberries; a mixture of raspberries and redcurrants, also uncooked; and blackberries, cooked as for gooseberries; but in this case I think that cream spoils the rich colour of the fruit and should be offered separately.

To me it is essential to serve fruit fools in glasses or in simple white cups, and with shortbread or other such biscuits to go with them.

ICED GOOSEBERRY FOOL

1 quart green gooseberries; ½ lb. white sugar; 1 pint of whipped cream; brandy or maraschino; vegetable greening; a little water; grated lemon peel.

'Stew very slowly one quart of green gooseberries with half a pound of white sugar and enough water to prevent fruit from burning. Rub through a hair sieve and use a very little vegetable greening to make it a pretty colour. (Add brandy or maraschino if required.) One pint of cream whipped stiff and grated lemon peel. Mix well together and freeze. Should take two hours to freeze and should be worked with a wooden spoon from time to time.'

Ruth Lowinsky, *Lovely Food, a Cookery Notebook*, Nonesuch Press, London, 1931

I find this recipe most interesting. The thirties was the decade when smart hostesses took to serving a great many dishes iced or frozen simply for the originality of the idea. In England at this time it was quite avant garde to possess a refrigerator. Iced camembert cream, frozen horseradish sauce, and tomato ice all belong to this period. I remember a cook of my childhood whose great dish was a *crème brûlée* in which the layer of glass-like caramel concealed, not the usual egg-thickened cream, but a delicate and softly frozen gooseberry fool.

Ruth Lowinsky's book is a true period piece, which is to say that in its time it was bang up to date. The recipes and the suggested menus evoke the days of English parlourmaids handing round every course in silver-plated entrée dishes far too big for the food they contained, while the illustrations of table decorations devised by Mr Thomas Lowinsky depict such conversation stimulators as 'two dead branches in an accumulator jar', or 'a spiral of chromium-plated steel pierced with holes through which the stems of flowers are passed'. Today's equivalents do not adorn our tables. They are worn by our guests. The clanking camisoles and the chain mail adornments of the sixties are certainly less static than the table decorations of the thirties; they exist surely for the same reason, to invite comment.

In sharp contrast the redundant vegetable greening and liqueurs in Mrs Lowinsky's gooseberry fool recipe hark back to Hannah Glasse and the mid-eighteenth century. Hannah Glasse's book, *The Art of Cookery Made Plain and Easy* was first published in 1747; in the 1751 edition appears what is possibly the first English printed recipe for an ice cream.[1] The formula is for a simple raspberry purée and cream mixture which today we should call a raspberry fool. Mrs Glasse directs that the cream be frozen in 'pewter basons'. What else are our fruit fools but the basis of modern cream ices or frozen desserts?

In the next recipe, the fool has amalgamated with the syllabub *and* the trifle, the gooseberry fool taking the place of the cake at the bottom of the dish. An attractive recipe.

GOOSEBERRY OR APPLE TRIFLE

'Scald a sufficient quantity of fruit, and pulp it through a sieve, add sugar agreeable to taste, make a thick layer of this at the bottom of your dish: mix a pint of milk, a pint of cream, and the yolks of two eggs: scald it over the fire, observing to stir it: add a small quantity of sugar, and let it get cold: then lay it over the apples or gooseberries with a spoon, and put on the whole a whip [a syllabub] made the day before. If you use apples, add the rind of a lemon grated.'

Elizabeth Hammond, *Modern Domestic Cookery and Useful Receipt Book, c.* 1817

The next recipe comes from a work compiled by two eighteenth-century London publicans.

TO MAKE GOOSEBERRY FOOL

'Put two quarts of gooseberries into about a quart of water, and set them on the fire. When they begin to simmer, turn yellow, and to plump, throw them into a cullender to drain out the water, and with the back of a spoon carefully squeeze the pulp through a sieve into a dish. Make them pretty sweet, and let them stand till they are cold.

1. No. There had been earlier published recipes, notably in Mary Eales' *Mrs Eales Receipts* 1718, and Vincent La Chapelle's *The Modern Cook* 1733. Both authors had derived their ice cream recipes from earlier French sources. Mrs Glasse's raspberry ice cream recipe, however, appears to be her own.

In the meantime, take two quarts of milk, and the yolks of four eggs beaten up with a little grated nutmeg. Stir it softly over a slow fire, and when it begins to simmer, take it off, and by degrees stir it into the gooseberries. Let it stand till it be cold, and then serve it up. If you make it with cream, you need not put any eggs.'

Francis Collingwood and John Woollams, *The Universal Cook and City and Country Housekeeper*, 1791

The main point of interest about the book from which the foregoing recipe is extracted is the French translation which appeared in Paris in 1810.

The flow of English translations from French cookery books has been well-sustained ever since the mid-seventeenth century when La Varenne's celebrated *French Cook* appeared in England. French kitchen terms peppered throughout English cookery books, and half-anglicized names of French dishes are no novelty to us. When for once the tide runs in the reverse direction we get a new view of our own cookery, and a revealing insight into the oddness of traditional names as they appear in another language.

In the case of *Le Cuisinier Anglais Universel ou Le Nec Plus Ultra de la Gourmandise* there are some interesting metamorphoses, as well as signs that the translator was defeated by the names of some of our cherished specialities, among them *le catchup* and *le browning* ('to even the most skilled of French cooks these sauces will be new', says the publisher's preface). The syllabub turns up as *Eternel Syllabub, syllabub solide*, and *syllabub sous la vache*.

La plume of the French translator gives a new aspect to several of our old sweet dishes, among them the trifle which as *bagatelle*, regains something of its lost charm. Cheesecakes also return to grace and elegance as *talmouses*. As for *folie de groseilles vertes* it is no longer perfidious Albion's frailty, serene and cool, but a wild whirl of summer gaiety and greenery.

I fancy that across the channel where Napoleon's wars were ravaging all Europe, our two innkeepers fell flat as pancakes, and were it not for the felicities of their translator they would scarcely be worth comment. All their recipes had been borrowed – by their own admission – from earlier works and their style is charmless. It is a relief to turn back to something with the flavour of originality, an evocation of a truly pastoral summer dish, half fruit fool, half syllabub.

TO MAKE CREAM OF SUNDRY KINDS OF FRUITS

'Take either currants, mulberries, raspberries or strawberries, sprinkle them with a little rose-water; press out the juice, and draw the milk out of the cow's udder into it; sweeten it with a little sugar, and beat it well with birchen twigs, till it froth up; then strew over it a little fine beaten cinamon, and it will be an excellent mess. You may do this with the juice of plums, gooseberries, apricots, figs, or any juicy fruit.'

The Family Magazine Containing Useful Directions in All the Branches of House-keeping and Cookery, 1741

Now two seventeenth-century gooseberry dishes:

TO MAKE GOOSEBERRY CREAM

'Codle them green, and boil them up with sugar, being preserved put them into the cream strain'd or whole scrape sugar on them, and so serve them cold in boil'd or raw cream. Thus you may do strawberries, raspas, or red currans, put in raw cream whole, or serve them with wine and sugar in a dish without cream.'

Robert May, *The Accomplisht Cook*, 1660

TO MAKE A GOOSEBERRY HUFF[1]

'Take a quart of green gooseberries boil them and pulp them thro' a sieve, take the whites of 3 eggs, beat them to a Froth, put it to the Gooseberries and beat it both together till it looks white, then take ½ pound refin'd sugar, make it into a Syrrup with Spring Water, boyl it to a Candy, [i.e. to the small thread] let it be almost cold then put it to the Gooseberries and Eggs and beat all together till tis all froth, which put into Cups or Glasses – Codlings [green apples] may be done the same way.

'N.B. Eleven Ounces of Codlin pulp'd thro' a sieve is a proper quantity to the above Eggs and Sugar.'

Dorset Dishes of the 17th Century, edited from MS. receipt books and published by J. Stevens Cox, The Toucan Press, Guernsey, 1967

BLACK FRUIT FOOL OR BLACK TART STUFF

This is a recipe adapted from a dish evidently popular three hundred years ago in the days of the Stuarts, when a purée of dried prunes, raisins and currants cooked in wine was used as a filling for tarts and

---

1. A redcurrant and whisked egg white confection made in a similar fashion was once a great favourite of my own. In the context huff means a puffed head.

pies. Recipes for this 'black tart stuff' as it was called appear in at least two cookery books of the second half of the seventeenth century. One of these books, *The Accomplisht Cook* of 1660 has already been quoted on pages 231 and 242. It is a most beautiful piece of cookery literature. The author, Robert May, worked in a number of grand and noble households, including that of the Countess of Kent, whose book of medical receipts appeared post-humously in 1653 under the title *A Choice Manual, Or Rare Secrets in Physick and Chirurgery*. Published together with *A Choice Manual* was a little book of cookery receipts entitled *A True Gentlewoman's Delight*, often also attributed, although probably wrongly, to the Countess of Kent.

Robert May gives several different variations on his 'black tart stuff' recipe, one of which includes damsons. *A True Gentle-woman's Delight* also gives a formula for black tart stuff. My own version is the result of experiments with these different recipes. I find it a delicious and refreshing cold fruit purée. As a pie filling it is rich and dark without the cloying and heavy qualities of mincemeat. It has also a certain originality which provides a small surprise at the end of the meal.

Exact proportions of the different dried fruits are not important, but as a rough guide, use ½ lb. of good large prunes, ¼ lb. of raisins (Spanish muscatels are the best for flavour and colour, stoneless Australian or South African raisins are cheaper) and 2 oz. of currants, plus ¼ pint of red table wine or ⅛ pint of port.

Put the prunes in an earthenware oven dish, with the wine and enough water to cover them. Leave them, in the covered pot, in a very slow oven, anything from gas no. ½ to 1 or 290°F., to gas no. 3 or 330°F., for 2 to 3 hours or longer, until they are very swollen and completely soft and have absorbed most of the liquid. During the final hour or so of cooking put the raisins and currants previously well washed, in a separate oven pot, and with water to cover them, to bake.

Stone the prunes, sieve them, with any remaining juice. Strain and discard the water from the raisins and currants. Sieve them. Mix the two purées together.

Serve well chilled in glasses, or in one large bowl, with a layer of thin pouring cream floated on the top, and with sponge or short-bread fingers.[1]

1. See the recipe on page 245.

When the purée is made a little extra port can be added by those who like a stronger flavour of wine.

These quantities fill six glasses of about 3-oz. capacity. The purée keeps well in the refrigerator, so it is economical to make a batch and store it.

A note for teetotallers: I have several times eaten another modern version of this dish in which black coffee rather than wine is used for flavouring the dried fruit.

QUINCE FOOL

Quarter and core the quinces but do not peel them; put them in a vegetable steamer – the kind known as an adaptable steamer, which looks a bit like a colander, and fits on the top of the saucepan, *not* a bain marie or double boiler – over a pan of water, and cover them. Steam until they are quite soft. Sieve them. Into the hot pulp stir caster sugar (about 6 to 8 oz. for 1½ lb. of quinces, but this is a matter of taste). When quite cold fold in about ⅓ to ½ pint of fresh cream.

This is my version of a quince cream recipe from the note book of Mrs Owen of Penrhos in Anglesey, 1695.

DRIED APRICOT FOOL

The way to get the maximum flavour out of dried apricots is to bake them slowly in the oven instead of stewing them. They emerge nicely plump, with a roasted, smoky flavour which I find irresistible; although only, it must be said, if they have been dried without the sulphur dioxide used as a preservative for dried fruit. To get good dried apricots it is nowadays necessary to shop for them in wholefood and health food stores.

Put ½ lb. of fine dried apricots to soak in water just to cover for a couple of hours – or overnight if it is more convenient. Cook them, in the same water and without sugar, in a covered oven-pot at a moderate temperature, gas no. 3, 330°F., for about an hour. Strain off the juice. Put the apricots through the coarse mesh of the vegetable mill, and into the resulting purée mix about 4 tablespoons of honey – the amount depends upon the quality of the apricots as well as upon your own taste – and then stir in about ¼ pint of thick, slightly whipped cream. A good addition to dried apricot fool is a spoonful or two of freshly ground almonds.

Serve chilled in glasses or cups. Enough for four.

RHUBARB FOOL

Rhubarb fool is made in just the same way as gooseberry fool, but needs an even larger proportion of sugar, preferably dark brown, and it is very necessary when the rhubarb is cooked to put it in a colander or sieve and let the excess juice drain off before the purée is made and the cream added.

Rhubarb fool is a very beautiful dish – and to me the only way of making rhubarb acceptable. The brown sugar, incidentally, gives rhubarb a specially rich flavour and colour.

A NINETEENTH-CENTURY TRIFLE

'Cover the bottom of the dish with Naples biscuits,[1] and macaroons broken in halves, wet with brandy and white wine poured over them, cover them with patches of raspberry jam, fill the dish with a good custard, then whip up a syllabub, drain the froth on a sieve, put it on the custard and strew comfits[2] over all.'

Frederick Bishop, *The Wife's Own Book of Cookery*, 1852

It is rarely appreciated that in Bishop's day, a Trifle was not a nursery pudding squashed anyhow into a common fruit bowl, but built up into a pyramid in an elegant stemmed glass compote dish. Crowned with its frothy whip and scattered with coloured comfits, the Trifle was a very pretty dish for a party. Eliza Acton, in *Modern Cookery* 1845, referred to a special trifle-dish. So did Mrs Beeton, in the first edition of *Household Management* 1861, and gave two illustrations of it, a black and white one on p.750, and a coloured one on plate VI. She garnished her built-up Trifle with strips of bright currant jelly, crystallised sweetmeats or flowers. Coloured comfits were rather old-fashioned, she thought. In her day cream was 1s. per pint and she estimated the total cost of her trifle at 5s. 6d.

ALMOND SHORTBREAD

A good and simple shortbread to serve with syllabubs, fruit fools, and creams.

3 oz. plain flour; 3 oz. unsalted butter; 1½ oz. of caster sugar; 1 oz. of ground almonds; ½ to 1 oz. of rice flour or cornflour.

Crumble the softened butter into the flour, sprinkling in the rice flour or cornflour at intervals, as and when the butter seems to be getting sticky. Add the almonds and the sugar.

1. At this period sponge fingers.
2. Sugar-coated coriander or caraway seeds.

The ingredients should not be worked too much. Grainy pieces will disappear in the cooking.

Spread the mixture into a 6-inch sandwich tin or tart tin with a removable base. Press it down lightly and smooth over the top with a palette knife. Prick the top surface with a fork.

Bake in the centre of a very slow oven, gas no. 2, 310°F., for an hour and a quarter, until the shortbread is a very pale biscuit colour.

Leave to cool in the tin, but before it is completely cold cut into small neat wedges. Enough for four people

Booklet published by Elizabeth David, 1969

*

In its original form my article on Syllabubs appeared in the very first number of Nova, *in March 1965. The historical recipes which I had included in my typescript were, however, omitted from the published article, and these, together with several for English fruit fools, and a new introductory essay, were published in* Queen *magazine in the summer of 1968, in the days of Hugh Johnson's editorship. On that occasion the article was illustrated with reproductions of Thomas Lowinsky's wonderful twenties designs for table centres, drawn originally for* Lovely Food, *his wife Ruth's book published by the Nonesuch Press in 1931.*

For its next reincarnation, I rearranged, revised and slightly augmented the text of the Queen *article, replacing the new introductory essay with the original one from* Nova, *and in 1969 published it in booklet form under the title* Syllabubs and Fruit Fools. *It was the last of a series of four little booklets which I published myself and sold to Elizabeth David Ltd. for the Pimlico kitchen utensil shop I had launched in 1965. Two years after the publication of the Syllabub book disagreements with my partners over policy matters led to my resignation as chairman and director of the firm and eventually to my total severance of all connection with it. When the booklets were finally sold out, I did not reprint them. The first of the series,* Dried Herbs, Aromatics and Condiments, *1967, formed the nucleus of my* Spices, Salt and Aromatics in the English Kitchen, Penguin *1970. Another,* The Baking of an English Loaf, *1969, an article first published in* Queen, *December 4th 1968, was eventually incorporated, much rewritten, in my* English Bread and Yeast Cookery, Allen Lane *1977. The fourth,* English Potted Meats and Fish Pastes, *1968, is reprinted in the present volume, pp.216–229. The retail price of the Herb and the Bread booklets was 2/6d, the Potted Meat and the Syllabub ones were all of 2/9d.*

I give these bibliographical details because from time to time I get asked for them by collectors and booksellers.

Operation Mulberry

Every August or early September for the last few years I have been lucky enough to receive a present of ripe mulberries from a magnificent old tree in the garden of Rainham Hall in Essex. I use them to make a Summer Pudding or a water ice. Last year I added a new dish of mulberries and almonds to the repertory.

SUMMER PUDDING OF MULBERRIES

For a small pudding, enough for four people, you need 1 lb. of home-made white bread at least two or three days old; 2 lb. of ripe mulberries; about 6 oz. of white sugar; a Pyrex soufflé mould of 20-oz. capacity.

Cook the mulberries with the sugar until the juice runs.

Line the mould with narrow, crustless slices of bread. These must fit the dish exactly, with no spaces for the juice to seep through. This task is made quite easy if you dampen the bread slightly so that it can be pressed into the shape you need.

Pour in the warm mulberries, with just a little of their juice, reserving the rest for later, and leaving enough room at the top for a covering layer of bread slices. When these are fitted into place put a flat plate or saucer *inside* the dish. On top put a 2-lb. weight. Transfer the pudding to the refrigerator, where you may safely leave it for several days. It is in fact all the better for a prolonged wait in the cold. The juice is best stored in the freezer.

Turn the pudding out into a deep plate or a dish with room to hold some of the juice reserved for pouring over it. Don't swamp it though.

With this most delicious version of summer pudding – raspberries and redcurrants make the next best – you need a jug of good rich cream of pouring consistency.

A note: if you don't make your own bread try white bread from a

Greek or Italian bakery. On no account use a factory loaf. I did once, in the interests of discovery. The experiment was expensive (a waste of good raspberries), disastrous and conclusive.

A MULBERRY AND ALMOND DISH

Mix 12 oz. to 1 lb. of mulberries cooked with sugar as above with 1½ to 2 oz. of fresh soft white breadcrumbs and 1½ to 2 oz. of skinned and finely ground almonds.

Serve chilled, in narrow goblets or white china cups, with a little cream floated on top.

The mulberry-almond-bread combination is a good one. It was suggested to me by an Italian recipe for a sauce or relish called *sapore de morone* which appears in *Epulario*, first published in Venice in 1516. According to Lord Westbury, *Handlist of Italian Cookery Books*, Florence, 1963, this work, attributed to Giovanni Rosselli, is in reality taken from the same Maestro Martino manuscript used in the earlier and better known *De Honesta Voluptate* by Bartolomeo Sacchi, printed in Venice in 1475.

I suspect that the mulberry sauce – we are not told for what manner of meat it was intended – may have originated somewhere in Asia Minor and was perhaps brought to Italy after the Venetian conquest of Constantinople in 1204 A.D. It could equally have come via Persia or Afghanistan where, as in Turkey, the berries of the white or silk mulberry are dried to provide a supply for the winter. In the *Epulario* sauce the berries – whether white or black we do not know – are uncooked, crushed lightly in a mortar, spiced with cinnamon and nutmeg – no sugar – and pressed through a fine cloth sieve together with the pounded almonds and breadcrumbs.

MULBERRY WATER ICE

I make this in the same way as a strawberry or raspberry water ice, except that mulberries need no additional lemon or orange juice.

Make a thickish syrup with 8 oz. each of sugar and water.

Purée 2 lb. of mulberries in a blender or food processor. Press them through a stainless steel wire sieve.

Mix the syrup and the mulberry pulp and chill in the refrigerator before turning into a mould, ice trays, or an electric sorbetière to freeze.

It was from the late Sir Harry Luke, author of that delightful and civilized book *The Tenth Muse* (Putnam, 1954, and revised edition 1962) that I learned of the beauty of mulberry ices.

MULBERRIES AS A DESSERT FRUIT

If you have just a few mulberries, not enough to make a pudding or an ice, arrange them in a little pyramid, if possible on shiny green leaves, on a plain glass compote dish, with a separate bowl of sugar. They are glorious. But beware the juice. It stains.

Petit Propos Culinaires No. 2, 1979

Foods of Legend

Refined or classic French cookery – call it haute cuisine if you must – and French regional, provincial, farmhouse and peasant styles of cookery cannot arbitrarily be isolated and set apart one from the other. All are interdependent and to a certain extent intermixed. Each borrows and learns from the other.

The transposition of a dish from one category into another happens in many different ways. For the sake of argument, let us say for example that the son of a humble couple in a Provençal village leaves home to train in the catering business. In the course of time he becomes one of the world's most famous cooks. At the height of his fame and glory he thinks with nostalgia of the rough country food of his childhood. He would like to reproduce for his customers a certain dish of sliced potatoes and artichoke hearts baked with olive oil and garlic and scented with wild thyme. So rustic a dish can hardly, he realizes, be offered to the fine ladies and gentlemen who frequent the elegant restaurant over which he presides. From force of habit he banishes the garlic and adds sliced truffles. It is a period in the history of cooking when the addition of truffles would make a poached mouse or a fricassee of donkey's ears acceptable to those rich and great ones who flock to eat the creations of this famous chef. They do not know that, for once, they will be eating what is almost a peasant dish. Truffles are one of the natural products of Provence. In a dish of potatoes and artichokes – another of the local products – they are by no means out of place. The olive oil of the country will not however be acceptable to Parisians or to Londoners. Butter must be used instead. Concentrated, clear meat juice, must, it goes without saying, be added. In the classic cooking of professionals meat juice or broth goes with everything, olive oil with nothing save salads, vinaigrette and mayonnaise sauces.

A poor Provençal family might find their great son's version of a familiar dish lacking in savour, although in its original form it would have made, with a saucerful of olives and perhaps a dish of fresh figs, an entire meal. To the customers of the Provençal village boy who is now the renowned and glorious Auguste Escoffier, potatoes, artichokes and truffles do not make even one course. They belong with a joint of meat. So Escoffier uses his vegetables as a foundation upon which to bake a choice little cut of spring lamb, a loin or best end of neck. For a festival or a wedding feast a very similar dish, a *gigot* of mutton on a bed of sliced potatoes, might have been taken by Madame Escoffier senior to the village baker's oven to cook. It would be no more, and no less, than the ancient *gigot boulangère* with a midi accent. Madame Escoffier's son gives it a more elegant name. To honour his compatriot, the Provençal poet Frédéric Mistral, he calls his creation *carré d'agneau Mistral*. He publishes the recipe in a book; and another of the myriad village dishes of France has entered the repertory of *la cuisine classique*.

Before long, wine scholars and menu compilers are gravely debating the question of which Bordeaux vintage will best harmonize with the lamb, the potatoes and the artichokes, wondering whether the presence of the truffles does not after all call for a burgundy.

Sometimes the rags to riches progress of a dish is reversed. A Parisian-born chef of the early nineteenth century brings to perfection – or to what at the time is considered perfection – a grandiose dish of sole in a white wine and cream sauce with a ceremonial garnish of freshwater crayfish, fried gudgeons, oysters, mushrooms and prawns impaled on ornamental skewers. The chef in question, who has perhaps first-hand knowledge of Normandy, and obtains his supplies of fish from the Norman coast, calls his creation *sole à la normande*. The recipe is modified and simplified by succeeding generations of cooks. Some hundred years later the great revival of regional specialities is initiated by a band of patriotic French men of letters fearful that the post-1918 influx of tourists demanding international palace hotel food (it is, alas, *le classique* which has opened the door to this dreariest of all styles of cooking) wherever they go will end in the annihilation of the typical specialities of the provinces of France. These entirely estimable men, among whom the prime movers are Curnonsky, Marcel Rouff and Count Austin de Croze, set to work compiling their wonderful catalogues and books concerning regional dishes and products, and their guides to the provincial restaurants where such things are served. At the same time the members of this happy band of pioneers do not hesitate to flay, in newspaper and magazine columns, the bad restaurateurs and the hoteliers who pander to ignorant tourists with mass-produced, characterless food.

One day these gentlemen, visiting a renowned restaurant in Rouen (or was it Caen, Trouville, Honfleur?) enjoy a modernized version of the original *sole normande*. The patron of the restaurant explains that a garnish of crayfish and oysters only is the right and true traditional one for *sole normande*. It is not long before this information gets into the newspapers and cookery books. An expert in Norman folklore proceeds to argue that the whole thing is too complicated. Cooks in the households of Norman seaside towns do not, he says, have freshwater crayfish at their disposal. They enrich their sole dishes with mussels and shrimps only; and they cook their fish in locally produced cider, not in expensive white wine imported from other regions.

It is a matter of months only before a learned historian unearths evidence which proves that the first sole normande was simply a mixture of fish boiled in a bucket of seawater on board the ship which took William of Normandy to Hastings. What the creation of the Parisian chef (his name is said to have been Philippe, owner of a restaurant in the rue Montorgueil) has lost in splendour it has gained in ancient antecedents and a background which will make a godsend for publicity men, compilers of travel literature, and the experts in picturesque magazine cookery. It is all good publicity for French tourism and the restaurants and hotels of Normandy. What is more, the proprietors of seaside cafés and catering establishments actually take up the recipe and produce their own versions of it. Who can say now that the dish is not, in fact, of ancient Norman lineage?

Because some local speciality has caught the imagination of tourists, it has, today, almost automatically come to be accepted as a great dish. Overestimation of the merits of a dish which relies purely on local conditions and ingredients for its charm will, in the end, kill it stone-dead. Take, say, from a *salade niçoise* the little pungent black olives of Provence, the fruity oil in the dressing, the sweet, ripe southern tomatoes, the capers and the brined anchovies which are all characteristic products of the region, and what is left? Little more than an English mixed salad . . .

To reproduce French cooking in England with any success at all it is best, I think, to go for dishes with less resounding reputations and less specialized ingredients. This should not be difficult. For every French regional dish of international repute there are a hundred comparatively unknown, equally interesting and more easily adaptable to differing conditions. Here are some recipes for such dishes. I learned about them during the course of visiting various wholesale food markets in France: visits which proved a great deal more instructive than a thousand meals in restaurants, however good, could ever be.

GRILLADE DES MARINIERS DU RHÔNE

This is just one version out of the score of recipes for this venerable dish which is not a grill at all and which you will scarcely find nowadays simmering away in the galleys of the great petrol barges which whirl down the Rhône to Marseille. But curiously enough this dish, although made with fresh meat rather than with left-over boiled beef, has much in its flavour and composition which makes it akin to the celebrated *miroton*, always reputed to be characteristic of the cooking of the Paris concierge.

Buy about 1½ to 2 lb. of a good lean cut of beef – topside is perhaps the best – and cut it into small steaks each weighing about 3 to 4 oz. The other ingredients are about 1 lb. of onions, 1 oz. of butter, 1 heaped teaspoon of flour, 2 or 3 tablespoons of chopped parsley, a clove of garlic, 3 tablespoons of olive oil, 1 of wine vinegar, 4 anchovy fillets, salt, pepper.

Slice the onions fairly fine. Put a layer of them in a not-too-deep earthenware casserole. On top put two or three of the steaks, sprinkled with salt and pepper. Then a layer of onions, another of meat and so on, finishing with a layer of onions. Work the butter and flour together. Divide it into tiny knobs. Spread them over the top of the onions and round the sides of the casserole. Cover with buttered paper and a lid, and cook in a very slow oven, gas no. 1, 290°F., for about 2 hours.

Mix the chopped parsley, garlic, olive oil, chopped anchovy fillets and vinegar to make a little vinaigrette sauce. Pour this mixture into the casserole. Replace the paper and the lid and cook another hour.

As you see, a primitive but excellent way of making a richly flavoured stew with a slightly thickened sauce but without the addition of stock, wine, or even water. The dish can of course be reheated without coming to any harm.

MUSEAU DE PORC EN SALADE

Now here is another extremely simple little dish, a dish which anyone who has a helpful butcher can make with very little trouble or expense. I saw it, and tasted it, for the first time, on a charcutier's stall in the market at Montpellier.

Ask your butcher to put a boned pig's cheek into brine for 24 hours. When you get it home, leave it soaking in cold water for an hour. Put it into a pot with an onion, a couple of carrots, 4 peppercorns, a bay leaf and a few parsley stalks. Just cover with fresh cold water and add a tablespoon of wine vinegar. Cook it very gently in a covered pot for about 1½ hours. Take it from the liquid, sprinkle it with oil, press it between two plates and leave it until the next day.

Cut it, rind included, into the finest possible slices. Mix it with a vinaigrette sauce made with a couple of chopped shallots, a couple of tablespoons of finely chopped parsley, a teaspoon of yellow French mustard, a little salt, 6 tablespoons of olive oil and 1 of wine vinegar. Add, just for the look of the thing, a half tomato, all pulp and seeds discarded, cut into tiny pieces.

Serve, as part of a mixed hors-d'œuvre, on a flat dish, strewn with more chopped parsley. There will be enough for 6 to 8 people.

FROMAGE NORMAND

The old Norman way – or one of the old ways – of making a cream cheese for dessert is to boil a pint of thick cream with a couple of tablespoons of sugar for about 5 minutes. If you like you can add a tablespoon or two of orange flower water. Turn the cream into a big bowl and leave it to get quite cold. You then whip the cream (it is easier if you have left it an hour or two in the refrigerator after cooling) and when it stands in peaks you can turn it in to the muslin or clean napkin with which you have lined an earthenware or metal cheese mould or drainer – which can be improvised by piercing holes in a cheap cake tin or in a tub-shaped carton – and leave it 3 or 4 hours, or overnight.

To serve you turn it out in to a shallow dish and eat it with sugar and, if you like, strawberry, raspberry, red currant or quince jelly. There will be enough for 6 to 8 helpings.

The Gourmet,[1] 1969

1. Journal of the Department of Hotel and Catering Administration and Technology, Hendon College of Technology.

The Markets of France: Cavaillon

It is a Sunday evening in mid-June. The cafés of Cavaillon are crammed. There isn't an inch to park your car. The noise is tremendous. In the most possible of the hotels – it goes by the name of Toppin – all the rooms are taken by seven o'clock. But the little Auberge La Provençale in the rue Chabran is quite quiet and you can enjoy a good little dinner – nothing spectacular, but genuine and decently cooked food well served – and go to bed early. The chances are you won't sleep much though, because Monday is the big market day in Cavaillon and soon after midnight the carts and lorries and vans of the big fruit farmers' co-operatives, of the market gardeners, of the tomato and garlic and onion growers, will start rattling and roaring and rumbling into the great open market in the place du Clos.

At dawn they will be unloading their melons and asparagus, their strawberries and red currants and cherries, their apricots and peaches and pears and plums, their green almonds, beans, lettuces, shining new white onions, new potatoes, vast bunches of garlic. By six o'clock the ground will be covered with *cageots*, the chip vegetable and fruit baskets, making a sea of soft colours and shadowy shapes in the dawn light. The air of the Place is filled with the musky scent of those little early Cavaillon melons, and then you become aware of another powerfully conflicting smell – rich, clove-like, spicy. It is the scent of sweet basil, and it is coming from the far end of the market where a solitary wrinkled old man sits on an upturned basket, scores and scores of basil plants ringed all around him like a protective hedge. With a beady eye he watches the drama of the market place. The dealers, exporters and wholesalers walking round inspecting the produce, discussing prices, negotiating; the hangers-on standing about in groups smoking, chatting; the market police and official inspectors strolling round seeing that all is in order.

On the whole the scene is quiet, quieter at least than you would expect considering that this is one of the most important wholesale fruit and vegetable markets in France, the great distributing centre for the *primeurs* of the astonishingly fertile and productive areas of the Vaucluse and the Comtat Venaissin – areas which less than a hundred years ago were desperately poor, inadequately irrigated, isolated for lack of roads and transport, earthquake-stricken, devastated by blights which destroyed the cereal crops and the vines.

It was with the building of the railways connecting Provence with Paris and the north, with Marseille and the ports of the Mediterranean to the south, that the possibilities of the Rhône and Durance valleys for intensive fruit and vegetable cultivation first began to be understood. New methods of irrigation, the planting of fruit trees in large areas where the vines had been stricken, the division of the land into small fields broken with tall cypress hedges as windbreaks against the scourging mistral, the ever-increasing demand in Paris and the big towns of the north for early vegetables, and the tremendous industry of these Provençal cultivators have done the rest. And to such effect that last year eighty thousand kilos of asparagus came into Cavaillon market alone between 15 April and 15 May; in the peak month of July three hundred tons of melons daily; five hundred tons of tomatoes every day in July and August. Altogether some hundred and sixty thousand tons of vegetables and fruit leave Cavaillon every year, about fifty per cent by rail, the rest by road. And Cavaillon, although the most important, is by no means the only big market centre in the neighbourhood. Avignon, Châteaurenard, Bollène, Pertuis, all dispatch their produce by special trains to the north; vast quantities of fruit are absorbed locally by the jam and fruit preserving industries of Apt and Carpentras; and every little town and village has its own retail vegetable and fruit market, every day in the bigger towns, once or twice a week in less populated places.

But now seven o'clock strikes in the market at Cavaillon. The lull is over. This is the moment when the goods change hands. Pandemonium breaks loose. The dealers snatch the baskets of produce they have bought and rush them to waiting lorries. A cartload of garlic vanishes from under your nose. A mountain of melons evaporates in a wink. If you try to speak to anybody you will be ignored, if you get in the way you'll be knocked down in the wild scramble to get goods away to Paris, London, Brussels, and all the great centres of northern and eastern France. Suddenly, the market place is deserted.

At eight o'clock you emerge from the café where you have had your breakfast coffee and croissant. The market place is, to put it mildly, astir once more. It is surrounded by vans and lorries disgorging cheap dresses and overalls, plastic kitchenware, shoes and scarves and bales of cotton, piles of plates and jugs, nails and screws and knives, farm implements and packets of seeds, cartons of dried-up-looking biscuits and trays of chemically-coloured sweets.

You dive down a side street where you have spied a festoon of pretty cotton squares, and there, under gaudy painted colonnades, lilac and orange, cinnamon and lemon and rose, in patterns more typical of Marseille or the Levant than of Cavaillon, the retail market stalls are already doing business. The displays seem rather tame after the wholesale market and there is not a melon to be seen. It is too early in the season, they are still too expensive for the housewives of Cavaillon. Five thousand francs a kilo they were fetching today, and a week later in London shops 12s. 6d. each for little tiny ones. But the street opposite the painted colonnades leads into the square where more and more food stalls are opening and the housewives are already busy marketing. Here you can buy everything for a picnic lunch. Beautiful sprawling ripe tomatoes, a Banon cheese wrapped in chestnut leaves, Arles sausages, pâté, black olives, butter cut from a towering monolith, apricots, cherries.

It is still early and you can drive out towards Apt and branch off across the Lubéron. The roads are sinuous but almost empty, and they will take you through some of the most beautiful country in Provence. Perched on the hillsides are typical old Provençal villages, some, like Oppède-le-Vieux, crumbling, haunted, half-deserted, others like Bonnieux with a flourishing modern village built below the old one, and up beyond Apt, through the dramatic stretch of ochre-mining country, the strange red-gold village of Roussillon appears to be toppling precariously on the edge of a craggy cliff. Round about here, the network of caves under the ochreous rocks has been turned into vast *champignonnières*, and at the modest little Restaurant David (no relation) you can eat the local cultivated mushrooms cooked *à la crème* or *à la provençale* with, naturally, olive oil, parsley and garlic. And the Rose d'Or, a little hotel opened only a few weeks ago, promises a welcome alternative to the establishments of Apt, Aix and Cavaillon.

POT-AU-FEU PROVENÇAL

A simple pot-au-feu is typical of the real old Provençal cooking of the days before Provençal specialities became chic restaurant food and got fussed up and transferred into goodness knows what fantasies. Even an inexperienced cook can make a pot-au-feu in its basic form. And with a little extra trouble it can be turned into a splendid party dish – not for a grand formal party to be sure, or even a buffet party, but the sort of meal for intimate friends when you can put all the food on a huge scrubbed kitchen table and everyone sits round and helps themselves. It is a heartening sight, evocative of all the sun and bright colours of Provence; it is economical because it is one of those composite dishes which you gradually build up, to which you can make additions or subtractions and for which the planning of the colours, flavours, extra salads, vegetables, sauces, becomes perfectly intoxicating – but steady, keep a hold, or you'll find you've made enough food for thirty, and you'll have to order another case of wine and invite twenty more guests . . .

For the basic pot-au-feu, then, you need 2½ lb. approximately of flank of beef, 2½ lb. of shoulder, middle neck or breast of lamb (it is the lamb which gives it its essentially Provençal character), 1 lb. of shin of veal. All these meats are best cooked with bone. The flavouring vegetables are 2 each of large carrots, leeks, onions and tomatoes; a bouquet of herbs consisting of parsley stalks, a piece of celery, a bay leaf and a crushed clove of garlic all tied together; 1 tablespoon of salt. If the pot-au-feu is for a special occasion you include as well a boiling chicken, but since so many kitchens aren't equipped with a soup pot large enough to hold a chicken at the same time as all the meat, this may have to be cooked separately.

Tie the beef and lamb into compact rolls or squares so that they retain their shape during cooking and will be easy to cut. Put them with the veal bone, and the chicken if there is room, into your biggest soup pot and cover with 4 or 5 pints of water. Bring gently to simmering point. As the grey scum rises, skim it off. When the scum becomes white and foamy, stop skimming. Put in the vegetables, the bouquet, the salt. At this stage you can add a glass of white wine if you have it to spare. Cover the pot. Cook at very low heat either on top of the stove or in the oven for 3 to 4 hours, until the chicken and meat are very tender. Take out the chicken and meat, put them in a deep dish and sprinkle them with olive oil and salt while they are still hot. The vegetables will be cooked to rags and can be discarded. Strain the stock into a bowl.

Next day, remove the fat from the stock (keep it for frying bread, potatoes, etc.) and if you have not already cooked the chicken, simmer it, with its giblets and feet, in the stock for about 3 hours. Or if you are using a roaster instead of a boiler, 45 to 50 minutes will cook it. As a matter of fact, although it is an extra extravagance from the point of view of fuel, the chicken will be very much nicer cooked the same day as it is to be eaten, before it has had time to harden up.

To serve the meat, you cut it all from the bones, slice it in very fine thin pieces, and keeping the beef, lamb and veal separate, sprinkle each with more oil, chopped parsley, shallots. Arrange them with the jointed chicken, all on one huge dish.

In bowls all round you have some or all of the following: a salad of chick peas, an aïoli, black olives, capers (these are the four typical, native Provençal dishes), a spicy tomato sauce, a grated carrot salad, a Jerusalem artichoke salad, potatoes, beetroot, celery, sweet red peppers, gherkins, hard-boiled eggs – it depends what is available, how many people you have to feed, on your own and your guests' tastes. And for a first course all you will need is either the broth from the pot-au-feu, which will have a very fine flavour and which you can thicken if you like with a little rice – there should be enough for seven or eight people – or perhaps a dish of mussels, or a light fish soup.

SALADE DE POIS CHICHES

Chick peas are those knobbly corn-yellow peas rather the shape of nasturtium seeds, which the Spanish call *garbanzos* and the Italians *ceci*. At one time they were very much cultivated in Provence and are still popular there. In England they can be bought in Soho shops; they make delicious soups and salads.

Soak ½ lb. of chick peas overnight in plenty of cold water into which you stir a tablespoon of flour. Next day put them in a saucepan with the same water, plus a half teaspoon of bicarbonate of soda. Simmer them for an hour. Skim and strain them. Rinse out the saucepan, fill it with 3 pints of fresh water, bring to the boil, add a tablespoon of salt, put in the chick peas and simmer another 1 to 2 hours, until the peas are perfectly tender and the skins beginning to break.

Strain them (keep the liquid – it will make a good basis for a vegetable soup), put them in a bowl and while still hot stir in plenty of olive oil, sliced onion, garlic, parsley, and a little vinegar. If you can't get chick peas, the same sort of salad can be made with haricot beans.

AÏOLI

Most readers will probably already be familiar with the famous garlic mayonnaise of Provence, so just as a reminder you will need, for eight people, a minimum of 2 large cloves of garlic – but more if you have avid garlic-eaters to entertain – 2 egg yolks, at least a half-pint of good olive oil, salt, lemon juice.

You first pound the garlic to a mash, then stir in the yolks, add a little salt, then the oil, exactly as for a mayonnaise. Lastly, the lemon juice. This beautiful golden ointment-like sauce is really the pivot and *raison d'être* of the whole affair, so you need plenty of it.

THE OLIVES AND CAPERS

The black olives of Provence are small, wrinkled, salty; all the tang of the South is in them. If you can't buy these little black olives in Soho, at least avoid the great brownish ones sold in most delicatessen stores; they really haven't anything of the same character. But there are two bottled brands (Sharwood's and Noel's) which are quite good.

As for capers, another typical product of Provence (the best are the *non-pareilles* from the Var and the Bouches du Rhône), buy the finest French ones. Simply serve them in tiny bowls or hors-d'œuvre dishes, or pile up little mounds of them beside the sliced lamb and beef.

COULIS DE TOMATES À LA MOUTARDE

This is really an alternative to the aïoli, in case you have anti-garlic guests. But it is an excellent sauce in its own right, hot with a boiled chicken, beef, lamb and fish, or cold as in the present case. Ingredients are 2 lb. of tomatoes, a small onion, 1 clove of garlic, 1 carrot, a little piece of celery top, half a dozen parsley stalks, a teaspoon of dried basil, a dessertspoon of salt, 2 tablespoons of olive oil, 4 teaspoons of yellow Dijon mustard.

Heat the oil in a wide shallow pan, put in the sliced onion, carrot, chopped celery and parsley stalks. After two or three minutes add the sliced tomatoes, garlic, basil and salt. Cook gently, uncovered, stirring from time to time, for about half an hour, until most of the moisture has evaporated and the tomatoes are in a pulp. Sieve the mixture in a food mill. Taste for seasoning – it may need sugar – then stir in, a little at a time, the mustard.

Vogue, January 1960

The Markets of France: Yvetot

Duclair is a little town on a loop of the Seine twenty kilometres outside Rouen towards Dieppe. It is not particularly picturesque and the main road and the ferry over the Seine make it noisy. But I always try to stay the night there on my way down through France and on the way back again because of the Hôtel de la Poste where the Swiss proprietor and his pretty Norman wife provide such a warm welcome and such good food. Their big airy dining-room overlooks the river, their delicious pâté of Rouen duckling cooked with port is brought to table in the gigantic old terrines in which it has been baked, their hors-d'œuvres are always fresh, well chosen, original and beautifully served, ducks and chickens are roasted on a spit in the old Norman fireplace in the kitchen.

And if you happen to arrive on a Monday evening you could see a typical Norman market, both wholesale and retail, at Duclair early on Tuesday morning. It is as good a way as any to the beginnings of an understanding and appreciation of any French province, to see the local markets in action, to watch the produce unloaded from the carts and vans, to hear the talk of the farmers and buyers in the cafés after the main business has been transacted. And to us, whose country markets are rapidly vanishing, the extraordinary activity and the variety of foodstuffs on sale in a little town of only three thousands inhabitants like Duclair, so few miles away from Dover, has a particular fascination.

One could almost go over there to do one's weekly marketing – or on into Rouen, where the big market day is also on Tuesday, and from where you could bring home butter made from unpasteurized cream, great bowls of *tripes à la mode*, and duck pâtés, and baskets full of big round Breton artichokes for a tenth of the price we have to pay here. And Norman cheeses too: genuine Pont-l'Evèque made on the farms of the Pays d'Auge from milk still warm from the cows; Livarot, that powerful and marvellous cheese which has been made in the district since the thirteenth century; even a good Norman Camembert can be found if you look. But progress is on the march in Normandy, and in a big way. It won't be long before cheeses such as these become rarities. More and more of the farms are going over to pasteurized milk, their produce is sent to the co-operatives, the butter and the cheese no longer have the characteristic ripe flavours one used to expect. On the whole, though, the Norman producers are acting with sense and foresight over the development of their dairy industry. They are frankly calling their new cheeses by new brand names, making them in different shapes and original packings, selling them on their own merits rather than attempting to pass them off as the great traditional products of an unmechanized and unstandardized age.

There are, of course, big areas of Normandy where the farmers are still producing milk, butter, cream and cheeses by the old methods. The outlet for these products are the local wholesale markets.

The great centre of the rich Pays d'Auge, also cider and Calvados country, is Vimoutiers, only a few kilometres from the cheese villages of both Camembert and Livarot. The big butter market is on Monday afternoons. The centre of the Bray district is Gournay, where over a hundred years ago Petit Suisse cream cheeses were evolved by a farmer's wife and a Swiss herdsman. There are now almost a dozen different varieties of these cream cheeses, and the Gervais factory, at Ferrières, absorbs something like 50,000 gallons of milk daily for the demi-sel and other fresh cheeses.

Yvetot is the great butter market of the Caux country and provides a sight worth seeing if you happen to be in the district on a Wednesday morning. Out of the vans are coming huge cones of butter fresh from the farms. It is made from ripened, unpasteurized cream, and divided into loaves of 35 or 70 kilos each; they are wrapped in crisp white cloths or in polythene wrappings and stacked in huge baskets or wire carriers. Each parcel of butter is tasted with a long scoop and then re-weighed before a buyer will accept it. On the long rows of stalls are ranged all sorts of fresh farm products – eggs, vegetables, salads, churns of cream, live chickens and ducks – brown Rouen ducks, black Muscovy ducks, white Pekin ducks, turkeys, baby chicks; one old woman has just one basket of produce for sale – eggs, a few fresh peas, and a bunch of green turnip-tops. But even this little collection of cottage garden produce won't change hands without some stern bargaining.

As for the farm butter, it is being borne away by the purchasers in the great baskets which look as if they might have been used by the Scarlet Pimpernel to smuggle refugee *aristos* out of Paris. Tomorrow this butter will be enriching many a roast chicken, thousands of omelettes and cakes and pastries, filling the kitchens of France with the incomparable scent of butter gently sizzling in a frying pan . . .

And indeed it is high time to think about lunch. There is Tôtes not far away on the Dieppe road, and the famous old Hôtel des Cygnes where Guy de Maupassant wrote *Boule de Suif* and where the proprietor appears the very embodiment of Norman robustness. At the Marée in the market place of Rouen there are delicious fish dishes, excellent food at the Beffroy in the rue du Beffroy, all the more unexpected because the place looks too like Ye Olde Bunne Shoppe to be true. But perhaps it is better to avoid Rouen, the midday traffic going in and coming out is too much of a worry. Better to drive a bit farther, down in to lower Normandy and the beautiful Vallée d'Auge, past old Norman farms and manors, through country thick with apple trees, and pastures so opulent and green that unless you have seen some of the raw, rebuilt little towns, it is hard to believe in the terrible devastation of only fifteen years ago.

At Orbec, twenty kilometres from Lisieux, is the Caneton, a restaurant which you know is going to be good as soon as you enter its doors – the smell is so appetizing – but it is small and not exactly unknown, so it is prudent to telephone for a table in advance. The *menu gastronomique* at the Caneton is generous and good value for 1800 francs, but a trifle fussy and rich, and a better choice for my taste is the *plat du jour*, with perhaps a duck liver pâté, or local *charcuterie*, to start with, which is what you see the inhabitants eating.

Vogue, February 1960

The Markets of France: Montpellier

'Buy a pound of choucroûte from a village charcutier. As you pass the municipal pump, pause a moment . . .'

Any English cookery writer who published a recipe opening with these words would be thought distinctly out of touch. The evocative sentence comes in fact from a little book called *La Cuisine en Plein Air* by that most adorable of French gastronomes, Dr Edouard de Pomiane. The little volume, which deals with cooking out of doors for motorists, cyclists, campers, walkers, and fishermen has never been translated into English and wouldn't be of much practical use to us if it were, because the majority of the recipes are based on the products to be bought at the 'village *charcutier*', an institution which doesn't exist in the British Isles.

It is only when one has haunted the markets of France and the food shops in the country towns and villages, watched the house-wives doing their shopping, listened to them discussing their pur-chases at the *pâtisseries* and the *charcuteries* that one realizes how much less they are tied to their kitchens than we had always been led to suppose.

The point is that in France no shame is attached to buying ready-prepared food because most of it is of high quality. The housewives and small restaurateurs who rely upon the professional skill of *charcutiers* and *pâtissiers* for a part of their supplies see to it that the pâtés and sausages, the little salads for hors-d'œuvre, the galantines and terrines and fish quenelles, the hams and tongues and pies, pastries and fruit flans, the petits fours and the croissants maintain high standards of freshness and excellence, and that any popular regional speciality of the district continues to be cooked with the right and proper traditional ingredients, even if the methods have been speeded up by the introduction of modern machinery.

Here in England we find little in our local delicatessen shop – the only approximation we have to the *charcutier* who sells many ready-prepared foods besides pork butchers' products – but mass-produced sausages, pork pies and fish cakes off a conveyor belt, piled slices of pale pink and blood-red flannel which pass respect-ively for cooked ham and tongue, bottles of pickled onions and jars of red cabbage in vinegar, possibly a potato salad dressed with synthetic mayonnaise and, with luck, some herrings in brine. In any French town of any size at all we find perhaps three or four rival *charcutiers* displaying trays of shining olives, black and green, large and small, pickled gherkins, capers, home-made mayonnaise, grated carrot salad, shredded celeriac in *rémoulade* sauce, several sorts of tomato salad, sweet-sour onions, *champignons à la Grec-que*, ox or pig's muzzle finely sliced and dressed with a vinaigrette sauce and fresh parsley, a salad of mussels, another of cervelas sausage; several kinds of pork pâté; sausages for grilling, sausages for boiling, sausages for hors-d'œuvre, flat sausages called *cré-pinettes* for baking or frying, salt pork to enrich stews and soups and vegetable dishes, pigs' trotters ready cooked and bread-crumbed, so that all you need to do is to take them home and grill them; cooked ham, raw ham, a galantine of tongue, cold pork and veal roasts, boned stuffed ducks and chickens . . . So it isn't difficult for the housewife in a hurry to buy a little selection, however modest, of these things from the *charcuterie*, and plus her own imagination and something she has perhaps already in the larder to serve an appetizing and fresh little mixed hors-d'œuvre.

When we visited the big open-air retail market in the upper town at Montpellier, there was an ordinary enough little *charcuterie-épicerie* stall offering the ingredients of what might be called the small change of French cookery, but to our English eyes it looked particularly inviting and interesting.

The atmosphere helped, of course. The sun, the clear sky, the bright colours, the prosperous look of this lively, airy university town and wine-growing capital; the stalls massed with flowers; fresh fish shining pink and gold and silver in shallow baskets; cherries and apricots and peaches on the fruit barrows; one stall piled with about a ton of little bunches of soup or pot-au-feu vegetables – a couple of slim leeks, a carrot or two, a long thin turnip, celery leaves, and parsley, all cleaned and neatly bound with a rush, ready for the pot; another *charcuterie* stall, in the covered part of the market, displaying yards of fresh sausage festooned around a pyramid-shaped wire stand; a fishwife crying pussy's parcels of fish wrapped tidily in newspaper; an old woman at the market entrance selling winkles from a little cart shaped like a pram; a fastidiously dressed old gentleman choosing tomatoes and leaf artichokes, one by one, as if he were picking a bouquet of flowers, and taking them to the scales to be weighed (how extra-ordinary that we in England put up so docilely with not being permitted by greengrocers or even barrow boys to touch or smell the produce we are buying); a lorry with an old upright piano in the back threading round and round the market place trying to get out. These little scenes establish the character of Montpellier market in our memories, although by now we have spent many mornings in different southern markets and have become accustomed to the beauty and profusion of the produce for sale and to the heavy smell of fresh ripe fruit which everywhere hangs thick in the air at this time of year.

Well, plenty of tourists spend their mornings in museums and picture galleries and cathedrals, and nobody would quarrel with them for that. But the stomach of a city is also not without its importance. And then, I wouldn't be too sure that the food market of a big city shouldn't be counted as part of its artistic tradition.

Where do they get their astonishing gifts for display, these French stall keepers? Why does a barrow boy selling bunched radishes and salad greens in the market at Chinon know by instinct so to arrange his produce that he has created a little spectacle as fresh and gay as a Dufy painting, and you are at once convinced that unless you taste some of his radishes you will be missing an experience which seems of more urgency than a visit to the Château of Chinon? How has a Montpellier fishwife so mastered the art of composition that with her basket of fish for the *bouillabaisse* she is presenting a picture of such splendour that instead of going to look at the famous collection of paintings in the Musée Fabre you drive off as fast as possible to the coast to order a dish cooked with just such fish? And what can there be about the arrangement of a few slices of sausage and a dozen black olives on a dish brought by the waitress in the seaside café to keep you occupied while your fish is cooking that makes you feel that this is the first time you have seen and tasted a black olive and a piece of sausage?

When one tries to analyse the real reasons for the respect which French cookery has so long exacted from the rest of the world, the French genius for presentation must be counted as a very relevant point, and its humble beginnings can be seen on the market stalls, in the small town *charcutiers*' and *pâtissiers*' shops, in the modest little restaurants where even if the cooking is not particularly distinguished, the most ordinary of little dishes will be brought to your table with respect, properly arranged on a serving dish, the vegetables separately served, the object of arousing your appetite will be achieved and the proprietors of the establishment will have made the most of their limited resources.

This in a sense is the exact reverse of English practice. We seem to exert every effort to make the least of the most. When you order a grilled Dover sole in an English restaurant it will very likely be a fine sole, fresh and well cooked. But when it is dumped unceremoniously before you with a mound of inappropriate green peas and a pool of cold tartare sauce spreading beside it on the hot plate, then your appetite begins to seep away . . .

To decorate a dish of smoked salmon, so beautiful in itself, with lettuce leaves, or to strew it with tufts of cress, is not to make that salmon which has cost 38s. a pound look as if it cost £3, but to belittle it so that you begin to feel it is some bargain basement left-over which needs to be disguised. Alas, where here is our celebrated capacity for understatement? Well, we have our own gifts, but the presentation of food is not one of them, and since French cooks and food purveyors so often appear to lose the lightness of their touch in this respect when they leave their native land and settle abroad, one can only conclude that the special stimulant which brings these gifts into flower is in the air of France itself. Does it sound trivial or over-rarified to make so much of such small points? I don't think anyone in full possession of their five senses would find it so.

Writing of the work of Chardin, whose most profoundly moving paintings are revelations of how trivial, homely, everyday scenes and objects are transformed for us when we see them through the eyes of a great painter, Proust says, 'Chardin has taught us that a pear is as living as a woman, a kitchen crock as beautiful as an emerald.' Since Proust wrote these words painters and writers have revealed other beauties to us – they have made us see the poetry of factory canteens and metro stations, the romance of cog-wheels, iron girders, bombed buildings, dustbins and pylons. But in the excitement of discovering these wondrous things we shall be poorer if we don't also give a thought now and again to the pear and the kitchen crock.

Vogue, March 1960

The Markets of France: Martigues

One of the meals we all enjoyed most during our journeyings round the markets of France last summer was a lunch in the end-of-the-world little town of Salin-de-Giraud on the edge of the Camargue. After a pretentious dinner and a bad night – it is rare, I find, to get through even a fortnight's motoring trip in France without at least one such disaster – spent in a highly unlikely establishment disguised as a cluster of Camargue guardian huts, we left before breakfast and spent a healing morning lost in the remaining lonely stretches of this once completely wild, mysterious, melancholy, half-land, half-water, Rhône estuary country.

Much of the Camargue has now been reclaimed, roads and bridges have been built, and huge rice fields have been planted. They have been so successful that from an initial yearly production of about 250 tons during the middle forties these rice fields now yield 145,000 tons a year and supply France with the whole of her rice requirements. It has been a great triumph for France's construction and agricultural engineers, a dazzling testimony to the industry and enterprise of a people who so often appear, to those who do not know them, to be in a perpetual state of political and economic chaos. One cannot but rejoice for France, and wholeheartedly admire the determination and ingenuity which has turned an almost totally waste land into a productive and prosperous one.

Alas, though, for the animals and the wild birds, for the legendary beasts which frequented the Camargue, for the shimmering lonely stretches of water, for the still heart of this mournful mistral-torn and mosquito-ridden country. The harpies from Paris running the road houses which must inevitably multiply will be a worse scourge than the mosquitoes. Owners of souvenir shops selling china Camargue bulls and plastic flamingoes and scarves printed with Provençal recipes will be more implacable than the mistral.

These rather gloomy thoughts were in our minds as we arrived, a bit soothed but still edgy, to find that the last ferry over the Rhône from Salin which would take us on to the road to Martigues had left at 11.30 and there would not be another until 2 o'clock. Forlornly we made our way to the local restaurant.

And there, instead of the omelette and the glass of wine which we had expected to swallow in a nervous hurry, we found the Restaurant La Camarguaise serving a well-chosen and properly cooked and comforting meal in a clean and high-ceilinged dining-room. The menu was 600 francs, and while the food was very simple it reminded me of what Provençal restaurants used to be like in the days before even the most ordinary of Provençal dishes became a 'speciality' listed on the menu as a *supplément* at 750 francs. There was an hors-d'œuvre of eggs and anchovies, there were hot grilled fresh sardines to follow, the vegetable course was *côtes de blettes*, the rib parts of those enormous leaves of the spinach family which we know as chard and which are much cultivated in the Rhône valley; the leaves themselves are cooked in the same way as spinach, the fleshy stalks and ribs were, on this occasion, sautéd in olive oil and flavoured with garlic and were delicious. The *bœuf Gardiane* which followed brought tears to our eyes; we had been over-wrought and dropping with fatigue, and while the food we had already eaten had cheered and comforted us, it wasn't until the cover was taken off the dish of beef stew and we smelt the wine and the garlic and the rich juices and saw the little black olives and the branches of wild thyme which had scented the stew laid in a little network over the meat, that the tension vanished. We ordered more supplies of the cheap red wine and decided that the 2.30 ferry would have to go without us.

Well, God bless the French lunch hour. It must have been nearly 5 o'clock when, having finally got the cars across that ferry, we eventually drove into Martigues in dazzling late afternoon sunshine to see the fishing boats come in.

In this still picturesque village, beloved and painted by generations of English as well as French artists, so charmingly, proudly, and absurdly known as the Venice of Provence – it is built on the Lagoon of Berre, west of Marseille – most of the inhabitants still live by fishing, and in spite of tremendous industrial development round about it is still comparatively unspoilt. It won't be for long. Martigues will soon be all but swallowed up in the new harbour constructions planned to stretch west from Marseille.

But for a little moment Martigues still stands, and we drink coffee on the quay as we wait for the boats to come in. Anthony is taking pictures of a faded blue warehouse door on which pink and coral and pale gold stars are hanging. They are starfish dried by the sun. Somewhere here in Martigues they are also drying something slightly more edible – the famous *poutargue*, compressed and salted grey mullet roes, a primitive speciality of Martigues whose origin goes back, they say, to the Phoenicians. It is made in Sardinia, too, and Crete, and for collectors of useless information, *poutargue*, or *botargo*, was among the dishes served at King James II's coronation feast. As a matter of fact we had some too, with a bottle of white wine for breakfast next day at M. Bérot's lovely restaurant the Escale, at Carry-le-Rouet, across the hills from Martigues and overlooking a real honest-to-goodness, glorious postcard Mediterranean bay.

The children watching us are also watching for the boats, and they have spotted the first of the fleet coming in. So have the cats. The *Yves-Jacky* chugs into her berth, ties up; the skipper's wife, ready at her post, wheels her fish barrow aboard. Almost before you can see what has come up out of the hold the fish is loaded on the barrow and trundled off at breakneck speed, followed by the small boys and the cats. The auction in the market place on the quay has started.

A few minutes later, in quick succession, come the *Espadon* and the *St-Jean* and the *Bienvenue*. The boats are blue, the nets are black, and the whole scene does remind me a little of the Adriatic, even if not precisely of Venice.

None of the boats have sensational catches today. This part of the Mediterranean is terribly overfished. A large percentage of Marseille's fresh fish supplies is brought from the North Sea and Channel ports. But still there are some fine and strange-looking fish gleaming with salt water and sparkling in the sun. There's a brown and red and gold beast called a *roucaou*; it's a bit like the famous *rascasse* which goes into the *bouillabaisse*, but larger. Here is a boxful of tiny *poulpes*, a variety of squid which never grow big and which are exquisite fried crisp in oil. There's a *langouste* or two, and some kind of silver sea bream which they call *sarde* round here, and some *baudroie*, that fish with the wicked antennae-like hooks growing out of its huge head – the fish they call *rana pescatrice* in Western Italy and *rospo* on the Adriatic, and angler or monk fish in England. The baby ones are as pretty and appealing as kittens with their little round heads. And there is a familiar friend, a gigantic turbot, and a long black fish with an arrow-shaped head. They call it *émissole* here, and to us it's a dogfish. There is a silver *loup de mer*, or sea-bass, and some big, rather touchingly ugly John Dories, called *St-Pierres* in France, because of the black St Peter's thumb marks on their sides.

Some of these big fish fetch big prices, two or three times as much as we would pay for them here, and they will go to the classy restaurants or the Marseille fish shops, but the boxes of little slithery bright pink fish called *demoiselles* and the miscellaneous collections of bony little rock fish, undersized whiting and other small fry, will go for very little. Most of the buyers are women – so is the auctioneer, a brawny, competent, good-humoured young woman with a Levantine cast of countenance and a thick Midi accent – who will re-sell them locally this very evening; any minute now the housewives of Martigues and Lavéra and round about will be turning them into *la soupe* or *la friture* for the evening meal.

Vogue, April 1960

The Markets of France: Valence

To drive from Lascaux of the prehistoric caves in the Dordogne right across country to Valence on the Rhône is possibly not the most expeditious way of getting from the deep south-west of France to the Mediterranean. But if time is not too desperately important it is one way of seeing a vast stretch of surprising and magnificent country, some interesting and unspoiled old towns, perhaps even of discovering some village in the heart of the still primitive agricultural Auvergne, some little-known hotel where one would like to stay instead of hurrying on, to which one would return another year. At the least, perhaps a country inn somewhere in the Limousin or the Cantal district will yield a new dish or a wine which was worth the détour. A *charcuterie* in Aurillac or Vic-sur-Cère or some other small but locally important town will possibly provide a pâté the like of which you never tasted before, or a locally cured ham, a few slices of which you will buy and carry away with a salad, a kilo of peaches, a bottle of Monbazillac and a baton of bread, and somewhere on a hillside amid the mile upon mile of golden broom or close to a splashing waterfall you will have, just for once, the ideal picnic.

Was it up here above Aurillac that one of our party found the best picnic place in France? A stretch of water, mysterious, still, full of plants and birds, away from the road, sheltered with silver birches, and with a stone table evidently waiting there especially for us?

We had driven from Montignac near Lascaux. We had stayed at the Soleil d'Or, a little hotel as warm-hearted as its name. We had eaten a good dinner – among other things a golden bolster of an omelette bursting its seams with truffles – and drunk some excellent red wine of Cahors and afterwards a glass of that remarkable *eau-de-vie* of plums called *Vieille Prune* which is one of the great Dordogne products – another is the odd and delicious walnut oil with which, if you are lucky, you may get your salad dressed.

In spite of all this, or perhaps because of it, we made an early enough start to reach Aurillac in plenty of time to buy our picnic lunch and see something of the old town. Had it been a Saturday we should have stayed to see the cheese market. For Aurillac is one of the centres for the distribution of the splendid cheese of Cantal, to my mind one of the best and most interesting in France. It is a cheese which has a texture not unlike a good Lancashire, and when properly matured a flavour which beats most modern English cheeses on their own ground. There is also a less interesting, creamy, unripened version called a *tomme de Cantal*, much used for cooking, especially in farmhouse potato and egg dishes.

After our picnic lunch we'll have to hurry. We must get across the Plomb du Cantal, into the Velay, and through the scruffy pilgrimage town of Le Puy. But I shall stop to buy some of those beautiful little slate-green lentils for which the district is famous and which a greedy guest of mine recently proclaimed as good as caviare – and also to telephone to Madame Barattero at the Hôtel du Midi at Lamastre to say we are coming for dinner.

Valence is the big shopping centre and market town for Lamastre. The wholesale fruit and poultry market opens before dawn on Saturday and is all packed up by seven o'clock in the morning. In the big retail market which opens later on the combined scents of ripe peaches and the fresh basil and thyme plants lying in heaps on the ground gave us our first sniff of Provence. But the plump little white ducks and the fresh St-Marcellin cheeses from the Isère, the exquisite black and green olives from Nyons which we bought for lunch tempted us to drive north or south-east of Valence instead of directly south.

The Drôme, the Tricastin, the Nyonsais regions are so different from Provence, so unfrequented early in the year, so interesting historically and architecturally . . . why hurry off to the south? The names of the little towns round about Valence ring like peals of bells compelling you to go and look at them. If, let us suppose, you were driving south from Mâcon or Bourge-en-Bresse (I would stay chez La Mère Blanc at Vonnas) you could drive through La-Tour-du-Pin, Saint-Rambert d'Albon, Beaurepaire d'Isère, Beaumont-les-Valence, La Garde-Adhémar, St-Paul-Trois-Châteaux – the three castles which gave their name to the Tricastin district – then down to Suze-La-Rousse and the tiny village of Donzère and its great nearby dam which is as wondrous and absorbing a spectacle in its way as any of the great Roman glories of this province through which, they claim, Hannibal marched with his Carthaginians – and presumably his elephants – two thousand one hundred and seventy-seven years ago.

The cooking of this mid-Rhône country is in a sense a cross-roads cooking. There are already the olive oil and the garlic and the aromatic herbs of Provence; there are the cream and the cheeses of the Dauphiné; there are the sumptuously cooked duck and chicken dishes of the Ardèche side of the Rhône. There are the crayfish and the creamy quenelles and the *charcuterie* which still belong a little to Lyon. And there are some old dishes entirely characteristic of this stretch of the Rhône itself and which have hardly spread farther than the villages and towns on the river banks. They are the dishes invented or popularized by the bargemen of the Rhône and their wives, and by the proprietors of the humble inns and *charcuteries* who used to cater for the men who worked the inland waterways. Such a dish is the *grillade des mariniers*, for which I have given a recipe on p.252 of the present volume.

BLETTES À LA CRÈME

This is a very everyday dish in the southern Rhône country. Just how good it is depends mainly upon how much care one takes over the cream sauce. For 1½ lb. of *blettes* or *poirée*, the chard which one sees displayed for sale in huge bundles in every market in the southern Rhône country make a cream sauce with 1½ oz. of butter, 2 tablespoons of flour, ¾ pint of milk, seasonings of salt, pepper and nutmeg and about 3 oz. of double cream.

Melt the butter; then, off the stove, stir in the flour. When it is smooth start adding the warmed milk, little by little. When the mixture looks creamy, return the saucepan to a very low heat, add the rest of the milk. Season lightly with salt, freshly milled pepper and a scrap of nutmeg. Let the sauce almost imperceptibly bubble for fifteen to twenty minutes, stirring frequently.

Now add the cream. The sauce should be very smooth, ivory-coloured and no thicker than cream. You can now if you like add a tablespoon or two of finely grated Gruyère or Parmesan cheese, just as a seasoning. And if your sauce has turned lumpy, press it through a sieve.

Clean the chard, discard the hard leaf stalks[1] and central veins, cook it in just a very little water, salt it lightly half way through the cooking. Drain it in a colander, press out excess moisture by putting a plate and weight on top. Chop it roughly.

In a *gratin* dish pour a little of your cream sauce. On top put the

---

1. Or save them for a separate dish. Cut into inch lengths and gently cooked in olive oil with a little garlic they are rather good.

chard and cover with the rest of the sauce. The *gratin* dish should be quite full. Spread a few tiny knobs of butter over the surface, heat in a moderate oven, gas no. 4, 350°F., for about 20 minutes, until the sauce is just faintly golden and bubbling.

Of course, all this is a trouble to do, but it makes an excellent and not very expensive first dish for a luncheon for four people. It is one I often serve before a simple meat dish, beef, lamb or veal, which is probably already cooking in the oven before the vegetable dish goes in.

Vogue, May 1960

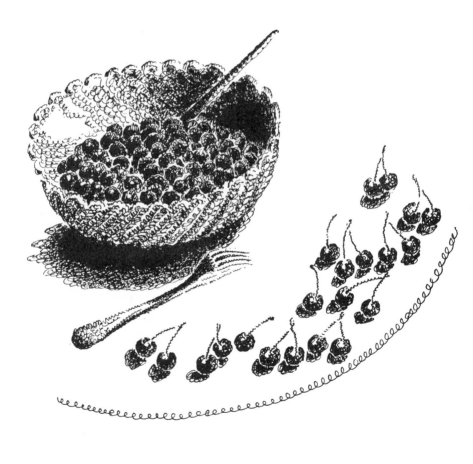

Oules of Sardines

What put the French fifty years ahead of any other nation when the sardine-canning industry developed in the nineteenth century was a combination of two circumstances; first, the fishermen of southern Brittany had evolved, for their own household consumption, a method of preserving their sardines which produced something more delicate than the primitive dried, salted and pressed fish of ancient Mediterranean tradition; they cooked their sardines in their own plentiful local butter or in olive oil imported from the south, packed them in clay jars called *oules*, and sealed them with more butter or oil. (The system sounds rather like the one used for preserving pork and goose in south-western France.) The delicacy came to be much appreciated by the prosperous shipbuilders and merchants of Nantes, the great trading port of the Loire estuary; and it was a Nantais confectioner, Joseph Colin, who in the early years of the nineteenth century first saw the possibilities of applying to the local method of preserving sardines the tinning process then being developed by a colleague, François Appert, by trade a confectioner-distiller, and by inclination an amateur chemist and scientist whose experiments with the preservation of food in bottles, jars and tins, hermetically sealed and then sterilized at high temperature, heralded the tinned-food era.

By 1824 Joseph Colin had established a sardine-tinning factory in the rue des Salorges at Nantes. The birth of the industry was attended by not unfamiliar wrangles, rivalries and complaints from the public. Colin's successful methods – he soon discovered that olive oil made the better preserving agent for sardines, and dropped the butter recipe – were almost immediately copied by competitors. In 1830 a Nantais restaurateur called Millet turned his establishment, situated in the heart of the residential quarter of the town, into a sardine-canning factory. The smell of the frying fish outraged the residents. Millet, brought to court in 1835, was forced to move his factory to the outskirts of the town. In 1838 another of Joseph Colin's rivals had the bright idea of taking into the firm a man who happened also to bear the name Joseph Colin; making him a partner, the firm proceeded to sell their products under precisely the same name as that of the originator. Another lawsuit followed – and put an end to the scandal.

For nearly fifty years sardine canning remained a French monopoly. It was not until the 1880s that competition from Spanish, Portuguese and American tinners, using cheaper processes and inferior grades of fish which were often not even true sardines, began to hit the French producers. By 1912 they felt driven into taking action to protect the industry from misrepresentation.

Sardines as understood in America and Canada were then and are still essentially a tinned product of which no equivalent in a fresh state exists in transatlantic waters; the only concession to exactitude obtained by the French from the American producers was that the place of origin of the tinned fish should be stated on their labels; and so the Americans have American-tinned herrings sold as Maine sardines, Canadian herrings labelled Canadian sardines, Norwegian sprats called Norwegian sardines and sometimes even Norwegian anchovies; so has arisen the confusion in the minds of the public as to whether or not there is actually and in fact any such animal as a sardine.

In England as well as in France matters are otherwise. The action brought in the English courts in 1912 by the French against an English importer selling Norwegian brisling (sprats) as sardines was finally settled in 1914 in favour of the French.

In England from that time on – which was presumably also the moment when the trade name of 'skippers' was invented for sprats – a sardine in a tin must be a sardine, and not a sprat or brisling, a herring or sild, a pilchard, an anchovy nor any other of the fish which belong to the same main family of Clupeas, but the *Sardinia pilchardus* or *Clupea* pilchardus Walbaum, the name by which the true sardine is now generally known. But just to add to the confusion there are several sub-divisions of the true sardine; the creature varies in numerous characteristics, as does the herring, according to the waters in which it is found, the food it eats, its degree of maturity. The Cornish pilchard is in fact a sardine, large and old and bearing only a small resemblance in appearance and flavour to the sardine of the Nantais canners, which is essentially a small and immature fish of which there are two main qualities, the finest not more than two years old – the age is indicated by rings on the scales – and measuring not more than seventeen centimetres from head to tail; the second, a year older and somewhat larger. The Portuguese sardine is again another variation, larger still and with one more vertebrae than the Breton sardine.

A director of Philippe et Canaud, the oldest existing and largest-producing sardine-canning firm of Nantes, had stern words to say about the way the English treat sardines. 'Our fine sardines,' he said, 'should not be cooked. At an English meal I was given *hot* sardines, on cold toast. It was most strange. They were my sardines and I could not recognize them. The taste had become coarse. Perhaps for inferior sardines . . . but ours are best just as they are. A little cayenne or lemon if you like, and butter with sardines is traditional in France, although they are fat, and do not really need it. But, please, no shock treatment.'

One sympathizes. Shortages and much-advertised cheaper replacements have rather made us forget that best-quality French sardines are products of some delicacy, a treat rather than an everyday commodity. Production is small – about one-fifth of that of Portugal – the process is expensive, the hazards a perpetual worry. A member of the Amieux family and of the famous firm which bears their name told me something about the sardine-canning business. It is chancy, a gamble almost, even after 140 years of existence.

Sardines are migratory fish; their habits are notoriously unpredictable; the catch is seasonal; the factories operate approximately from May to October only; for several years there may be – and have been – shortages; then perhaps suddenly a glut. In a good year the Amieux firm will can up to 30,000 tons; in a poor one output may be as little as 6,000 tons. And since the sardine is one of the most perishable of all fish, depending for its delicacy upon its absolute freshness, the Nantais firms, who all deal in many other products besides sardines, have established special factories on the coast and close to the Breton and Vendéen fishing ports such as Douarnenez, the Ile d'Yeu, the Sables d'Olonne, St-Guénolé, Quiberon, Le Croisic, La Rochelle. Once into port, the sardine fishers rush their catches to auction; 15,000 kilos is the minimum quantity of any use at any one time to the Amieux factories. Raced from auction to factory, the sardines are decapitated and degutted, rinsed, plunged into a mild brine – made with salt from the Breton salt marshes – for anything from a few minutes to half an hour according to size; rinsed again, arranged on great grids, dried briefly in a current of warm air, rapidly fried (no more than a few seconds in the sizzling oil), drained, packed in their tins, covered with fresh olive oil selected by an expert taster for the purpose; the sardines are going to mature in that oil, and acquire some of its flavour; its quality is of prime importance. Finally, as required by French law, the sealed tins are stamped with code figures which indicate the date of tinning, and then sterilized at a temperature of 112°C.

In essentials, the present-day French process is the same as the one evolved by Joseph Colin, the sardine-tinning pioneer; other and cheaper methods have been tried; some, such as the Portuguese one of steaming instead of frying the sardines, have proved successful and popular; but the French canners consider that for finesse of flavour and texture, the olive-oil-frying system has never been equalled.

Ideally, the Nantais producers say, sardines in olive oil would be kept at least a year before they are passed on to the consumer; and after two years are at their best. Nowadays, though, unless one were to lay down stocks of sardines, one would not get them in this condition. The 1962 season has been a comparatively good one, but it follows five poor sardine years on the Brittany and Vendée coasts; the entire production has been going out to the wholesalers and retailers within months.

Dried and salted sardines were known it seems to the Romans. In the days of the Empire the Sardinians traded their product all over Italy and as far as Gaul. When the sardine fishing industry got under way on the Atlantic coasts of the Vendée and Brittany, round about the sixteenth century, much the same primitive methods of preservation must have been used. Henry IV, the Béarnais who so often crops up in the mythology of French gastronomy, was apparently inordinately fond of salt sardines. By the seventeenth century the French Treasury was already exacting taxes from the sardine industry which included among its activities the sale of by-products such as oil for lamps and for the tanners, obtained from pressed sardines, and manure from the debris of the fish to be salted.

The Spectator, 12 October 1962

*

As a postscript to Oules of Sardines, *written twenty-two years ago, I should like to quote from an article entitled* What is a Sardine, *written by Alan Davidson and published by him in* Petits Propos Culinaires No. 2,[1] *August 1979. The question of the legitimate use of the name sardine and of how widely it may be used had recently been the subject of discussion in the Codex Alimentarius Com-*

---

1. Prospect Books, 45 Lamont Road, London, s.w.10.

mission of the Food and Agriculture Organisation of the United Nations:

'*The starting point of any such discussion must be* the sardine, Sardina pilchardus *(Walbaum). Young specimens of the fish are the archetypal sardines. (Older ones, incidentally, are pilchards.) But the name sardine has also been applied for a very long time to two close relations,* Sardinella aurita *and* Sardinella maderensis. *Both of these are in areas where* Sardina pilchardus *is found; and it requires some expert knowledge to tell them apart.*'

To summarise the rest of Alan Davidson's report, the Commission concluded that eighteen other species also qualify as sardines, a conclusion which seems to me a thoroughly confusing one since among the eighteen are Clupea harengus, *the Atlantic herring,* Sprattus sprattus, *the sprat, and one called* Sardinella longiceps, *which the Indian authorities were seeking to introduce into the already numerous company. Mr Davidson, having eaten* Sardinella longiceps, *whether in or out of a tin he doesn't say, thought that it had a good claim on the basis 'of what technical people call its 'organoleptic' qualities, by which they mean its appearance, texture, flavour, etc'. The Commission, however, in spite of their findings, decided that any tinned sardine other than* Sardina pilchardus *must be labelled with the name of a country, a geographic area, the species, or the common name of the species, e.g. sprat. So all the Commision's deliberations bring us back, more or less, to what I wrote all those years ago, and Alan Davidson very rightly comments that while keeping an open mind about the merits of the various species, potential consumers 'would do well to pay particular attention to the other contents of the can, which will often be of greater importance than any small difference between the qualities of the fish themselves'. Indeed. You may, for example, find tins of sardines in olive oil in France, Spain and other olive growing areas, but, for the English market, it would seem that sardines of whatever variety are more usually canned in groundnut or cotton seed oil, or in tomato sauce.*

Trufflesville Regis

On Saturday morning the entire main shopping thoroughfare of the Piedmontese market town of Alba in the Italian province of Cuneo is closed to traffic. The stalls are set up in the middle of the street, and the awnings stretch right across it from pavement to pavement. Coming from the big piazza Savona you pass first stall upon stall of clothes, bales of cloth, household wares, plastics, and, on the ground, huge copper polenta pots. The vegetable, fruit, and cheese stalls fill the vast piazza at the far end of the street and ramble right round and to the back of the great red *duomo*. (There are some very remarkable carved and inlaid choir stalls in Alba's cathedral. The artist, Bernardo Cidonio, has created magnificent fruitwood panels showing the local landscapes, castles and towers, architectural vistas, and still-lifes of the fruit and even of the cooking pots of the region. These treasures, dating from 1501, unheralded by guide-books, shouldn't be missed.)

At this season in Alba there are beautiful pears and apples, and especially interesting red and yellow peppers, in shape rather like the outsize squashy tomatoes of Provence, very fleshy and sweet, a speciality of the neighbourhood. What we have really come to Alba to see and eat, though, are white truffles, and these are to be found in the poultry, egg, and mushroom market held in yet another enormous piazza (Alba seems to be all piazzas, churches, red towers, and white truffles), and will not start, they say, until nine-thirty. In the meantime there are baskets of prime mushrooms to look at and to smell, chestnut and ochre-coloured *funghi porcini*, the cèpes or *Boletus edulis* common in the wooded country of Piedmont, and some fine specimens of the beautiful red-headed *Amanita caesarea*, the young of which are enclosed in an egg-shaped white cocoon, or volva, which has earned them their name of *funghi uovali*, egg mushrooms – although in Piedmont, where everything possible is kingly, the *Amanita caesarea* are *funghi reali*, royal mushrooms. They are *oronges* considered by some French fungi-fanciers as well as by the Piedmontese to be the best of all mushrooms.

In Piedmont the royal mushroom is most commonly eaten as an hors-d'œuvre, sliced raw and very fine, prepared only when you order it. Since few Piedmontese restaurateurs supply printed menus, expecting their clients to be familiar with the specialities, it is well for tourists to know that they won't get fungi unless they ask for them. The basket will then be brought to your table, you pick out the ones you fancy, making as much fuss as possible about the freshness and size, instruct the waiter as to their preparation (*funghi porcini* are best grilled), and they are charged according to weight.

As far as the beautiful salad of tangerine-bordered, white-and-cream cross-sections of *funghi reali* is concerned, normally it is seasoned only with salt, olive oil, and lemon juice, but at this season you have to be pretty quick off the mark to prevent the Piedmontese in general and the Albesi in particular from destroying this exquisite and delicate mushroom with a shower of *tartufi bianchi*.

It is not that the white truffles, which are not white but putty-coloured, are not entirely marvellous and extraordinary. It is simply that their scent is so overpowering and all-penetrating that nothing delicate can stand up to their assault. The one creation evolved by the Piedmontese that accords perfectly with the white truffle is the famous *fonduta*, a dish made from the fat, rich Val d'Aosta cheese called Fontina, cut into cubes and steeped in milk for an essential minimum of twelve hours, then cooked, by those very few who have the knack, to a velvety, egg-thickened cream with an appearance entirely guileless until the rain of truffles, sliced raw in flake-fine slivers with a special type of *mandoline*-cutter, descends upon it. There is something about Fontina cheese, a hint of corruption and decadence in its flavour, that gives it a true affinity with the rootless, mysterious tuber dug up out of the ground.

The black truffles (*Tuber melanosporum*) of Périgord are, traditionally, sniffed out by pigs. In Provence and the Languedoc, dogs are trained to locate and indicate the presence of truffles by scratching the patches of ground that conceal them. In Piedmont the white truffle (*Tuber magnatum*) is located in the same way. In the village of Roddi, not far from Alba, there is a training establishment for truffle hounds. Most of the dogs are mongrels. Valuable property, these Bobbis and Fidos, to the farmers and peasants who go about their truffle-digging secretively by dawn light, bearing their little hatchets for extracting the treasure from the earth. No system of truffle cultivation in the technical sense has ever yet been evolved, but according to Professor Gagliardi and Doctor Persiani in their Italian book on mushrooms and truffles, truffles can be and are propagated successfully by the reburying of mature truffles and spores close to the lateral roots of oaks and beeches, and in chalky ground with a southerly aspect. In five to ten years the chosen area may or may not yield a truffle harvest. Truffle veins peter out in forty to fifty years; laying truffles down for the future seems to be a sensible precaution.

The season for the true *tartufi bianchi* is brief. It opens in September. During the second week of October, Alba is in full fête with banquets, speeches, visiting celebrities, and its very own truffle queen. By November the truffles are at their most potent and plentiful. By the end of January the ball is over.

In the Morra family's Hôtel Savona in Alba, visitors staying in rooms on the side are likely to be wakened early during the truffle season. The Morra canning and truffle paste factory starts up at six in the morning. It is not so much the noise, a very moderate one as Italian noises go, that gets you out of bed, as the smell of the truffles being bashed to paste, emulsified with oil, and packed into tubes for a sandwich spread. 'Truffle paste? Is there such a thing?' asks a *cavaliere* whose little shopwindow in the main street of Alba is pasted over with newspaper clippings and announcements to the effect that he is the *principe dei tartufi*. Certainly, somebody is due to succeed the Morra dynasty, still regarded as kings of the Alba truffle domain, even though the Morra manner of running a hotel and restaurant (its Michelin star must be the most misplaced of any in the whole Guide) is not so much regal as reminiscent of a Hollywood gangster-farce. All the same, the Morra truffle paste not only exists but does retain something of the true scent and flavour, which tinned whole truffles rarely do.

Contradiction and confusion in all things concerning the white truffle are normal in Alba, where the most harmless questions are met with evasive answers and where, for all the information one would ever be able to extract from the truffle dealers, the things might be brought by storks or found under gooseberry bushes. In the market there is no display of the truffle merchants' wares. The knobbly brown nuggets are not weighed out and are not even to be seen unless you are a serious customer. Some three dozen silent men in sombre suits stand in a huddle outside the perimeter of the poultry market. Only if you ask to see the truffles will one of these truffle men extract from his pocket a little paper- or cloth-wrapped parcel. You buy by nose and a sound, dry appearance.

About the storage of truffles the Albesi are comparatively communicative, if not very enlightening. 'What is the best way to keep *tartufi*?'

'You wrap them in a piece of stuff . . .'

Another dealer interrupts, 'No, you keep them in a jar of rice.'

The *cavaliere* says this is nonsense. Rice, he says, makes the truffles wet, and they must have air. (Nobody here seems to have heard of the Bolognesi method of keeping truffles dry in sawdust or wood shavings.) The *cavaliere* says jauntily that the ones we buy from him will last ten days. They are packed in tissue paper in four-inch-square packing cases. They have so much air that on the drive back to Turin from Alba we are nearly strangled by the smell. It is glorious, but it is dissipating itself, and the truffles are weakening with every kilometre. By the time we get them back to London in three days they will be ghosts.

The *cavaliere*'s ten days was a hefty overestimation, but his recommendation of the cooking at the Buoi Rossi (The Red Ox), the unmodernized Piedmontese country-town inn in the via Cavour, was worthwhile. In the quiet old courtyard, with its characteristic vista of Piedmontese arches and open loft stacked with the copper-red corncobs, we drank a bottle of red Dolcetto, a local wine and a dry and genuine one, and ate some bread and butter spread with truffles. (This is one of the best ways of eating them if you can ever persuade a Piedmontese to allow you such a simple treat.) We returned three days running for meals.

The Red Ox is not mentioned in Michelin and is a simple *albergo-ristorante* where honest, decent, and cheap food, which includes a genuine *fonduta*, is to be had. There were also delicious pears baked in their skins and sprinkled with coarse sugar, and fresh, fat *fagioli alla regina*, oven-cooked. The local wines are all they should be. In typical Italian fashion the *padrona* was unable to tell us more about her first-class vintage Barolo than that it comes from her cousin, one Enrico Borgogno, a grower in Barolo itself, and that it was, she thought, ten years old. The finer points of vintages and vintage years do not preoccupy Italian inn-keepers. Unless it is standardized and commercialized out of all recognition, two bottles of precisely the same growth are likely to resemble each other in about the same degree as the black truffle of Périgord resembles the white one of Piedmont.

The Compleat Imbiber 7, 1964

The Magpie System

An organization we could do with at Christmas time is one which would provide packing depots – boutiques perhaps they would be called – places to which all one's miscellaneous presents could be taken, made up into seemly parcels and entrusted to the shop for postage or dispatch.

Parcel-wrapping stations in big stores are fine as far as they go but since one can hardly ask them to pack things bought in other shops, that isn't quite far enough. I was thinking particularly about hampers of food and wine. The roof under which one would be able to buy *everything* one would like to put into such parcels doesn't exist; my hampers would be based on a lot of small things; some cheap, some less so; they would be Christmas stockings really, not hampers, and one rule would be that everything should be the very best of its kind, and that means you have to go to specialist shops, like, for instance, Moore Brothers (of the Brompton Road and Notting Hill) for coffee, three or four different kinds in labelled parcels (all ready-made hampers contain fine quality tea, which is all very well for friends abroad, but silly in England; you can buy good tea anywhere; good coffee is infinitely more rare) which would include Mocha, Java, Blue Mountain. Then there would be little packets, neat *and* gaudy, of those spices which are not always easy to come by even in a city which not all that long ago was the centre of the entire world spice trade.

The spice importing-exporting centre appears to have moved to North America, and the English supermarketeers (and how sensible of them) have been quick to see the possibilities of American- and Canadian-packed whole spices, such as coriander seeds, allspice berries, cumin and fennel seeds, cinnamon sticks and ginger root. As a matter of fact, by buying one large packet of pickling spice you get, if you can identify them, a good selection of these spices (not the cumin or fennel seeds, though) which grocers are always denying they have in stock. For a phial of fine whole saffron – even I wouldn't need a professional packer for that – a well-found chemist is the best bet. Then, inevitably, an expedition to Soho and Roche of 14 Old Compton Street, the only shop selling the envelopes of herbs dried and packed on the stalk – wild thyme, basil, thick fennel twigs, which contain the right true essence of all the hills of Provence. And one could do worse than buy a gallon or two of their beautiful olive oil, and decant it into clear wine or liqueur bottles for presents.

*

Half the charm of the magpie system of shopping is that one comes across unexpectedly pretty and festive-looking things for so little money; in the window of the Empire Shop in Sloane Street there is a pyramid of white candy sugar in rocky lumps, so irresistibly decorative that one would like to hang them on the tree; and inside the shop, by-passing the chain-dairy goods which have somehow strayed in, are dark and dazzly genuine Indian chutneys, garnet-bright Jamaican guava jelly, English quince, Scottish rowan, and squat jars of shiny lemon curd.

Indeed, to think no further than how to make up hampers of jams and jellies, marmalade and honey would still be to have and to give plenty of entertainment.

Dark French heather honey from the Landes is one which I know to be especially aromatic, and there must be some fifty more different kinds of honey at least to be bought in London. Fortnum's seem to have the most dazzling choice; there can be found (if you dodge the gift packs, the china beehives, the peasant pottery) honey from Hungary and Guatemala, California and Canada and Dalmatia, from Buckfast and Jamaica, from Mexico, Sicily, Greece, Scotland, Italy, Ireland and Spain; and every aromatic flower of which one has ever heard has apparently fed those bees; lime flowers and rosemary, acacia, wild thyme, white clover, orange blossom and lemon and wild roses. With all their colours and different degrees of opacity or translucence, some creamy as white cornelian and some clear and golden as Château d'Yquem and some bronze as butterscotch, they have the allure which Christmas presents ought to have. Three Kings' presents perhaps. Just the quality which things in ready-made-up hampers hardly ever possess.

*

Those bottles of indeterminate sherry and port, Christmas puddings and tins of tea and fancy biscuits are survivals from the days when such things were distributed by Ladies Bountiful to old retainers, retired nannies and governesses and coachmen who would probably much rather have had a couple of bottles of gin. Well, wouldn't you? And really one would have to have quite a grievance against somebody before one felt impelled to give them a hamper – this is one from the list of a great West End store a year or two ago – containing one tin each of chicken, ox-tongue, steak, cocktail sausages, shrimps, ham, crab, dressed lobster and steak pie, plus one box of assorted cheese, and all costing 63s. Then there was the writer of a handout I once received from a public relations firm flogging Italian tomato products whose Christmas hamper idea was for two tins of tomato juice packed in a beribboned wicker basket, price about 21s. as I remember, which would make, they ventured to suggest, a gift acceptable to 'elderly people or neighbours'. As Christmas approaches, people (and neighbours, too, I dare say) do tend to rather morbid ideas about others. But that bad?

*

I'm not sure about the precise technical distinction between mushrooms and *champignons*, but Fortnum's hampers this year have come out in a rash of tinned *champignon* butter and *champignon* bisque; and here and there in the parcels directed at overseas customers are ready-made *crêpes Suzette* brought over from the United States; perhaps pancakes travel exceptionally well, and if they don't, they are, at any rate in Fortnumese, 'Conversation Pieces of memorable quality.' Harrods' man seems to have been bemused by dates in glove boxes and something called Bakon Krisp; Selfridges are bent on spreading the joyful tidings that you can buy shoestring potatoes in tins; Barkers' cheese hampers would be rather sensible, except that Prize Dairy Stilton *and* Assorted Cheese Portions seem to make such unlikely basketfellows.

Inconsistency is characteristic of all Christmas hampers, but at least Christopher's, the wine merchants of 94 Jermyn Street, is one firm which has eliminated it from their Christmas lists this year. A case containing a bottle of Manzanilla and two tins of Spanish green olives stuffed with anchovies, all for 25s., makes sense; so does a bottle of Sercial Madeira and two large jars of turtle soup for £2, and a bottle of champagne, plus a tin of foie gras for two, at 45s., or a bottle of Club port and a jar of Stilton for 44s., are better value by a good deal than the contents of most store-chosen hampers, and since Messrs Christopher's also sell first-pressing Provence olive oil and Barton and Guestiers fine white wine vinegar, it shouldn't be beyond the ingenuity of their directors to devise a salad-making or kitchen case which would be cheap and imaginative.

The Spectator, 23 November, 1962

Traditional Christmas Dishes

How the food of a past age tasted seems to us almost impossible to imagine. We know roughly what our ancestors' kitchens were like, what sort of pots they cooked in and what fuel they used. We have their cookery books and recipes and ample evidence of how their meals were composed. All this still doesn't convey to us what the food tasted like to them.

The reproduction of dishes cooked precisely according to the recipes of a hundred or two hundred years ago is a fairly pointless undertaking, not only because our tastes, our methods of cookery and our equipment have so toally changed but because even the identical ingredients would no longer taste the same. Period clothes for the stage inevitably bear the stamp of contemporary fashion, however much trouble the designers and the cutters have taken over the authentic detail. So it is with food. And I always feel a bit dubious when I read about traditional English puddings and pies, cakes and creams, pickles, hams, cheeses and preserves being made 'precisely according to a 300-year-old recipe'. Even were this really so, I can't help thinking our ancestors would have considerable difficulty in recognizing them. Chemical feeding stuffs and new systems of breeding and fattening animals for market, vegetables and fruit grown in artificially fertilized soil, the pasteurizing of milk and cream, the production of eggs from battery hens, the refining of salt and flour, the substitution of beet sugar for cane, the preservation of fish by modern methods, and even the chlorination of water – in what way these developments have caused our food to deteriorate or to improve is not under discussion here, but certainly they have changed the nature of almost every single ingredient which comes into our kitchens.

In *La Cuisine de Tous les Mois*, a cookery book published in the nineties by Philéas Gilbert, a great teaching chef and one of Escoffier's collaborators, is to be found the following very relevant observation. 'Cookery,' says Gilbert, 'is as old as the world, but it must also remain, always, as modern as fashion.' And as Christmas is the season when rather more improbable talk than usual goes on about what is called 'traditional English fare' I have tried to take Philéas Gilbert's hint and to produce recipes which, while based on the old ones, are modern in treatment. It is a system which works so long as the spirit of the recipes is preserved, for then we do get some sense of a continuing tradition into our cookery, avoiding the farcical effect produced by 'traditional' recipes made up almost entirely of synthetic or substitute ingredients. I have not forgotten that recipe sent out a few years ago by a publicity firm and said by them to have been dropped by Richard the Third's cook on the field of Bosworth. (A careless crowd, Richard and his followers.) By a fascinating coincidence this recipe called for the use of a highly advertised brand of modern vegetable cooking lard.

On the other hand, methods, quantities, and, especially, seasonings, have to be modernized, or all we get is a sort of folk-weave cooking perilously close to that hilarious land of which Miss Joyce Grenfell is queen, with the American advertisements of the British Travel Association for hand-maidens.

SPICED BEEF FOR CHRISTMAS

This recipe has perhaps a somewhat unrealistic sound, but it is a lovely one; it is not exactly a recipe of kitchenette cookery, but those who have the space and the patience will find it well worth doing once in a while. Beef dry-pickled with spices, very different in flavour from the brine-pickled beef of the butchers, used to be a regular Christmas dish in a great many English country houses and farms. 'This is more a Christmas dish than any other time of the year,' says John Simpson, cook to the Marquis of Buckingham, in his *Complete System of Cookery* (1806), 'not but it may be done any time, and is equally good.' He calls it rather grandly *Bœuf de Chasse*, but under the names of Hunting Beef or Beef *à l'Écarlate*, or simply Spiced Beef, various forms of the recipe have certainly been known for at least three hundred years.

In former times huge rounds of beef weighing upwards of 20 lb. were required to lie in pickle for 3 to 4 weeks. Today, a modest 5 to 12 lb. piece will be ready for cooking after 10 to 14 days. Here are two prescriptions for the spices for varying quantities of meat. The presence of juniper berries among the pickling spices makes the recipe somewhat unusual. They appear in old recipes from Yorkshire, Cumberland, Wales and Sussex – those areas, in fact, where junipers grow wild on the hills. They can be bought from grocers who specialize in spices, such as Selfridges, and Coopers of Brompton Road.

For a 10 to 12 lb. joint		For a 5 to 6 lb. joint
5 to 6 oz.	light brown Barbados or other cane sugar	3 oz.
1 oz.	saltpetre (to be bought from chemist's)	½ oz.
6 oz.	coarse kitchen salt	4 oz.
2 oz.	black peppercorns	1 oz.
2 oz.	juniper berries	1 oz.
1 oz.	allspice berries (also known as pimento and Jamaica pepper. To be bought from the same shops as the juniper berries).	½ oz.

For cooking the beef you will need only water, ½ to 1 lb. of shredded suet, and greaseproof paper or foil. Ask the butcher for the best quality round or silverside beef and explain to him what it is for. He will probably be incredulous but will know how to cut and skewer it.

First rub the beef all over with the brown sugar and leave it for two days in a glazed earthenware bread crock or bowl. Crush all the spices, with the salt and saltpetre, in a mortar. They should be well broken up but need not be reduced to a powder. With this mixture you rub the beef thoroughly each day for 9 to 14 days according to the size. Gradually, with the salt and sugar, the beef produces a certain amount of its own liquid, and it smells most appetizing. But keep it covered, and in a cool airy place, not in a stuffy kitchen.

When the time comes to cook the beef, take it from the crock, rinse off any of the spices which are adhering to it, but without sousing the meat in cold water.

Put it in a big deep pot in which it fits with very little space to spare. Pour in about ½ pint of water. Cover the top of the meat with the shredded suet; this is a great help in keeping the meat moist during cooking. In the old days the pot would now have been covered with a thick crust made from a pound of flour and 2 oz. of lard, but this can be dispensed with – two or three layers of greaseproof paper or foil being used instead, to make sure there is no evaporation of juices. Put the lid on the pot. Bake in a very low oven, gas no. 1, 290°F., for 4 to 5 hours according to the size of the joint. Take it from the oven carefully, for there will be a lot of liquid round the beef. Let it cool, which will take several hours. But before the fat sets, pour off all the liquid and remove the beef to a board.

Wrap it in foil or greaseproof paper and put another board or a plate on top, and a 2- to 4-lb. weight. Leave until next day.

The beef will carve thinly and evenly, and its mellow spicy flavour does seem to convey to us some sort of idea of the food eaten by our forebears. Once cooked, the beef will keep fresh a considerable time. 'A quarter of a year,' one cook says. At any rate it will certainly keep 10 to 14 days in an ordinary larder if it is kept wrapped in clean greaseproof paper. Those who feel that all this really is too much of an undertaking will be interested to know that beef spiced according to the same recipe, and ready for cooking, will be on sale at Harrods butchery counter during December.

GINGER CREAM

A recipe adapted from a much more elaborate one given by John Simpson; it provides a useful way of using some of the ginger in syrup which one gets given at Christmas time.

Ingredients are a pint of single cream, 5 to 6 egg yolks, a strip of lemon peel, a sprinkling of cinnamon and nutmeg, 3 or 4 tablespoons of sugar, 2 tablespoons each of the ginger syrup and the ginger itself, finely chopped. Put the spices and lemon peel into the cream and bring it to the boil. Beat the yolks of the eggs very thoroughly with the sugar. Pour the hot cream into the egg mixture, stir well, return to the saucepan and cook gently, as for a custard, until the mixture has thickened. Take the pan from the fire, extract the lemon peel, go on stirring until the cream is cool. Add the syrup and the chopped ginger.

Leave it in the refrigerator overnight, then, stirring well so that the ginger does not sink to the bottom, pour it into little custard glasses, small wine glasses, or coffee cups. There will be enough to fill 8 glasses.

If you subtract a quarter pint of cream from the original mixture, adding the same quantity of whipped double cream when the custard is quite cold, and freeze it in the foil-covered ice-trays of the refrigerator (at maximum freezing point) for 2 hours, this makes a very attractive ice cream.

Vogue, December, 1958

*

GOOSE WITH CHESTNUTS AND APPLES

The chestnuts and apples are prepared like a stuffing, but they don't go into the goose, they are cooked separately. This is because if you are going to have your goose cold, a stuffing is too fat-soaked from the bird to be attractive, whereas if it is baked separately in a terrine or a pie dish it comes out almost like a *pâté* and can be cut into nice even slices as an accompaniment, and all you will probably need besides is a big bowl of salad (endive, celery, and beetroot is a good one) and baked potatoes for those who have given up caring about their weight.

To start on the chestnuts – about 1½ lb. Score them right across on the rounded side, preferably with a broken-off, but still sharp knife which isn't going to be ruined in the process. Put them in a baking tin, half at a time, and cook them in a moderate oven for 10 to 15 minutes. Take out a few and, to shell and skin them, squeeze each nut in your hand so that the shell bursts. Then it comes off quite easily with the aid of a sharp knife, sometimes bringing the inner skin with it, sometimes not. And if this inner skin will not come away easily, leave it, do not hack at it. When all except these resistant ones are done, put them in a basin and pour boiling water over them. This should succeed in loosening the skins. Put the chestnuts in a saucepan with ½ pint of milk and 4 tablespoons of water and simmer them for about half an hour, or until they are quite soft.

Meanwhile peel, slice and core 4 sweet apples, and stew them in a little water until they are almost in a purée. Drain the liquid from the chestnuts, break them up roughly but do not mash them. Mix them with the apples, add a ¼ lb. of minced lean veal, 2 finely chopped shallots, 2 tablespoons of parsley, a very little salt, freshly milled pepper, and a well-beaten egg. Turn into a buttered pie dish or terrine, which you put, covered with a buttered paper, into the oven at the same time as the goose, and take out after about 1½ hours.

If you have bought your goose a day or two before you intend to cook it, it will benefit from being well rubbed with coarse salt night and morning, left in a cool larder, and the salt carefully wiped off before cooking. But if the weather is muggy this procedure is not advisable. Most Christmas birds have been killed a good deal in advance and once out of the poulterers' cold rooms are best cooked as soon as possible, unless your refrigerator is large enough to hold them.

Put the goose on a rack in the largest baking tin which will get into the oven, because a lot of fat runs out of the bird while cooking. Cover it with an oiled paper or foil, and bake it 2½ to 3 hours for a goose weighing about 8 lb. drawn and dressed (13 to 14 lb. gross weight). During the final half hour turn the heat very low and remove the paper so that the skin turns golden.

The fat from the bird should be separated from the juices and poured off into a bowl, for it is very valuable for frying; the juices can be mixed with wine-flavoured stock from the giblets to make a sauce for the goose.

House and Garden, December 1958

Welsh Doubles

'My aim', wrote Lady Llanover in her *Good Cookery*, published in 1867, 'has been to preserve or restore all the *good* old habits of my country, and utterly repudiate all immoral introductions which ruin the health as well as imperil the soul—'

Lady Llanover's country was South Wales, her particularly beloved part of it the estate of Llanover near Abergavenny in the county of Monmouthshire. It was at Llanover that, as Augusta Waddington, she was born and brought up. In 1823, as the twenty-year-old bride of young Benjamin Hall, M.P. for Newport, it was close by her girlhood home that she and her husband settled. It was at Llanover that she spent the greater part of a lifetime which spanned the entire nineteenth century, from 1802 to 1896.

Formidably industrious, endowed with a high sense of duty towards her dependants and her husband's constituents, Augusta Hall devoted also immense energy to the study of Welsh traditions and agriculture, to local folklore, music, literature, husbandry, cookery, and housekeeping.

After the death of her husband, created Baron Llanover as a reward for his labours as Commissioner of Works (it was during his term of office in the eighteen-fifties that the Westminster clock tower was completed. It is to Benjamin Hall that Big Ben owes its nickname) Lady Llanover evidently settled down to the writing of her cookery book. We can take it that everything she set down was first-hand, noted from direct observation and practical experience. When she gives recipes for rice bread, barley cakes, leek and plum broth, chicken and leek pie with cream, Welsh salt duck, Gwent short cakes (made of a dough shortened with sheep's-milk cream in preference to butter) her authority is indisputable, her recipes always fully, if sometimes rather confusingly, described.

It is fortunate for us that Lady Llanover recorded such recipes – as she recorded, in the water colours[1] for which her name is chiefly remembered, the now extinct regional costumes of South Wales – for they do not appear in other published works, and but for *Good Cookery* might well be entirely forgotten.

We hear a lot these days of a renaissance of English cooking. As far as restaurants are concerned does this really amount to much more than the obvious? A syllabub (wrongly presented) here, an authentic smoked haddock (price 35s. 6d. a portion) there, aren't going very far toward the re-creation of a tradition.

Among national recipes which could, and should, be rescued from oblivion many are to be prised out of forgotten cookery books. One of the most interesting and successful, for example, of Lady Llanover's Welsh recipes is for a duck salted for three days and cooked in a double boiling pan.

Of this utensil, known as a 'double', Lady Llanover gives drawings and a detailed description. It was a large double boiling pan, one fitting *inside* the other, the inner one light and made of tin, the outer of heavy iron and one inch larger in circumference. Both were fitted with covers and the whole contrivance could be used for oven cooking as well as for boiling.

Although Lady Llanover implies that 'doubles' (the term reminds me of Sir Kenelm Digby's 'dubble ones are the Best' when he prescribes violets in a recipe for metheglin), known in Wales as *ffwrn fach*, were commonplace in Welsh kitchens, one suspects that her own had been made to her particular specifications, probably by the local blacksmith. Her kitchen was equipped with both oval and round doubles. In them many of her dishes were cooked. Veal was oven-baked in the outer one, rabbits and chickens were jugged in the 'double', pickled beef was baked in it, tongues simmered in the same way as the salt duck. Maintaining throughout her book that one of the cardinal points of good cooking is the retention and

---

1. These are to be seen in the National Library of Wales at Aberystwyth.

Lady Llanover, by Mornewick, reproduced by kind permission of the Warden of Llandovery College

concentration of all natural savours and juices rather than enrichment or sophistication by the extraneous addition of butter, cream and stock, Lady Llanover rejected the eternally-simmering stock-urn so dear to her contemporaries. 'I don't possess one', she says of a stock-pot, 'and if I did I *would not use it.*' To a generation brought up to believe that all kitchen virtue resided in the liquor produced from the stock-pot, Lady Llanover, although perfectly right, was proclaiming herself something of a heretic. In her repudiation of the marvels of Victorian progress and the products of what she called 'mechanical talent' she was also reactionary. Or was she a visionary? To those of us who today yearn increasingly for authenticity and natural food, she appears sometimes to be writing of the 1960s rather than of the 1860s.

Many of the recipes in *Good Cookery*, now a very scarce book, are buried in the main part of Lady Llanover's text. This is written, not with entire success, in the form of a dialogue between two fictitious characters of whom one, the Hermit of St Gover, is Lady Llanover's own mouthpiece. His foil is the Traveller, a Candide-like innocent from London, introduced for the purpose of making naïve assertions to be seized upon by the Ancient and demolished as evidence of the folly and ignorance to be expected of those exposed to life in the metropolis.

From this tract for the times, the accounts, quoted below, of the author's own Welsh cheese made from a mixture of ewe's and cow's milk are of particular interest. The Welsh salt duck and the toasted cheese recipes come from the appendix of straightforward recipes which occupies the final fifth of Lady Llanover's four-hundred-and-eighty-page volume.

WELSH SALT DUCK

'For a common sized duck, a quarter of a pound of salt to be well rubbed and re-rubbed, and turned on a dish every day for three days, then wash all the salt off clean, put it in a "double" with half a pint of water to the pound, and let it simmer steadily for two hours. Salt boiled duck with white onion sauce, is much better than roast duck.'

Lady Llanover's white onion sauce, although an unusually mild one, made on a basis of milk and water in which onions have been boiled, rather than with the onions themselves, seems to me not quite appropriate with duck. This point apart, the salt duck formula is one I have been using for many years. I find it better as well as simpler than any other known duck recipe. Far more subtle than the eternal duck with orange, it has, curiously, affinities with Chinese duck cookery. The pre-salting of the bird produces, as promised by Lady Llanover, a very fine-flavoured duck. Even for a plain roast duck, a day's salting works an immense improvement.

For the cooking of the duck my own method of improvising a 'double' is to place the duck, as directed by Lady Llanover, in water in a deep oval baking pan. This is placed in a large baking tin also containing water. Very steady, slow oven cooking – 2 hours at gas no. 2, 310°F. – gives better results than simmering on top of the stove. If, during the final half-hour of cooking, the duck is left uncovered the skin will be baked to a nice golden crispness; and my own inclination is to let the bird cool in its cooking liquid, eat it cold, and serve with it nothing but the simplest of salads. In the summer, crisp Webb's lettuce is best, in the winter a bowl of honeydew melon cut into cubes and seasoned with nothing more exotic than a few drops of lemon juice and a sprinkling of fine sugar.

When I wrote of this recipe many years ago in the *Sunday Times*, an old lady of my acquaintance who had spent her early married life at Llandaff near Cardiff told me that she remembered Welsh salt duck very vividly and said that she had eaten it more than once at the house of neighbours. Another correspondent, however, wrote demanding to know upon what authority I had based my statement that the dish was of Welsh origin. This lady was herself Welsh, but came from North Wales, and in a further letter said she had never heard of Lady Llanover, nor of her book, nor of her paintings.

Was Welsh salt duck entirely a dish of South Wales? Was it preserved from oblivion by Lady Llanover? Does anyone still cook it?

One last point should, I think, be made. It is sad, but necessary, to say that mass-market frozen ducklings will not do for the salting method. They are flabby-fleshed, immature (one can't help wondering whether Lady Llanover would not have put them into the category of 'immoral introductions') and lacking in savour. The old recipe of the Principality demands a fully grown, fat, well-fed bird weighing, with head and giblets, not one ounce under six pounds and preferably rather more.

SHORT CAKES OF GWENT AND MORGANWG

'One pound of flour, three ounces of currants well picked and washed, a little sugar (and spice if liked); mix into a thick batter with one pint of sheep's-milk cream, butter the tin of a Dutch oven and drop it in and bake before the fire. Care must be taken in turning; it can be cut in any shape. Cream of cow's milk may be used but sheep's-milk cream is best for these cakes.'

The Welsh name of these short cakes is *teisen frau Gwent a Morganwg*. Of sheep's-milk cream, and sheep's-milk cheese, there is much talk and a good deal of interesting detail in *Good Cookery*. That the milking of ewes was little practised in England in the late nineteenth century although well-understood in parts of Wales is clear from the words Lady Llanover puts into the Traveller's mouth:

'I confess that when the Hermit first told me that his best cheese owed its superiority to the addition of sheep's milk, I thought he was jesting; and although I saw the ewes being milked, and admired the Arcadian scene, I supposed, in my ignorance, that the milk was to feed the calves. But I am now fully aware that the milk of that valuable animal [the Welsh sheep], when mingled with that of the cow, produces cheese which is not only excellent to eat new, but, when old, is more like Parmesan than anything else I ever tasted.

'His lambs were sold when I was with him, about the beginning of July, at three to four months old. The ewes were then milked for three months. They were twenty-four in number, and they gave on an average twenty-four quarts a day. The proportions for cheese were one quart of ewe's milk to five quarts of cow's milk. Six quarts of ewe's milk to thirty quarts of cow's milk made a cheese, weighing from twelve to fourteen pounds, of a most superior quality, with the sharpness so much admired in Parmesan.'

According to Lady Llanover, the authentic Welsh toasted cheese was made with this part ewe's milk, part cow's milk cheese. Given that the only Welsh cheese now on the market is so-called Caerphilly made in the cheese factories of the West country, it is not easy to see how we could revive anything like an authentic version of the recipe given by Lady Llanover. Some people swear by Double Gloucester for toasted cheese. I prefer Lancashire. At any rate it is interesting to know how the dish was prepared a century ago:

WELSH TOASTED CHEESE

'Welsh *toasted* cheese, and the *melted* cheese of England are as different in the mode of preparation as the cheese itself. Cut a slice of the real Welsh cheese made of sheep's and cow's milk, toast it at the fire on both sides, but not so much as to drop: toast a piece of bread, less than a quarter of an inch thick, to be quite crisp, and spread it very thinly with fresh cold butter on *one* side (it must not be saturated with butter) and lay the toasted cheese upon the bread and serve immediately upon a very hot plate.'

Finally, a jam recipe which is worth a trial:

RHUBARB JAM

'Boil an equal quantity of rhubarb cut up, and gooseberries before they are quite ripe, with three-quarters of a pound of crystallized moist sugar to one pound of fruit. When boiled, it will make an excellent jam, similar to apricot.

'It will keep some time in a cool place, tied down as usual.'

This recipe, Lady Llanover adds, was given to her by 'the venerable Mrs Faulkner of Tenby, South Wales, aged ninety-three, for many years landlady of the principal hotel there, then the White Lion'. It sounds like a very worthwhile early summer preserve. Could it really be 'similar to apricot'? Probably at any rate more similar than the gooseberry fool served to me at a riverside inn last summer was to gooseberry fool. It seemed to have been made with tinned gooseberry juice and flour – complete with lumps. One answer to the pudding problem would be to offer jam and cream rather than travesties of honourable old English sweet dishes.

Wine and Food, Summer 1965

*

Readers interested in more of Lady Llanover's recipes will find some relevant to Welsh oatcake and bread baking in my English Bread and Yeast Cookery, 1977, *and something about the author herself as well as her recipes in Mrs Bobby Freeman's* First Catch Your Peacock; *Freeman Image Imprint, 1980.*

Too Many Cooks

The cool blonde on the jacket picture of the centenary edition of Mrs Beeton keeps reminding me of Swinburne's Proserpine: crowned with calm leaves, she stands, who gathers all things mortal with cold immortal hands.

White-sweatered, Lux-washed, pale hands pink-tipped she sits (actually), this implacable girl, at her pale blue laminated-plastic-topped table, weighing out flour while a machine is whisking the eggs and any minute the automatically controlled cooker will ring a bell to say its oven is ready for more food. For all the interest or animation shown by the cook she might indeed be gathering in mortals or for that matter operating a switchboard or dishing out stamps at the Post Office.

Messrs Ward Lock bought the copyright of *Household Management* from Sam Beeton in 1867 and have owned it ever since. I wish they had seen fit to include in their centenary edition a few notes on the life and extraordinary work of the dazzlingly competent young woman who wrote it. Untrained in cookery but for a pastry-making course and the housekeeping she had learned while helping to look after her mother's and stepfather's families of twenty younger children, Isabella Mayson married Samuel Beeton when she was twenty. At twenty-one she had already started compiling and editing the work which, as *Beeton's Book of Household Management*, was published in 1861, when she was twenty-five. During these four years she bore two children, ran her household, led an active social life, supported her husband in his business activities, travelled abroad, and contributed translations of French novels as well as articles on fashion, cookery and other household subjects to Sam Beeton's *Englishwoman's Domestic Magazine*. Just before the birth of her fourth child in 1865 she had corrected final proofs of the dictionary version of the book which had already become a phenomenal success. A week later, barely twenty-nine, she died.

No fewer than fifty-five experts are credited for their work on this new edition of her book – now renamed *Cookery and Household Management*, in case the customers might think the latter doesn't include the former. And when so many hands have been at work on a book the result is bound to be uneven and to suffer from contradictions, errors of fact, and some confusion. I should indeed like to see any such compendious volume which didn't. Even the great *Larousse Gastronomique* is sometimes inconsistent and occasionally incorrect.

So I do not complain really of details such as the schoolgirl French – *glace à l'eau de grappes* for grape water ice and *crème fouetté* for frothy sauce (milk, eggs, sherry) are two fair enough examples – you can find others on page after page – or that foreign recipes are sometimes slapdash and misleading – chicken roasted with bacon and served with bread sauce and gravy is described as French style; and you just cannot hope to explain a regional dish like bouillabaisse in one short paragraph. The statement that Camembert cheese comes from Brittany is a slip which shouldn't have got by, as is the suggestion that three snipe make six helpings, and a brace of grouse five or six. And I suppose there *are* people who would believe that the best dressing for a potato salad is a cold béchamel mixed with egg yolk and vinegar, and who makes dishes like Brussels sprouts salad, Ugli cocktail, Sardine Rissolettes and Coconut Mould.

All the same, too much space is occupied by expendable recipes. To cookery students – who will find this book for years to come in their training college libraries – the inclusion of a separate section of recipes from the original work and Mrs Beeton's own instructions on, for example, roasting, would have been of the greatest interest. Copies of the 1861 edition are very scarce,[1] and I find it quite astonishing that Ward Lock have not had sufficient historical sense to give students a chance to see some of its contents for themselves. Surely they couldn't have been afraid of comparison between the achievement of fifty-five trained and experienced domestic experts and that of one young amateur cook aged twenty-five?

However, general principles are on the whole concisely explained and important details like the making of breadcrumbs, the clarifying of fat, the egging and crumbing of fish for frying are briskly written and easy to find. The section on stock is most sound. Bread making, yeast cookery generally, cake and scone mixing and baking, fresh milk cheeses, and the chapters on marmalades and fruit bottling strike me as most valuable. I wish that bad faults in some of the other cookery chapters had not made me doubt the validity of the whole.

Surely what we look for in *Household Management* are authoritative and decisive answers to the basic cookery problems likely to

1. But see my note p. 308.

arise every day. We feel that Mrs Beeton promises us the godlike wisdom of a revered professor combined with Nanny's protective comfort. We don't get it.

Out of this gigantic volume, consider just one aspect of cookery. One which touches us all. Just suppose one is a young person with little experience of shopping for food or of cooking it. One wants to produce a decent, conventional English meal. One looks up the recipe for roast beef. It calls for 'a joint suitable for roasting' and gives one system of timing for meat on the bone and another for a boned joint. No indication of whether one should buy 2 lb. of meat or ten. One turns to the general instructions relative to beef cookery. Where do they say what is or is not a joint suitable for roasting? Sirloin is mentioned. Topside and top rump can be 'cooked in the oven with a small quantity of water', 'it is common today for silverside to be roasted but it is . . . eminently suitable for salting and boiling'. The fore ribs and back ribs require 'rather more care in roasting, that is to say a lower heat, a longer time and the addition of a little water to the pan'. 'The top ribs and flat ribs come half-way between the two types of cut and may be very slowly roasted.' Back to the recipe. The temperature given for roasting after the initial sealing of the meat is a medium hot one – gas no. 5, 380°F. – but the inexperienced won't know what this implies. Fat is demanded for basting, but not a mention of 'a little water' or of what timing and temperature to apply for a 'very slowly roasted joint'. No beginner and, if I know anything about cookery-book readers, which I do, extremely few old hands are going to have any idea that they must turn to yet another part of the book to find more paragraphs on roasting, slow-roasting, braising, grilling . . . And even then – I don't think they'll extract the necessary information before they go out shopping. What is needed is a table showing which cuts are, and especially which are *not*, suitable for roasting, and why.

When we get to the cheaper cuts, these are competently explained in the beef section, and the differences in cooking quality between cuts from the fore and hindquarters indicated. Too many of the recipes, however, call for nothing more specific than 'stewing steak' or 'lean beef'. Nowadays, if housewives want good value for money and the best results from their recipes they *must* be taught to ask the butcher – the one who can and will help them is now very rare – for the appropriate cut of meat.

As for veal, the editors can hardly be blamed for shirking a diagram or picture of veal cuts – the proper method of veal cutting is a sore subject to English butchers. But they might at least have had a crack at telling us how to get escalopes properly cut.

In 1960, when young people really are crying out for technical knowledge, it is not enough to say that what is needed for *escalopes viennoises* is 1¼ to 1½ lb. fillet of veal cut into six slices, or to tell the reader that 'once the preceding facts about beef, pork and lamb have been acquired there is little to be added on veal'.

It's not that I'm all that set on the *real* Mrs Beeton's book. In many ways I prefer that of her predecessor Eliza Acton, who, in her *Modern Cookery*, published in 1845, was the first English writer to go into the minutest of detail in her recipes and who first used the concise and uniform system of setting them out which was later adapted by Mrs Beeton. But the great points about Isabella Beeton's *Household Management* were the clarity and detail of her general instructions, her brisk comments, her no-nonsense asides. No doubt she was sometimes a governessy young woman. That was just what made her voice the voice of authority. Mrs Beeton commands . . . Her pupils obey. When she says, for example, of a steak and kidney pudding recipe that because the meat is cut up into very small pieces 'this pudding will be found far nicer and more full of gravy than when laid in large pieces on the dish' – well, you jolly well do what she says and if you can't be bothered you know you've only yourself to blame for poor results. What young Mrs Beeton knew instinctively was that if instructions to the inexperienced are going to be effective they must be given in decisive terms. Nobody ever learns anything from a teacher who can't make up her own mind.

The Spectator, 21 October 1960

Isabella Beeton and her Book

Isabella Mayson, eldest of Benjamin and Elizabeth Mayson's four children, was born in 1836. When she was seven her young widowed mother married Henry Dorling, Clerk of the Course at Epsom. He too had four children by his previous marriage. In the course of time Mr and Mrs Dorling produced thirteen more.

From the bondage of helping with the housekeeping for this

'living cargo of children', as she herself once described her step-family, Isabella escaped at the age of twenty into marriage with Sam Beeton. Sam was an erratic, neurotic, exceptionally bright and publicity-minded young publisher. Without delay, his bride was set to work for him.

At the age of twenty-one she had already started collecting and compiling recipes, and writing and editing all the general information and instructions which eventually appeared in *Beeton's Book of Household Management*.

During the four years she devoted to this task, four years, as she told readers in her preface, 'of incessant labour', she was also contributing translations of French novels, articles on fashion as well as cookery and other domestic subjects to her husband's *Englishwoman's Domestic Magazine*, running her household, leading an active social life, keeping in close touch with her own 'large private circle', and travelling abroad. She also, during these years, bore two sons and suffered the loss of the first of them three months after his birth.

Here, one begins to see, was a young woman with capacities and intelligence, drive and will-power far and away beyond the ordinary.

Household Management first appeared in book form in 1861. Isabella was then twenty-five. In 1863, her second child died – he was three years old – and her third was born. In January 1865, she completed work on a dictionary version of the book which had already become an undreamed-of success. On the 29th of January, Isabella gave birth to her fourth son. A week later, in her twenty-ninth year, she died.

In 1867, Sam Beeton, as a result partly of injudicious publishing ventures, but mainly owing to the disastrous failure of the Overend, Gurney Bank, found himself in a serious financial plight. He was also gravely ill with consumption and mentally still suffering from the grief and shock of his wife's death. He had relied so heavily upon her support and advice that without her he was lost. He now signed away to Messrs Ward, Lock and Tyler, the publishers with whom he had already been associated, all his own copyrights, including that of his wife's book and its subsidiaries.

And we shall never know how different a course English household cookery might have taken had the successive directors of this publishing house not turned the book they had bought from Sam Beeton into something far more than the best-seller it already was –

into what eventually became the great British domestic legend of the twentieth century.

To that legend Ward, Lock's editors very largely contributed. Mrs Beeton's own recipes were for sound, solid, sensible, middle-class mid-Victorian food. In many cases they were more economical and produced dishes of less finesse than those of her predecessor, Eliza Acton, from whom she had borrowed the admirable system of setting out the ingredients, the quantities, and the timing of the recipes in a uniform and concise manner. For, although it seems incredible now, Eliza Acton's *Modern Cookery*, published by Longmans in 1845, was the first English cookery book in which such instructions were given. Alexis Soyer, from whose books Mrs Beeton also learned, was another celebrated writer of the same period who endeavoured to establish order in these matters. But Soyer was a man of diffuse interests and inconstant genius. It was the singleness of purpose animating Eliza Acton, her methodical mind and meticulous honesty which made her cookery book then, and makes it even still, far and away the most admired and copied in the English language.

So far as one knows, Miss Acton and Mrs Beeton never met. Isabella would have been only nine years old when *Modern Cookery* was published. By the time *Household Management* appeared Miss Acton was dead.

It is ironic that almost the only part of Mrs Beeton's original book which remained constant, whatever the other changes made in the successive editions, was that system of setting out the recipes which she had adapted from Miss Acton.

For twenty years, Ward, Lock left *Household Management* more or less alone to sell itself, simply bringing out, in 1869, and with Sam Beeton's co-operation, a new edition with minor revisions and additions – mainly in the non-cookery sections of the work. About half a dozen different abridged volumes of Mrs Beeton's cookery instructions and recipes were also launched on the market. These ranged from *Mrs Beeton's Every Day Cookery and Housekeeping Book* at 3s. 6d. down to *Beeton's Penny Cookery Book* which comprised 'Recipes for Good Breakfasts, Dinners and Suppers at a cost varying from Ten Pence to Two Shillings a Day for Six Persons'. Before long, every category of literate household in the land was catered for by one or other of the Beeton cookery books.

In 1888 appeared a new and much revised edition of *Household Management*. It contained over sixteen hundred crammed pages –

the original had been eleven hundred odd – and the claim made for it was that it provided *all of Mrs Beeton* and a lot more besides. This was not strictly true. A number of Mrs Beeton's original instructions had been curtailed, and others, less sound, substituted – the piece on the household stock-pot was particularly scarifying – written, one suspects, by a lady journalist specializing in domestic matters other than cookery.

Most of the recipes were now given French as well as English titles, for in spite of her sound knowledge of the language, Mrs Beeton had evidently not thought it necessary to supply French names for her English dishes. Ward, Lock kitchen French, with its latest and most remarkable flowering of 1960 was not Isabella Beeton's invention.

In the 1888 edition also appeared for the first time those sections on foreign dishes with recipes so unconvincing and anglicized that they must, I think, be held at least partly responsible for the muddled ideas about continental cookery held by generations of English housewives and their not very good plain cooks. 'Mrs Beeton says so, so it must be right.' But Mrs Beeton had not said so, and her personality and beliefs were no longer quite clearly defined in the book which now bore her name. Gentility and suburban refinement had crept in; they were the keynotes of the colour plates of truly astonishing late Victorian china and glass, table decorations and furniture. An illuminating piece of English domestic taste, this 1888 edition. It was the period of Japonaiserie run to raging chaos, of tiered bamboo tables and *jardinières*, of octagonal teapots and porcelain sardine boxes encrusted with plum blossom, lovebirds and chrysanthemums.

In 1906, all change again. This time it was a professional chef, C. Herman Senn, who was employed to re-edit the cookery sections. This edition was a completely revised one. It was a volume of over two thousand pages, weighing about six pounds.

Handsomely printed, on heavy paper, the book now had new colour plates of a very high standard of printing and colour processing. They were also very pretty. Some of them showed elegant and wonderfully festive Edwardian tables. Draped with fine linen, loaded with flowers, ice-pails, and red-shaded candles and festooned with garlands, not a living soul could have found room to sit down at them. But how rich and bright they now appear to us.

And here for the first time too were the plates demonstrating the art of setting an invalid tray. On crisp white hemstitched cloths we see the plated toast racks and crystal butter dishes, the starched napkins and tall *cloisonné* vases – two to a tray – filled with swaying roses and carnations, the engraved-glass tumblers, the befrilled cutlets, the whirls of creamed potato, the neatly rolled little omelettes and the individual creams and jellies which have become almost symbolic of a dream world of lovely willowy women, wax pale in lilac silk tea gowns, far too frail to descend to the dining room for dinner. (As a matter of fact they would have had to have been pretty brawny to balance one of those trays on their knees.)

Herman Senn, who had been chef at the Reform Club and subsequently adviser to the Food and Cookery Association, had written many cookery books of his own. He now proceeded to recreate an image of Mrs Beeton as the most *recherché* and extravagant cook of all time. On to her down-to-earth housewife's recipes he grafted his own brand of Edwardian professionalism. Masses of refined little things in dariole moulds, any amount of aspic jelly and truffles, cream puddings, iced soufflés, mousses, jellies and gâteaux galore. Senn also enlarged the section of American and colonial dishes first introduced in the 1888 edition and which included the famous Australian recipe so often attributed to Mrs Beeton herself. Fish Klosh (½ a lb. of cold Trumpeter), Baked Flathead, Parrot Pie (1 dozen paraqueets) and roast Wallaby are jokes trotted out whenever anyone wants a little fun at Mrs Beeton's expense. And there are plenty of other laughable little items which may very well have been responsible for some characteristic beliefs and habits of English cooks. The statement for example that 'as regards the food of the upper classes the cookery of France is now almost identical with that of England', the instructions to make coffee with 1 tablespoon to the half-pint of water, the assertion that 'Parmesan is . . . usually made with goat's milk', the recipe in which scallops are boiled for an hour . . .

Nevertheless the 1906 *Mrs Beeton* was a wonderful and beautiful book and is still greatly beloved by any one lucky enough to possess it. And any cook or housewife who wanted traditional English household cookery and sound, reliable cakes and pies and puddings could still needle out a certain number of the good old recipes from the mass of frills and fantasies supplied by Herman Senn.

Because, for all his faults – and today it is easy enough to pick holes – Senn was a fine editor. The 1906 edition may not have been Mrs Beeton, but it added up to a coherent whole. And it completely established the legend of Mrs Beeton's omnipotence in kitchen matters. Right on into the nineteen-thirties, by which time scarcely anything of the original work remained, it was still possible for the publishers to let the reader infer that Mrs Beeton was still alive and co-operating with the revision of her work. The note by Sam Beeton (he himself died in 1877) appended to the prefaces of the 1869 and 1888 editions in which he referred to 'my late wife' was expunged from the 1906, never again to re-appear.

Not in the skilfully-worded prefaces, not in the publisher's notes, not in the quotes from famous writers, not even in a comment by Sir Mayson Beeton (the son after whose birth she died) about his mother's work, was she ever referred to as 'the late' Mrs Beeton. The image of a formidable old dragon in black silk and white bonnet, still telling us to be up betimes, to wash up as we go along and not to chatter about trivial household affairs, still presided over thousands of English kitchens.

A century has passed since the first appearance of *Household Management*. The publishers have had no alternative but to admit that Mrs Beeton herself has now been replaced by fifty-five trained and experienced domestic experts.

It was scarcely to be expected that the work turned out by such a team, lacking one master guiding spirit, would have anything like the personality and vitality of that produced by one young woman possessed of a burning conviction of what should be said and the ability to say it in clear and unmistakable terms.

I do not propose here to write the obituary of *Household Management*. The editors and publishers have done that for themselves.

In vain one looks for some small sign of the historical sense which might have infused life into this mammoth volume. But the publishing house which so largely created the Mrs Beeton legend have utterly muffed their chance of showing the public and more especially students of cookery and domestic history how that legend originated and grew.

In their 1960 volume of one thousand three hundred and forty-four 9½ by 6½ inch pages the publishers who have found Mrs Beeton's name such a steady source of income for ninety-three years have not even thought to reproduce one single one of those original recipes which, whether we, or they, or the editors like them or not, belong irrevocably to the history of English cookery. The omission is hard to forgive.

Wine and Food. Spring 1961

The above article was written at André Simon's request, to celebrate the centenary of the publication in book form of Household Management. *At the time, as I complained, Mrs Beeton's original recipes were out of reach of the general public. About four years later, however, Messrs. Jonathan Cape, more imaginative than Messrs. Ward Lock brought out a facsimile edition of the 1861* Household Management *which then became cheaply available to all. Copies may still be bought from Prospect Books of 45 Lamont Road London SW10.*

Index

Page numbers in bold type refer to recipes

Acton, Eliza:
  English Bread Book, 136
  Modern Cooking, 10, 35–6, 245,
    303, 306
Adair, Robin, 165, 166, 170, 172–4
Adrian, Leslie, 10
Aïoli, **259–60**
Alba, 280–3
Albóndigas, 95
Alexandria, 23, 159
Ali Baba, 184, 185
Almond:
  and mulberry dish, **248**
  shortbread, **245–6**
Alose à l'oseille, 64
American food, 137–9, 159, 231
Amory, G., 112
Anacapri, 113, 214
Anchovy, 100, 128
  butter, **168**
Andrieu, Pierre, *Fine Bouche*, 143–5
Anisette, with fish, **190–92**
Apicius, 183, 184
Appert, François, 275
Apples, 105
  baked, 34, 36
  Bramleys, 34–7
  with game, 34–5
  with honey and cumin, 184, 185
  with lemon and cinnamon, **105**
  purée, **35–6**, 37
  sauce, **35–6**, 37
  trifle, **240**
  varieties for cooking, 34–7
Apricots, dried, 244
  fool, **244**
Arbroath smokies, 217–18
Artichauts Escoffier, **61–2**
Asher, Gerald, 84, 85, 93
Asparagus, 210n.
  wild, 107–8, 111, 112
Australian food, 307
Austrian food, 132–3
Avignon, 51, 79–80
Azzalin, Ugo, *Alcune Menestre
  Venete*, 108n.

Babinski, Henri, 175
Baillie, Lady Grisell, *The Household
  Book of*, 236–7
Barattero, Madame, 53–63
Barnett, Lady, 47
Basil, 33
Beaujolais, 42, 101
Beaumes de Venise, 83–5
Bedford, Sybille, 126
Beef:
  grillade des mariniers du Rhône,
    252, 273
  roast, stewed, 153
  salt, 222
  spiced, **288–90**
  stews, 153, **252**, 273
Beerbohm, Max, 162, 229
Beeton, Mrs Isabella, *Household
  Management*, 10n., 26–7, 245,
    300–9
Beeton, Sam, 300, 304–5, 307
Beetroot, 178, 182
Benton, Peggie, 181
Berenson, Bernard, 117
Bernard, Madame, 66
Big Ben, 293
Bini, Giorgio, *Names of
  Mediterranean Fish*, 141
Bird's custard, 229–30
Bishop, Frederick, *The Wife's Own
  Book of Cookery*, 245
Black fruit fool, **242–4**
'Black tart stuff', **242–4**
Blackberry fool, **239**
Blencowe, Anne, *Receipt Book*,
    201
Blettes (chard), 58, 77, 268
  à la crème, **273–4**
Bogue (*boops boops*), 141
Boni, Ada, *La Cucina Romana*, 108,
    110–11
Borrow, George, *Wild Wales*, 219
Boulestin, Marcel, **162–74**, 213
  The Best of, 167, 172–3
  The Conduct of the Kitchen, 165,
    166, 169

Evening Standard Book of Menus,
  166, 168
The Finer Cooking, 171–2
Having Crossed the Channel, 165,
  170–71
Myself, My Two Countries, 173,
  174
A Second Helping, 164–5
Simple French Cooking, 164
What Shall We Have Today?, 165
Bozzi, Ottorina Perna, *Vecchia
  Brianza in Cucina*, 112
Brandy, 187, 188–90
Brazier, Mère, 70–72
Bread:
  English, 74, 75, 135–7, 247
  French, 74, 75, 203
  home-baked, 135–7
Breadcrumbs, 37–9
Breakfasts, 91, 219
Bream, 142
Briand, Aristide, 172
Brianza, 108, 112
Brien, Alan, 10
Brill, 141, 191
Brillat Savarin, Jean-Anthelme de, 178
Brisse, Baron, 192
British: *see* English food;
    Restaurants; Scottish food;
    Welsh food
Brown, Helen, *West Coast Cook
  Book*, 137–9
Bruscandoli, 106–13
Bryson, Bill, 14n.
Buckland, Anne, *Our Viands*, 211
Burgundy, white, 16, 52
Bute, 4th Marquis of, *Moorish
  Recipes*, 143
Butter, clarified, 218, 220–21

Cairo, 23
Camargue, 267–8
Cameron, Ida, 26
Cantal cheese, 272
Capers, 260
Capri, 123–4, 129–30
Carrier, Robert, 36
Carter, Ernestine, 10, 13
Catalonia, 91–93
Cauliflower cheese, 41
Cavaillon, 255–7

Cecil, Lord David, *Max*, 229
Cenci, 117
Chablis, 101
Char, 225
Chard (*blettes*), 58, 77, 268
  à la crème, 273–4
Chardin, Jean-Baptiste, 267
Charvillat, *chez*, 64
Chase, Joanna, 16
Cheese (*see also* Cream cheeses):
  DISHES:
  fondues, fonduta, 117, **157–8,
    160**, 161, 281, 283
  omelette Molière, 52
  sauce, 117–18
  toasted, **299**
  tranches au fromage, **180**
  Welsh rabbit and toasted cheese,
    161, **299**
  wines with, 52
  TYPES:
  British, 160–2, 298–9
  French, 77–8, 156–61, 261–2,
    271–2
  Italian, 118, 205–6, 281
  German, 159, 162
  Swiss, 157
Chestnuts, 292
Chick pea salad, **259**
Chicken:
  livers: *crostini*, 116–17; potted,
    222–3; with spaghetti, 115–16
  potted, with ham, **222**
  poularde: de Bresse, 71; *en vessie*,
    59–60
  poulet rôti, 62
Child, Julia, *Mastering the Art of
  French Cooking*, 169
Chocolate, 66
Choucroûte, 184, 263
Christmas, 102, 283–6, **287–93**
Christopher's, 286
Cidonio, Bernardo, 280
Cipriani's, Torcello, 106–7
Clams:
  Coos Bay Clam Cakes, 138
  tinned, 29
Clarified butter and fats, 218, 220–21
Clark of Tillypronie, Lady, *Cookery
  Book*, 205
Cocktail party food, 207, 220

Cod's roe, smoked, paste, 277, 228
Cognac, 187, 188–90
Colette, 162
Colin, Joseph, 275–6, 278
Collingwood, Francis, and John
    Woollams, *The Universal Cook*,
    240–41
Compleat Imbiber, 9, 14, 66,
    187–92, 280–3
Connolly, Cyril, 217
Connolly, Major Matthew, 217–18,
    219
Conserva di peperoni, 114–15
Cordon Bleu School, 34, 88
Cornas, 82
Cornish Fairings, 30
Côte Rôtie, 82
Cottage cheese, 205
Coulis de tomates à la moutarde, 260
Courchamps, Comte de, **191–2**
Courgette *gratin*, 47
Crab, 226
    boiling, 32–3
    potted, 226
Cream and milk cheeses, 104,
    203=7, 253
    croûtons, 207–8
    fromage normand, 253
    milk, 205–7
    Osborne, 205
    snow, 204
Creams:
    fruit (sundry kinds), **242**
    ginger, 290
    gooseberry, 242
Crème brûlée, 239
Croft-Cooke, Rupert, *Exotic Food*, 109
Crostini, **116–17**
Croûtons:
    cream cheese, 207
    à la marinière, 87
Croze, Count Austin de, 250
Cuisine et la Pâtisserie Bourgeoises,
    La, **109–10**
Cumberland sauce, 154
Curnonsky (Maurice-Edmond
    Sailland), 250
Custard, 229–30

David, Elizabeth:
    booklets, 229, 246–7

English Bread and Yeast Cookery,
    246, 299
French Country Cooking, 91, 93
French Provincial Cooking, 9, 15,
    17, 55, 62, 66, 71, 182
Italian Food, 214
Mediterranean Food, 22
Spices, Salts and Aromatics in the
    English Kitchen, 212, 246
Summer Cooking, 135
Davidson, Alan:
    Mediterranean Seafood, 10
    Seafish of Tunisia . . ., 10, 139–42
    What is a Sardine, 278–9
    See also Petits Propos Culinaires
Dentice, 141
Diat, Louis, 40
Digby, Sir Kenelm, *The Closet of*,
    231, **232**, 234, 294
Dods, Meg (Mrs Johnstone), *The*
    Cook's and Housewife's
    Manual, 219, 220, 226, **234–5**
Dominic, Peter, 9
Dordogne, 74, 271
Dorset Dishes of the 18th Century,
    234
Dorset Dishes of the 17th Century,
    242
Double (boiler), 294, 296
Douglas, Norman, 13, 120–33,
    139–40
    Alone, 123, 128
    Birds and Beasts of the Greek
        Anthology, 133
    Late Harvest, 123
    Old Calabria, 120, 123
    Siren Land, 123, 129
    South Wind, 123
    Together, 123, 133
    Venus in the Kitchen, 124–32
Dried fruit, **242–4**
Drummond, J. C., and Anne
    Wilbraham, *The Englishman's*
    Food, 134
Duck, Welsh salt, **294–7**
Dumas, Alexandre, 192
Durrell, Lawrence, 78

Eales, Mary, *Receipts*, 240n
Eggs:
    œufs à la neige, 80

scrambled, with haddock, 169
wine with, 51, 52
See also Omelettes
Encyclopedia of Practical Cookery,
   212
English food, 41, 134, 153–6, 208–
   11, 277, 279, 287–8, 300–9
and foreign recipes, 11, 25–7, 92,
   241, 301, 306
See also Restaurants
Epulario (Maestro Martino), 248
Escoffier, Auguste, 154, 179, 195–6,
   212, 214–16, 250, 287
Everlasting syllabub, 231, 235
Ewes' milk cheeses, 77, 298–9

Farley, John, *The London Art of*
   Cookery, 221
Fennel, 104, 191
with Parmesan, 104–5
seeds, 127
Fieldhouse, Harry, 17
Fields, Gracie, 124
Fireman's Apron, 39
Fish, shellfish, 85–90, 139–42, 176,
   270–1, 275–9
anisette with, 190–2
pastes, 216–17, 225–8
potted, 225–8
Florentine fennel with Parmesan,
   104–5
Florio, John, 119n.
Flour, 136–7
Fondues and *fonduta*: see Cheese
   (dishes)
Fontina cheese, 118, 281
Fools, fruit, 237–46
Fools, fruit, 237–46
Fowler, H. W., 14n.
Frampton, Judith, 232–4
Franche-Comté cheese and *fondue*,
   77, 157–8, 161
Freeman, Mrs Bobby, *First Catch*
   Your Peacock, 299
Frittata con i loertis, 112
Fromage normand, 253
Fruit fools, 237–46
Frying, 51, 220
Fungi, 280–1

Galantines, 58

Game:
potted, 223–4
See also Pheasant
Geoduck, 138
Gigondas, 80, 82, 84
Gilbert, Philéas, *La Cuisine de Tous*
   les Mois, 287
Gin, 190
Ginger cream, 290
Ginny (Guinea) pepper, 119n
Glasse, Hannah, *The Art of Cookery*
   Made Plain and Easy, 199, 240
Glyka, 29
Go, 9, 17, 192–7
Goldsmith, Oliver, 198
Goose:
roast, 292–3
Gooseberry:
cream, 242
fools, 238–42
huff, 242
trifle, 240
Gourmet, 120–4, 249–53
Greek Anthology, the, 124, 133
Greek food, 22–3, 29, 151
Green, Patricia, 66
Greene, Graham, 125, 130
Grenfell, Joyce, 288
Grillade des mariniers du Rhône, 252,
   273
Grilling in breadcrumbs, 37–9
Grouper, 142
Grouse, potted, 223–4
Guégan, Bertrand, translation of
   Apicius, 183
Guérard, Michel, 11, 181–2, 184,
   185n.
Guinness, 160

Ham, potted, 222
Hammond, Elizabeth, *Modern*
   Domestic Cookery, 238, 240
Hampers, Christmas, 283–6
Hannibal, 272
Harper's Bazaar, 9
Heath, Ambrose, *Good Food*, 190
Henry IV (of France), 278
Henry VIII, 198
Herbal Review, 106–12
Herbert, Colonel Kenney, 10

Herbodeau, Eugene, and Paul
  Thalamas, *G. A. Escoffier*, 216
Hièly's, 79
Hill, Derek, 117, 119
Honey, 285
  tomato, 213
Hop-shoots, 108–13
House and Garden, 9–10, 85–7,
  292–3
Hughes, Therle, *Sweetmeat and Jelly
  Glasses*, 237n.

Ice cream, 240
  ginger, 290
India, 10, 195
Italian:
  food, 14, 89–90, 98–119, 121–2,
    281–3
  wines, 101–5, 282

Jam, 47, 151, 285
  rhubarb, 299
  tomato, 212–13
James II, 269
James, Henry, *A Little Tour of
  France*, 72
Jewish cookery, 181–2
John Dory, 141, 191, 270
Johnson, Hugh, 17, 246
Junket, 206

Kaufeler, M., 39
Kent, Countess of, *A Choice Manual*
  and *A True Gentlewoman's
  Delight*, 243
Kipper paste, 227
Kiwi fruit, 210n.

La Chapelle, Vincent, *The Modern
  Cook*, 240n.
La Varenne, François Pierre, *French
  Cook*, 241
Laboureur, J. E. 164, 165
Lamastre, 53–62, 272
Lamb:
  breast of, Ste. Ménéhould, 38–9
  carré d'agneau Mistral, 250
  gigot bouilli, 153–4
Lancaster, Osbert, 126

Larousse Gastonomique, 301
Latini, Antonio, *Lo Scalco alla
  Moderna*, 119
Lawrence, D. H., 131
Left-overs, 146, 153
Lehmann, John, 22
Lemons, 198–201
  cheese-cake, 200
  curd, 199–200
  grating, 199
  juice, 198–9, 202
  pie, 200–1
  preserved, 201
  syllabub, 234
Lentils, 198, 272
Leslie, Miss, *Complete Cookery*, 213
Levin, Bernard, 10
Llanover, Lady, *Good Cookery*, 161,
  293–9
Lobster, 187, 189
  boiling, 31–2
  Courchamps, 190–2
  potted, 226
Locust bread, 143
Lowinsky, Ruth, *Lovely Food*, 239–
  40, 246
Lowinsky, Thomas, 239, 246
Luke, Sir Harry, *The Tenth Muse*, 10,
  150–1, 248
Luppoli, 108, 110–11, 112
Lyon, 71–2

McGovern, William, 98n.
MacIver, Susannah, *Cookery and
  Pastry*, 238
Mackenzie, Faith Compton, 126
McNeill, Marian, *The Scots Kitchen*,
  235
Manzoni, Alessandro, 112
Marples, Ernest, 148n.
Martigues, 267–70
Mason, Charlotte, *The Lady's
  Assistant*, 111
Maupassant, Guy de, 263
May, Robert, *the Accomplisht Cook*,
  231–2, 238, 242, 243
Mayonnaise, 25–7, 191
Mazapan, 96
Mediterranean food, 21–5, 91–7,
  198, 207
  See also Provençal

Mendl, Lady, *Recipes for Successful Dining*, 186
Merle's *Domestic Dictionary*, 226
Middle East food, 21–5, 143, 248
Mikes, George, 19
Milk cheeses: *see* Cream cheeses
Mistral, Frédéric, 250
Molière, Omelette, 52
Montpellier, 263–5
Mont-St-Michel, 49
Moorish food, 143
Morra truffle paste, 282
Morris, Cedric, 165
Mortimer, Raymond, 56
Moules, 86–90, 191
Muffet, Dr, *Health's Improvement*, 108–9
Mulberries, 247–9
  and almond dish, **248**
  cream, **242**
  as dessert, **249**
  sauce, **248**
  summer pudding, **247**
  water ice, **248**
Muscat de Beaumes de Venise, 84–5
Museau de porc en salade, 253
Mushrooms, 86–7, 280–1
  baked, **33–4**
Mussels, 86–90, 191
Mutton, boiled, 153–4

Nantes, 13–14, 88–9, 275–8
Néo-Physiologie du Goût, 192n.
Newnham-Davis, Colonel, 192–7
Nicholas, Elizabeth, 17
Normandy, 49–50, 75, 86–7, 250–1, 253, 261–3
Nova, 9, 13, 17, 203–12, 219, 246

Œufs à la neige, 80
Olive oil, 26–7, 68, 83–4, 198, 275, 279, 284, 286
Oliver, Raymond, 156–7
Olives, 48, 96–7, 260
Omelettes, 50–2
  hop-shoot, **112**
  Molière, **52**
Orioli, Pino, **126**
Owen, Mrs, of Penrhos, **244**
Oxford English Dictionary, 237n.
Oysters in wine, **132**

Pa y all, 91–3
Pain d'écrevisses sauce cardinal, 59, 61
Paris, 89–90, 149, 178
Park Railings, 39
Partridge, potted, 223
Pasta, 115–17, 123, 128, 205
Pastry, short crust, 200–1
Peas, 59
Pellaprat, Henri, *Le Poisson dans la Cuisine Française*, 88–9
Penzance, 30
Pepper, Beverly, *Pot-Luck Cookery*, 146–7
Peppers, 78, 113–14
  conserva di peperoni, **114–15**
Perrier, Bernard, 62–3
Petits pois à la française, 59
Petits Propos Culinaires, 15, 66–74, 113–19, 247–9, 278–9
Pheasant, 189–90
  à la Hannibal, 133
Picarel, 141
Picnics, 72–4, 184
Piedmont, 157, 280–3
Pigeon, 143
Pimentos: *see* Peppers
Pipérade, 170, 171
Piperna, 119
Pisanelli, Baldassare, *Della Natura dei Cibi*, 109
Pissaladière, 76, 98–100
Pizza, 11, 40, 76, 91–2, 98–100
Poirée: see Blettes
Pois chiches, **259**
Polish cookery, 178, 181–2
Pomiane, Dr Edouard de, 175–85, 263
  Cooking in Ten Minutes, 181, 184
  Cooking with, 181, 185
Porc aux pruneaux, 63–6
Pork:
  pig's cheek, **253**
  museau de porc en salade, **253**
  porc aux pruneaux, 63–6
  spare-ribs, **39**
  stuffed and rolled, **102–3**
Port-Salut, 161
Portuguese cooking, 210
Postgate, Raymond, 25
Potatoes, 77
  gratin dauphinois, **77**

Pot-au-feu, 153, 257–9
Potted foods, 216–29
    chicken, with ham, 222
    chicken livers, 222–3
    crab, 226
    fish (pastes), 216–17, 225–8
    game, 223–4
    ham, with chicken, 222
    kipper, 227
    lobster, 226
    pork, 224
    rillettes, 224
    salmon, 225–6
    salt beef, 222
    sardine, 168, 227
    serving, 219–20
    smoked cod's roe, 227, 228
    smoked haddock, trout etc., 227
    smoked salmon, 227
    storage, 218–19
    tongue, 221
    tunny, 228
    venison, 222
'Potter, A', *Pottery*, 216
Poulard, Madame, 50
Poularde:
    de Bresse, 71
    en vessie, 59–60
Poutargue, 269
Powell, Anthony, *The Kindly Ones*,
    149
Praga, Mrs Alfred, *Dainty Dinner
    Tables*, 186–7
Price, Pamela Vandyke, 17
Proust, Marcel, 267
Provençal:
    food, 46–8, 49, 79, 82–5, 210, 249
        –50, 255–60, 267–71, 273
    wines, 52, 82–5
Prunes, 242–4
Prunier, Madame, 12
Pulses, 198, 259
Punch, 11, 39–41

Quails à la normande, 35
Queen, 246
Quiches, 11, 39–40, 70, 92–3
Quince fool, 243

Raffald, Elizabeth, *The Experienced
    English Housekeeper*, 222,

    225–6, 234
Ras el hanoot, 143
Raspberry:
    cream, 242
    fool, 238
    summer pudding, 247–8
Ravioles, 77–8
Ray, Cyril, 9, 10, 14, 66
Red mullet, 133
Redcurrant:
    fool, 239
    summer pudding, 247–8
Renaudet, Benjamin, *Les Secrets de la
    Bonne Table*, 153–6
Rennet, 206
Restaurants:
    in Britain, 41–8, 80, 102, 148–9,
        155, 165, 172–4, 192–7, 209–
        11, 217–18, 219, 266, 294, 299
    in France, 41, 46, 49–84, 86, 88–
        90, 143–5, 149, 156, 165–6,
        170, 177–8, 189, 203–4, 209,
        271
Rhône, 58, 272–3
Rhubarb fool, 245
Rice, 117–19
    See also Risotti
Richard III, 288
Ricotta, 206
Rillettes, 224
Ris de veau, 59
Riso:
    in bianco, 119
    ricco, 118–19
    secco, 118–19
Risotti, 107, 110, 112
Romano's, Burano, 107
Rome, 109–10
Ross-on-Wye, 20–21
Roubaud, Château, 81, 82
Rouff, Marcel, 250
Russell, Leonard, 15, 16, 135, 147

Sacchi, Bartolomeo, *De Honesta
    Voluptate*, 248
Saffron, 97, 129, 284
Saint-Ange, Madame E., *Livre de
    Cuisine*, 35, 169
Saintsbury, George, 223
Salads, 138
    museau de porc en salade, 253

salade de pois chiches, **259**
tomato, 94–5, 208, 210
Salmon, potted, **225–6**
Salt:
  beef, potted, 222
  duck, Welsh, **294–7**
Sardenara casalinga, **98–100**
Sardines, 13, 275–9
  butter, 168, 227
Sauces:
  apple, 35–6, 37
  cheese, **117–18**
  coulis de tomates à la moutarde,
    260
  for fish, **190–2**
  mulberry, 248
  tomato, 118–19, 210–11, 260
  au vin du Médoc, 66
  See also Aïoli; Mayonnaise
Saucisse en feuilletage, 61
Sausages, yellow, **132**
Scallops, 182–3, 191, 307
Scappi, 109n.
Scott, Sir Walter, 234
Scottish food, 235, 236, 238
Scott-James, Anne, 14n.
Scurfield, George and Cecilia, *Home
  Baked*, 135–7
Seafood: see Fish
Seneca, 127
Senn, Herman, 26–7, 306–8
Shad, 64
Shellfish: see Fish
Shortbread, almond, **245–6**
Shortcake, Gwent, **294, 298**
Simon, André, 16, 17, 166–7, 217
Simpson, John, *Complete System of
  Cookery*, 288, 290
Simpson, N. F., 22
Smith, E., *Complete Housewife*, 231
Smoked fish pastes, **227, 228**
Smollett, Tobias, 134, 136
Sole normande, **250–1**
Soups, 168
  crème vichyssoise, 40
  au fromage, 158
  hop-shoot, 110–11, 112
  thickened with bread, 17–18
  vegetable, 59
  zuppa di luppoli, 108, **110–11**
Soyer, Alexis, 154, 305

Spaghetti with chicken livers and
  lemon, **115–17**
Spain, 92, 93, 94–7, 208–9
Spectator, 9–11, 14, 19–39, 41–8,
  82, 94–7, 137–42, 148–56, 185
  –7, 275–8, 283–6, 300–303
Spiced beef, **288–90**
Spices, 284
Spinach *à la crème*, **273–4**
Stevenson, R. L., 237
Stock, 167–8, 296
Stores, 22–5, 27–9, 145–7
Stout, in cooking, 160
Strawberry:
  cream, **242**
  fool, 238
Summer puddings, **247–8**
Sunday Dispatch, 9
Sunday Times, 9, 10, 11, 15, 98–100,
  134–7, 143–5, 147, 175–81,
  184
Sutcliffe, Dorothy, 36–7
Suzanne, Alfred, *La Cuisine Anglaise*,
  154–5
Sweetbreads, 59
Swinburne, Algernon, 300
Swiss food, 25, 157, 179–80
Syllabubs, **229–37, 241**

Table decoration, 185–7, 239–40,
  306–7
Taramasalata, **227, 228**
Tarragon, 153, 192
Thalamas, Paul: see Herbodeau,
  Eugene
Thompson, Sir Henry, 136
Thyme, 119
Tinned and packet foods, 22–4, 27–
  9, 40–1, 210–11, 213–16, 264,
  275–9
Tomatoes, 208–16
  coulis de tomates à la moutarde,
    260
  à la crème, **178**
  honey, **213**
  preserve (jam), 212–13
  tinned, 24, 211, 212, 214–16
  salads, 95–6, 208, 210
  sauces, 118–19, 210–11, 260
Tongue, potted, **221**

Toulouse-Lautrec, Comtesse Mapie de, **161**
Tours, 63–6
Tranches au fromage, 180
Tree, Herbert Beerbohm, 229
Trifle, 229–30, 237, 241
  apple, **240**
  gooseberry, **240**
  19th-century, **245**
Tripe, 39
Truffles, 14, 249–50, 281–3
Tunny fish butter, **228**
Turner, E. S., *What the Butler Saw*, 148

Utensils, 51
Uzès, 76–81

Valence, 271–3
Vaucluse, 82–5, 255
Veal:
  braised, with carrots, **169–70**
  kidneys *à la liégeoise*, 190
Vegetables, 104–5, 170–71, 182–3
Venice, 106–8, 112–13, 142
Venison, potted, **222**
Verdier, Ernest, *Dissertations Gastronomiques*, 211
Viel, Robert, 50
Vine leaves, and baked mushrooms, **33–4**
Vogue, 9, 16, 53–66, 115n., 255–75, 287–90
Vongole, tinned, 29
Vorarlberg, 133–4

Walls' pies and sausages, 11, 12, 27–8
Wartime and rationing, 11, 19–21, 24, 137, 159, 216

Water ices, **248**
Waugh, Evelyn, *Black Mischief*, 46
Welsh food, 159, **161**, **294–8**
  Welsh rabbit and toasted cheese, **161**, **299**
Westbury, Lord, *Handlist of Italian Cookery Books*, 248
Whisky, in cooking, 187–90
White, Sam, 149
Whitehorn, Katharine, 10
Wilbraham, Anne, *see* Drummond, J.C.
Willy (Henry Gauthier-Villars), 162–3
Wine:
  dessert and sweet, 84–5, 104–5, 117
  with egg and cheese dishes, 51 52–3
  temperature, 42, 102–3
  with vegetables, 104
  women and, 16, 46, 127
  See also Italian; Provençal
Wine and Food, 53, 124–133, 156–74, 198–201, 293–9, 300–9
Wine and Food Society, 216
  Quarterly, 17
Wine Mine, 9, 101–6
Wine waiters, 46, 127
Withers, Audrey, 9, 16, 53, 55
Woollams, John: *see* Collingwood, Francis

Yellow sausage, 133
Young, Barbara, **234**
Yvetot, 262

Zuliani, Mariu Salvatori de, *A Tola Co i Nostri Veci*, 112
Zuppa di luppoli, 108, 110–11